CA Proficiency 2

Taxation 2 (RoI)

2019–2020

CHARTERED
ACCOUNTANTS
IRELAND

Published in 2019 by
Chartered Accountants Ireland
Chartered Accountants House
47–49 Pearse Street
Dublin 2
www.charteredaccountants.ie

ISBN: 978-1-912350-26-1

Typeset by Deanta Global Publishing Services
Printed and bound by CPI Group (UK) Ltd, Croydon, CR0 4YY

FSC www.fsc.org MIX Paper from responsible sources FSC® C013604

Contents

PART THREE CAPITAL ACQUISITIONS TAX

PART FOUR CORPORATE TAXATION

Chartered Accountants Ireland *Code of Ethics*

Chartered Accountants Ireland's *Code of Ethics* applies to all aspects of a Chartered Accountant's professional life, including dealing with corporation tax issues, capital gains tax issues, capital acquisitions tax issues and stamp duty issues. The *Code of Ethics* outlines the principles that should guide a Chartered Accountant, namely:

- Integrity
- Objectivity
- Professional Competence and Due Care
- Confidentiality
- Professional Behaviour.

As a Chartered Accountant, you will have to ensure that your dealings with the tax aspects of your professional life are in compliance with these fundamental principles. Set out in **Appendix 2** is further information regarding these principles and their importance in guiding you on how to deal with issues which may arise throughout your professional life, including giving tax advice and preparing tax computations.

Part One

Capital Gains Tax

1

Capital Gains Tax: Introduction, General Principles and Administration

Learning Objectives

After studying this chapter you will be able to:

- Advise on and apply the general principles for the computation of capital gains tax (CGT) liabilities.
- Advise on the payment of CGT and the filing of returns.
- Identify "development land" for CGT purposes and apply the relevant restrictions to any such disposals.
- Determine and apply the appropriate treatment of capital losses.

Chartered Accountants Ireland's *Code of Ethics* applies to all aspects of a professional accountant's professional life, including dealing with capital gains tax issues. Further information regarding the principles in the *Code of Ethics* is set out in **Appendix 2**.

Students should also be aware of the issues around tax planning, tax avoidance and tax evasion, and these are discussed in **Appendix 3.**

1.1 The Basic Charge to Capital Gains Tax

Legislation introduced taxation on capital gains arising from the disposal of chargeable assets on or after 6 April 1974. The legislation has been modified by amendments contained in subsequent Finance Acts.

The charge to capital gains tax (CGT) is now contained in the Taxes Consolidation Act 1997 (TCA 1997). There are four basic elements that must apply before the provisions relating to the taxation of capital gains come into operation. These are as follows:

- there must be a **disposal**;
- of an **asset**;
- by a **chargeable person**;
- after **5 April 1974**.

The extent to which gains are chargeable, and losses are allowable, depends on the location and nature of the asset and the person's tax residence, ordinary residence and domicile (see **Chapter 2**).

1.2 Disposal

In order for a liability to CGT to arise, a disposal of an asset must take place or must be deemed to take place. A disposal for these purposes will occur in each of the following situations:

1. On the sale of an asset.
2. On the sale of part of an asset (part disposal – see **Section 1.6.5**).
3. On the gift of the whole or part of an asset.
4. On the receipt of a capital sum resulting from the ownership of an asset, e.g. receipt of compensation for damage or injury to assets or receipt of a capital sum in return for forfeiture or surrender of rights.
5. On the capital sum received as consideration for use or exploitation of assets.
6. On the transfer of an asset to a trust or a corporate body.
7. On an exchange of assets in a barter transaction.
8. On the occasion of the entire loss or destruction of an asset, e.g. if a painting is destroyed in a fire, there is a disposal of the painting whether or not any insurance proceeds are received.
9. Where an asset becomes negligible in value and Revenue allows a claim for loss relief, there is a deemed disposal of the asset (see **Section 1.14.8**).

1.3 Assets

For the purpose of CGT all forms of property are assets, including options and property created by the person disposing of it (e.g. copyrights, patents and goodwill), debts and foreign currency. Specifically included is an interest in property, e.g. a lease. The basic rule is that any capital asset of an individual or company is a chargeable asset unless it is specifically exempt from CGT or corporation tax on chargeable gains. Specifically included is an interest in property, e.g. a lease.

1.4 Chargeable Persons

CGT is charged on gains realised by individuals, partnerships and trusts. Companies are assessed to CGT on disposals of development land only. Other capital gains realised by companies are also chargeable gains but are assessed to corporation tax and not CGT.

1.5 Rate of Tax, Date of Payment and Returns

1.5.1 Rate of CGT

CGT is charged by reference to the **year of assessment for individuals**. A CGT year of assessment is the same as an income tax year (i.e. up to 6 April 2001 it ran from 6 April to following 5 April each year; the tax year 2001 covers the period 6 April 2001 to 31 December 2001; and the tax year 2002 and subsequent tax years is the **calendar year**).

The rate of **CGT for 2019 is 33%**. The rates of CGT for previous years are listed in **Appendix 1**, Table 16. A 10% (20% for disposals in 2016) rate of CGT applies to disposals of certain business assets qualifying for revised entrepreneur relief (see **Section 4.8**).

1.5.2 Date of Payment

Self-assessment applies to CGT. There is no requirement for preliminary tax to be paid in respect of CGT.

For 2019, a person's CGT liability is payable in two amounts. The first amount, known as "**tax payable for the initial period**", is payable on or before **15 December in the tax year**. "Tax payable for the initial period" means the **tax which would be payable for the tax year if it ended on 30 November in that year instead of 31 December**. By deeming the tax year to end on 30 November, this means that all reliefs, e.g. losses carried forward from previous years or the annual exemption amount, are taken into account in calculating the person's chargeable gains and, thus, their CGT liability for the period.

The second amount, known as "**tax payable for the later period**", is payable on or before **31 January after the end of the tax year**. "Tax payable for the later period" means the **tax payable for the tax year less tax payable for the initial period**.

Example 1.1

An individual disposes of an asset in June 2019 giving rise to a chargeable gain of €10,000 and disposes of a second asset in December 2019 giving rise to a chargeable gain of €8,000. The individual had a loss forward of €3,000 from the disposal of shares in 2018. CGT is payable by the individual as follows:

Tax Payable for Initial Period

	€
Chargeable gains 01/01/2019 – 30/11/2019	10,000
Less: losses from 2018	(3,000)
Less: annual exemption	(1,270)
Taxable gain	5,730
CGT @ 33%	1,891

Tax Payable for Later Period

	€
Total chargeable gains in 2019	18,000
Less: losses from 2018	(3,000)
Less: annual exemption	(1,270)
Taxable gains	13,730
CGT @ 33%	4,531
Less: tax payable for initial period	(1,891)
Tax payable for later period	2,640

CGT for 2019 is payable as follows:

	€
On or before 15 December 2019	1,891
On or before 31 January 2020	2,640

It should be noted that tax due for the initial period is calculated **ignoring any losses that might arise in the tax year after 30 November**. Accordingly, where capital losses arising in the period 1 December to 31 December exceed chargeable gains arising in the same period, a refund of CGT will be due. Assuming, in the above example, the asset disposed of by the individual in December 2019 gave rise to an allowable loss of €4,000, the individual would still be required to pay CGT of €1,891 on 15 December 2019. However, after the end of the tax year he would be entitled to claim a refund as follows:

continued overleaf

	€
Total chargeable gains in 2019	10,000
Less: allowable losses in 2019	(4,000)
Less: losses from 2018	(3,000)
Less: annual exemption	(1,270)
Taxable gains	1,730
CGT @ 33%	571
Less: tax payable for initial period	(1,891)
Refund due	(1,320)

1.5.3 Returns

A return of chargeable gains must be made on or before 31 October in the year following the year of assessment, i.e. for 2019 the return must be made by 31 October 2020. If filing using the Revenue Online System (ROS), the 31 October deadline is usually extended to mid-November. This return will normally be made on a **Form 11** (the self-assessment annual income tax return) where the individual pays income tax under the self-assessment system; or on **Form CG1** where the individual is not within the self-assessment system for income tax purposes.

Failure to submit this return on time will result in the application of a **surcharge** of 5% of the CGT liability or €12,695, whichever is the lower, if filed within two months of the due date. The surcharge is 10% or €63,485, whichever is the lower, if the return is filed more than two months after the due date.

It should be noted that if an individual deliberately or carelessly files an incorrect return on or before the due date for the filing of the return, then the individual is deemed to have failed to file the return before the due date unless the error in the return is remedied on or before the due date for the filing of the return. However, if the individual becomes liable to a tax-geared penalty (see **Section 29.2.2**) in respect of an error in the return and pays the penalty due, a surcharge is not payable. If an individual files an incorrect return on or before the due date for the filing of the return, but does so neither deliberately nor carelessly and it comes to the individual's attention that the return is incorrect, then the individual is deemed to have filed the return after the due date unless the error in the return is remedied without unreasonable delay.

With effect from 1 July 2009, interest on overdue tax is charged at the rate of 0.0219% per day or part of a day (approximately 8% per annum). Prior to this date, the daily rate was higher.

1.6 Computation of Gain or Loss

1.6.1 General

The capital gain is the difference between:

1. the **consideration for the disposal** of the asset or the deemed consideration (e.g. **market value** in the case of a gift or disposal between connected persons); and
2. the **cost of acquisition** of the asset or its **market value** if not acquired at arm's length (e.g. property acquired by way of inheritance or gift).

If any part of the sales consideration is taken into account in computing income tax profits or losses, it is excluded from the amount under 1. above.

Any expenditure that is allowable as a deduction from income tax profits, or that would be so allowable if the asset had been employed as a fixed asset of a trade, is excluded from 2. above.

Allowable expenditure for CGT purposes is confined to expenditure included on capital account, i.e. it excludes expenditure deductible in calculating income. It includes the following:

1. **Incidental costs of acquisition or disposal**, e.g. agent's commission, stamp duty, valuation costs, cost of transfer or conveyance, auctioneers', accountants' or solicitors' fees and advertising costs.
2. Any cost associated with the **creation of an asset** that was not acquired, e.g. copyright, goodwill of a business.
3. Expenditure incurred for the purposes of **enhancing the value** of the asset and which is reflected in the state of the asset at the time of disposal, e.g. improvements to property. To be allowable, the expenditure must neither have been abortive nor must its value have wasted away before the disposal of the asset. Expenditure incurred in establishing, preserving or defending an owner's title or interest in an asset is allowable within this definition.

The basic layout of the CGT computation is shown below.

CAPITAL GAINS TAX COMPUTATION FOR 2019

	€	€
Sales proceeds (or market value)	X	
Less: incidental costs of sale	(X)	
		X
Deduct allowable costs:		
Costs of acquisition (or market value)		
(indexed if applicable – see **Section 1.6.2**)		(X)
Enhancement expenditure (indexed if applicable)		(X)
Gain		X
Deduct: reliefs		(X)
Deduct: losses		(X)
		X
Deduct: annual exemption (see **Section 1.9**)		(1,270)
Taxable gain		X
CGT payable: taxable gain × CGT rate		X

If there is a contingent liability, it is ignored and the gain or loss is calculated as if this liability did not exist. If the contingency happens after the CGT liability has been paid, then at that stage the gain or loss is recalculated to include a deduction for the liability. This will typically lead to a repayment of CGT overpaid.

1.6.2 Indexation Relief

The legislation introduced indexation relief to permit the effects of inflation to be taken into account in computing chargeable gains on disposals of assets. However, it is only available for assets acquired before 2003.

The relief operates by permitting the cost of any asset (including enhancement expenditure) to be adjusted for inflation by reference to the increases in the Consumer Price Index over the period of ownership of the asset.

The provisions introducing indexation relief also introduced another fundamental change in the law relating to the taxation of capital gains. **All assets owned at 6 April 1974 are deemed to have been disposed of and immediately re-acquired at their market value at that date.**

The deemed disposal and re-acquisition at 6 April 1974 of assets held on that date means that, for the purposes of applying the indexation multiplier, such assets are regarded as acquired in 1974/75 and their base cost is their 6 April 1974 market value. The multiplier effectively measures the change in the level of the Consumer Price Index from the mid-February preceding the year of assessment in which the asset is disposed of. The table of indexation factors for CGT is included in the tax reference material included at **Appendix 1** at the end of this textbook.

When using the tables, you should note that the tax years up to 2001 ran from 6 April to 5 April. The 2001 tax year was 6 April 2001 to 31 December 2001. All years since then are January to December.

Indexation relief is **only available in respect of the period of ownership of an asset up to 1 January 2003**. Accordingly, assets acquired in 2003 or subsequent years will not qualify for any indexation relief. Where assets acquired in 2002 or prior tax years are sold in 2003 or subsequent years, the cost of such assets is indexed using the multipliers applicable for disposals in 2003.

The following important points should be noted about indexation relief:

1. Indexation relief applies to **all** assets without exception, but is restricted to a significant degree in the case of development land.
2. Indexation relief cannot increase an allowable loss to an amount greater than the actual monetary loss. The allowable loss is restricted to the actual loss.

Example 1.2
Mary bought shares for €1,000 in June 2000. She sold them for €800 in August 2019. What is the allowable loss?

		€
Proceeds		800
Cost	€1,000 @ 1.144	(1,144)
"Loss"		(344)

As Mary made an actual loss of €200, the allowable loss is €200.

3. Indexation relief cannot convert a monetary gain into an allowable loss. In these circumstances, the disposal is at "no gain/no loss", i.e. effectively the disposal is ignored for tax purposes.

Example 1.3
Joe bought shares for €1,000 in June 2000. He sold them for €1,100 in May 2019. What is the taxable gain?

		€
Proceeds		1,100
Cost	€1,000 @ 1.144	(1,144)
"Loss"		(44)

As Joe made an actual gain, the disposal is at "no gain/no loss".

4. The interaction of indexation relief and the use of a 6 April 1974 valuation instead of cost can result in an actual monetary gain or loss being increased. In such circumstances, as at 2. above, the taxable gain or allowable loss is restricted to the actual gain or loss.

   Similarly, the interaction of indexation relief and the use of a 6 April 1974 valuation instead of cost can result in the conversion of an actual monetary gain into a loss, or an actual monetary loss into a gain. In such a scenario, as at 3. above, the disposal is deemed to be at no gain/no loss.

1.6.3 Enhancement Expenditure

Where enhancement expenditure has been incurred on an asset and is **reflected in the asset at the date of disposal**, the original cost and the cost of each subsequent item of **enhancement expenditure** is deductible. The chargeable gain is calculated as the difference between the various items of expenditure (i.e. both original cost and enhancement expenditure as adjusted for indexation) and the sale proceeds. Enhancement expenditure is **indexed** from the date **when it was incurred**.

Example 1.4

A public house was acquired in November 1998 at a cost of €450,000. Enhancement expenditure was incurred as follows:

		€
(1)	November 1999	100,000
(2)	November 2001	15,000
(3)	November 2003	10,000

The public house was sold in September 2019 for €1,850,000.

Computation of Taxable Gain

		€	€
Sale proceeds			1,850,000
Deduct:			
Allowable costs:			
1998/99 expenditure:	€450,000 @ 1.212	545,400	
1999/00 expenditure:	€100,000 @ 1.193	119,300	
2001 expenditure:	€15,000 @ 1.087	16,305	
2003 expenditure:	€10,000	10,000	(691,005)
			1,158,995
Annual exemption			(1,270)
Taxable gain			1,157,725

1.6.4 Special Rules Relating to Allowable Deductions

1. Treatment of Interest

Interest payments in general are not allowable deductions in the computation of capital gains. There is one specific exception to this rule. The exception is made in the case of a **company** that incurs **interest on money borrowed to finance the construction of any building, structure or works.** Such interest will be allowed as a deduction to the extent that the company has charged to capital the interest on the borrowed funds and no deduction was, or could have been, availed of by the company for the interest in computing its profits for the purposes of corporation tax.

2. Value-added Tax (VAT)

Where a person acquires a chargeable asset and the acquisition is liable to VAT, then the cost of the asset for CGT depends on whether or not the acquirer is entitled to claim "input credit" in respect of the VAT. If the acquirer cannot claim input credit, the cost of the asset is the VAT-inclusive price. Where the acquirer can claim input credit, the cost of the asset is the VAT-exclusive price. In other words, if VAT can be reclaimed it is no longer a cost.

3. Insurance Premiums

Insurance premiums paid to protect against damage to an asset are specifically **not an allowable deduction**.

4. Foreign Tax

Where the person making a disposal of a foreign asset incurs a charge to foreign tax and the foreign tax is incurred in a country with which Ireland has a **double taxation treaty**, relief is given by deducting the foreign tax paid from the Irish CGT, i.e. **credit relief**.

Example 1.5

Jones realised a gain of €500,000, after annual exemption, on the disposal of a property in Paris in March 2019. The French CGT payable was €80,000. The computation is as follows:

	€
Chargeable gain	500,000
Irish CGT payable @ 33%	165,000
Less: credit for French CGT paid	(80,000)
Balance of Irish CGT payable	85,000

Where the person making a disposal of a foreign asset incurs a charge to foreign CGT on the gain arising and **no double taxation relief** is available for the foreign CGT suffered, then the **foreign CGT may be deducted** in computing the amount of the gain that is chargeable to Irish CGT.

Example 1.6

Smith sold a capital asset located in Libya, a country with which Ireland does not have a double taxation treaty, for €900,000. The indexed cost of the asset was €398,730. The Libyan tax paid on the capital gain was €80,000. The computation is as follows:

	€
Total sale proceeds	900,000
Less: foreign CGT	(80,000)
Net proceeds	820,000
Less: indexed cost	(398,730)
Less: annual exemption	(1,270)
Taxable	420,000
Irish CGT @ 33%	138,600

5. Grants

No deduction is allowed in computing chargeable gains for any expenditure that has been met by the provision of government, public or local authority grants (whether Irish or foreign).

1.6.5 Part Disposal

We have seen earlier that the partial disposal of an asset is a chargeable event for CGT purposes. Where a portion of an asset is sold, the sale proceeds are known but the issue arises as to **how much of the original cost of the asset is allowable as a deduction when computing the chargeable gain or allowable loss arising on the part disposal.**

TCA 1997 provides that the **portion of the original cost** of the total asset that is allowed against the consideration received on the part disposal is to be confined to the proportion of the original cost of the asset that the value of the part being disposed of bears, at the time of disposal, to the market value of the whole asset. The formula is, therefore:

$$\text{Original Cost} \times A/(A + B)$$

where A is the amount of the proceeds of the part disposal (or market value, if appropriate), and B is the market value of the portion of the asset that is retained.

Example 1.7

Assume an asset cost €1,000 on 1 September 2019 and that nine months later part of the asset was sold for €600. The market value of the remainder of the asset is €700. The chargeable gain in respect of the disposal would be computed as follows:

	€
Sale proceeds	600
Less: allowable cost €1,000 × €600/(€600 + €700)	(462)
Chargeable gain	138

Note: the balance of the cost of €538 (€1,000 − €462) will be the allowable cost deductible in calculating any gain arising on the disposal of the remainder of the asset.

Example 1.8

Asset cost €10,000 on 10 April 1982. Part of the asset was sold on 10 November 2006 for €27,000. At that time, the market value of the remainder of the asset was €50,000. The remainder of the asset was sold on 1 November 2019 for €30,000.

The individual is married. Calculate the CGT liability for 2019.

		€
Proceeds		30,000
Cost:	€10,000 − [€10,000 × €27,000/(€27,000 + €50,000)] × 2.253	(14,630)
		15,370
Annual exemption		(1,270)
Taxable gain		14,100
CGT due @ 33%		4,653

There is no requirement to apportion any expenditure that, on the facts, is wholly attributable to the asset or part of the asset that is disposed of; or wholly attributable to the asset or part of the asset that remains undisposed of.

1.6.6 Application of Market Value

Normally where a disposal is at arm's length and the consideration is known in money terms, the consideration is accepted for CGT purposes. However, where the transaction is:

1. between connected persons, as defined in law, the *main* people being:
   (a) **Spouse** (husband or wife), **civil partner** and **relatives** (brother, sister, uncle, aunt, niece, nephew, ancestor or lineal descendant (including stepchild or adopted child)). It should be noted that the definition of "relative" does not include cousins.
   (b) **In-laws**, i.e. husband, wife or civil partner of a relative or husband, wife or civil partner of a relative of the person's spouse or civil partner.
   (c) **Partners**, i.e. a person is connected with any person with whom s/he is in partnership and with the spouse or relative of his/her partners.
   (d) **A company** is connected with another person if that person has control of the company or if that person and the persons connected with him together have control of the company, with companies under common control being connected persons;
2. not at arm's length (e.g. gift);
3. for a consideration that is not valued in money terms or that is a barter transaction;
4. the acquisition or disposal of an asset, wholly or partly, for a consideration that cannot be valued;
5. the acquisition of an asset by way of a distribution of property in specie from a company, e.g. in a winding up situation; or
6. the acquisition of an asset in connection with an office or employment, or in recognition of past services from an office or employment,

the market value is then deemed to be the consideration for the purpose of determining the chargeable gain or allowable loss.

1.7 Time of Disposal

The time/date of disposal for CGT purposes is determined by reference to special rules contained in TCA 1997. The date of disposal determines the rate of CGT that applies, e.g. gains arising on the disposal of assets on or after 6 December 2012 are subject to CGT at 33% (see **Section 1.5.1**). The date when a gain accrues determines when the CGT must be paid, e.g. CGT arising on gains accruing in October 2019 must be paid by 15 December 2019. The date of disposal and the date a gain accrues is the same date. Briefly, the rules for the date of disposal are as follows:

1. In the case of an **unconditional contract**, the date of the contract is the relevant date irrespective of the date of the conveyance or transfer of the asset (i.e. "the closing date" is not relevant).
2. In the case of a **conditional contract**, the general rule is that the date of the disposal for the purposes of CGT is the date on which the condition is satisfied. A conditional contract is a contract that is subject to a condition that must be satisfied before there is a binding contract between the parties, e.g. a contract for the sale of land that is subject to planning permission being granted in respect of the land.

3. In the case of **gifts**, the date of disposal is the date on which the property effectively passes, e.g. in the case of the gift of a chattel, the date that the chattel is delivered is the date of disposal for CGT purposes. This rule also applies to gifts into settlements.
4. In the case of **compulsory purchase orders**, the date of disposal is the date the compensation is received. (The law was different for compensation received prior to 1 January 2016. This is beyond the scope of this textbook.)
5. In **compensation cases**, the effective date is usually the date of receipt of the compensation, e.g. the date of receipt of insurance proceeds on the destruction of an asset.

1.8 Location of Assets

The legislation contains rules for determining the location of assets. These rules are particularly relevant to **an individual who is not Irish domiciled but who is resident or ordinarily resident** in the State (i.e. the Republic of Ireland). Such an individual is chargeable to CGT on chargeable gains accruing on the disposal of assets situated outside the State only to the extent that the gains are remitted to this country. Accordingly, it will be important for such an individual to establish that the gains were realised from the disposal of assets that were, in fact, situated outside the State. The following are the main rules that apply:

1. Rights or interests in **immovable** or **tangible movable property** are situated where the property is situated.
2. In general, **debts** are situated in Ireland if the creditor is resident in Ireland. **A judgment debt** is situated where the judgment is recorded.
3. **Shares or securities** issued by a government, governmental authority or municipal authority are situated in the country where that authority is established.
4. **Shares in, or securities of, a company incorporated in the State** are situated in the State.
5. **Other registered shares and securities** are situated where they are registered and, if registered in more than one register, where the principal register is situated.
6. **Goodwill** of a business is situated at the place where the trade, business or profession is carried on.

1.9 Annual Exemption

Individuals (not companies) are entitled to an annual exemption of **€1,270**. If the **chargeable gains** do not exceed €1,270 for 2019, no tax is due. If the gains exceed €1,270, only the excess is chargeable.

If an individual is married or in a civil partnership, **each** spouse or civil partner **is entitled to the €1,270 allowance**. If one spouse or civil partner does not avail of the allowance, it ***cannot*** be transferred to the other spouse or civil partner. Furthermore, this allowance cannot be carried forward to subsequent years if it is not used in the current year.

Example 1.9

An individual sold the following in March 2019:

(a) a building for €100,000, which had cost €75,000 on 1 October 1997;
(b) shares in an unquoted trading company for €20,000, which had cost €1,000 on 1 March 1990.

		€
Building:	Proceeds	100,000
	Cost €75,000 @ 1.232	(92,400)
		7,600
Shares:	Proceeds	20,000
	Cost €1,000 @ 1.503	(1,503)
		18,497
Summary		
Total gains		26,097
Less: exemption		(1,270)
		24,827
CGT due @ 33%		8,193

Example 1.10

Holly and Robin are married. During 2019 they had the following disposals:

- on 5 July, Holly sold shares for €12,000 – original cost was €11,500 on 5 March 2012;
- on 8 August, Robin sold a building for €350,000 – original cost was €290,000 on 7 January 2008.

As both assets were acquired post-2003, there is no indexation.
Holly had a capital gain of €500 (€12,000 – €11,500).
Robin had a capital gain of €60,000 (€350,000 – €290,000).

Holly can claim an annual exemption of €1,270. As her gains are less than €1,270, she has no CGT liability.

Robin can claim an annual exemption of €1,270. However, he cannot claim for the part of Holly's exemption that she could not use. Therefore, his CGT liability is 33% × (€60,000 – €1,270), i.e. €19,381.

1.10 Spouses and Civil Partners

1.10.1 General

Each spouse or civil partner is a separate "person" for CGT purposes and their gains or losses should be computed separately. The residence and domicile status of each spouse or civil partner must be considered individually to decide whether or not that person is chargeable to CGT.

1.10.2 Charge to Tax

The chargeable gains accruing to a married woman in any year of assessment during which she is **"living with her husband"** will be assessed on the husband unless an application for separate assessment for CGT purposes has been made or the couple elect for any assessments to be raised on the wife. As references to a man, married man or husband can be taken as references to a woman, married woman or wife, as the case may be, and vice versa, spouses in same-sex marriages are included within this provision. The net gains that accrue in a year of assessment to civil partners **living together** are charged on the nominated civil partner unless either civil partner has applied to be charged separately.

1.10.3 Disposal by One Spouse or Civil Partner to the Other

A disposal of an asset from one spouse or civil partner to the other **does not give rise to a CGT liability**, provided that the couple are living together for tax purposes, i.e. they are not separated (see **Section 1.10.7**). The asset is deemed to have passed from one to the other at a value that gives rise to no gain or no loss. On a subsequent disposal of the asset to a third party, there is a **chargeable gain or allowable loss by reference to the whole period of ownership by both spouses or both civil partners, and indexation to be applied is determined accordingly. There are two exceptions to this exemption:**

- where the asset concerned forms part of the inventories of either spouse or civil partner; or
- where the spouse or civil partner who acquired the asset could not be taxed in the State for the year of assessment in which the acquisition took place in respect of a gain on a subsequent disposal in that year by that spouse or civil partner.

In these two situations, there is a disposal and the consideration is always deemed to be the market value, regardless of the values agreed between the spouses or civil partners.

1.10.4 Principal Private Residence

Only one residence can qualify for exemption (see **Section 4.7**). Where a married couple or two civil partners have two residences, **they must jointly nominate one as their principal private residence**. If a principal private residence passes from one spouse or civil partner to another (by sale, gift or on death), the period of ownership should be treated for the purposes of the principal private residence relief as beginning at the date of acquisition by the spouse or civil partner who first acquired the residence.

1.10.5 Separate Assessment

If either spouse or civil partner makes an election for separate assessment before 1 April in the year following the year of assessment, then separate assessment will apply for the earlier year of assessment and for all subsequent years of assessment until it is withdrawn. A notice withdrawing an election for separate assessment must be made before 1 April in the year following the year of assessment to which the notice relates.

1.10.6 Losses

The general rule where a married couple are living together in the year of assessment is that the net chargeable gains accruing to one spouse for that year of assessment should be reduced as far as possible by any unutilised allowable losses accruing to the other spouse (taking into account losses brought forward) for the same year of assessment. The same rule applies to civil partners.

Example 1.11: Year of Marriage

Date of marriage is 1 October 2019. The gains and losses accruing are as follows:

	Husband	Wife	
	€	€	
1 January 2019 to 30 September 2019			
Net chargeable gains	4,800	100	
Net allowable losses		(200)	disposal prior to marriage
1 October 2019 to 31 December 2019			
Net chargeable gains	0	25	
Taxable gains	4,800	(75)	Net Losses

The wife's net losses for 2019 are set off against the husband's gains, the husband being assessed for the year on €3,455 (i.e. €4,725 less the €1,270 exemption).

By making an application before 1 April following the year of assessment, a spouse or civil partner may decide that their net loss accruing in that particular year of assessment shall be carried forward for set-off against his or her future gains instead of being set-off against the other's net gains accruing in the year. A fresh application is needed in respect of the losses of each year.

1.10.7 Separated and Divorced Couples

As outlined at **Section 1.10.3**, for a married couple or civil partners to benefit from the exemption on disposal of a capital asset between spouses or civil partners, they must be living together.

Year of Separation

Although technically a couple must be living together for the exemption to apply, Revenue practice is that any assets transferred in the year of separation are transferred at no gain/no loss (subject to the exceptions for trading inventories and spouse or civil partner not within the charge to Irish CGT outlined at **Section 1.10.3**). If there is a loss in the year of separation, the loss of one spouse or civil partner may be used by the other.

Years Following Separation

A charge to CGT does not arise where a person disposes of an asset **to a spouse or civil partner** as a consequence of a **legal obligation** under a **Deed of Separation** or an **Order of a Court**, including on a divorce or dissolution (subject to the exceptions for trading inventories and spouse or civil partner not within the charge to Irish CGT outlined at **Section 1.10.3**).

This means that each asset is treated as being disposed of for an amount that gives rise to neither a gain nor a loss in the hands of the spouse or civil partner disposing of the asset. The spouse or civil partner acquiring the asset is deemed to acquire the asset on the same day and at the same cost as the spouse or civil partner who originally acquired it.

Spouses and civil partners continue to be connected persons following a separation. All disposals between spouses following a separation that takes place after the year of separation, or outside of a legal deed of separation/court order, will be deemed to be at market value regardless of the actual consideration (see **Section 1.6.6**), and CGT will be calculated in the normal way. Following a divorce or dissolution, a couple cease to be connected persons as they are no longer married or in a civil partnership.

Example 1.12
Joe and Anne separate. As part of a deed of separation, Joe transfers the following assets to Anne:

- shares worth €100,000 (which he had purchased 10 years previously for €20,000);
- his interest in the family home (cost €30,000 20 years previously).

Joe will not be liable for any CGT on either of these disposals to Anne, regardless of whether the transfers take place in the year of separation or subsequently.

If Anne subsequently sells any of the shares, she will be liable for any CGT which arises. The gain will be calculated as if she had purchased the shares herself, 10 years previously, at the original cost of €20,000.

Example 1.13
Jack and Jill, who were married for years, separated permanently on 7 January 2012.

On 5 April 2012 Jack transferred to Jill shares in ABC Plc valued at €20,000, which he had acquired in 2008 for €5,000. In 2013, Jack transferred to Jill shares in XYZ Plc valued at €25,000 and which he had acquired in 2007 for €2,500. On 5 March 2019, Jack and Jill were granted a decree of divorce. The Order giving effect to the divorce provided that Jill's interest in an investment property the couple had jointly acquired in 2009 should be transferred to Jack. Jill's interest in the investment property was transferred to Jack on 1 May 2019. Jack sold the property in November 2019.

Jack would not have been liable to CGT on the transfer of shares in ABC Plc to Jill in 2012 as this was the year of separation. Jill is deemed to have acquired these shares for €5,000 in 2008. Jack would have been liable to CGT on the transfer of shares in XYZ Plc valued at €25,000 to Jill in 2013. The inter-spousal exemption did not apply as they were not living together. Jill is treated as acquiring these shares in 2013 for €25,000.

Jill will not be liable to CGT on the disposal of her interest in the investment property to Jack as it is made under an Order of a Court. The gain on the disposal of the property by Jack in November 2019 will be calculated as if Jack had purchased the entire interest in the property in 2009.

1.11 Partnerships

Dealings in partnership assets are treated as dealings by the individual partners and not by the firm. Therefore, chargeable gains or allowable losses accruing on the disposal of partnership assets are apportioned among the partners in accordance with their profit-sharing ratio. An individual's share of a partnership allowable loss may, therefore, be set-off against private gains and vice versa.

Partnership goodwill is a chargeable asset and consequently a gain on the disposal by a partner of his share of a firm's goodwill is chargeable.

The special rules relating to disposals between connected persons will apply on disposals and acquisitions between partners, as partners are deemed to be connected persons. In addition to a person being connected with all his/her business partners, that person is also connected with the husband/wife/civil partner/relatives of any of his/her partners.

"Relative" is defined as brother, sister, uncle, aunt, niece, nephew, ancestor, lineal descendant, stepchild or an adopted child.

Example 1.14

A and B are in partnership, sharing profits and losses 60% and 40% respectively. In November 2019 the partnership disposed of a building it had originally acquired for €30,000 in June 1983. It realised €100,000 on disposal.

Computation of Gain

	€
Sale proceeds	100,000
Deduct: cost €30,000 @ 2.003	(60,090)
	39,910
Apportioned as to A: 60% × €39,910	23,946
Apportioned as to B: 40% × €39,910	15,964
	39,910

Each partner would be entitled to claim any personal capital losses against the above gains and, of course, would be entitled to claim their annual personal exemption.

1.12 Connected Persons

1.12.1 Meaning of Connected Person

Where there is a transaction between "connected persons", the consideration is **deemed to be the open market value**. Any consideration agreed between the connected persons is ignored for the purposes of computing chargeable gains or allowable losses. The definition of connected persons in section 10 TCA 1997 is very broad. The following are the *main* persons:

1. **Spouse, Civil Partner, Relatives and In-laws:** relative includes brother, sister, uncle, aunt, niece, nephew, ancestor, lineal descendant (including stepchild or an adopted child), but it does not include a cousin. In-laws include spouse or civil partner of a relative, or spouse or civil partner of a relative of the person's spouse or civil partner. In the two instances where an inter-spouse or inter-civil partner transaction is regarded as a disposal (i.e. where the asset concerned forms part of the inventories or where the spouse or civil partner who acquired the asset could not be taxed in the State), the spouses or civil partners are regarded as connected persons and the inventories or other assets are deemed to be transferred at open market value, no matter what consideration is agreed between the spouses or civil partners.
2. **Partners:** a person is connected with any person with whom he/she is in partnership and with the spouse/civil partner or relatives of his/her partners.
3. **Company:** a company is connected with another person if that person has control of the company or if that person and the persons connected with him together have control of the company. Companies under common control are also connected persons.

1.12.2 Losses

Where a disposal to a connected person results in an allowable loss, that loss may only be **set-off against chargeable gains on disposals to the same connected person**.

1.12.3 Treatment of a Series of Transactions between Connected Persons

If an individual owns a number of assets and the value of the assets taken together is greater than the sum of the individual assets, and if those assets are then sold in separate transactions to the same connected person, the value of each asset sold is the higher proportionate value of the total assets and not the lower value of that individual asset. This is an anti-avoidance rule that does not arise frequently.

1.13 Development Land

1.13.1 Introduction

Disposals of "development land" made on or after 28 January 1982 are subject to special CGT treatment involving restrictions of indexation relief and loss relief. Principal private residence relief may also be restricted (see **Section 4.7.4**).

It should also be noted that Irish resident companies are only assessed to CGT on disposals of development land (see **Chapter 19**), all other disposals by Irish resident companies are assessed to corporation tax.

"Development land" is defined in section 648 TCA 1997 as: "Land in the State, the consideration for the disposal of which, or the market value of which at the time at which the disposal is made, exceeds the current use value of that land at the time at which the disposal is made, and includes shares deriving their value or the greater part of their value directly, or indirectly, from such land, other than shares quoted on a Stock Exchange."

The **"current use value"** of land at any particular time is defined as: "The market value at that time, if the market value were calculated on the assumption that it was, at that time, and would remain unlawful to carry out any development in relation to the land other than development of a minor nature." Development of a minor nature is one for which no planning permission is required.

A similar definition is also provided in relation to shares in an unquoted company that derive their value, or the greater part of their value, directly or indirectly from land.

The rate of CGT applicable to development land is the normal rate, i.e. 33%.

1.13.2 Restriction of Indexation Relief

In the case of development land acquired prior to 6 April 1974, indexation may only be applied to such part of the market value of the asset at 6 April 1974 as is equal to the "current use value" of the asset on that date.

In the case of development land acquired after 6 April 1974, **indexation relief may only be applied to the part of the consideration paid on purchase that relates to the "current use value"** of the asset together with the appropriate portion of total incidental costs of acquisition at that date.

Enhancement expenditure incurred after acquisition can be treated as an allowable cost when calculating the CGT liability. However, indexation relief does not apply to this enhancement expenditure.

Example 1.15

		€
Sale proceeds: development land 1 August 2019		150,000
Original cost of acquisition 1 January 1973		10,000
Total market value 6 April 1974		30,000
Current use value at 6 April 1974		14,000
Enhancement expenditure May 1986		5,000
Capital Gains Tax Computation 2019	€	€
Sale proceeds		150,000
Deduct: current use value at 6 April 1974		
€14,000 indexed @ 7.528	(105,392)	
Balance of market value at 6 April 1974	(16,000)	
Enhancement expenditure May 1986	(5,000)	
		(126,392)
Chargeable gain		23,608
Deduct: annual exemption		(1,270)
Taxable gain		22,338
CGT @ 33%		7,372

Example 1.16

		€
Sale proceeds: development land 1 August 2019		200,000
Original cost of acquisition 1 July 1982		40,000
Current use value 1 July 1982		21,000
Incidental costs of acquisition		1,000
Enhancement expenditure June 1986		3,000
Capital Gains Tax Computation 2019	€	€
Sale proceeds		200,000
Deduct:		
Current use value on purchase €21,000 indexed @ 2.253	47,313	
Incidental costs referable to current use value:		
$€1{,}000 \times \frac{21{,}000}{40{,}000} = €525$ indexed @ 2.253	1,183	
Balance of original cost	19,000	
Balance of incidental costs	475	
Enhancement expenditure	3,000	(70,971)
Chargeable gain		129,029
Deduct: annual exemption		(1,270)
Taxable gain		127,759
CGT @ 33%		42,160

1.13.3 Restriction of Loss Relief

Normally allowable losses for CGT may be set-off against other chargeable gains realised in the same year of assessment or, alternatively, carried forward against chargeable gains in future years. The legislation relating to development land provides that allowable **losses on assets other than development land may not be set-off against gains arising on the sale of development land**. However, allowable **losses arising on the disposal of development land may be offset against the gains arising on any type of chargeable asset.**

1.13.4 Disposals of Development Land for €19,050 or Less

The special CGT rules relating to restriction of indexation and loss reliefs that normally apply to sales of development land do not apply where **the total sales consideration** (not the amount of the gain) for disposals of development land by an individual **does not exceed €19,050 in any year of assessment**. It should be noted that this special relief is restricted to individuals and is not available to companies.

1.14 Losses

1.14.1 General

Losses are computed in the same manner as gains. If the asset is sold for less than the allowable cost of acquiring and enhancing the asset, then it is disposed of at a loss and that loss is an allowable loss. However, if the asset disposed of is an exempt asset, then the loss is not allowable. At **Section 4.1** it states that Irish Government securities are exempt assets, so a loss on such a security is not an allowable loss. An allowable loss may arise in certain circumstances even where the asset is not disposed of, e.g. a loss arising from the value of an asset becoming negligible. Subject to certain specific exceptions, allowable losses may not be carried back prior to the year of assessment in which they are incurred. They may not be set-off against taxable income.

In general, a loss is an allowable loss if, had there been a gain on the disposal of the asset, the gain would have been a chargeable gain.

Allowable losses arising must be set-off against chargeable gains accruing in the same year of assessment against gains chargeable at the highest rate of tax first, insofar as this is possible, and to the extent that there is an unutilised balance, the losses must be carried forward and set-off against chargeable gains arising in the earliest **subsequent** year.

All available loss relief must be utilised before relief for the €1,270 annual exemption may be taken.

Example 1.17

An individual has the following gains/losses for 2019:

			€
15 January	Asset 1	Gain	4,000
23 May	Asset 2	Gain	2,000
17 August	Asset 3	Loss	(4,000)
29 November	Asset 4	Gain	3,000

continued overleaf

The individual has allowable losses forward of €2,000 from 2018. Loss relief will be claimed as follows:

	Total
	€
Chargeable gains	9,000
Deduct: 2019 allowable losses	(4,000)
Deduct: allowable losses forward	(2,000)
	3,000
Deduct: annual exemption	(1,270)
Taxable gains	1,730
CGT due @ 33%	571

1.14.2 Carry-back of Losses Terminal Relief

The general rule is that capital losses cannot be carried back to earlier years. An exception to this rule is made in the case of **losses that accrue to an individual in the year in which he dies**. These losses may be carried back and set against gains of the three years of assessment preceding the year of assessment in which the individual died.

Example 1.18
Mr X dies on 31 August 2019. In the period 1 January 2019 to 31 August 2019, Mr X made disposals of assets and realised allowable losses of €5,000.

The losses of €5,000 will first be available for set-off against any chargeable gains assessed on Mr X in 2018, then against any chargeable gains in 2017 and, finally, against any chargeable gains in the tax year 2016. Any overpaid tax will be repaid by the Revenue.

1.14.3 Losses on Chattels

We will see later (at **Section 4.2**) that where a chargeable chattel is disposed of for less than €2,540, any loss on the disposal should be computed as if the consideration for the disposal had been €2,540.

1.14.4 Losses between Connected Persons

Where a disposal to a connected person results in an allowable loss, that loss may only be **set-off against chargeable gains on disposals to the same connected person**.

1.14.5 General Restrictions on Loss Relief

The following general rules apply in relation to relief for capital losses:

1. Losses may not be set-off against gains of an earlier year of assessment except in the case of losses accruing to an individual in the year of death.
2. Relief may not be given more than once in respect of any capital loss.
3. If the loss is realised and relief could be given for that loss against income profits (e.g. by way of a balancing allowance), then no relief is available for that loss against chargeable gains (see example in **Section 1.14.6**).
4. A loss accruing to a person who is not resident or ordinarily resident in the year of assessment is not an allowable loss for CGT purposes unless, if a gain had accrued instead of a loss on the disposal, the person would have been chargeable on the gain. Thus, in general, relief for capital losses arising to non-resident persons is limited to losses incurred on the disposal of:

(a) land in the State;
(b) mineral assets in the State;
(c) rights in the Irish Continental Shelf;
(d) shares of an unquoted company deriving their value from assets at (a) to (c) above; and
(e) assets of a business carried on in the State through a branch or agency.

5. There is no loss relief available in respect of assets situated outside the State for non-domiciled individuals who are assessed on the remittance basis.
6. Indexation cannot increase a loss (see **Section 1.6.2**).
7. The substitution of market value at 6 April 1974 for cost cannot increase a loss (see **Section 1.6.2**).

1.14.6 Losses on Assets Qualifying for Capital Allowances

Expenditure which qualifies for capital allowances represents an allowable cost for CGT purposes. However, to the extent that a loss on an asset has been covered by capital allowances no further relief is allowed for CGT purposes.

Example 1.19

Cost of factory (qualifying for industrial	€
buildings allowance)	150,000
Sale proceeds	120,000
Capital losses	30,000

Assuming the tax written down value of the building is €100,000, a balancing charge of €20,000 will arise. The capital loss allowable is restricted as follows:

	€	€
Capital loss		30,000
Allowances claimed	50,000	
Balancing charge	(20,000)	
Net allowances granted		(30,000)
Allowable capital loss		Nil

If the written down value of the building was nil, then the allowable capital loss would still be nil, i.e.

	€	€
Capital loss		30,000
Allowances claimed	150,000	
Balancing charge	(120,000)	
Net allowances granted		(30,000)
Allowable capital loss		Nil

In general, **capital losses arising on the sale of assets qualifying for capital allowances will only be allowable for CGT purposes to the extent, if any, by which they exceed the capital allowances granted for income tax purposes** (including any balancing allowance). Such an unlikely situation might arise, e.g. in the case of a sole trader who used an asset partly for business and partly for private use. In such a case a capital loss arising on disposal would not be fully relieved by way of a balancing allowance (due to restriction for private element) and some measure of CGT loss relief might then be available.

1.14.7 Losses and Development Land

The restriction of losses is detailed at **Section 1.13.3** above.

1.14.8 Negligible Value Claims

Where a person owns a capital asset, the value of which is now negligible, the person may make a claim to Revenue for relief for the unrealised loss. Even though there is no disposal of an asset, if the Inspector is satisfied that the value of an asset has become negligible, the Inspector may allow relief for the loss. The loss relief is allowed when the claim is made. On a strict interpretation of the law, a loss under this provision is allowable only in the year of claim. In practice, however, a claim made within 12 months of the end of the year of assessment (or accounting period for a company) for which relief is sought will be allowed by Revenue, provided that the asset was of negligible value in the year of assessment or accounting period concerned. The word 'negligible' is not defined and has its normal meaning, i.e. not worth considering; insignificant.

Example 1.20

Joe owns two assets. The first is 1,000 shares in a bank, which he bought for €15 per share, and which are now worth 50c per share. The second asset is 1,500 shares in Defunct Ltd, which he bought for €10 per share. A liquidator has been appointed to Defunct Ltd and it is insolvent.

Joe is entitled to make a claim for the loss of €15,000 (1,500 × €10), and this will be allowed by the Inspector as the shares have negligible value. While he has suffered a very significant unrealised loss on the shares in the bank, the shares have more than negligible value and, therefore, he cannot get relief for the unrealised loss. He can only get relief if he sells the bank shares.

1.15 Death

The assets that a deceased person was competent to dispose of are deemed to be acquired on his or her death by the personal representatives or by the beneficiary at the **market value at the date of death**. The deemed transfer at market value at date of death does not give rise to a chargeable disposal for CGT purposes and, accordingly, no liability will attach to the estate of the deceased in respect of any gains realised on the asset over their lifetime. The converse is also true in that no allowable losses are crystallised on a death. The **base cost** for the purposes of a subsequent disposal, by the personal representatives or by the beneficiaries, of an asset acquired on death will be the market value at the date of death. This is subject only to the exception that if the death occurred prior to 6 April 1974, then the market value at 6 April 1974 will form the base cost.

Questions

Review Questions

(See Suggested Solutions to Review Questions at the end of this textbook.)

Question 1.1

1. Maurice purchased a holiday home for €20,000 on 2 February 1985 and subsequently sold it on 30 November 2019 for €80,000. Incidental legal costs on purchase amounted to €600, and €750 on sale.
2. Vincent bought shares in a Plc in December 1991 for €1,200. He sold the shares for €9,300 on 1 April 2019.

3.

		Cost	Date of Purchase	Market Value @ 06/04/74	Sale Proceeds
		€		€	€
(a)	John sold a capital asset on 31/12/2019	7,600	June 2001	N/A	7,800
(b)	Philip sold a capital asset on 31/12/2019	3,000	July 1980	N/A	2,700
(c)	Paul sold a capital asset on 31/12/2019	5,700	June 1973	5,800	5,500
(d)	Oliver sold a capital asset on 31/12/2019	15,000	July 1980	N/A	18,000

Requirement
Compute the CGT due or allowable losses in each case. Assume that the individuals had no other realised gains or losses during the year.

Question 1.2

1. James constructed a hotel in July 1992 for €260,000. He received a capital grant from the State of €10,000. Additional expenditure was incurred as follows:

		€
August 2001	Repair roof	3,000
May 2005	Three new bedrooms added	90,000

James sold the hotel on 31 May 2019 for €650,000. James had no other capital gains during 2019.

2. Declan purchased a public house on 6 April 1998 for €85,000. Additional expenditure was incurred as follows:

	€
Additional games room 6 August 2001	20,000
Additional lounge bar 1 February 2004	39,250

Declan sold the public house for €400,000 on 1 July 2019. Declan had no other capital gains during 2019.

Requirement
Compute the CGT payable by James and Declan in each case (assume that the 33% rate of CGT applies).

Question 1.3

Joe Loss died on 27 July 2019. In the period 1 January 2019 to 27 July 2019 he made disposals of three assets as follows:

		€
Asset 1:	Chargeable gain	1,500
Asset 2:	Chargeable gain	200
Asset 3:	Allowable loss	(7,500)

In the four previous years of assessment, Joe had been assessed on net chargeable gains (after the annual exemption).

	€
2018	100
2017	150
2016	250
2015	1,000

Requirement
Compute the relief available to Joe in respect of the net loss incurred by him in the year of death. Take the annual exemption at €1,270 for all years.

Question 1.4

Michael Gain made the following disposals of Plc shares on 6 October 2019.

	Cost	**Date Purchased**	**Proceeds**
	€		€
1,000 Courtaulds Plc	888	06/11/1974	1,162
1,550 Box Plc	1,732	07/05/1981	1,662
500 Cox Plc	1,693	07/12/1993	16,000
400 Nox Plc	623	01/03/2006	1,305

Michael is not married and had no other chargeable gains during 2019.

Requirement
Compute chargeable gains (if any) made by Michael and the CGT payable (if any) for 2019.

Question 1.5

Derek Cotter is 49 years old and has completed the following capital transactions for the year ended 31 December 2019. He has lived in Ireland all his life.

1. On 12 January 2019 he sold a 5% holding, with a market value of €50,000, in the family tanning business to his sister for €40,000. Derek had inherited the shares from his father in January 2000 when they had a market value of €8,000.
2. On 5 February 2019 he sold his holiday home in Florida for €320,000. Derek had acquired the property for €110,000 on 30 October 1999.
3. On 5 May 2019 he sold shares in a Plc for €30,000. Derek had purchased the shares for €50,000 in April 2002.
4. On 10 December 2019 he sold a house (not his principal private residence) in Foxrock, Dublin, for €2,000,000. Derek had acquired the house and garden in December 1992 for €300,000. Derek sold the garden of one acre for €500,000 on 30 April 2001. The remainder of the house and garden was valued at €1,000,000 on 30 April 2001. The house did not have any development value at 10 December 2019.
5. On 21 December 2019 he gifted an antique chair to his nephew, Tom. The chair had been purchased for €2,600 on 3 December 2001. On 21 December 2019 the chair was valued at €3,500.

Requirement
Compute Derek's CGT liability for the tax year 2019 and state the due dates for the payment of this liability (assume that the 33% rate of CGT applies to all gains).

2

Territoriality Rules

Learning Objectives

After studying this chapter you will be able to:

- Apply the territoriality rules for CGT as influenced by a person's residence, ordinary residence and domicile, and the location of the asset.
- Identify and apply the rules for temporary non-residence for CGT purposes.

2.1 Recap – Rules on Resident, Ordinarily Resident and Domiciled

Liability to CGT depends on an individual's residence, ordinary residence and domicile, as well as the location and nature of the asset. At CA Proficiency 1, students studied income tax and the rules as to when an individual is:

- resident;
- ordinarily resident; and
- domiciled.

The charge to CGT also depends on whether an individual is Irish resident, ordinarily resident and/or domiciled. To recap, the meaning of these terms is set out below.

"Resident"
An individual is resident in the State in any tax year of assessment in which he or she:

- is present in the State for a total of 183 days or more;
- is present in the State for more than 30 days in that year, and was present for more than 30 days in the preceding tax year, and in that year and the previous year taken together spends 280 days or more in the State; or
- elects to be so resident, being in the State in that year with the intention, and in such circumstances that make it likely, that they will be resident in the following year of assessment.

"Ordinarily Resident"
An individual is ordinarily resident in the State in any tax year of assessment in which they have been resident in the State in the three previous years of assessment. Once an individual becomes ordinarily resident, they remain so until a year of assessment in which they have been non-resident in each of the three previous years of assessment.

"Domicile"

"Domicile" is a legal term. Briefly put, a person's domicile is the country where they are deemed to have their permanent home in law. This is normally the country in which they reside with the intention of remaining permanently. It should be stressed, however, that an individual may be domiciled in a country without actually residing in it.

2.2 Individual is Resident or Ordinarily Resident

An **Irish domiciled** individual who is **resident or ordinarily resident** in the State for 2019 (1 January to 31 December 2019) is chargeable to CGT on **worldwide** chargeable gains made on the disposal of assets.

A **foreign domiciled** individual who is **resident or ordinarily resident** in the State is liable on all **Irish gains** but only on **foreign gains to the extent that they are remitted to the State**, i.e. the remittance basis applies. There is **no loss relief available in respect of assets situated outside Ireland for non-domiciled individuals who are assessed on the remittance basis.**

Where an individual is taxed on a remittance basis, the rate of CGT that applies to remitted gains is the rate of CGT which applied when the disposal was made.

> ***Example 2.1***
> Hans Vervoort is a Belgian domiciled individual who has been resident in Ireland for many years. On 22 October 2012, when the Irish rate of CGT was 30%, Hans disposed of a property in Belgium. Hans did not remit the proceeds from this disposal to Ireland until 2019. Hans will be liable in 2019 to Irish CGT at 30% on the gain that arose on the disposal of the property.

Anti-avoidance legislation provides that, where a non-domiciled individual transfers outside the State to his or her spouse or civil partner, any of the proceeds of the disposal of any assets on which chargeable gains accrue and, on or after 24 October 2013, any amounts are received in the State that derive from that transfer, then the amounts will be deemed to have been received in the State by the non-domiciled individual and therefore are liable to Irish CGT.

While an Irish domiciled person who is non-resident, but is still ordinarily resident, is liable to Irish CGT, Irish domiciled individuals had been able to avoid Irish CGT by being resident in certain tax treaty countries. However, there is an anti-avoidance rule that charges to tax certain disposals by temporary non-residents (see **Section 2.4**).

2.3 Individual is not Resident and not Ordinarily Resident

An individual who is neither resident nor ordinarily resident is not liable to Irish CGT on the disposal of an asset unless it is a disposal of a specified Irish asset, i.e. disposals of foreign assets or Irish non-specified assets are outside the charge to CGT for an individual who is neither resident nor ordinarily resident. However, the disposal may be caught under the temporary non-resident anti-avoidance rules dealt with at **Section 2.4**.

2.3.1 Specified Irish Assets

Gains arising on the disposal of certain **specified Irish assets** are chargeable to CGT irrespective of the residence or ordinary residence of the owner. The specified assets are:

1. Land and buildings in the State.
2. Minerals in the State or any rights, interests or other assets in relation to mining or minerals or the searching for minerals, including exploration or exploitation rights within the limits of the Irish Continental Shelf.
3. Unquoted shares deriving their value, or the greater part of their value, from 1. or 2. above.
4. Assets situated in the State that, at or about the time when the gains accrued, were used for the purposes of a trade carried on in the State through a branch or agency, or were used, held or acquired for use by, or for, the purposes of the branch or agency.

You will recall that an individual is ordinarily resident in the State if resident in the State for the preceding three tax years. To become non-ordinarily resident, the individual must not be resident for at least three tax years. Therefore, if an individual wishes to avoid Irish tax on the disposal of a foreign asset or on an Irish asset that is not a specified asset, the individual must become both non-resident and non-ordinarily resident. This would mean that the individual would have to be non-resident for three tax years before the Irish CGT could be avoided under this general rule.

Example 2.2
During 2019, Mary made the following disposals:

1. Gain of €10,000 on sale of shares in Irish Plc, a company quoted on the Irish Stock Exchange.
2. Gain of €100,000 on sale of land in Galway.
3. Gain of €50,000 on sale of shares in UK Plc, a company quoted on the London Stock Exchange.
4. Loss of €5,000 on sale of shares in Completely Irish Plc, a company quoted on the Irish Stock Exchange.
5. Loss of €8,000 on sale of shares in Lyons Plc, a company quoted on the Paris Stock Exchange.

If Mary is Irish domiciled and resident or ordinarily resident, she is liable to Irish CGT on all the gains and is allowed loss relief for all the losses.

If Mary is not Irish domiciled, but is resident or ordinarily resident, she is liable to Irish CGT on Irish gains only (i.e. 1. and 2.) and allowed loss relief for Irish losses only (i.e. 4.). Mary will be liable to Irish CGT on the foreign gain (i.e. 3.) if she remits the gain to the State. She will not be entitled to relief for the foreign loss (i.e. 5.).

If Mary is not resident or ordinarily resident, she is liable on specified assets only and therefore is taxable only on 2. and is not entitled to relief for either of the losses.

2.3.2 Administration, including Withholding Tax

Due to the difficulty of collecting CGT due by non-residents, Revenue can issue a notice of assessment at any time, including before the end of the tax year. In this instance the CGT is due either two months after the making of an assessment or three months from the date of disposal, whichever is later.

In respect of certain specified assets, where a tax clearance certificate is not provided by the person making the disposal, the law provides for a withholding tax of **15%** of the purchase price to be withheld by the purchaser and paid directly to Revenue on behalf of the vendor. The purchaser is required to pay the withholding tax and submit information relating to the acquisition of the asset to the Collector-General within 30 days of the payment of the consideration for the asset. The vendor of the asset is entitled to offset the amount deducted against any CGT due on the disposal.

Assets that are potentially liable to the withholding tax are:

- land and buildings in the State;
- minerals in the State or any mineral or mining rights;

- exploration or exploitation rights in a designated area;
- unquoted shares deriving their value from any of the above assets; and
- goodwill of a trade carried on in the State.

While tax law only refers to land, under the Interpretation Act 2005 land is defined, and includes, houses and buildings and any estate, right or interest in or over land. Therefore, any reference to land includes any building(s) on that land.

The requirement to withhold tax of 15% only applies where the **value** of the asset disposed of **exceeds €500,000 or, in the case of a house or apartment, exceeds €1 million**. If an asset exceeding this value is sold in parts to the same person or connected persons, then those disposals are to be treated as one disposal. Where a deduction cannot be made from the purchase price because the consideration is in non-monetary form, the purchaser is still required to pay the 15% withholding tax, but it is recoverable by the purchaser from the vendor. This provision, in relation to consideration in a non-monetary form, does not, however, apply in the case of gifts as Revenue may assess the tax on the donee, i.e. the recipient of the gift.

A vendor may complete a form CG50 and apply for a clearance certificate to receive the proceeds without any withholding tax implications. The Inspector will issue a clearance certificate (CG50A) if satisfied that:

- the vendor is resident in the State;
- no CGT is due on the disposal; or
- the vendor has already paid the CGT due on the disposal of the asset and there is no CGT outstanding from a previous disposal of the asset.

While an Irish resident can obtain the clearance certificate prior to paying any CGT due on the disposal, non-residents must pay any CGT due if they want to receive the clearance certificate and avoid the 15% withholding tax.

2.4 Temporary Non-residents

2.4.1 Background

There is an anti-avoidance rule to tax Irish domiciled individuals who are temporarily non-resident and who would otherwise not pay Irish CGT due to tax treaty protection. This law seeks to prevent individuals who expect to make a gain on the disposal of shares from avoiding Irish CGT by becoming non-resident or becoming tax resident in a treaty country, disposing of the shares so that no Irish CGT is payable, and then returning to Ireland within a few years. If the person is, for more than five consecutive tax years, not tax resident in Ireland, then this anti-avoidance provision does not apply.

2.4.2 Liability to Irish Tax

The law imposes a CGT charge in respect of a *deemed* disposal of "relevant assets" owned by an individual on the last day of the tax year for which the individual is taxable in the State prior to becoming taxable elsewhere.

"Relevant assets" are a holding in a company that, when the person ceases to be chargeable to CGT in the State (i.e. the last day of the tax year in which the person departs),

- is **5% or more by value** of the **issued share capital** of the company; or
- has a **value in excess of €500,000**.

If a person disposes of all or part of such relevant assets during a period of five tax years or less, during which he or she is outside the charge to CGT under normal rules, the person will be liable to CGT on this disposal as if the person had disposed of those assets, or that part of those assets, on the last day of the tax year in which he/she was resident before departing, i.e. 31 December. For example, if a person leaves in December 2019 and becomes resident again in 2025, there could be a charge under this legislation if the disposal of the relevant assets takes place in the years 2020–2024 inclusive. If the individual waited until 2026 to become resident again, there would be no charge.

While the gain on the deemed disposal arises before the individual ceases to be resident in the State,

- the actual gain is calculated using the actual market value on the date the relevant assets are subsequently disposed of; and
- for self-assessment purposes the gain is required to be included in the individual's tax return, and the CGT in respect of it accounted for, in the year in which the individual again becomes taxable in the State.

Credit will be given in respect of any foreign tax payable on an actual disposal of the assets where such tax is payable in a territory with which Ireland has a double taxation treaty.

Therefore, this CGT charge will only arise if the individual:

- is Irish domiciled and has been Irish tax resident prior to departing temporarily from the State;
- disposes of relevant assets (i.e. certain shares) in the intervening years and only to the extent of the disposal; and
- is not taxable in the State in respect of any gains on the disposal of relevant assets for a period of five years or less before again becoming so taxable.

Example 2.3

Richie Rich owns 40% of the shares in Teleireland Ltd. These shares cost him €200,000 in 1999/2000. On 30 June 2019, he is offered €50 million for his shares. A friend has told him that if he goes to live in Portugal in 2019 and disposes of the shares in 2020, then he will not have any CGT liability on the sale, provided he is regarded as tax resident only in Portugal under the terms of the Ireland/Portugal double taxation treaty, even if he returns to the State in a couple of years' time.

If Richie Rich does as his friend suggests and is non-resident for five years or less between the year of departure and the year of return, and he disposes of the shares in this intervening period, then he would still be liable to CGT in the year in which he returns.

Assuming the shares are worth €51 million on 31 December 2019 and that he sells them for €52 million in June 2020 (and ignoring the annual exemption), the gain will be calculated as follows:

		€
Deemed proceeds:	market value at date of sale (June 2020)	52,000,000
Cost of shares:	€200,000 @ 1.193	(238,600)
Gain		51,761,400

If, however, Richie Rich remained non-resident for more than five years from the year of departure to the year of return, then this anti-avoidance rule would not apply and he would not be liable to CGT.

Questions

Review Questions

(See Suggested Solutions to Review Questions at the end of this textbook.)

Question 2.1

Jacques, a French domiciled individual, has been resident in Ireland since September 2009. During 2019 he made the following disposals.

(a) Disposed of 8,000 shares in a French family trading company for €65,000 on 15 May 2019. Jacques had acquired 16,000 of these shares in August 1994 for €60,000. Jacques used €10,000 of the proceeds received to improve his Dublin home. The remaining €55,000 he put on deposit in a bank in Paris.

(b) Disposed of a UK rental property for €200,000 on 1 October 2019. Jacques acquired this property in November 1997 for €180,000. He carried out extensive renovations on the property in the period January/February 1998, which cost €30,000 in total. He lodged the proceeds in his bank account in Dublin.

(c) Disposed of H Plc shares for €24,000 on 3 December 2019. Jacques had acquired these shares in June 1998 for €8,025. H Plc is an Irish company.

Jacques did not have any chargeable gains in 2018. He did, however, incur a loss of €15,000 on the sale of shares in a German trading company. Jacques remitted the proceeds from this sale to an Irish bank account.

Requirement
Calculate Jacques's CGT liability for 2019 (assuming the 33% rate of CGT applies to all disposals).

3

Shares

Learning Objectives

After studying this chapter you will be able to:

- Calculate CGT on share disposals in accordance with specific rules for ascertaining which shares are sold and the appropriate base cost of the shares.
- Advise on the tax relief available on certain employee share option schemes.

3.1 Introduction

Shares present special problems when attempting to compute gains or losses on disposal. Consider the scenario in **Example 3.1**.

Example 3.1

Joe bought the following shares in X Ltd:

	€
1,000 in January 2007 for	2,000
1,000 in January 2012 for	8,000

If Joe sells 1,000 shares today, what determines the cost of acquisition of the shares for CGT purposes?

The general rule is that disposals of shares are to be identified with purchases on a first in/first out (FIFO) basis, i.e. the longest held shares are deemed to be disposed of first. In the example above, the shares purchased first are deemed to be sold first – so Joe's cost of acquisition (base cost) for CGT purposes is €2,000. The FIFO rule offers the taxpayer the maximum advantage as indexation relief is applied to those assets owned for the longest period (see **Example 3.2** below).

Example 3.2

Ordinary shares in Abbott Limited, a trading company

		Number	Cost
			€
May 1981	Bought	100	100
July 1982	Bought	300	300
May 1986	Sold (FIFO)	(100)	
7 April 1989	Bought	400	425
May 1991	Bought	500	600 (i.e. €1.20 each)
May 2013	Sold	(300)	
June 2019	Sold	(525)	Sale proceeds €21,000

The disposals are dealt with on the following basis:

1. **May 1986 disposal:** the FIFO rule applies and the 100 shares sold are deemed to be those purchased in May 1981.
2. **May 2013 disposal:** the sale of 300 shares in May 2013 is deemed to be a disposal of the 300 shares acquired for €300 in July 1982.
3. **June 2019 disposal:** the sale of 525 shares in June 2019 for €21,000 would give rise to the following gains. Two separate disposals are deemed to have taken place:

	€
(a) Disposal of 400 shares acquired on 7 April 1989	
Proceeds: 400 @ €40 (i.e. sale price per share)	16,000
Deduct: €425 indexed @ 1.503	(639)
Chargeable gain	15,361
(b) Disposal of 125 shares out of the 500 originally acquired in May 1991 at a total cost of €600.	
Proceeds: 125 @ €40 (i.e. sale price per share)	5,000
Deduct: cost $\frac{125}{500} \times 600 = €150$	
Original cost of 125 shares: €150 indexed @ 1.406	(211)
Chargeable gain	4,789

The CGT liability is therefore:

	€
Total chargeable gains	20,150
Deduct: annual exemption	(1,270)
Taxable gains	18,880
CGT @ 33%	6,230

3.2 Rights Issues

A shareholder may be entitled to purchase additional shares in a company based on their existing shareholding in that company, i.e. by way of a rights issue. The shares acquired will form part of the original block of shares when applying the FIFO rule – they are effectively deemed to be part of the original holding. However, as the cash paid for the additional shares was paid at a later date than the original holding was acquired, the cash paid is treated as enhancement expenditure for indexation relief purposes.

Example 3.3

Jim acquired 1,000 €1 ordinary shares in Axel Plc on 1 May 1989 for €1,000.

On 1 June 1993 he acquired a further 2,000 shares for €5,000.

On 1 January 1997 Axel Plc made a rights issue of 1 for 5 at a price of €3 per share issued.

On 1 May 2019 he sold 1,600 shares at €50 each.

Step 1: Identify the make-up of Jim's holding, prior to the sale on 1 May 2019.

		No. of shares	Cost
Holding acquired 1 May 1989			€
	Shares @ €1	1,000	1,000
	Rights issue @ €3 (Note)	200	600
		1,200	
Holding acquired 1 June 1993			
	Shares @ €1	2,000	5,000
	Rights issue @ €3 (Note)	400	1,200
		2,400	

Note: 1996/97 rights issue of one new share for every five shares held (1:5) is deemed to be acquired at same time as the original holding.

Step 2: Apply the FIFO rule to the holdings acquired on 1 May 1989 and on 1 June 1993 to determine which shares are deemed to be disposed of in the sale on 1 May 2019.

The 1,600 shares sold are comprised of:

1,200	Shares from holding at 1 May 1989
400	Shares from holding at 1 June 1993 (i.e. 1/6th of total June 1993 holding)
1,600	

The disposal is treated as the separate disposal of two distinct holdings, those acquired in May 1989 and June 1993.

(a) Disposal of 1,200 shares of May 1989 holding

	€	€
Sale proceeds: 1,200 @ €50		60,000
Deduct:		
Original 1,000 shares cost €1,000		
Indexation: May 1989 @ 1.503	1,503	
Rights issue 200 shares cost €600		
Indexation: January 1997 @ 1.251	751	(2,254)
Chargeable gain		57,746

(b) Disposal of 400 shares of June 1993 holding

Sale proceeds: 400 @ €50		20,000
Deduct:		
Original June 1993: 2,000 shares × 1/6 = 333 shares.		
Cost of 333 shares @ €2.50 each = €832 indexed @ 1.331	1,107	
Rights issue 400 shares × 1/6 = 67 shares.		
Cost of 67 shares @ €3 each = €200		
Indexation: January 1997 @ 1.251	250	(1,357)
Chargeable gain		18,643

continued overleaf

Summary	
Gain applicable to May 1989 holding	57,746
Gain applicable to June 1993 holding	18,643
	76,389
Deduct: annual exemption	(1,270)
Taxable gain	75,119
CGT @ 33%	24,789

3.3 Bonus Issues

A shareholder may acquire, at no cost, additional shares in a company based on their existing shareholding in that company, i.e. by way of a bonus issue. The shares acquired will form part of the original block of shares when applying the FIFO rule – they are effectively deemed to be part of the original holding. As no consideration was paid for the additional shares there is no further deductible expenditure for CGT purposes. As no consideration is paid by the shareholders on receipt of the bonus shares, the complex calculations necessary in the case of rights issues are not required.

Example 3.4

Joe originally acquired 1,000 shares on 1 June 1990 for €2,000.

On 1 June 1994, he bought 500 more at a cost of €1,500.
On 1 January 1996, a bonus issue of 2 for 5 was made.
On 1 June 2019, Joe sold 2,000 shares for €20 each.

Prior to the sale on 1 June 2019, Joe's total holding of 2,100 shares was made up as follows:

	No. of shares	Cost
		€
Holding 1 June 1990		
Original acquisition	1,000	2,000
Bonus issue	400	0
	1,400	2,000
Holding 1 June 1994		
Original acquisition	500	1,500
Bonus issue	200	0
	700	1,500

Computation

The 2,000 shares sold are deemed to have been comprised of:

(a) the holding of 1,400 acquired 1 June 1990 for €2,000;
(b) 600 of the holding of 700 shares acquired 1 June 1994 for a total of €1,500.

	€
Sale proceeds: 1,400 shares @ €20 each	28,000
Allowable cost: €2,000 @ 1.442	(2,884)
Chargeable gain	25,116
Sale proceeds: 600 shares @ €20 each	12,000
Allowable cost: 600/700 × €1,500 = €1,286 @ 1.309	(1,683)
Chargeable gain	10,317

Note: above gains are subject to the annual exemption.

3.4 Acquisition within Four Weeks of Disposal and Disposal within Four Weeks of Acquisition

These are anti-avoidance provisions designed to prevent taxpayers benefiting by the creation of artificial losses. The transactions involved are commonly referred to as "bed & breakfast" transactions.

3.4.1 Acquisition within Four Weeks of Disposal

In this situation a loss accrues to a person on the disposal of shares and that person then re-acquires shares of the same class within four weeks of the disposal.

In this case, the loss on the shares can only be offset against the gain on the re-acquired shares, i.e. the loss cannot be used against other gains but can only be used when the new shares are disposed of and only against a gain on those shares (if any) and not against any other gains.

Example 3.5
Harry owns 1,000 shares in X Ltd, which he originally purchased at €5 each. On 30 December 2019 the shares are quoted at €1 each. Harry does not wish to sell his 1,000 shares as he believes they will rise in price in the future, but, at the same time, wishes to claim loss relief for the paper loss he has suffered. He cannot do this unless he has a realisation, i.e. a disposal. Accordingly, he arranges to sell his 1,000 shares at €1 each on 30 December 2019 on the understanding that his stockbroker will re-purchase a further 1,000 shares on the market two to three days later. Accordingly, Harry will realise a loss of €4,000 on the disposal which, in the absence of anti-avoidance provisions, would be available to set-off against any gains he has realised in 2019. In addition, he will also still own 1,000 shares in X Ltd.

The legislation prevents the utilisation of the loss by Harry by providing that as the disposal and re-acquisition of the same class of shares took place within four weeks, then the loss arising in 2019 can only be set against the subsequent gain arising on the disposal of the shares which have been re-acquired, i.e. the loss cannot be set against other gains in 2019 or any subsequent year.

Where the number of shares so re-acquired is less than the number of shares disposed of, a proportion of the loss is available for offset in the normal manner. This proportion is the same proportion of the loss on the disposal as the number of shares not re-acquired bears to the number of shares disposed of.

3.4.2 Disposal within Four Weeks of Acquisition

In this situation a person acquires shares and within four weeks after the acquisition disposes of shares of the same class. In this case, the FIFO rule is set aside in relation to the disposal within four weeks, and the shares sold are treated as being those which were acquired within the four-week period. In other words, the 'last in/first out' (LIFO) rule replaces the FIFO rule. It should be noted that LIFO replaces FIFO in all situations where there is an acquisition of shares followed by a disposal of the same class of shares within four weeks of the acquisition, even where the FIFO rule would not result in a loss.

Example 3.6
Joe owns 3,000 shares in a company that have fallen in value by €20,000 since they were purchased. He has other realised gains in the tax year of €30,000 and wishes to offset the losses accrued on his holding of 3,000 shares, but also wishes to retain the investment.

Joe therefore purchases a further 3,000 shares in the company, which he sells within four weeks. If FIFO applied, the disposal of the 3,000 shares would be deemed to come out of the original holding of 3,000 shares purchased at the higher price, thereby realising a loss of €20,000 to set against his other realised gains of €30,000.

continued overleaf

However, the existence of the anti-avoidance rule means that he is treated as selling the most recently acquired shares (LIFO applies) and his gain or loss on disposal will be calculated on that basis. Therefore the loss of €20,000 is not available.

Where the number of shares disposed of exceeds the number of shares acquired within the four-week period, the excess comes within the normal FIFO rule.

These provisions also apply to married persons and civil partners living together, thus preventing one spouse or civil partner from selling the shares on the open market and having the other spouse or civil partner re-acquire the shares.

3.5 CGT Treatment of Employee Share Options

A share option is the right to subscribe, at a specified price, for a specified number of shares in the employer's company during a specified period of time. The income tax treatment of share options has been covered in your CA Proficiency 1 course. You will recall that different tax treatments apply depending on whether the share option scheme is approved or unapproved.

3.5.1 General CGT Treatment of Employee Share Options

An **employee is subject to income tax on the exercise** of a share option and, **possibly, on the grant of the option,** depending on the exercise period.

For CGT purposes, **any gain that is chargeable to income tax is treated as being an additional consideration given by the employee for the shares acquired on the exercise of the option and is an allowable deduction when calculating any gain/loss on a disposal of the shares.**

Example 3.7

Patrick is granted an option by his employer, XYZ Plc, to subscribe for 1,000 €1 ordinary shares at a price of €1 each at any time in the following eight years. He is granted this right by reason of his employment at a time when the shares are valued at €3 each. Some time later Patrick exercises the option, at a time when each €1 ordinary share in XYZ Plc is worth €10, and takes up the 1,000 shares in XYZ Plc.

At the **date of grant** of the option, Patrick is chargeable to income tax on the difference between the option price (€1 per share) and the market value (€3 per share) – total €2,000 taxable at his marginal rate (as the option is longer than seven years).

At the date of exercise of the option he is chargeable to income tax on the full gain, with credit for the tax paid at the date of grant of the option, i.e. **he is charged to income tax on the difference between the amount paid for the shares (€1 per share) and the market value at the date of exercise of the option (€10 per share) – €9,000, with a credit for the tax paid on the gain of €2,000.** He has effectively been charged to income tax on €9,000: €2,000 at the date of grant and €7,000 at the date of exercise.

What is Patrick's base cost for his shares should he now choose to dispose of them?

	€
Actual sum subscribed	1,000
Gain chargeable to income tax to be treated as consideration	9,000
Total	10,000

If Patrick disposed of his shares immediately for €10,000 on exercising his option (which is a frequent occurrence in practice, since employees often cannot finance the holding of the shares they acquire under option schemes), **he would have no gain and no loss for CGT.**

3.5.2 Key Employee Engagement Programme (KEEP)

Finance Act 2017 introduced the Key Employee Engagement Programme (KEEP) to facilitate the use of share-based remuneration to attract and retain key employees in unquoted companies. KEEP provides for an exemption from income tax, USC and PRSI on the gain arising on exercise of a qualifying share option by a qualifying individual to acquire shares in a qualifying company in the SME sector, provided certain conditions are met by both the company and the individual throughout the period from the date of the grant to the date of exercise. Tax on such shares will be deferred until the shares are disposed of and CGT will be payable on the gain arising on the difference between the sales proceeds received and the price paid on exercise for the shares. The relief applies to qualifying share options **granted** in the period from 1 January 2018 to 21 December 2023.

Qualifying Share Options

A qualifying share option is a right granted to an employee or director of a qualifying company to purchase a predetermined number of shares at a predetermined price where the following conditions are met:

- the shares must be new, ordinary fully paid-up shares in a qualifying company;
- the shares cannot carry any current or future preferential rights to dividends, assets on a winding up or redemption;
- the option price at date of grant cannot be less than the market value of the same class of shares at that date;
- there must be a written contract in place setting out the number and type of shares, the option price, and the period during which the options can be exercised;
- options cannot be exercised within 12 months of grant other than in limited circumstances;
- options cannot be exercised more than 10 years from the date of grant; and
- the share option must have been granted for bona fide commercial purposes, the main purpose of which is to recruit or retain employees in the qualifying company, and not part of a tax avoidance scheme or arrangement.

Qualifying Company

The company must:

- be incorporated in the State or in an EEA state and must be resident in the State or carry on business in the State through a branch/agency;
- exist wholly or mainly for the purpose of carrying on a qualifying trade;
- at the date of the grant:
  - be an SME (i.e. less than 250 employees, annual turnover less than €50 million, and/or balance sheet not exceeding €43 million), and
  - total market value of issued but unexercised qualifying shares options cannot exceed €3 million;
- from date of grant to date of exercise:
  - be an unquoted company, other than a ESM or its equivalent in a EEA/DTA country, and
  - not be a company in difficulty under EU state aid rules.

A holding company can qualify if its business consists wholly of the holding of shares in a qualifying company that is a directly held 100% subsidiary.

A qualifying company is required to make an annual return to Revenue giving details of all options granted and exercised in the year.

Qualifying Trade
A qualifying trade is defined as trading activities other than excluded activities, such as:

- adventure or concerns in the nature of trade;
- financial activities;
- specified professional service companies;
- dealing in shares and other financial assets;
- dealing in or developing land, building and construction;
- forestry;
- coal, steel and shipbuilding.

Specified professional services include medical, dental, architectural, accountancy, geological and legal services. The qualifying trade must be undertaken on a commercial basis with a view to the realisation of profit, the profits or gains of which are charged to tax under Case I of Schedule D.

Qualifying Individual
A qualifying individual is a full-time employee or director of the qualifying company who is required to work a minimum of 30 hours per week for the company. This applies for the duration from date of grant to date of exercise. The employment must be capable of lasting at least 12 months from the date of grant of the share option. These working time conditions are deemed to be satisfied if the share options are exercised within 90 days of leaving the employment.

An individual will cease to qualify if they, together with connected parties, directly or indirectly become the beneficial owner of more than 15% of the ordinary share capital during the option period. If an individual ceases to qualify during the option period they will be assessed to income tax, PRSI and USC on any gain arising on the exercise of the option granted.

Limits on the Relief
Finance Act 2018 increases the limits on qualifying share options granted to qualifying individuals; however, the changes are subject to a Ministerial Commencement Order, which is not yet signed into legislation. Accordingly, the current limits remain as set down in Finance Act 2017. The market value of all shares in respect of which qualifying share options have been granted to an employee or director cannot exceed:

- €100,000 in any one tax year;
- €250,000 in any three consecutive tax years; or
- 50% of the annual emoluments of the qualifying individual in the year of assessment in which the option is granted.

Example 3.8
Hannah works full-time as a food scientist for Veganberries Ltd, a small, Irish-incorporated and tax-resident company. She earns €75,000 per annum. At 1 January 2019, the company grants her the option to acquire shares in the company. The shares are valued at €1 at 1 January 2019 and the option price is €1 per share. She can exercise her option anytime between 1 April 2020 and 31 March 2024. The maximum share options are the lower of:

- €100,000 in 2019;
- €250,000 in 2019, 2020 and 2021; or
- €37,500, being 50% of annual emoluments in the year of the grant.

Hannah is granted options on 30,000 shares at €1 each.

Example 3.9
Following on from **Example 3.8**, Hannah decides to exercise the option at 1 March 2024 when the market value is €6 per share.

In the absence of any relief, Hannah would be assessed to income tax, PRSI and USC at her marginal rate (52%) on the difference between the amount paid for the shares and their market value at the date of exercise:

30,000 × (€6 – €1) @ 52% = €78,000

As Hannah, the company and the share options fulfil all of the KEEP conditions, this gain is exempt from income tax.

Hannah sells the shares immediately. Ignoring the annual exemption and assuming she does not qualify for revised entrepreneur relief, Hannah is liable to CGT of:

30,000 × (€6 – €1) @ 33% = €49,500

In essence, Hannah has saved €28,500 in tax.

Questions

Review Questions

(See Suggested Solutions to Review Questions at the end of this textbook.)

Question 3.1

Louise, a single person, disposed of 5,000 shares in Tedu Ltd, a trading company, for €15,000 in June 2019. She acquired 4,000 shares in July 2004 for €1.50 per share. In October 2005 the company declared a 1: 2 bonus issue.

Requirement
Calculate Louise's CGT liability for 2019.

Question 3.2

On 2 May 2019, Lorraine McCarthy, a single person, gifted 10,000 shares in Arco Ltd, a trading company, to her sister, Mary. Lorraine had acquired her shares in Arco Ltd as follows:

1 July 1972	6,000 shares @ 19c each
1 November 1983	Rights issue 2 for 1 @ 34c each

She took up her rights issue fully.

At 6 April 1974 the shares were worth 22c each, and at 2 May 2019 they were worth €1.68 each.

Requirement
Compute Lorraine's CGT liability for 2019 (assume that the 33% rate of CGT applies).

Question 3.3

Martin Doyle, a married man, acquired 4,000 ordinary shares in Dublin Ltd, a trading company, in May 1973 for €1,000. The market value of each share at 6 April 1974 was 75c. On 6 January 1988, Dublin Ltd made a rights issue to existing shareholders. The offer was 1 share for every 2 held at a rights price of €3 per share. Martin took his full entitlement under the rights issue. The market value per share after the rights issue was €4.

On 6 July 2019, Martin sold 1,500 shares in Dublin Ltd to his wife, Orla, and 900 shares to his only son, Gerry, for €1,500 and €900, respectively. The market value of each share on that date was €10.

On 6 October 2019, Martin sold the balance of his shares on the market for €12 each.

Requirement
Compute CGT payable by Martin Doyle (assume that the 33% rate of CGT applies).

4

Exemptions and Reliefs

Learning Objectives

After studying this chapter you will be able to:

- Identify, advise on and apply the appropriate CGT treatment to disposals of particular assets that qualify for exemption or relief, including:
  - government securities exemption;
  - chattels exemption;
  - site to a child exemption;
  - certain land and buildings acquired from 7 December 2011 to 31 December 2014;
  - miscellaneous exemptions;
  - principal private residence relief; and
  - revised entrepreneur relief.

4.1 Securities of Government, Local Authorities and Semi-State Bodies

This exemption includes all Government securities, land bonds, stock of Local Authorities and securities issued by semi-State bodies such as the ESB, Bord na Mona, Housing Finance Agency, Bord Gáis Éireann and An Post. That is to say, no chargeable gain or allowable loss can arise on their disposal.

4.2 Non-wasting Chattels Sold for €2,540 or Less

A non-wasting chattel is defined as "tangible movable property" that has a predictable useful life of **more than 50 years**. Though the term "tangible movable property" is not defined, it covers, for example, paintings, antiques, postage stamps, etc.

A gain arising to an **individual** on the disposal of non-wasting chattels is exempt if the consideration does not exceed €2,540. It is the consideration **after deduction of expenses of sale** that is compared with €2,540 for the purposes of this exemption.

Where the consideration exceeds €2,540, there is a marginal relief that restricts the "tax payable" to one half of the excess of the proceeds over €2,540. The CGT is first calculated as if no marginal relief is to apply (deducting the annual exemption of €1,270 if applicable). This figure is then compared to the maximum CGT payable as calculated using the marginal relief formula and the lesser amount is the CGT liability. The annual exemption is only taken into account to the extent that it cannot be used against other chargeable gains.

Example 4.1
A work of art was bought for €100 and sold for €1,900 in August 2019. There is no chargeable gain.

Example 4.2
Assume no indexation relief applies, i.e. asset acquired after 31 December 2002 and the annual exemption was used against other chargeable gains.

	Situation A	**Situation B**
	€	€
Sale proceeds	2,550	2,590
Cost	(1,400)	(2,550)
Chargeable gain	1,150	40
Less: exemption	(Nil)	(Nil)
Gain	1,150	40
CGT @ 33%	379	13
Half the excess of sale proceeds over €2,540	5	25
CGT payable	5	13

Where a loss is incurred on the disposal of a chattel for less than €2,540, the allowable loss is restricted by deeming the **consideration** to be exactly €2,540.

Think about this carefully, as it is **not quite** the opposite of relief for gains. There the **tax payable** must not exceed half the excess over €2,540; the **allowable loss** is limited to the excess of cost over €2,540.

Compare **Examples 4.1** and **4.2** relating to gains with **Example 4.3** below.

Example 4.3

		€	€
Two works of art	Sale proceeds	1,400	1,900
	Cost	(2,600)	(2,600)
Actual loss		(1,200)	(700)
Allowable loss – in each case cost less €2,540		(60)	(60)

Note: in such circumstances, expenses of sale are added to the allowable loss and not deducted from the consideration for the purpose of the €2,540 limit. If the expenses on each sale were €30, the allowable loss would be increased to €90.

Note: the €2,540 exemption rule does not apply to currency and commodity futures in addition to **not** applying to wasting assets.

4.3 Wasting Chattels

A gain arising on the disposal of tangible movable property, which is a wasting asset, does not give rise to a charge to tax.

A "wasting chattel" is defined as a chattel with a **predictable life not exceeding 50 years**, for example, livestock, bloodstock, private motor car, yachts, aeroplanes and caravans. These assets include durable consumer goods that waste away over their lifetime and whose residual value is negligible so that gains will not normally arise on their ultimate disposal. Plant (other than plant that is a work of art) and machinery is always to be regarded as having a predictable life of less than 50 years and is always a wasting asset. Accordingly, antique plant or machinery, e.g. an antique clock or a vintage car, is deemed for tax purposes to have a predictable life of less than 50 years, even though in reality such an asset may be older than 50 years. However, a work of art, which includes a picture, print, book, manuscript, sculpture, piece of jewellery, furniture or similar object, is not a wasting asset and therefore is subject to the treatment outlined at **Section 4.2**.

The exemption is **not** given, however, where the chattels are business assets used in a trade or profession **and** which qualify for capital allowances. The reason for this is that capital allowances up to the full cost of those assets are given for income tax purposes. Even if capital allowances were not claimed, the exemption will still not operate if the allowances **could** have been claimed.

No loss claim is available in respect of assets qualifying for capital allowances. If the asset is sold for less than its cost, its capital allowances (including a balancing allowance where necessary) could be claimed and double relief cannot be given.

4.3.1 Treatment of Wasting Chattels that have Qualified for Capital Allowances

As outlined above, the exemption from CGT on gains realised from the disposal of wasting chattels does not apply to the extent that the chattels have qualified for capital allowances.

If the entire asset has qualified for capital allowances and the allowances have not been restricted due to private usage, then any loss arising on disposal of the asset will not be allowable for CGT purposes as it will have been effectively relieved for income tax or corporation tax purposes.

Example 4.4

	€
Business equipment cost	10,000
Tax WDV at date of sale	2,000
Sale proceeds	4,500
Computation	
Sale proceeds	4,500
Cost	(10,000)
"Loss"	(5,500)
Loss allowed for CGT purposes	Nil

The loss of €5,500 has already been fully relieved for income tax purposes as follows:

	€
Original cost	10,000
Less: tax WDV at date of sale	(2,000)
Capital allowances granted during period of ownership	8,000 (A)
Sale proceeds	4,500
Less: tax WDV at date of sale	(2,000)
Balancing charge on disposal	2,500 (B)

Capital allowances granted A – B = €5,500

If a wasting asset is sold and the asset has qualified without restriction for capital allowances purposes, then any gain arising after indexation relief has been taken into account is fully chargeable to CGT.

Example 4.5

	€
Business equipment cost	1,000
Tax WDV at date of sale	Nil
Sale proceeds	4,500

Asset owned by single individual for four years. Assume the indexation factor to be applied is 1.8.

Computation of gain

	€
Sale proceeds	4,500
Cost €1,000 @ 1.8	(1,800)
Chargeable gain	2,700

Note: the total capital allowances granted during the period of ownership will be recaptured on sale by means of a balancing charge.

4.4 Disposal of a Site to a Child

There is a CGT exemption, under section 603A TCA 1997, where a parent or the civil partner of a parent **disposes of a site to a child** (or certain foster children) of the parent on or after 6 December 2000 for the purpose of enabling the child to **construct a dwelling** house on the land and which is to be **occupied by the child as their only or main residence**. Such a disposal is **exempt** from CGT provided the market value of the site at the date of the disposal does not exceed €500,000. The site area is limited to one acre (0.4047 hectare) (excluding the area of the house to be built). Finance Act 2018 amended the definition of a "child of the parent" to include the spouse/civil partner of the child concerned, so allowing the child's spouse or civil partner to benefit from the relief with effect from 1 January 2019. References to "child" below should therefore be read as including the child's spouse or civil partner.

Where a site that qualified for exemption is subsequently disposed of to any person other than a spouse or civil partner and the land does not contain a dwelling house that:

1. was constructed by the child since the time of the acquisition of the land; **and**
2. has been occupied by the child as their only or main residence for a period of three years,

then the chargeable gain that would have accrued to the parent is treated as accruing to the child.

Where the transfer of a site has qualified for exemption, a further transfer of another site to that child will not qualify for exemption unless the chargeable gain that would have accrued on the transfer of the first site is treated as accruing to the child.

4.5 Certain Land and Buildings Acquired between 7 December 2011 and 31 December 2014

Section 604A TCA 1997 provided an exemption from CGT on gains arising on the disposal of land and buildings in the State and the EEA (EU plus Norway, Iceland and Liechtenstein) if the property was acquired between 7 December 2011 and 31 December 2014 and held for seven years, with tapered relief if the asset was sold after that date. Finance Act 2017 reduced the seven-year holding period to four years for disposals on or after 1 January 2018 and provides full exemption for gains arising on disposals made in the period between four and seven years after the asset was acquired. Where the property is owned for more than seven years before disposal, tapered relief applies as before.

To qualify for relief the property must be:

- acquired in the period 7 December 2011 to 31 December 2014;
- at a consideration equal to its market value or, if acquired from a relative (sibling, parent, ancestor, descendant, uncle, aunt, niece or nephew), at a consideration not less than 75% of the market value at the date of acquisition; and
- continue in the ownership of the person who acquired that land or buildings for at least four years from the date of acquisition;
- the income, profits or gains from the land or buildings must subject to Irish taxation; and
- there must be no tax arrangements in place which give additional tax relief beyond that which would be available if no tax arrangements were in place.

Example 4.6

In October 2014, Patrick, who is Irish resident and domiciled, acquired an investment property in Dublin for €250,000. Patrick pays Irish income tax on the rental income. In August 2018 he entered into a contract for the disposal of the property for €425,000.

What are the CGT implications for Patrick?

Having entered into a contract for the sale of the property in August 2018, the disposal will not be exempt from CGT as he has not held the property for at least four years. He will be liable to CGT of €57,750, ignoring the annual exemption (i.e. €425,000 – €250,000 @ 33%).

If Patrick had not entered into the contract for the disposal until November 2018, the gain on disposal would have been exempt from CGT as he would have held a qualifying property for at least four years and less than seven years.

Example 4.7

Sheila acquired an investment property in Dublin on 1 March 2013 for €180,000. She pays Irish income tax on the rental income. On 1 March 2021, Sheila sells the property for €315,000. What are the CGT implications (ignoring the annual exemption)?

A portion of the gain will be exempt (i.e. reflecting seven years' "exempt" ownership):

Ownership:	1 March 2013 to 1 March 2021 = 8 years
Exempt:	1 March 2013 to 1 March 2020 = 7 years

Sale proceeds	€315,000
Cost	(€180,000)
Gain	€135,000
Exempt part of gain:	
€135,000 × 7/8	(€118,125)
Chargeable gain	€16,875
CGT @ 33%	€5,569

4.6 Miscellaneous Exemptions

The law provides that certain gains are **exempt** from CGT. The *main* exempt gains are as follows:

1. Bonuses payable under Post Office instalment savings schemes.
2. Winnings from betting, lotteries, sweepstakes or games with prizes.
3. Sums obtained as compensation or damages for any wrong or injury suffered by an individual in his person or in his profession or in his vocation. This exemption extends to damages for personal or professional wrong, or injuries such as libel and slander.
4. Gains on disposals of fine art objects with a market value of at least €31,740 and which were on loan and displayed in an approved gallery or museum for not less than 10 years are exempt from CGT.

4.7 Principal Private Residence (PPR) Exemption

4.7.1 Introduction

The general rule is that a gain accruing on the disposal of an individual's principal private residence (PPR) is exempt from CGT. Grounds up to one acre (0.4047 hectares) (exclusive of the site of the house) around the house are included as exempt property. If there is more than one acre of land, then the acre to be taken is that which would be most suitable for occupation and enjoyment with the residence.

Only one house per person qualifies for exemption, and spouses or civil partners count as one person for this purpose. A person with two or more residences will nominate which one will qualify for relief by giving notice to the Inspector of Taxes within two years of the beginning of the period of ownership of the two or more residences. Unless such notice is given, the Inspector may decide the matter, subject to the taxpayer's rights of appeal within 21 days to the Tax Appeals Commission.

If the owner of the PPR rents out a room in the PPR and qualifies for rent-a-room relief, this will not reduce any relief due under these provisions.

4.7.2 Occupation and Deemed Occupation of PPR

Full exemption from CGT is granted only where the owner has occupied the house throughout the period of ownership. Where occupation has been only for part of the period of ownership, the exempt part of the gain is the proportion given by the formula:

$$\frac{\text{Period of occupation post-6 April 1974} \times \text{chargeable gain}}{\text{Total period of ownership post-6 April 1974}}$$

Any period before 6 April 1974 is ignored. The **period of occupation is deemed to include certain periods of absence** provided:

1. the individual has **no other exempt residence** at the time; and
2. the period of absence was both preceded by, and followed by, a period of occupation.

It is not necessary for the periods of occupation to immediately precede and follow the periods of absence. It is enough that there was occupation at some time before and after absence. The periods of absence deemed to be periods of occupation subject to the above condition are:

- **any periods** in which the owner was required by their employment to **work wholly outside Ireland**; and

- any period **not exceeding four years,** or any periods that together do not exceed four years, throughout which, because of the individual's place of work or a condition of employment being a condition reasonably imposed to secure the effective performance by the employee of the employee's duties, the individual had to reside away from their home. Where such periods exceed four years, only four years are deemed to be periods of occupation.

There is also a general rule whereby **the last 12 months of ownership are included in the period of occupation** as long as the owner was in occupation at some time during the period of ownership.

In addition to the deemed periods of occupation set out in the legislation, by concession Revenue also provides for two further periods of deemed occupation as follows:

1. Any period of absence during which:
   (a) the individual (who normally lives alone) was receiving care in a hospital, nursing home or convalescent home, or was resident in a retirement home on a fee-paying basis, and
   (b) the private residence remained unoccupied (or only occupied by a relative rent-free for the purpose of security or maintaining the house in a habitable condition),
   should be treated as a period of occupation.
2. Where an individual has a house constructed on land they already own, provided the house is completed within a year of the acquisition of the land and occupied as the individual's PPR by the individual, the period from the date the land was acquired and the house was first occupied shall be treated as a period of occupation of the house as a main residence.

It should be noted that in the case where full exemption is not available, partial relief will apply to reduce the liability of any chargeable gain arising.

Example 4.8

Owen Gough bought a freehold house for €6,000 on 1 April 1985. He lived in it until 30 September 1995 when he moved into a rented flat. He let the house until he sold it on 1 October 2019 for €220,000.

In the period 30 September 1995 to 1 October 2019, there is one year's deemed occupation, i.e. the last 12 months of ownership. Therefore, the CGT liability is:

	€
Proceeds	220,000
Cost: €6,000 @ 1.819	(10,914)
Chargeable gain	209,086
Less: exempt portion:	
$\frac{10.5 \text{ years} + 1 \text{ year}}{34.5 \text{ years}} \times €209{,}086$	(69,695)
Chargeable gain	139,391
CGT @ 33%	45,999

It is assumed that the annual exemption has been utilised against other gains.

If, alternatively, there is a loss, then the loss on the PPR is not allowable. However, if there would only be a partial exemption if the house were sold at a gain, e.g. the house had only been a PPR for part of the period of ownership, then a similar part of the loss is disallowed, but the balance is allowable.

> ***Example 4.9***
> Una bought a house for €250,000 on 1 May 2009. She lived in it until 1 May 2011 when she let it. On 1 May 2019 she sold the house.
>
> If she sold it for €300,000, her capital gain would be:
>
> | | € |
> |---|---|
> | Proceeds | 300,000 |
> | Cost | (250,000) |
> | Gain | 50,000 |
> | Exempt portion: | |
> | $\frac{2 \text{ years} + 1 \text{ year}}{10 \text{ years}} \times €50{,}000$, i.e. 3/10 × €50,000 | (15,000) |
> | Chargeable gain | 35,000 |
>
> This would be added to any other gains and her CGT for 2019 would be calculated, net of any capital losses and annual exemption.
>
> If she sold it for €210,000, she would have a loss of €40,000.
>
> As it was her PPR for part of the time she owned it, the fraction of the loss which is not allowed is the same fraction of any gain which would be taxed, i.e. 3/10ths of the loss (€12,000) is not allowed. The balance (€28,000) is an allowable loss.

If part of the house is used for the purpose of a trade or profession, the gain may be apportioned, and the part used for the trade is not exempt (see **Section 4.7.5**).

4.7.3 House Occupied by Dependent Relative

The legislation extends the PPR exemption to a gain arising on the disposal of a private residence owned by an individual and occupied by a dependent relative as their PPR.

To qualify for the relief, the following conditions must be satisfied:

1. The house must have been provided to the dependent relative rent-free and without any other consideration.
2. For complete exemption, the house must have been occupied by the dependent relative as their sole private residence throughout the full period of ownership.
3. The house must be occupied by a dependent relative of the individual claiming the relief.

A "dependent relative", in relation to an individual, means:

(a) a relative of the individual, or of the wife or husband of the individual, who is incapacitated by old age or infirmity from maintaining himself or herself; or
(b) a person, whether or not he or she is so incapacitated, and:
   (i) who is the widowed father or widowed mother of the individual or of the wife or husband of the individual, or
   (ii) who is the father or mother of the individual or of the wife or husband of the individual and is a surviving civil partner who has not subsequently married or entered into another civil partnership.

Relief is also given where the residence is occupied by a dependent relative of a civil partner of the individual claiming the relief, provided that all the other conditions are satisfied.

For any particular individual, only one house can qualify for the relief at a particular time. However, in the case of married couples or civil partners, relief can be claimed by each spouse or civil partner in respect of a disposal of a PPR owned by the spouse or civil partner and occupied in accordance with the conditions of the relief by a dependent relative **of that spouse or civil partner**. For example, a married couple/civil partnership could have three PPRs: their own, and one for a dependent relative of each spouse/civil partner.

Relief is also available on the disposal of a house by the trustee of a trust where the house was settled property and it was occupied by a beneficiary of the trust under the term of the trust deed.

4.7.4 Restriction of PPR Exemption – Development Land

The CGT exemption available on the disposal of one's PPR is restricted when the gain is derived from the disposal of a residence that is deemed to be "development land" for CGT purposes (see **Section 1.13**). Only the portion of the gain that refers to the **increase in the "current use value" of the residential property is exempted from CGT**. The balance of the gain arising is effectively treated as a gain on disposal of development land. If there are incidental costs of acquisition or disposal, they are to be apportioned between the current use value element and the "hope value" element.

Example 4.10
A private individual sells their residence with grounds on 1 June 2019 for €350,000. The individual had owned the residence since June 1998 when it cost €20,000. The sale proceeds of €350,000 are deemed to be split as to €200,000 current use value and €150,000 "hope value". The June 1998 cost of €20,000 is to be split as to €12,000 current use value and €8,000 "hope value".

	CUV	Hope Value
	€	€
Sale proceeds	200,000	150,000
Cost 1998/99		
CUV @ 1.212	(14,544)	
Hope value 1998/99		(8,000)
Gain	185,456	142,000
PPR relief	(185,456)	
Chargeable gain	Nil	142,000

4.7.5 Restriction of PPR Exemption – House Used Partly for Trade

Where a PPR is also used partly in the carrying on of a trade or profession, PPR relief is available only on the portion of the house used as a residence. PPR relief is calculated by:

$$\frac{\text{Period of occupation}}{\text{Period of ownership}} \times \text{Gain} \times \%\text{ used as residence}$$

Example 4.11
Gerry Skelly purchased a house on 1 July 1973 for €10,000 exclusive of €1,000 costs. From 1 July 1973 to 1 February 1990, Gerry occupied approximately 75% of the house as his PPR; the remaining portion was used solely for his veterinary surgeon's practice.

Gerry took rented accommodation for both his private residence and veterinary practice with effect from 1 February 1990. On 30 June 2019 he sold the house for €350,000 (gross). Costs amounted to €15,000.

Mr Skelly is married. The market value of the house at 6 April 1974 was €15,000.

continued overleaf

Computation of CGT for 2019

	€	€
Sale proceeds	350,000	
Less: costs of sale	(15,000)	335,000
Allowable cost:		
Market value at 06/04/74 €15,000 indexed @ 7.528		(112,920)
Gain		222,080
PPR relief: $\frac{202}{543}$ × €222,080 × 75%		(61,962)
Chargeable gain		160,118
Deduct: annual exemption		(1,270)
Taxable gain		158,848
CGT @ 33%		52,420

Note:

	Period of ownership	
06/04/74 to 01/02/90	15 years 10 mths occupied	190 mths
01/02/90 to 30/06/18	28 years 5 mths	341 mths
01/07/18 to 30/06/19	1 year deemed occupied	12 mths
Total		543 mths

Alternatively, if Gerry Skelly advised your manager that he occupied the house from 1 July 1973 to 1 February 1992 and you knew from the tax file that he ceased to occupy the house on 1 February 1990, what should you do?

As you know that the information is not correct and your client must have made a mistake, you should advise your manager of the correct date based on the file and the calculation on that basis so that he can raise it with Gerry Skelly and give him the correct tax computation.

4.8 Revised Entrepreneur Relief

Section 597AA TCA 1997 (introduced by Finance Act 2015) provides for a revised entrepreneur relief under which a reduced **rate of CGT of 10%** (was 20% for disposals in 2016) applies in respect of chargeable gains on the disposal of **chargeable business assets** made by a **relevant individual** on or after 1 January 2016, up to **a lifetime limit of €1 million of gains**. There are conditions to be satisfied in relation to the asset being disposed of and the individual.

Note: the original entrepreneur relief (section 597A TCA 1997) still exists and is available if it is more favourable to the taxpayer, but is beyond the scope of this textbook.

4.8.1 The Reduced Rate of 10%

Provided the conditions are satisfied, from 1 January 2016 the first €1 million of gains is taxed at a reduced rate, which, since 1 January 2017, is 10%.

Example 4.12
On 6 February 2019, Helen disposes of shares that are chargeable business assets, and she satisfies all of the other conditions for revised entrepreneur relief. Helen has not previously disposed of any chargeable business assets. The shares are sold for €1.5 million. Ignoring the annual exemption, what would Helen's CGT liability be if she realised a gain of:

(a) €800,000?
(b) €1.3 million?

(a) **Gain of €800,000** As Helen qualifies for revised entrepreneur relief and her gain is less than €1 million, she is taxed at 10% on the gain. Capital gains tax is €800,000 @ 10% = €80,000.

(b) **Gain of €1.3 million** As Helen qualifies for revised entrepreneur relief she is taxed at 10% on the first €1 million of the gain. The balance is taxed at the standard CGT rate of 33%. Therefore, CGT is:

€1,000,000 @ 10%	€100,000
€300,000 @ 33%	€99,000
Total	€199,000

4.8.2 Relevant Individual

The relief only applies if the individual is a "relevant individual", i.e. the individual has held the asset for a continuous period of three years out of the five years prior to the disposal.

4.8.3 Chargeable Business Asset

To qualify for revised entrepreneur relief, there must be a disposal of a "**chargeable business asset**" by an individual. "Chargeable business asset" means:

1. An asset used for the purpose of a "qualifying business" carried on by the individual. (A "qualifying business" is any business that is not in the business of holding investments, holding development land or the developing or letting of land.)
   This would include, for example, goodwill, buildings, plant and machinery.
2. Ordinary shares in a company where the following conditions are satisfied:
   (a) the individual owns not less than 5% of the ordinary share capital of the company;
   (b) the individual has been a director or employee of the company, or a group member, in a managerial or technical capacity for a continuous period of at least three of the five years before the disposal;
   (c) during the three-year period working for the company, or group company, the individual was required to spend not less than 50% of their working time working for the company, or group company.

   Shares in a holding company can qualify for relief. A holding company is a company whose business consists wholly or mainly of holding shares in 51% subsidiary companies.

The legislation specifically states that chargeable business assets do not include:

(i) shares held as investments;
(ii) development land;
(iii) any asset that would not give rise to a chargeable gain if sold (e.g. inventory);
(iv) goodwill transferred to a company if, immediately after the transfer, the individual is connected with the company (e.g. incorporation of sole trade); or

(v) shares transferred to a company if, immediately after the transfer, the individual is connected with the transferred company.

Goodwill and shares referred to in (iv) and (v) above, will however qualify as chargeable business assets if it would be reasonable to consider that the disposal was made for bona fide commercial reasons and did not form part of a scheme or arrangement the main purpose, or one of the main purposes, of which was tax avoidance. If arrangements are made to circumvent the connected parties test, the reduced rate of CGT will not apply.

4.8.4 Summary of Conditions

For the disposal of a **sole trader business**, the 10% rate applies if the following conditions are satisfied:

1. The business is a qualifying business (i.e. the business does not consist of holding investments, holding development land or developing or letting land).
2. The sole trader has disposed of chargeable business assets (for example, goodwill, buildings and plant and machinery used for the business).
3. The disposal was for bona fide commercial reasons and did not form part of a scheme or arrangement the main purpose of which was to avoid tax in circumstances where the sole trader disposed of goodwill to a company and is connected with the company immediately after the transfer.
4. These assets have been held for a continuous period of three years out of the five years prior to the disposal.
5. The lifetime limit on gains since 1 January 2016 of €1 million has not been exceeded.

For the disposal of **shares** in a company, the 10% rate applies if the following conditions are satisfied:

1. The business of the company is a qualifying business (i.e. the business does not consist of holding investments, holding development land or developing or letting land).
2. The individual is disposing of chargeable business assets – they are ordinary shares and they own at least 5% of the ordinary shares.
3. The disposal was for bona fide commercial reasons and did not form part of a scheme or arrangement the main purpose of which was to avoid tax in circumstances where the disposal is of shares to another company and the individual is connected with the transferred company immediately after the transfer.
4. The shareholder has owned the shares for a continuous period of three years out of the last five years.
5. The shareholder has been a director or employee of the company in a managerial or technical capacity for a continuous period of at least three of the last five years before the disposal.
6. During the three-year period working for the company, the shareholder was required to spend not less than 50% of their working time working for the company.
7. The lifetime limit on gains since 1 January 2016 of €1 million has not been exceeded.

Example 4.13
Emily and her spouse, Hugh, set up a distribution business, Together Ltd, in 2011. Each owns 50% of the shares in the company. Emily works full-time as managing director for the company; Hugh is a non-executive director of the company. They have been offered €2.1 million for the company by Takeover Ltd, an unconnected company, which would generate a gain of €1 million each.

continued overleaf

Ignoring the annual exemption, what would be the CGT payable by Emily and Hugh?

Condition	**Company**	**Emily**	**Hugh**
Qualifying business?	Yes – distribution		
Ordinary shares?		Yes	Yes
Owns at least 5%		Yes	Yes
Connected after disposal?		No	No
Held for 3 of last 5 years?		Yes	Yes
During 3 of last 5 years, have:			
– managerial role,		Yes	No
– for not less than 50% of working time?		Yes	N/a

Emily satisfies all of the conditions, therefore she will pay CGT of €1 million @ 10% = €100,000.

Hugh's situation is different. Although most of the conditions are satisfied, he has not worked for the company in a managerial or technical capacity so he is not entitled to the 10% rate. Therefore Hugh will pay CGT of €1 million @ 33% = €330,000.

4.8.5 Other Matters

The relief applies to disposals of shares in public and quoted companies, provided that the conditions are satisfied.

If there is a company reorganisation that qualifies for tax relief, any period of ownership of, and working for, the original company will be taken into account in determining whether or not the three-year test is satisfied. However, any period of being a sole trader before incorporation is ignored, i.e. the company must be trading, etc. for three years before the 10% rate can apply. Also, if the shareholder owns an asset that is leased to and used by the company, that asset does not qualify for this relief.

Where there is a transfer of a business to a company, and relief under section 600 TCA 1997 is claimed (see **Chapter 5**), the reduced rate of 10% will not apply to any portion of a gain relating to non-share consideration, unless it is reasonable to consider the transfer is done for bona fide commercial reasons and not as part of a tax avoidance arrangement or scheme.

Retirement relief (see **Chapter 6**) also contains a definition of chargeable business assets, which is specific for the purposes of that relief and should not be confused with its meaning under revised entrepreneur relief. Also, where an individual satisfies the conditions for retirement relief and revised entrepreneur relief, the individual will claim retirement relief but the relieved gain will use up part (or all) of the €1 million gain that may be taxed at 10% under this relief. For example, say Joe disposes of chargeable business assets giving rise to a gain of €1 million and Joe qualifies for both retirement relief and revised entrepreneur relief. The taxable gain of €1 million is fully relieved under retirement relief and he pays no tax. Even though he has not claimed the 10% rate, he has realised gains of €1 million, since 1 January 2016, on the disposal of chargeable business assets and therefore he cannot benefit from the 10% rate of tax on any subsequent disposals of chargeable business assets.

If an individual has gains taxed at 10% and 33% during the tax year and has losses (forward or current year), the losses are offset first against gains taxed at 33% and then against gains taxed at 10%.

Questions

Review Questions

(See Suggested Solutions to Review Questions at the end of this textbook.)

Question 4.1

Philip Even is married, and during the tax year 2019, he completed the following transactions:

1. On 1 July 2019 he gave a gift of a painting to his wife. He bought the painting in June 1988 for €8,000 and its current market value is €17,000.
2. On 1 September 2019 he sold two acres of development land to his son, John, for €10,000. The land has planning permission for residential development. The market value of the land on 1 September 2019 was €200,000. He originally bought it on 1 June 1982 for €5,000. At that date the current use value of the land was €3,000.
3. He sold a small farm for €260,000 on 1 June 2019. He originally acquired the farm by gift from his wife on 25 December 1992. The farm has been let by Philip for the last 10 years. The market value of the farm at that date was €50,000. The farm is not development land. His wife originally acquired it for €32,000 on 1 July 1990.
4. He sold his entire holding of Irish Government National Loan Stock on 1 July 2019 for €8,000. He had originally acquired it for €6,100 on 1 February 2012.
5. He sold an antique necklace for €1,500 on 7 August 2019. He had bought the necklace nine months earlier for €1,100.
6. He sold a painting on 8 August 2019 for €900. He had bought the painting in January 2006 for €1,200.
7. He gifted one of his commercial properties to his mother on 1 August 2019. The market value of the property at that date was €875,000. He originally bought the property on 1 January 1983 for €50,000. In June 1989 he extended the property at a cost of €60,000. In March 2008 he further extended the property at a cost of €50,000.
8. He sold a second piece of development land on 1 October 2019 for €18,000. He had acquired this land four months earlier for €10,000.
9. On 1 June 2019 he sold an antique vase for €1,800. He had bought the vase for €700 in June 1992.

Philip had agreed unutilised losses forward at 1 January 2019 of:

(i) losses unrelated to development land of €6,000;
(ii) losses in respect of disposals of development land of €1,500.

Requirement
Compute Philip Even's CGT liability for 2019.

Question 4.2

(a) Mrs O'Sullivan sold a large freehold commercial property on 6 October 2019. She had owned it for many years and it had been continuously let to tenants at a commercial rent. The details given to you are:

	€
Disposal proceeds	1,585,000
Legal costs of disposal	12,500
Agent's commission	7,000

The property had been extended on 6 June 1994 at a cost of €162,000. The agreed value at 6 April 1974 was €60,000.

Requirement (a)
Calculate the chargeable gain in respect of the above disposal.

(b) Mrs O'Sullivan had 10 acres of development land adjoining a housing estate. She acquired the land in June 1970 for €5,000. She has received an offer for the land of €1.8 million. The market value of the land at April 1974 was €25,000 and its current use value at that date was €12,500.

Requirement (b)
Calculate the CGT payable on the assumption the land is sold for €1.8 million on 31 May 2019. (Ignore the annual exemption.)

Question 4.3

Bill O'Rourke bought a substantial residence on one acre of land in Rathgar, Dublin, on 6 April 1986 for €75,000. His incidental costs on purchase were €4,251.

Bill accepted an offer from a developer and signed a contract for sale on 10 June 2019 for the residence and one acre at a selling price of €1.68 million. Incidental costs of disposal were €18,000. The value of the property as a residence at the date of disposal was €800,000.

Throughout the period of ownership, Mr O'Rourke had used the property as his PPR.

Requirement
Compute the chargeable gain in respect of Bill's disposal.

Question 4.4

On 5 January 2019, Mr Smart, a single man, sold a shop premises that he had owned as an investment. The sale price was €695,000 and costs of disposal amounted to €7,000. He had never occupied the premises himself and had never carried on a trade in the property.

The premises had been purchased in 1973 and was professionally valued at €10,000 as at 6 April 1974. Enhancement expenditure of €12,000 was incurred on 6 December 1991.

On 1 June 2019, Mr Smart also sold a holiday cottage to his nephew for €16,000. Mr Smart had purchased the cottage on 6 July 1987 for €25,000. The market value of the cottage on 1 June 2019 was €20,000.

Requirement
Advise Mr Smart of his CGT liability, if any, for the tax year 2019, giving reasons for your conclusions.

Question 4.5

Christine Martin, a single woman, entered into the following transactions during 2019.

1. On 1 August 2019, she disposed of a derelict shop for €224,000. The property was adjacent to a shopping centre that wished to expand. The current use value of the property at the date of disposal was €80,000. Auctioneer's fees amounted to €3,100. Christine had purchased the property in March 1992 for €63,000, its then current use value, and it has been vacant since then. Christine used €40,000 of the sale proceeds to repay the outstanding mortgage on the property.
2. On 20 October 2019, she sold 2,000 shares in MAX Plc for €4.50 each. She had acquired 1,500 shares in March 1995 for €6,800. In July 1997 MAX Plc had a rights issue of 1 for 5 at €3.50, which Christine took up. In January 1998, MAX Plc had a 1 for 2 bonus issue of shares, immediately after which the shares were valued at €2.50 each.
3. On 5 May 2019, she disposed of a painting for €2,600. She had inherited the painting on the death of her mother on 20 December 2004, at which date it had a value of €1,900. The painting was a family heirloom that was considered to have a value of €100 on 6 April 1974.

Requirement
Compute the CGT payable by Christine Martin for 2019.

5

Transfer of a Business to a Company

Learning Objectives

After studying this chapter you will be able to:

- Advise on the CGT exposure for a sole trader transferring the business to a company upon incorporation.
- Advise on the potential deferral of CGT arising on the transfer of a business to a company and the future base cost of shares in the company.

5.1 Sole Trader Transfers Trade to Company

Where a sole trader carries on a trade, the individual owns all the assets of the trade, including the capital assets. If any capital assets are disposed of, the individual sole trader must calculate a gain or loss on the disposal and pay any CGT due. If the individual sole trader decides to incorporate the business, i.e. transfer the trade, including some or all of its assets and liabilities, to a company, then the individual will typically have a disposal of capital assets (e.g. goodwill, building, machinery, etc.) to the company and therefore will have to consider the CGT implications and any reliefs – see **Section 5.2** below. When transferring the assets, it is critical to remember that this is a disposal between connected parties and therefore all assets must transfer at market value, including goodwill. This chapter deals with the taxation of these gains and the relief that is available, provided the conditions are satisfied.

When the assets are transferred to the company, they now belong to the company. If the capital assets are subsequently sold by the company, it will be liable to corporation tax (capital gains tax in the case of development land) on any gain in excess of the market value of the assets at date of transfer. **Chapter 24** deals with companies and capital gains.

5.2 Relief Available

As an individual and a limited company are separate legal entities, the transfer of business assets to a company by an individual will be a chargeable event for CGT purposes. That is, the disposal of capital assets, such as goodwill, buildings and machinery, by the individual to the company may trigger a CGT liability for the individual. However, under section 600 TCA 1997, CGT on the disposal of business assets to a company may be deferred, provided the business and all its assets (or all its assets other than cash) **are transferred in consideration for the issue of shares in the company** (see **Example 5.1** below). To avail of this relief, the business must be transferred as a going concern to the company. The deferral continues until the shares are disposed of by the individual who transferred the assets to the company (see **Example 5.3** below).

As with many CGT reliefs, the relief will not apply unless it is shown that the transfer has been effected for bona fide commercial reasons and does not form part of any arrangement or scheme of which the main purpose, or one of the main purposes, is avoidance of liability to tax.

The net gain on the transfer of the chargeable assets to the company is calculated in the usual way, and the proportion appropriate to any cash or deemed cash consideration is assessed immediately. The balance of the total net gain, i.e. the deferred gain, is apportioned rateably over the shares received, thereby reducing the base cost of the shares for the purposes of any subsequent disposal. The allowable cost of future disposals of the shares for the purposes of indexation is the original cost of the shares (at the time they are first issued) less the amount of the deferred gain.

If any liabilities of the trade, such as trade payables, are taken over by the company, then this is treated as a cash payment to the former proprietor and the deferred gain is reduced accordingly. Similar treatment applies if part of the consideration is satisfied by the creation in the company of a loan account in favour of the individual.

When the normal gain arising on the transfer of the chargeable assets to the company has been calculated, the amount to be deferred is calculated by applying the formula:

$$\frac{\text{Value of shares}}{\text{Total consideration}} \times \text{Chargeable gain (after indexation relief)}$$

If more than one class of shares is issued, the deferred gain is deducted from the cost of the shares on the basis of the relative market values of each class of shares at the time of acquisition.

Note: the greatest problem many students have with this topic is an accounting/shares issue and not a tax issue, i.e. how to value the shares. Once you remember that the value of the shares is the difference between the market value of the assets and the amount received in cash and deemed cash (e.g. liabilities taken over), then the computation is significantly easier.

Example 5.1

Mr X transferred his business, with all its assets other than cash, to a company on 30 November 2019. He had acquired the business on 5 December 1999. In consideration for the transfer, the company, X Ltd, issued 10,000 ordinary shares at par fully paid and paid Mr X €600,000 in cash. Mr X has not previously disposed of any chargeable business assets.

At the date of transfer the balance sheet of the business was as follows:

		€
Assets:	Goodwill at cost	29,000
	Inventories	250,000
	Buildings	250,000
	Cash	50,000
		579,000
Liabilities:	Trade payables	100,000
	Capital account	479,000
		579,000

continued overleaf

At the date of transfer the market value of the assets was as follows:

	€
Goodwill	250,000
Inventories	300,000
Buildings	1,300,000
	1,850,000
Trade payables	(100,000)
Net value of assets transferred	1,750,000

The market value of the assets was €1,850,000. The cash (€600,000) and deemed cash (payables €100,000) totalled €700,000. Therefore, the shares are worth €1,150,000 (€1,850,000 – €600,000 – €100,000).

The cost of the chargeable assets at acquisition on 5 December 1999 was as follows:

	€
Goodwill	29,000
Buildings	250,000

The chargeable gains are computed as follows:

	Dec 1999	Index	Adjusted Base Cost	Current Market Value	Chargeable Gain
	€		€	€	€
Inventories (not chargeable – gain liable to income tax)					
Goodwill	29,000	1.193	34,597	250,000	215,403
Buildings	250,000	1.193	298,250	1,300,000	1,001,750
					1,217,153

Deferred gain:

$$\frac{\text{Value of shares issued}}{\text{Total consideration}} \times €1,217,153$$

$$\frac{€1,150,000}{€1,850,000} \times €1,217,153 = €756,609 \text{ deferred gain}$$

Chargeable gain:	€
€1,217,153 – €756,609	460,544
Less: annual exemption	(1,270)
	459,274

This gain will be taxed at 33% unless Mr X satisfies the conditions required for revised entrepreneurs' relief, which would reduce the CGT rate to 10%.

Allowable cost of shares for future disposal:	€
Cost of shares	1,150,000
Less: deferred gains	(756,609)
Base cost for subsequent disposals of the shares issued to Mr X	393,391

There is a Revenue concession that, where an individual transfers a business to a company in exchange for shares only and assets exceed liabilities, bona fide trade payables taken over will not be treated as consideration. See **Example 5.2** below.

Example 5.2

Ms Y transferred her business, with all its assets (other than cash) and liabilities, to a company on 30 June 2019. In consideration for the transfer, the company, Y Ltd, issued 10,000 ordinary shares at par fully paid.

At the date of transfer the balance sheet of the business was as follows:

		€
Assets:	Inventories	250,000
	Buildings (at cost)	250,000
	Cash	50,000
		550,000
Liabilities:	Trade payables	100,000
	Capital account	450,000
		550,000

At the date of transfer the market value of the assets was as follows:

	€
Goodwill (Note 1)	250,000
Inventories	300,000
Buildings (Note 1)	1,300,000
	1,850,000
Trade payables	(100,000)
Net value of assets transferred	1,750,000

Note 1: the business was set up in June 1990. The building was bought at that time. The goodwill has no base cost as it was not acquired.

The chargeable gains are computed as follows:

	Cost June 1990	Index	Indexed Cost	Market Value	Gain
	€		€	€	€
Inventories (not chargeable – gain liable to income tax)					
Goodwill	Nil			250,000	250,000
Buildings	250,000	1.442	360,500	1,300,000	939,500
					1,189,500

Under the Revenue concession, where an individual transfers a business to a company in exchange for **shares only,** and assets exceed liabilities, **bona fide trade payables taken over will not be treated as consideration**. As this transfer satisfies these conditions, all of the gain may be deferred.

Allowable cost of shares for future disposal:	€
Cost of shares	1,750,000
Less: deferred gains	(1,189,500)
Base cost for subsequent disposals of the shares issued to Ms Y	560,500

Example 5.3

On 31 July 2019, Bill sold his 15,000 ordinary shares in FCS Ltd to Buy Ltd for €300,000. Bill had acquired these shares on 31 March 1999 when he transferred all his business assets, other than cash, and liabilities to FCS Ltd in exchange for 15,000 ordinary shares of €1 each in FCS Ltd and €25,000 cash.

Bill's balance sheet at 31 March 1999 read as follows:

		Cost	Market Value at 6 April 1974	Market Value at 31 March 1999
	€	€	€	€
Premises (at cost – 19 August 1970)		10,000	18,000	200,000
Goodwill		15,000	8,000	100,000
Receivables		13,000	N/A	13,000
Inventories		12,000	N/A	18,000
Cash		4,000		
		54,000		331,000
Less: payables	5,000			
Tax due	1,000	(6,000)		
		48,000		

At 31 March 1999 FCS Ltd had agreed to pay payables €5,000 and taxation €1,000 on behalf of Bill.

What is the chargeable gain arising from this transaction in 2019?

To calculate the CGT on Bill's disposal in 2019 it is necessary to calculate the base cost of the shares when he acquired them at 31 March 1999. Bill received the shares in 1999 in consideration for transferring his business to the company, FCS Ltd. Therefore, we must first calculate the deferred gain that arose on the transfer of his business to the company in return for the shares in FCS Ltd at 31 March 1999.

Disposal 31 March 1999 (disposal of business)

		€	€
Value of assets transferred at 31 March 1999			331,000
Taken in cash		25,000	
Debts paid by FCS Ltd		6,000	31,000
Value of shares (balance)			300,000
Proportion of consideration taken in shares		300 / 331	
Premises: 06/04/74 value: €18,000 @ 6.215		111,870	
Proceeds		200,000	
Gain			88,130
Goodwill: 06/04/74 value: €8,000 @ 6.215		49,720	
Proceeds		100,000	
Gain			50,280
{Receivables}			
{Inventories}	No chargeable gain		
{Cash}			
	Total chargeable gains		138,410

continued overleaf

Bill would have claimed relief to the extent that the sale proceeds were taken by way of shares in the company. In effect, this relief consisted of a deferral of the CGT payable on the amount of the consideration taken in the form of shares in the company.

Deferred gain: $\frac{300}{331} \times €138,410 = €125,447$

The deemed share value for future disposals following the application of the relief is calculated as follows:

	€
Value of shares	300,000
Less: deferred gain	(125,447)
Base cost of shares for CGT	174,553

Disposal 31 July 2019 (shares)

	€
Sale proceeds	300,000
Cost €174,553 @ 1.212	(211,558)
Chargeable gain	88,442

Bill will be assessed to CGT on this chargeable gain in 2019.

This relief merely defers some or all of the CGT arising on the disposal of a business by an individual. It is important to remember that such a disposal may also entitle the individual to claim other CGT reliefs, such as revised entrepreneur relief (see **Chapter 4**) as demonstrated in the following example, and retirement relief (see **Chapter 6**).

Example 5.4

Mr Harris carried on a wholesale distribution business from 8 May 1990 to 5 May 2019.

With effect from 6 May 2019, Mr Harris agreed to merge his business with a similar one carried on by Mr Hoyle. The merger is for bona fide commercial reasons and not as part of an arrangement the main purpose of which would be to avoid tax. A new company, H&H Ltd, will take over their businesses as going concerns.

Proceeds for disposal of Mr Harris's assets will be as follows:

(1) Goodwill valued at €60,000 is to be satisfied by issue of 50,000 €1 ordinary shares in H&H Ltd, valued at €50,000 and €10,000 cash. The market value of goodwill at 8 May 1990 acquired on purchase of business was €5,000.

(2) Receivables and inventories as per the balance sheet at 5 May 2019 are €8,000 and €10,000, respectively. Inventories per balance sheet was valued at historical cost. Having regard to current cost prices, it was agreed that inventories would be taken over at a value of €12,000. Mr Harris agreed to take 10,000 ordinary shares and €10,000 cash for these two items. There were no other business assets.

What is Mr Harris's CGT liability for 2019 on the basis that this was his only disposal for that year, and that he has not previously disposed of any chargeable business assets? Indicate the cost of shares in H&H Ltd for CGT purposes.

continued overleaf

	€	€
Consideration – goodwill		60,000
Market value at 8 May 1990: €5,000 × 1.442		(7,210)
Gain		52,790
Value of assets transferred (€60,000 + €8,000 + €12,000)	80,000	
Amount taken other than in shares (i.e. cash)	(20,000)	
Amount taken in shares	60,000	
Gain chargeable in 2019: $\frac{20}{80} \times$ €52,790		13,198
Less: annual exemption		(1,270)
		11,928
CGT @ 10%		1,193
Cost of shares	60,000	
Less: deferred gains (€52,790 – €13,198)	(39,592)	
Base cost for CGT purposes	20,408	

5.3 Limitations on the Relief

1. The fact that liabilities of the trade taken over by the company are treated as cash consideration for the purposes of calculating the deferral relief seriously reduces the benefit to be gained from claiming the relief.
2. Capital gains that arise in a company in effect suffer CGT twice: once on the company on disposal of the asset by the company; and again on the shareholder on disposal (by sale or liquidation) of the shares. Thus, appreciating assets, such as land and buildings, are open to an effective double charge to CGT if owned by a company.
3. The relief is not available unless all the assets of the trade, including land and buildings, are transferred to the company. An exception for cash was noted above.
4. The deferred gain reduces the base cost of the shares in the event of a subsequent disposal. However, if it is the individual's intention to benefit from retirement relief (see **Chapter 6**) or to never sell the shares, then this is not a concern.
5. Neither revised entrepreneur relief (**Section 4.8**) nor retirement relief (**Chapter 6**) will apply to reduce the CGT on the non-share based proportion of the gain unless the transfer is done for bona fide commercial reasons and not part of a tax avoidance scheme. However, as relief under section 600 itself will only apply if the transfer is done for bona fide commercial reasons and not as part of a tax avoidance scheme, this condition will generally be satisfied.

Questions

Review Questions

(See Suggested Solutions to Review Questions at the end of this textbook.)

Question 5.1

Jack O'Dowd has run a successful retail business for a number of years. To facilitate expansion of the business he decided to form a limited company, O'Dowd Ltd. The business (i.e. all assets and liabilities) was transferred to O'Dowd Ltd on 30 June 2019 in exchange for 200,000 €1 ordinary shares and cash of €50,000. The cash was left outstanding on a loan account. Jack has not previously disposed of any chargeable business assets.

The balance sheet of the business immediately prior to the transfer was as follows:

	€	€
Warehouse at cost (purchased May 1981)	120,000	
Depreciation to date	(12,000)	108,000
Plant and machinery at cost	46,000	
Depreciation to date	(14,000)	32,000
Receivables	117,000	
Inventories	48,000	
Payables	(55,000)	
Net current assets		110,000
		250,000
Jack O'Dowd's capital account		250,000

Market values as at 30 June 2019 were as follows:

	€
Warehouse	400,000
Plant and machinery (Note 1)	40,000
Goodwill (Note 2)	130,000
Net current assets	110,000

Notes:

1. The market value of no individual item exceeded its original cost.
2. The value of goodwill was ascertained by professional valuers. It relates entirely to the business as it was built up over the years by Jack.

Jack sold an antique vase on 5 December 2019 for €88,000. The vase had cost €7,000 in 1972 and had a market value on 6 April 1974 of €10,000. He sold shares in ABC Plc for €5,000 on 7 December 2019, which cost him €10,000 on 9 July 1998. Jack, who is single, has no other disposals in the year ended 31 December 2019. He had a capital loss forward of €10,000.

Requirement

(a) Calculate the CGT liability of Jack O'Dowd for the tax year 2019.

(b) State when this CGT liability is payable.

(c) Calculate the base cost of the shares in O'Dowd Ltd for CGT purposes.

6

Retirement Relief

Learning Objectives

After studying this chapter you will be able to:

- Explain the principles of, and conditions for, CGT retirement relief.
- Determine the availability of CGT retirement relief on disposal of shares and other business assets to a child and calculate the relief due.
- Determine the availability of CGT retirement relief on disposal of shares and other business assets to a person other than a child and calculate the relief due.

6.1 Introduction

Certain gains arising on the disposal of "qualifying assets" by an individual who is at least 55 years of age may be exempt from CGT if certain conditions are satisfied. There is no requirement that the individual in question actually retires. The amount of relief available depends upon whether the assets are disposed of to the taxpayer's children as defined or, alternatively, to third parties (see **Sections 6.5** and **6.6** respectively).

If retirement relief is claimed, the annual exemption of €1,270 is not due for other disposals in the year of assessment, i.e. there is no annual exemption in the year retirement relief is claimed, including any marginal relief claim.

The relief will not apply to disposals to third parties where the sole or main purpose of the disposal of qualifying assets is the avoidance of tax and not for genuine commercial reasons.

6.2 Assets Qualifying for Relief

Relief is available in respect of disposals of **qualifying assets**. The main qualifying assets, excluding farmland which has been rented to a tenant, are:

1. **Chargeable business assets** of the individual owned by them for at least 10 years ending with the date of disposal, and which have been their chargeable business assets throughout this 10-year period. The requirement for **10-year ownership does not apply to assets that are tangible, movable property**, e.g. movable plant and equipment.

In the context of retirement relief, chargeable business assets are **assets used for the purposes of a trade, profession, farming or employment carried on by the individual, or by the individual's family company**. Note that the definition of chargeable business assets for retirement relief differs from its definition under revised entrepreneur relief (see **Section 4.8**).

While stocks (inventories) and debtors (receivables) are assets used for the purposes of the trade, any gain on disposal of these assets is not subject to CGT. They are therefore not considered to be chargeable assets for this purpose.

Goodwill is a chargeable business asset for retirement relief purposes. However, as with revised entrepreneur relief (**Section 4.8.3**), the legislation provides that goodwill will not be a chargeable business asset if the goodwill is disposed of to a company and the individual is connected with the company immediately after the disposal unless it is reasonable to consider that the transfer was done for bona fide commercial reasons and not as part of a tax avoidance arrangement or scheme. This bona fide test for goodwill is in addition to the general bona fide test detailed in **Section 6.1**.

Assets not employed for the purposes of a trade, such as assets held as investments (shareholdings or rented property), are not chargeable business assets.

2. **Shares owned by the individual in a trading or farming company that is the individual's family company**. To qualify, the following conditions must be satisfied:

   (a) the shares must have been owned by the individual for at least 10 years ending on the date of the disposal;
   (b) the shares must be in a company that has been a trading or farming company, and the individual's "family company" for at least 10 years ending on the date of the disposal; and
   (c) the individual has been a working director of the company for at least 10 years, during which time the individual has been a full-time working director for at least five years;
   (d) if the shares are transferred to a company and the shareholder remains connected with the transferred company, retirement relief will not apply unless it is reasonable to consider that the transfer was for bona fide commercial purposes and not a part of a scheme or arrangement to avoid tax. This bona fide test for shares is in addition to the general bona fide test detailed in **Section 6.1**.

   Note: the 10-year period for which the individual must have been a working director of the company does not have to be the 10-year period ending with the date of the disposal.

   The legislation provides the following definitions:

   - **Family company** A company in which the individual claiming relief controls:
     - at least 25% of the voting rights; or
     - at least 10% of the voting rights and at least 75% of the total voting rights (including the individual's own 10%) are controlled by members of the individual's family or a member of the family of their spouse or civil partner.

     "Family", for this purpose, means the individual's spouse or civil partner, or a brother, sister, ancestor or lineal descendant of the individual or their spouse or civil partner.
   - **Full-time working director** A director who is required to devote substantially the whole of their time to the service of the company in a managerial or technical capacity.
   - **Trading company** A company whose business consists wholly or mainly in the carrying on of a trade or trades. It also applies to professions.

3. Shares owned by the individual in a company that is a **member of a trading group, the holding company** of which has been the individual's **family company**. Conditions 2(a)–(d) above and the definitions of family company and full-time working director also apply to these shares. The specific terms are defined as:

   - **Holding company** A company whose business (disregarding any trade carried on by it) consists wholly or mainly of the holding of shares or securities in one or more companies that are 75%'subsidiaries.
   - **75% subsidiary** A company is a 75% subsidiary of another company if not less than 75% of its ordinary share capital is owned directly or indirectly by that other company.
   - **Trading or farming group** A group of companies consisting of the holding company and its 75% subsidiaries, the business of whose members consists wholly or mainly of carrying on a trade(s).

   As the relief applies to the disposal of shares by an individual, it generally covers the sale of shares in a holding company.

4. **Land and buildings, machinery or plant** that the individual has owned for a period of not less than **10 years** ending with the disposal and which:
   (a) was **used throughout that period** for the purposes of the relevant company (i.e. the family company referred to in **2. and 3.** above); and
   (b) is **disposed of at the same time and to the same person as the shares** in the family company.

   Personally owned assets can qualify for retirement relief provided that they were used for the business of the company and are disposed of at the same time and to the same person as the shares in the company. This is similar to the rule that applies in capital acquisitions tax (CAT) business relief (see **Section 14.6.3**). Unlike CAT business relief however, there is no requirement that the vendor should have control of the company whose shares are being sold in order for assets let to the company to qualify for retirement relief.

   The definition of qualifying assets also includes certain farming and fishing payments and assets.

In applying the 10-year tests, the following periods can be taken into account.

1. The period of ownership by the individual's spouse or civil partner is treated as a period of ownership by the vendor.
2. The period of use by the spouse or civil partner of the individual where the spouse or civil partner is deceased is treated as a period of use by the vendor.
3. The period immediately before the death of a deceased spouse/civil partner, throughout which the deceased was a full-time working director is counted as a period when the vendor was a full-time director.
4. Continuity of ownership is available where new business assets replace older business assets, i.e. the period of ownership of old assets is taken into account when a disposal of new assets takes place. In other words, the period of ownership of both old and new assets are aggregated in determining the qualifying 10-year period.
5. The period of ownership of the business prior to incorporation by the individual will qualify as a period of ownership and throughout which they were a full-time working director if the individual was entitled to "transfer of a business to a company" relief.

6. The period that an individual was a director of a company will be deemed to include the period during which the individual was a director of another company where, under a scheme of reconstruction or amalgamation, shares in that other company were exchanged for shares in the first-mentioned company.
7. As indicated above, it is not necessary to satisfy the 10-year test in the case of tangible movable property.

6.3 Disposal of Sole Trader Business

If the sole trader, who is aged 55 or more, only owns chargeable assets which are used for the purposes of the trade and the assets (other than tangible movable property) have been owned for at least 10 years, then full relief may be available. However, if the proceeds on the disposal of these chargeable business assets exceed €750,000 (or €500,000 if the individual is at least 66 years old) and the disposal is to someone other than a child, then either marginal relief applies or no relief is available (see **Section 6.6**).

Example 6.1
Anna, aged 56, disposes of her sole trader business for €800,000 to an unconnected third party, Gregoria Ltd. The value is derived from the following assets and liabilities:

	€
Premises	600,000
Goodwill	90,000
Equipment	50,000
Receivables	100,000
Inventories	70,000
Liabilities	(110,000)
	800,000

Anna set up the business in 2001, when she bought the premises.

Does Anna qualify for retirement relief?

- She is at least 55 years of age.
- She has owned the chargeable business assets (other than the equipment, which is tangible movable property) for at least 10 years.
- The chargeable business assets have been used in the business for at least 10 years.

Anna does therefore qualify for retirement relief. Is full or marginal relief available to her?

- The value of the chargeable business assets is €740,000 (€600,000 + €90,000 + €50,000), i.e. it does not exceed the €750,000 limit. (Remember, receivables and inventory are not subject to CGT and so are not considered chargeable business assets for retirement relief.)
- She is less than 66 years of age.
- As Anna is not connected with the company after the transfer of goodwill to the company, the goodwill qualifies as a chargeable business asset for retirement relief purposes.

Therefore, Anna qualifies for full relief and the disposal of the business is exempt from CGT.

Example 6.2
Tom, aged 58, disposes of his sole trader business for €900,000 to an unconnected third party. The value is derived from the following assets and liabilities:

	€
Premises	600,000
Goodwill	90,000
Equipment	50,000
Investment (cost €50,000 in 2005)	80,000
Receivables	100,000
Inventories	90,000
Liabilities	(110,000)
	900,000

Tom set up the business in 2000, when he bought the premises.

As Tom is at least 55 but not 66 years old, has owned the chargeable business assets (other than equipment) for at least 10 years and the value of the chargeable business assets is not greater than €750,000 (it is €740,000, i.e. €600,000 + €90,000 + €50,000), Tom is exempt from CGT on disposal of the trade assets. However, the disposal of the investment is liable to CGT because it is not a chargeable business asset, i.e. used for the purpose of the trade. On the basis that this is his only chargeable disposal in 2019 his CGT is:

	€
Proceeds	80,000
Cost	(50,000)
Gain	30,000
CGT @ 33%	9,900

No annual exemption available in 2019 as retirement relief applies in 2019.

6.4 Disposal of Shares

If the assets subject to disposal are shares in a family company or a holding company that is a family company, then the following points are relevant.

Where shares are sold and the company owns assets comprised of chargeable and non-chargeable business assets (within the definition specific to retirement relief), only a portion of the gain qualifies for retirement relief. The amount of the gain that qualifies for relief is the proportion of the gain which the value of the company's **chargeable business assets** bears to the value of the company's **total chargeable assets**, i.e.:

$$\text{Gain on disposal of shares} \times \frac{\text{Value of chargeable business assets}}{\text{Value of total chargeable assets}}$$

where total chargeable assets is chargeable business assets plus assets held as investments.

Where the shares are disposed of to someone other than a "child" (see **Section 6.6**), in determining whether the consideration limit has been exceeded, sale proceeds are apportioned between the value of the company's **chargeable business assets and other chargeable assets that are not chargeable business assets**, i.e.:

$$\text{Sale proceeds of shares} \times \frac{\text{Value of chargeable business assets}}{\text{Value of total chargeable assets}}$$

Example 6.3 – Family trading company

John owns 100% of the shares in Durun Ltd. The company's assets have the following market values:

	€
Land and buildings	700,000
Equipment	10,000
Goodwill	30,000
Inventories	30,000
Trade receivables	40,000
Quoted investments	50,000
	860,000
Deduct: liabilities	(60,000)
	800,000

Assume that all the conditions for retirement relief are met and that John, aged 58, is disposing of the shares to an individual who is not a child. Therefore, the limit on proceeds from qualifying assets is €750,000.

The sale proceeds to be taken into account for the purposes of determining whether or not retirement relief applies is calculated as follows:

$$\text{Sale proceeds of shares} \times \frac{\text{Chargeable business assets}}{\text{Total chargeable assets}}$$

$$€800{,}000 \times \frac{(€700{,}000 + €10{,}000 + €30{,}000)}{(€700{,}000 + €10{,}000 + €30{,}000 + €50{,}000)} = €749{,}367$$

As the portion of sales proceeds representing chargeable business assets is less than the €750,000 lifetime limit for retirement relief on disposals to persons other than a child, retirement relief may be claimed on the portion of the gain relating to chargeable business assets.

The portion of the gain qualifying for retirement relief will be calculated as follows:

Gain on disposal of shares × €740,000/€790,000

In the case of a holding company, the formula would take into account the asset position of the whole trading group, i.e.:

$$\text{Sales price of shares in holding company} \times \frac{\text{Value of chargeable business assets of trading group}}{\text{Value of total chargeable assets of trading group (excluding shares in other group members)}}$$

6.5 Disposal to a "Child" (section 599 TCA 1997)

6.5.1 Individual Aged 55 to 65

Section 599 TCA 1997 permits unlimited retirement relief on disposals of qualifying assets to a child of the individual, where the individual is aged between 55 and 65 years old.

In addition to natural children, stepchildren and adopted children, the definition of "child" includes:

- A child of the civil partner of the individual.
- **Nieces** or **nephews** who have **worked substantially on a full-time basis for five years ending with the date of the disposal** in the business or company also qualify. The reference to nephew/niece does *not* include nephews/nieces of the spouse or civil partner of the individual disposing of the asset.
- A foster child who resided with and was under the care of and maintained at the expense of the individual making the disposal for a period of five years, or periods that together amounted to five years, up to the time that such foster child reached 18 years of age. A claim cannot be based on the uncorroborated testimony of one witness.
- A **child of a deceased child** of the individual or the civil partner of the individual, a child of the civil partner of a deceased child of the individual and a child of the civil partner of a deceased child of the civil partner of the individual.

For the purposes of any subsequent sale by the child, the child is deemed to have acquired the assets at **market value** at the **date of disposal**.

If the child **disposes of the assets within six years** of the date they acquired the assets, the "child" will have to pay the CGT that would have been payable by the individual had the individual not qualified for section 599 relief (retirement relief on a disposal to a child). In such circumstances you should check if the individual would have qualified for section 598 retirement relief or marginal relief (see **Section 6.6**) or revised entrepreneur relief (see **Section 4.8**) when computing the CGT now payable by the child in respect of the original disposal by the individual who qualified for retirement relief. This CGT is payable in addition to any CGT arising on any gain that the child realises on the disposal of the assets by the child.

Example 6.4: Transfer of shares to a child

Andrew, who is aged 60, transferred his 100% shareholding in his wholesale company to his daughter, Louise, in 2019. The market value of the shares at the date of transfer was €800,000. He had acquired the shares in January 1983 for €1,000. He was a full-time director of the company and the company held no investment assets.

The conditions for retirement relief are met and, as the disposal is to his child and Andrew is aged between 55 and 66 years, there is no limit on the amount of the proceeds. Therefore, no CGT is due. If Louise were to dispose of the shares within six years, she would have a liability to CGT on her disposal and also on the original disposal by her father to her.

Example 6.5: Transfer of shares to a child

Paddy, who is aged 57, is in a civil partnership with Joe. He transferred his 100% shareholding in Paddy Ltd, a trading company, to Joe's daughter, Carol, in August 2019. The market value of the shares at the date of transfer was €1 million. Paddy had not previously disposed of any chargeable business assets.

The shares were acquired 15 years ago for €40,000. Assume an indexation factor of 2.5. Paddy was a full-time working director of the company throughout the period of ownership.

continued overleaf

The market value of the assets of the company at the date of transfer were:

	€
Premises	450,000
Goodwill	350,000
Inventories and receivables	300,000
Investments	150,000
	1,250,000
Payables	(250,000)
Net value	1,000,000

As Paddy is less than 66 years of age and because Carol is the daughter of Paddy's civil partner, Joe, this is a disposal to a "child" and there is no limit on the proceeds.

	€
Deemed proceeds	1,000,000
Cost €40,000 @ 2.5	(100,000)
Gain	900,000
Less: retirement relief:	
$€900{,}000 \times \frac{€450{,}000 + €350{,}000}{€450{,}000 + €350{,}000 + €150{,}000}$	(757,895)
Chargeable gain	142,105

CGT @ 10% = €14,210.

Paddy also satisfies the conditions for revised entrepreneur relief (see **Section 4.8**), therefore the 10% rate of CGT applies

6.5.2 Individual Aged 66 or Over

With effect from 1 January 2014, if the individual is aged 66 or over, retirement relief is only available on qualifying assets with a value up to €3,000,000. Any excess is subject to CGT. The limit of €3,000,000 is in respect of all disposals to children, as defined, by a parent while the parent is aged 66 or over. Once the limit has been used, there is no further relief.

Example 6.6

Joanne Phelan is 65 years of age. She has a very successful trading company, Prime Limited, the shares in which she has owned for over 30 years. She has been a full-time working director of the company during that time. The only chargeable assets of the company are chargeable business assets for retirement relief. The company is worth €10 million. Joanne has not previously disposed of any chargeable business assets. The shares cost €5,000 and the indexation factor is, say, 4. She advises you that she is going to retire when she is 66, in 2020, and give her shares to her son, Jack. Advise her as to the CGT implications of disposing of the shares to Jack in 2019 (when she is 65) versus 2020 (when she is 66), assuming no change in value of the company or in tax law.

If Joanne disposes of the shares in 2019, she will have no taxable gain as all the conditions for retirement relief have been satisfied. If Jack sells the shares within six years, he will have to pay the CGT Joanne did not pay in addition to any CGT due by him.

If she disposes of the shares in 2020 when she is at least 66, there will be relief but it will only be given as if the consideration for the disposal had been €3 million. Therefore, assuming no change in the value of the company, the rate of tax, etc., her CGT would be calculated as follows:

continued overleaf

	€
Deemed consideration	10,000,000
Indexed cost: €5,000 × 4	(20,000)
Gain	9,980,000
Relief: €3,000,000 – €20,000	(2,980,000)
Taxable gain	7,000,000
CGT @ 10% of €1,000,000 (Note)	100,000
@ 33% of €6,000,000	1,980,000
Total CGT payable	2,080,000

Therefore, by disposing of the shares in 2019, Joanne has avoided CGT of €2.08 million. If Jack sells the shares within six years, he will have to pay the CGT that Joanne did not pay in addition to any CGT due by him.

Note: the 10% rate of CGT would apply to €1 million of the gain as the conditions for revised entrepreneur relief (see **Section 4.8**) will also be satisfied.

6.6 Disposal to Person Other than a "Child" (section 598 TCA 1997)

6.6.1 Individual Aged 55 to 65

Section 598 TCA 1997 provides for retirement relief on disposals of qualifying assets to a person other than a child, where the individual is aged between 55 and 65 years old and the sales proceeds do not exceed €750,000. There is no clawback of retirement relief on disposals to a person other than a child (unlike the six-year stipulation for disposals to a child). This is a lifetime limit. The assets may be sold piecemeal over a number of years, but if the aggregate consideration for all the qualifying assets sold since 6 April 1974 exceeds €750,000, then the relief will be withdrawn from all disposals that qualified for relief under this section.

Note: **qualifying assets** only include assets in respect of the disposal of which retirement relief could have been claimed. Accordingly, disposals of business assets by the individual before he reached age 55 are ignored in determining whether the €750,000 (or €500,000) limit has been breached.

Example 6.7: Disposal of sole trader business

Sam, a sole trader aged 65, sold his business to Barry, an unconnected person, for €250,000 in October 2019.

		Market Value 6 April 1974
	€	€
Freehold	150,000	2,000
Goodwill	19,000	3,000
Investments	20,000	1,000
Receivables	71,000	
Payables	(10,000)	
	250,000	

Freehold and goodwill are exempt as under €750,000.

Investments	20,000
€1,000 @ 7.528	(7,528)
	12,472
CGT @ 33%	4,116

No annual exemption is available as retirement relief applies in 2019.

Example 6.8: Family trading group Da-Jo Holdings Ltd

David and Joe Sheahan (brothers), both aged at least 55 but less than 66, own a successful Irish trading group. The trade has grown from humble beginnings when Joe and David set it up for almost nothing – assume Joe's indexed cost of acquisition is €1,000. The group is now valued at an estimated €7 million (on the basis of the trade/goodwill and asset portfolio within the group). The group structure is as follows:

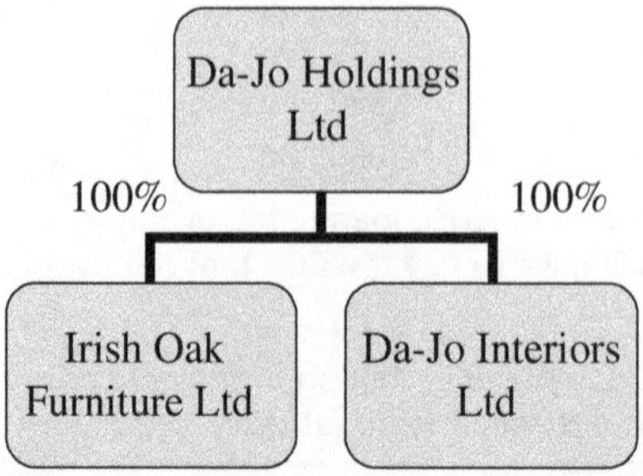

Da-Jo Holdings Ltd is a 100% parent of both companies in the group. **David owns 90% of Da-Jo Holdings Ltd and Joe owns 10%**. They have owned the company shares for over 20 years. Both men devote all their working time to the group's business and have been directors of Da-Jo Holdings Ltd since the 1980s. Joe wishes to sell his 10% holding to an unconnected third party for €0.7 million. Joe has not previously disposed of any chargeable business assets.

Requirement Compute the retirement relief available if the chargeable business assets of the group are €5.5 million, and the chargeable assets of the group that are not chargeable business assets are €0.5 million.

Assets available in the group

	€
Chargeable business assets of the group	5.5m
Chargeable assets that are not chargeable business assets	0.5m
Non-chargeable assets (net)	1.0m
Market value of the group	7.0m

Retirement relief is available to Joe on his 10% holding as he satisfies all the conditions. The proceeds re qualifying assets are:

$$\frac{€700{,}000 \times €5{,}500{,}000}{€6{,}000{,}000} = €641{,}667$$

€641,667 is within the €750,000 limit; however, part of the gain does not qualify for relief as some of the chargeable assets are not chargeable business assets. Therefore the taxable gain is as follows:

	€
Proceeds	700,000
Indexed cost of shares assumed	1,000
Gain on sale of shares	699,000
Retirement relief: €699,000 × €5.5m/€6m	(640,750)
Chargeable gain	58,250
CGT @ 10% (Note)	5,825

Note: the 10% rate of CGT would apply as the conditions for revised entrepreneur relief (see **Section 4.8**) are also satisfied.

Marginal relief applies where the proceeds of disposal are in **excess of €750,000**. In such cases, the CGT payable cannot exceed half the excess of the aggregate proceeds over €750,000 (or €500,000, if appropriate).

Example 6.9: Disposal of shares

Joe is married and aged 65. He bought shares in a family trading company in 1975/76 for €1,000. He has been a full-time working director since then. He sold the shares in October 2019 for €780,000 to an unconnected third party. Joe has not previously disposed of any chargeable business assets.

The net assets of the company at the date of sale were as follows:

		€
	Factory	645,000
	Goodwill	125,000
	Receivables	60,000
	Liabilities	(50,000)
		780,000
Proceeds		780,000
Cost:	€1,000 @ 6.080	(6,080)
		773,920
	Less: annual exemption	(1,270)
		772,650
	CGT @ 10%	77,265

The 10% rate of CGT applies as the conditions for revised entrepreneur relief (see **Section 4.8**) are also satisfied.

The maximum CGT liable if retirement relief marginal relief were to apply would be:

€780,000 – €750,000 = €30,000 × 50% = €15,000

Therefore retirement relief should apply.

When considering whether or not the lifetime limit of €750,000 has been exceeded, the following should be noted:

1. Qualifying assets transferred to a spouse/civil partner are included at market value. Thus, while the transfer of a qualifying asset to a spouse/civil partner will not be a chargeable disposal for CGT purposes, it may restrict the relief available.
2. Disposals of qualifying assets to "children" are not included.
3. If the disposal arises due to the receipt by an individual of a payment made by a company on the acquisition of its own shares, which is not treated as a distribution but as a capital disposal (see **Section 7.3** for the conditions to be satisfied), this capital receipt will be treated as coming within the scope of retirement relief and will therefore be taken into account for the purpose of the €750,000 threshold.

Example 6.10: Disposal of sole trader business

A newsagent, aged 58, who meets the conditions for retirement relief, gives one of his two shops to his wife (market value €700,000) and sells the other shop to an unconnected third party for €90,000 (allowable indexed cost, say, €30,000). Both shops were owned for 11 years and disposed of on 1 May 2019.

	€
Market value of transfer to wife	700,000
Sale to third party	90,000
Total proceeds	790,000
Excess proceeds over €750,000	40,000
Max. CGT liability (€790,000 − €750,000) × 1/2	20,000
CGT if no retirement relief:	
CGT on transfer to wife	Exempt
CGT on disposal to third party:	€
Sale proceeds	90,000
Less: indexed cost	(30,000)
Gain	60,000
Less: annual exemption	(1,270)
Taxable	58,730
CGT @ 10% (Note 1)	5,873

Notes:

1. Revised entrepreneur relief applies (see **Section 4.8**) as the asset is a business asset that has been owned for at least three of the last five years and, assuming the newsagent has not sold any other business assets since 31 December 2016, cumulative gains on the sale of business assets do not exceed €1 million. The 10% rate of CGT applies.

   As the CGT liability computed in the normal way is below €20,000, marginal relief does not apply.

2. If retirement relief had applied, no annual exemption of €1,270 would be due.

6.6.2 *Individual Aged 66 or Over*

With effect from 1 January 2014, the proceeds limit is €500,000 instead of €750,000.

Example 6.11

Carol Edwards has a very successful trading company, Edwards Limited, the shares in which she has owned for more than 10 years. She has been a full-time working director of the company during that time. The only chargeable assets of the company are chargeable business assets for retirement relief. The company is worth €740,000. The shares cost €1,000 in 2005. Carol has not previously disposed of any chargeable business assets. She advises you that she is going to retire during 2019 and sell her shares to Purchase Limited. Advise her as to the capital gains tax implications of disposing of the shares in 2019, (a) if she sells in February when she is 65 years of age; or (b) in May when she is 66.

Sell in February 2019 (aged 65)

If Carol disposes of the shares to someone other than her "child" in February 2019, when she is 65, she will have no taxable gain as all the conditions for retirement relief have been satisfied and the proceeds do not exceed the limit of €750,000.

continued overleaf

Sell in May 2019 (aged 66)

If she disposes of the shares in May 2019 when she is 66 years of age, again all the conditions will be satisfied, but the proceeds limit will be only €500,000. As the proceeds limit is exceeded, she may qualify for marginal relief. Her maximum tax will be limited to

(€740,000 – €500,000) × ½ = €120,000

This is compared to the CGT she would pay if retirement relief did not apply.
CGT payable if retirement relief does not apply:

	€
Proceeds	740,000
Cost (no indexation (2005))	(1,000)
Gain	739,000
Annual exemption	(1,270)
Liable to CGT	737,730
CGT @ 10% (Note)	73,773

Note: the 10% rate of CGT applies as the conditions for revised entrepreneur relief (see **Section 4.8**) are also satisfied.

As the CGT payable is less than it would be using the marginal relief formula, marginal relief does not apply. Therefore, she will pay €73,773 of CGT. However, by disposing of the shares in February 2019, instead of May 2019, Carol would avoid paying **any** CGT and would thereby save €73,773.

Example 6.12

Sean O'Brien is 67 years of age. He has a very successful trading company, O'Brien Limited, the shares in which he has owned for over 30 years. He has been a full-time working director of the company during that time. At all times, the only chargeable assets of the company are chargeable business assets for retirement relief. In 2016, when Sean was 63, he disposed of 50% of the shares in O'Brien Limited to Jones Limited for €300,000. He qualified for retirement relief and so did not have to pay CGT of €97,591. Now in 2019, when he is 68, he is disposing of the remaining 50% of his shares in O'Brien Limited to Jones Limited for €400,000. Advise him as to the CGT implications of disposing of the shares to Jones Limited in 2019, on the basis that the indexed cost of 50% of the shares in the company is €3,000. Sean did not dispose of any chargeable business assets in 2019.

All the conditions for retirement relief have been satisfied by Sean. However, as the proceeds limit is €500,000 and he has received proceeds of €700,000 (€300,000 + €400,000) since he was 55 years of age, he will have to pay the CGT on the disposal in 2018, and there will be a clawback of all the relief granted in 2016; or alternatively, marginal relief may apply if this results in a lesser amount of CGT being payable.

CGT before marginal relief

CGT would be calculated as follows:

	€
Disposal in 2019	
Proceeds	400,000
Indexed cost	(3,000)
Gain	397,000
Annual exemption	(1,270)
Liable to CGT	395,730
CGT @ 10% (Note)	39,573
2016 CGT as retirement relief no longer available	97,591
Total CGT payable	137,164

Note: the 10% rate of CGT applies as the conditions for revised entrepreneur relief (see **Section 4.8**) are also satisfied.

Marginal relief

The maximum tax is: (€700,000 – €500,000) × ½ = €100,000

Therefore marginal relief will apply and Sean will pay CGT of €100,000 (rather than €137,164).

6.7 Summary of Conditions to be Satisfied

The summary below sets out the key issues only and does not deal with all issues which may arise. Therefore, it is important to read all of the chapter.

6.7.1 Sole Trader

- At least 55 years of age.
- Owned chargeable business assets for at least 10 years (plant and machinery – no minimum period; replacement of assets allowed), or owned by spouse or civil partner and individual for 10 years.
- Proceeds limit of €750,000 (or €500,000 if aged 66 or over) on qualifying assets if disposed of to someone other than a child. If the disposal is to a child and the individual disposing of the assets is aged 66 or over, there is a limit of €3,000,000 on the proceeds that can qualify for retirement relief.
- Must be for genuine commercial reasons and not the avoidance of tax.

If there are any chargeable assets which are not chargeable business assets, any gain on these assets will be taxable.

6.7.2 Shareholder

- At least 55 years of age.
- Shares owned for at least 10 years ending on the date of the disposal (or owned by spouse or civil partner and individual for 10 years; if qualified for transfer of business to a company, can include period as sole trader).
- Shareholder cannot be connected with the transferred company if the disposal is to another company, unless it is reasonable to consider the transfer was for bona fide commercial purposes and not part of a scheme to avoid tax.
- Shares in trading company or trading group.
- Shares in family company (at least 25% or, alternatively, 10% with 75% owned by family).
- Working director for at least 10 years, of which at least five years were full-time (or working by spouse or civil partner if spouse or civil partner is deceased; if qualified for transfer of business to a company, can include period as sole trader).
- Proceeds limit of €750,000 (or €500,000 if aged 66 or over) on qualifying assets if disposed of to other than a child (remember to count the value of a building if it is transferred separately – see **Section 6.7.3**). If the disposal is to a child and the individual disposing of the assets is aged 66 or over, then there is a limit of €3,000,000 on the proceeds that can qualify for retirement relief.
- Must be for genuine commercial reasons and not the avoidance of tax.

Even if the relief is due, if there are any chargeable assets in the balance sheet of the company and these are not chargeable business assets, then there is only part relief, i.e. chargeable business assets/total chargeable assets.

6.7.3 Land, Buildings, Plant and Machinery Owned by an Individual and used by the Family Company

- At least 55 years of age.
- Owned land, buildings, plant or machinery for at least 10 years ending with the date of the disposal.

- Land/buildings/plant used by family/trading company for at least 10 years ending with the date of disposal.
- Disposed of land, etc. at same time and to same person as shares in family trading company.
- Shares in family/trading company must also qualify for retirement relief.
- Proceeds limit of €750,000 (or €500,000 if aged 66 or over) on qualifying assets if disposed of to other than a child (remember to count the value of the shares – see **Section 6.7.2**). If the disposal is to a child and the individual disposing of the assets is aged 66 or over, then there is a limit of €3,000,000 on the proceeds that can qualify for retirement relief.
- Must be for genuine commercial reasons and not the avoidance of tax.

Questions

Review Questions

(See Suggested Solutions to Review Questions at the end of this textbook.)

Question 6.1

On 1 August 2019, Jim Hughes, who is 60 years old, transferred 20% of his 100% shareholding in his family trading company to his son, Paul. The market value of the 20% is €800,000. Jim had acquired these shares in the family company on 1 December 1984 when their market value was €40,000. He has been a full-time working director since 1984 and has not previously disposed of any chargeable business assets.

Requirement

(a) Compute the CGT payable in respect of this transaction, indicating the year for which it will be assessed and by whom it will be payable.

(b) If Paul Hughes, who is single, were to sell his 20% of the private company for €900,000 on 1 December 2019, what would be the CGT liability and by whom would it be payable?

Question 6.2

For the past 40 years Sean Humbert, aged 63, has operated Tara Foods Ltd as a very successful company in the catering sector. Sean is now considering, in December 2019, the transfer of his business by way of gift to his only son, Michael. Sean has been a full-time working director of the company since it was incorporated in 1987, with himself as the 100% beneficial owner. Sean has not previously disposed of any chargeable business assets.

The share capital of the company comprises 100 ordinary shares of €1 each. Sean subscribed for his shares at par value in July 1987. Of the 100 shares, 99 are registered in Sean's name and the remaining share is registered in the name of Sean's wife, and is held in trust for Sean.

The shares in Tara Foods Ltd carry a current value of €800,000, derived from the following assets and liabilities:

	Market Value
	€
Goodwill	600,000
Equipment	50,000

Inventories	40,000
Trade receivables	25,000
Quoted investments	120,000
Trade payables	(35,000)
	800,000

The property from which the company operates is owned personally by Sean and it is his intention to transfer the property to Michael by way of gift, in addition to the shares in Tara Foods Ltd. The property was purchased by Sean for €28,000 in July 1987. The current market value of the property is €300,000.

Requirement

(a) Set out your views on Sean's eligibility for retirement relief on the proposed transfer of his shares and business premises to Michael. The basis for your views should be outlined together with an indication of the amount of relief available in the circumstances as set out.

(b) Compute the CGT liability that will arise if Sean makes the proposed transfers to Michael.

(c) Under what circumstances would the retirement relief claimed at (b) be withdrawn?

(d) How would Revenue recover the CGT due should the retirement relief fail to be clawed back?

Question 6.3

On 1 November 2019, on the occasion of his 60th birthday, Colin, a widower, made the following gifts:

	Notes	**Market Value at 1 November 2019**
(a) To his son Sean:		
100% of the shares in an unquoted trading company, Crawford Sportswear Ltd	1.	€500,000
Premises occupied by Crawford Sportswear Ltd	1.	€250,000
(b) To his daughter Esther:		
A holiday cottage in France	2.	€120,000
Cash		€50,000
(c) To his wife's sister Jean:		
An antique brooch	3.	€3,000

Notes:

1. Crawford Sportswear Ltd is engaged in the sale of sportswear. Colin had carried on this trade as a sole trader since 1980 until he incorporated Crawford Sportswear Ltd on 1 January 2010. On 1 January 2010 Colin transferred the entire assets and liabilities of the trade, other than the cash and the shop premises, to Crawford Sportswear Ltd in exchange for shares in the company. On 31 December 2009, the market value of the trade's assets and liabilities were as follows:

	Market Value
	€
Premises*	125,000
Fixtures and fittings*	50,000
Goodwill	80,000
Inventories	120,000
Receivables	25,000
Cash	10,000
Payables	110,000

* Colin acquired the premises on 1 June 1980 for €20,000. Following the transfer of the business to Crawford Sportswear Ltd, the premises were let at full market rent by Colin to the company. The market value of no single item of fixtures and fittings exceeded its original cost at 1 January 2010.

Colin has always been a full-time working director of the company.

At 1 November 2019, all of the company's assets consisted of assets in use, and which have always been in use, for the purpose of the company's trade.

Apart from the disposals set out above, Colin has not previously disposed of chargeable business assets.

2. Colin inherited the holiday cottage in France from a French cousin. Colin's cousin died on 10 October 1983, when the cottage was valued at €25,000. A number of complexities arose in the administration of his cousin's estate and the legal ownership of the cottage was not transferred to Colin until 11 January 1985, when the cottage was valued at €30,000.
3. Colin had inherited the brooch from his wife on her death on 1 December 2005. The brooch was then valued at €2,400. Colin's wife had inherited the brooch from her own mother in May 1987 when the brooch was valued at €1,500.

Requirement
Calculate Colin's CGT liability for 2019 on the assumption that no other assets were disposed of during the year.

7

Acquisition by a Company of its Own Shares

Learning Objectives

After studying this chapter you will be able to:

- Apply the CGT (and income tax) rules appropriate to the purchase by a company of its own shares.

7.1 Overview

A company is legally entitled to acquire/buy back its own shares or shares of its parent company. A company, particularly a quoted company, might do this if its management were of the view that the shares were good value at present; an unquoted company might do this **if a shareholder wished to dispose of shares and another shareholder did not want to buy the shares**.

We will see in **Chapter 25** that if the shareholder is an individual, any distribution out of assets of the company in respect of shares, except any part of it which represents a repayment of capital, is a distribution for tax purposes, i.e. the difference between what the shareholder subscribed for the shares and what he/she is now receiving is taxable under Schedule F. The income tax liability is typically at 40%, plus Universal Social Charge of up to 11% and PRSI at 4%.

Chapter 9 of Part 6 TCA 1997 sets out the tax treatment of an acquisition by a company of its own, or its holding company's, shares. Where the relevant conditions are satisfied, the sale of the shareholder's shares is subject to CGT treatment rather than income tax treatment. The law deals separately with quoted and unquoted companies.

7.2 Quoted Companies

A buyback (including the redemption, repayment and purchase) of its own shares by a quoted company (or of its own shares by a subsidiary of a quoted company) is not treated as a distribution. Consequently, the disposal of the shares by the shareholders(s) concerned is within the charge to CGT.

There is a condition that must be satisfied by quoted companies, i.e. a share buyback must not be part of a scheme or arrangement, the main purpose (or one of the main purposes) of which is to enable the owner of the shares to participate in the profits of the company, or of any of its 51% subsidiaries, without receiving a dividend. If this condition is not satisfied, the share buyback is treated as a distribution. Quoted companies must include in their annual corporation tax return details of any share buybacks undertaken in an accounting period, indicating whether or not the buyback is to be treated as a distribution.

7.3 Unquoted Companies

Where an unquoted trading or holding company buys back its own shares (or its holding company's shares) from a shareholder who is not a dealer in those shares, the payment made to the shareholder is, subject to certain conditions being satisfied, not to be treated as a distribution. As the payment is not to be treated as a distribution, **CGT treatment** applies to the shareholder's disposal of the shares.

7.3.1 Conditions to be Satisfied

The conditions that **must** be satisfied if such a purchase is not to be treated as a distribution are:

- The company must be a trading company or a holding company of a trading company.
- The motive test, i.e. the acquisition of the shares by the company must be wholly or mainly for the **benefit of the trade** of the company or any of its 51% subsidiaries. See **Appendix 7.1** for an extract from Revenue's *Tax and Duty Manual*, Part 06-09-01: Acquisition by a company of its own shares, dealing with its interpretation of "the benefit of the trade" test.
- The buyback must not be part of a scheme or arrangement the purpose of which is to enable the shareholder to participate in the profits of the company or any of its 51% subsidiaries without receiving a dividend.
- The vendor of the shares, if an **individual**, must be **resident and ordinarily resident** for the year of assessment in which the shares are bought back; if the vendor is a **company**, it must be **resident** in the accounting period in which the shares are bought back. This ensures that the vendor is within the charge to Irish CGT.
- The vendor must have **owned the shares throughout a five-year period** ending with the date of the buyback. The period of ownership of a spouse or civil partner living with a vendor at the date of the buyback is aggregated with that of the vendor. However, where an Approved Profit Sharing Scheme has appropriated the shares to a participant, the period is reduced to three years. If the vendor inherited the shares from the previous owner, the vendor's period of ownership is deemed to include the period of ownership of the previous owner. In addition, where the shares are inherited, the required period of ownership is reduced to three years.
- Where the vendor's shareholding in a company is not fully purchased, redeemed or repaid, then generally his/her **shareholding** and entitlement to **share of profits** must be **substantially reduced**. Both the nominal value of shareholding and the profit entitlement must, after the sale of the shares, be reduced **by at least 25%**.

Example 7.1

D Ltd has an issued share capital of 100,000 €1 ordinary shares, of which E holds 20,000 (that is, 20/100ths or 20%). If E sells 5,000 shares to D Ltd, D Ltd's issued share capital is reduced for tax purposes to 95,000 shares, of which E holds 15,000, a fraction of 15/95ths or 15.79%.

Thus, although E has sold 25% of the original holding, E's percentage holding has been reduced by only 21%, and the buyback will not qualify for CGT treatment (i.e. it will be treated as a distribution). To achieve a reduction of 25%, E would need to sell 5,890 shares.

- The **vendor is not connected with the company**, or group company, after the buyback, i.e. the vendor and the vendor's associates must not, after the buyback of the shares, be entitled to more than 30% of the capital, voting rights or assets on a winding up of the company.

  There is a very long definition of an associate in the law. The **main** people are:

  - a husband and wife or civil partners living together are associated with one another and a person under the age of 18 is an associate of his or her parents and their spouses or civil partners (no other relatives are treated as associated);
  - a person who has control of a company is associated with that company;
  - two companies which are controlled by the same person are associated.

  The legislation states that in order for CGT treatment to apply, the vendor is only required to reduce their shareholding by 25% and also provides that the vendor must not be entitled to more than 30% of the share capital of the company after the buyback. Thus the legislation envisages situations where a vendor continues to have a shareholding in the company. However, as set out in **Appendix 7.1**, Revenue's interpretation of how it sees the "benefit of the trade" test being satisfied does not envisage the vendor continuing to have a shareholding in the company of in excess of 5%. In practice, therefore, in order to satisfy the "benefit of the trade test" so that CGT treatment will apply, the vendor will generally have to reduce their shareholding to 5% or less. Furthermore, Revenue's view is that the shareholder should also cease to be a director of the company in order for the "benefit of the trade" test to be satisfied. In this context, Revenue state that it would be acceptable for a shareholder to stay on as a director for no longer than six months after the sale of their shares.

7.3.2 *Buyback of Shares to Pay Inheritance Tax*

The various conditions necessary for a buyback not to be treated as a distribution are waived where it can be shown that shares had to be disposed of in order to discharge inheritance tax in respect of an inheritance by that shareholder of the company's shares or to repay borrowings used to pay the inheritance tax. For this rule to apply, the shareholder must not otherwise have been able to discharge the inheritance tax owed without undue hardship.

Example 7.2

Harry and Peter, two Irish resident and ordinarily resident individuals, set up Super Friends Ltd in 1994 to sell electronic equipment. Harry owns 80% of the shares, while Peter owns 20%. The company has been very profitable and now has revenue reserves of €2 million. Harry believes that the success of the company is due totally to his efforts. He believes that Peter does not really contribute to the success of the company and is more interested in his golf handicap. There have been a number of acrimonious board meetings and as a result Harry has decided to "buy out" Peter. Peter is happy to dispose of his shares provided that he receives €1 million and pays CGT at 33%, or 10% if revised entrepreneur relief applies (see **Section 4.8**), and not the higher tax on income.

If Harry were to buy the shares, he would need €1 million. As Harry does not have that amount of cash, he would have to either borrow the money (which would have to be repaid) or get money from the company (on which he would be liable to income tax).

If Super Friends Ltd bought back the shares from Peter, then Harry would own all the shares without having to find the cash to actually buy the shares. Peter will be liable to income tax on the cash received from Super Friends Ltd in excess of the amount he contributed for the shares. However, if he satisfies the following conditions, he will be liable to CGT on the gain, and not income tax:

continued overleaf

1	Trading or holding company?	Yes
2	Will the acquisition benefit the trade?	Yes, there is disagreement between shareholders
3	Is Peter resident and ordinarily resident in Ireland in 2019?	Yes, resident and ordinarily resident
4	Has Peter owned the shares for five years?	Yes
5	Is Peter selling all his shares, or at least substantially reducing his shareholding?	Yes, he is selling all his shares
6	Is Peter not connected with Super Friends Ltd after the disposal?	Yes

As all the conditions have been satisfied, Peter will be liable to CGT on the disposal of the shares to Super Friends Ltd.

7.3.3 Other Issues

Even though the buyback is not treated as a distribution for the shareholder, it is a distribution for the purposes of the close company surcharge (see **Chapter 26**), i.e. it would reduce the amount liable to the surcharge. It does not matter whether the buyback is treated as a distribution or a capital gain – there is no tax deduction for the company.

In respect of treasury shares:

- treasury shares that are not cancelled by a company are treated as cancelled immediately when they are acquired by the company;
- no allowable loss arises on cancellation of treasury or other shares by a company, regardless of whether the shares are actually cancelled or are treated as cancelled for tax purposes; and
- reissues of treasury shares are treated as new issues of shares.

A return is required to be made to the Inspector by companies that buy back their own shares or acquire their holding company's shares, where such companies consider exemption from the distribution treatment applies to those acquisitions. The time limit for making such a return is nine months from the end of the accounting period in which the acquisition takes place. There is provision for penalties for failure to make returns.

Appendix 7.1: Extract from Revenue's *Tax and Duty Manual,* Part 06-09-01: Acquisition by company of its own shares

The following is taken from Appendix II of the *Tax and Duty Manual*, Part 06-09-01: Acquisition by a company of its own shares. It outlines Revenue's guidance on the application of the trade benefit test.

"Revenue will normally regard a buy-back as benefiting the trade where for example:

- There is a disagreement between the shareholders over the management of the company and that disagreement is having or is expected to have an adverse effect on the company's trade and where the effect of the transaction is to remove the dissenting shareholder
- The purpose is to ensure that an unwilling shareholder who wishes to end his/her association with the company does not sell the shares to someone who might not be acceptable to the other shareholders.

Examples of this would include:

- An outside shareholder who has provided equity finance and wishes to withdraw that finance.
- A controlling shareholder who is retiring as a director and wishes to make way for new management.
- Personal representatives of a deceased shareholder where they wish to realise the value of the shares.
- A legatee of a deceased shareholder, where she/he does not wish to hold shares in the company.

The above examples envisage the shareholder selling his/her entire shareholding in the company and making a complete break from the company. If the company is not buying **all** the shares owned by the vendor or if the vendor is selling all the shares but retaining some connection with the company (e.g. directorship) it would seem unlikely that the transaction would benefit the company's trade.

However, there may be situations where:

- For sentimental reasons a retiring director of a company wishes to retain a small shareholding in the company. In this context, **Revenue would consider that a small shareholding would not exceed 5% of the share capital of the company**.
- A controlling shareholder in a family company is selling his/her shares to allow control to pass to his/her children but remains on as a director for a specified period purely because his/her immediate departure from the company at that time would otherwise have a negative impact on the company's business. **Revenue would consider that the specified period that the director remains with the company should not exceed 6 months**.

In such circumstances it may still be possible for the company to show that the main purpose is to benefit its trade.

Given that the underlying concept is that the buy-back will benefit the company's trade, consideration will be given as to whether the proposed manner of funding the buy-back will place the company in a weak financial position. Where the manner of paying for the shares leaves the company in a position where, for example, it would be undercapitalised or its cash flow situation jeopardised this would unlikely to be considered to be of benefit to the trade.

In some circumstances it may be necessary for the company to borrow in order to pay for the share buy-back. It is accepted that, in principle, where the buy-back is to be funded or part funded by a loan that this will not in itself mean that the trade benefit test isn't satisfied. However, where any such borrowing would seem to materially weaken the company's financial situation it is very unlikely that a positive advance opinion will be given."

Questions

Review Questions

(See Suggested Solutions to Review Questions at the end of this textbook.)

Question 7.1

Alan Doyle has been a director of Annally Ltd since the company was incorporated in August 1990. The company is a large importer of toys from the Far East, which it distributes in Ireland and the UK.

Alan is 60 years old and intends retiring from the business shortly. His original investment in company shares was €10,000 in €1 ordinary shares. There was no share premium account. His brothers, Mark and Colm, also own 10,000 €1 shares between them, and they will continue to run the company as directors after Alan's retirement.

Alan has recently had his shares valued and was pleasantly surprised to discover that they are worth €600,000. He has asked Mark and Colm to purchase these shares, but they have told him that they do not have sufficient funds.

You have been approached for advice on the possibility of the company acquiring its own shares from Alan.

Requirement

(a) State the conditions that must be in place in order that the proceeds from a company acquiring its own shares can be treated as a share disposal for CGT purposes.
(b) Compute Alan's liability to CGT if all the conditions are met.
(c) State the tax consequences for Alan and the company if the conditions are not met.

Part Two

Stamp Duty

8

General Principles and Conveyance or Transfer on Sale

Learning Objectives

After studying this chapter you will be able to:

- Advise on and calculate the stamp duty implications of certain transactions involving certain written documents either executed in the State or relating to property situated in the State.
- Advise on the stamp duty administrative requirements and the implications of non-compliance.

Chartered Accountants Ireland's *Code of Ethics* applies to all aspects of a Chartered Accountant's professional life, including dealing with stamp duty issues. As outlined at the beginning of this textbook, further information regarding the principles in the *Code of Ethics* is set out in **Appendix 2**.

Students should also be aware of the issues around tax planning, tax avoidance and tax evasion, and these are discussed in **Appendix 3**.

8.1 Background

Prior to 15 December 1999, the law governing stamp duties was contained in the Stamp Act 1891 and the Stamp Duties Management Act 1891, with subsequent Finance Acts amending and adding to these provisions. The Stamp Duties Consolidation Act 1999 (SDCA 1999) was brought into law with effect from 15 December 1999, consolidating the legislation into a single Act and subsequent Finance Acts.

8.2 Charge to Stamp Duty

Section 2 SDCA 1999 provides that any "instrument" specified in Schedule 1 to the SDCA that is:

1. **executed in the State**; or
2. relates to any **property situated in the State**; or
3. relates to any matter or thing done, or to be done, in the State

is chargeable with stamp duty, subject to exemptions provided for in the Act.

An explanation of the meaning of these terms and the wording used is required, and is given below.

8.2.1 Instrument

While an instrument is defined as "including every legal document", the important thing to note is that it is a written document of some sort that acts as a mechanism for doing something. Accordingly, **where no written document is produced, no stamp duty can arise.**

For example, oral agreements that are not then put into writing or transactions executed by conduct (such as delivery) do not attract stamp duty. Nor do agreements recorded on film, tape, etc.

> ***Example 8.1***
> Pat and Catherine agree that Pat will buy Catherine's collection of antique books for €10,000. No written agreement was drawn up and, accordingly, no stamp duty arises.

8.2.2 Schedule 1 SDCA 1999

Schedule 1 SDCA 1999 lists instruments of various types and describes the stamp duties attaching to them. Any instrument not falling within Schedule 1 is not subject to stamp duty. Certain instruments which do not themselves fall within Schedule 1 are deemed to be instruments within it for stamp duty purposes (e.g. conveyance of a gift).

Stamp duty can be one of two types:

1. *Ad valorem* – where the amount of stamp duty depends on the value of the consideration or property affected by the instrument concerned (e.g. land).
2. Fixed – where the instrument attracts a set amount of stamp duty regardless of the value of the property affected by the transaction (e.g. cheque).

8.2.3 Executed in the State

Executing an instrument means doing whatever is necessary to make the instrument operable or effective. For most written agreements, this means signing the agreement. In some cases instruments are not executed until signed and sealed (e.g. deed of convenant).

> ***Example 8.2***
> An agreement is signed in Killarney to transfer ownership of a painting kept in Bermuda from one party to another. The agreement is subject to Irish stamp duty as it is executed in the State, i.e. in the Republic of Ireland.

8.2.4 Property Situated in the State

The rules relating to where property is situated are the same as those for CGT (see **Section 1.7.1**). In summary, the legal status of various types of property is as follows:

Property	**Location**
Shares in registered form	Where share register is kept
Simple contract debts	Where debtor resides*
Land and buildings	Where located
Goodwill	Where business is carried on
Patents/trademarks	Where registered

* The rule for the location of debts is different from the rule for CGT purposes. For CGT purposes, a debt is located in Ireland only if the creditor is resident in Ireland. The stamp duty legislation does

not state the location of different types of property, so general legal principles apply. Under general legal principles a debt is located where the debtor is resident.

> ***Example 8.3***
> An agreement is signed in Chicago to transfer the ownership of a building in Dundalk. The document is stampable as it relates to property situated in the State.

8.2.5 "Any matter or thing done, or to be done, in the State"

This a very wide provision that rarely arises in practice. The view of the Revenue Commissioners in relation to this criterion is that the instrument and/or the underlying transaction should relate to, or involve, a substantive action or obligation to be carried out or undertaken in the State. For example, where an instrument is executed abroad and the only connection with the State is that one of the parties is an Irish resident, the Revenue Commissioners' view is that in such a case the instrument would not be liable to duty.

8.3 Payment and Returns

8.3.1 When is Stamp Duty Payable?

Stamp duty is payable within 30 days of execution of the instrument concerned. However, as a matter of practice, Revenue extends this date so that the duty on the instrument must be paid **within 44 days** of the date of first execution of the instrument.

8.3.2 Who is Liable to Pay Stamp Duty?

In theory, it is a matter for agreement between the parties to the transaction as to who is responsible for the stamp duty, the "accountable person". The legislation does contain provisions to decide who the "accountable person" is, in the event that the Revenue Commissioners has to sue for the stamp duty, as follows:

- the purchaser or transferee in the case of a transfer on sale;
- the lessee in the case of a lease;
- either party in the case of a gift or sale at undervalue (voluntary disposition *inter vivos*).

Where a person buys shares in a public company through a stockbroker, the stamp duty is collected by the stockbroker and paid to Revenue. Where a person buys shares in a private company, the person dealing with the share transfer document, for example the accountant, will deal with collecting the stamp duty and paying it to Revenue. Where a person buys land and buildings, the solicitor will convey the property and will collect the stamp duty and pay it to Revenue.

8.3.3 e-Stamping via ROS

Under e-stamping, a person uses ROS (Revenue Online Service) to file the stamp duty return and pay stamp duty online and receive a stamp certificate as part of that online transaction. This stamp certificate is printed and attached to the instrument, to denote the instrument as stamped.

Alternatively, the statutory return may be filed in paper format. However, this is only allowed where Revenue has excluded a person from the requirement to file electronically, i.e. where the accountable person:

- does not have sufficient access to the internet to comply with the requirements; or
- in the case of an individual, is prevented by age or mental or physical infirmity from being able to comply with the requirements.

8.3.4 Self-assessment

Similar to other taxes, under self-assessment for stamp duty the accountable person (usually the purchaser) files the return, calculates and pays the stamp duty and may be subject to audit at a later stage. As with other taxes, if the accountable person has a doubt about the application of stamp duty law to a particular transaction, the person can lodge an "expression of doubt". If Revenue does not agree with the position adopted by the accountable person, he/she has a right of appeal against Revenue's decision.

Under self-assessment, a return must be filed within 30 days of the date of the execution of the document in question, although in practice Revenue will accept that a return is filed on time if it is filed up to 44 days after the date of execution. If a return is not filed on time, there is a fine of €3,000 plus a surcharge of:

- 5% of the stamp duty liability or €12,695, whichever is lower, if the return is filed within two months of the due date, i.e. within 92 days from the date of execution; and
- 10% of the stamp duty liability or €63,485, whichever is lower, if the return is filed more than two months after the due date, i.e. after 92 days from the date of execution.

As with other taxes, if stamp duty is paid late, interest is payable at 0.0219% per day or part of a day.

8.4 Conveyance or Transfer on Sale

A conveyance is an instrument whereby ownership of any property, immovable or movable, tangible or intangible, is transferred from one person to another.

The term "conveyance" is usually thought of as being the document that transfers ownership in land following the signing of contracts for sale. However, it has a much wider meaning. For instance, it includes court orders. The term "on sale" implies that two considerations have been satisfied:

1. there has been an agreement to sell the property with all the necessary conditions of contract law satisfied (offer, acceptance, consideration); and
2. the consideration is in the form of money.

In Schedule 1 SDCA 1999, there are three heads of charge for conveyances or transfers on sale. The two of importance here are:

1. "Conveyance or transfer on sale of any stocks or marketable securities".
2. "Conveyance or transfer on sale of any property other than stocks or marketable securities".

8.4.1 Stocks and Securities

For stamp duty to arise under this head, there must be a sale (including a gift) of stocks or securities.

Stamp duty is chargeable at 1% of the consideration, rounded down to the nearest euro, subject to a minimum payment of €1. There is an exemption on share transfers where the duty involved is €10 or less.

Example 8.4
Paul sells shares in Damascus Ltd, an Irish incorporated private company, to Peter for €1,250.

	€
Stamp duty liability: 1% × €1,250	12.50
Stamp duty	12.00 (rounded down)

The stamp duty due would be payable by Peter (the purchaser).

The instrument (document) that is the conveyance for these purposes is the share transfer form. Generally the transfer or conveyance on sale of shares and marketable securities of **a company not registered in the State** is **not subject to Irish stamp duty**. This is provided that the conveyance is not executed in the State, nor does it relate to:

1. any Irish immovable property;
2. any Irish-registered stocks and marketable securities.

Stocks must be in a company registered in the State or relate to Irish immovable property.

Finance Act 2017 introduced a new stamp duty anti-avoidance section that applies the 6% stamp duty rate on the disposal of certain shares deriving their value from non-residential property (which is beyond the scope of this textbook).

Issue of Shares by a Company
Where an Irish company issues shares in return for cash, this is not liable to stamp duty.

Purchase by a Company of its Own Shares
Technically, when a company purchases its own shares, a liability to stamp duty arises. In practice, however, shares in unquoted companies can be converted into redeemable shares and redeemed. No stamp duty arises on redemption of these shares.

Alternatively, the shares can be bought back on foot of a contract or share purchase agreement. If the shareholder and the company enter into an agreement and the shareholder simply hands over the share certificates to the company, there is no need for a stock transfer form and no duty is charged.

8.4.2 Property Other than Shares

The most common example of stamp duty arising under this head is on sales of land and buildings. Sales of freehold land, transfers of business property (e.g. goodwill) and assignments of leasehold interests in land are also covered under this head of charge. The creation of a leasehold interest is charged under the "lease" heading.

The rates of stamp duty applicable depend on whether the property is residential property or non-residential property. In either case, it is the purchaser who pays the stamp duty, not the vendor.

Residential Property
With effect from 8 December 2010 the rates of stamp duty, as set out in **Appendix 1**, are **1% on the first €1,000,000 of the consideration and 2% on the balance**, rounded down to the nearest euro.

Example 8.5

Mary buys a residential property with a value of €1,250,000. The stamp duty payable by Mary is as follows:

	€
First €1,000,000 @ 1%	10,000
Balance €250,000 @ 2%	5,000
Total	15,000

Non-residential Property

In the case of non-residential property, such as commercial buildings, farms, land and goodwill, the rate is 6% of the consideration, rounded down to the nearest euro, for instruments executed on or after 11 October 2017 (previously the rate was 2% from 7 December 2011 to 10 October 2017). Transitional provisions apply to instruments executed after 11 October 2017 and before 1 January 2018 where a binding contract was entered into before 11 October 2017 (instrument must contain a certificate to this effect in such form as Revenue specifies).

Mixed-use Property

In the case of a mixed-use property, the consideration must be apportioned on a just and reasonable basis between the residential and non-residential parts of the property.

Example 8.6

Susan buys a shop and an apartment over the shop for €900,000. The estate agent advises that the value of the shop is €750,000 and the apartment is €150,000. The stamp duty payable by Susan is:

Shop (€750,000 @ 6%)	€45,000
Apartment (€150,000 @ 1%)	€1,500
Total stamp duty	€46,500

8.5 Gifts – Deemed Conveyance on Sale

Certain transfers are deemed to be "conveyances on sale" for stamp duty purposes, even though the consideration is not in the form of money. A conveyance of property by way of gift is not a conveyance on sale as there is no sale; however, it is a deemed conveyance on sale for stamp duty purposes. The consideration is the market value of the property conveyed.

This is a point of particular importance in estate planning when assessing whether assets should be gifted now or transferred as part of a person's estate by inheritance. Stamp duty is payable in relation to a gift. No stamp duty arises on inheritance.

Example 8.7: No stamp duty arises on foot of an inheritance

Mr X approaches you for advice in relation to whether or not he should gift Irish shares worth €200,000 to his brother now, or provide that his brother will receive the shares on his death by way of an inheritance.

Stamp duty implications if he gifts now: €200,000 @ 1% = €2,000.

This will be a liability of Mr X's brother.

Stamp duty implications if it is an inheritance: no stamp duty payable by Mr X's brother on receipt of the shares by inheritance.

8.6 VAT on Property

Where VAT is charged on the acquisition of a property, it is the amount of consideration exclusive of VAT that is liable to stamp duty.

The supply of property is subject to VAT at 13.5% when it:

- is supplied for consideration in the course of business;
- has been developed in the 20-year period prior to the supply; and
- is considered to be 'new'.

Development, other than minor development, essentially makes a property 'new' for VAT purposes if it is either:

1. a completed property supplied within five years of its development (five-year rule), or
2. a second and subsequent supply of a property within five years of its development if it has not been occupied for 24 months in total (two-year rule).

Example 8.8

James owns a warehouse and in 2019 work is carried out that converts the warehouse to a serviced office space. After the work is completed, James sells the property. The sale is subject to VAT at 13.5% as the building is developed and has been made 'new'.

Kudos Ltd purchased the property for €908,000, including VAT.

Calculate the VAT charged by James on the disposal of the property and stamp duty payable by Kudos Ltd on its acquisition.

Consideration (including VAT)	€908,000
VAT (€908,000/1.135 × 13.5%)	€108,000
Consideration (excluding VAT)	€800,000
Stamp duty @ 6%	€48,000

Minor development can be described as development that does not (and is not intended to) adapt the property for a materially altered use, provided that the cost of such development does not exceed 25% of the consideration for the (subsequent) supply of the property.

Any supply of a developed, but incomplete, property within 20 years of when the development ceased is subject to VAT at 13.5%. The sale of residential properties by a developer or builder is always liable to VAT at 13.5%.

The following supplies of property are generally **exempt**:

- sales of undeveloped land;
- old, completed properties or buildings (greater than five years from completion);
- second-hand properties less than five years old and not within two years of occupation.

The letting of property is also VAT-exempt.

Example 8.9

Eoin (a farmer) owns a 20-acre undeveloped field. In 2019, he sells the field to Vincent, aged 52, for €400,000.

The sale is not liable to VAT as the field is not developed.

Vincent will pay stamp duty @ 6%, i.e. €24,000.

Where a property is supplied when it is no longer considered 'new', the supply is exempt from VAT. The vendor is therefore not obliged to charge VAT. However, the seller and the purchaser may jointly opt to tax the supply if they are both carrying on businesses in the State. Where the option to tax is exercised, the purchaser must account for the VAT on the supply on the reverse charge basis.

VAT on property is a complex area of tax law and specialist VAT on property advice should be sought before a transaction is complete.

Questions

Review Questions

(See Suggested Solutions to Review Questions at the end of this textbook.)

Question 8.1

Frank is considering acquiring the following assets:

(a) Shares in an Irish Plc at a cost of €30,000.
(b) Shares in a US Plc at a cost of €20,000.
(c) Land in Galway for €80,000.
(d) An apartment in Kilkenny for €120,000.

Requirement
Frank would like advice regarding whether any stamp duty is payable and, if so, the amount payable.

Question 8.2

The following transactions have taken place in September 2019:
(a) Ann Murphy bought an apartment for €200,000 on 1 September.
(b) Frank Gibbons received a gift of shares in an Irish private company from his brother on 5 September. The market value of the shares is €300,000.
(c) Ciara Cawley bought a new house for €567,500, inclusive of 13.5% VAT, on 11 September.

Requirement
Advise each of these individuals as to the amount of stamp duty payable and the date by which it must be paid.

9

Exemptions and Reliefs

Learning Objectives

After studying this chapter you will be able to:

- Identify and advise on the main exemptions from stamp duty.
- Advise on the availability of certain reliefs from stamp duty, including young trained farmer relief, transfers of farmland between relatives relief, and transfers between associated companies relief.

9.1 Exemptions

The **main** exemptions from stamp duty are as follows:

1. Transfers of Government stocks.
2. Wills.
3. **Conveyance or transfer of property between spouses or civil partners.** This exemption applies provided the spouses or civil partners are legally married or in a civil partnership (even if they are separated); it is only after divorce or dissolution of the civil partnership that a conveyance or transfer becomes liable to stamp duty. Furthermore, upon divorce or dissolution of a civil partnership, any transfer of property made under an Irish court order (or a foreign court order recognised as valid in the State) is also exempt from stamp duty.
4. Conveyance, transfer or lease of land made for **charitable purposes** in the State or Northern Ireland.
5. Any instrument for the sale, transfer or other disposition of **intellectual property**, as defined. Intellectual property includes patents, trademarks, copyright, registered designs, inventions, domain names, etc. (The definition of intellectual property is the same as the definition of intangible assets for corporation tax purposes in **Chapter 20, Section 20.11**).
6. Conveyances of **immovable property situated outside the State** (subject to some conditions).

9.2 Reliefs

9.2.1 Young Trained Farmer Relief

Under section 81AA SDCA 1999, there is a full relief from stamp duty on a transfer of an interest in land to a "young trained farmer" up to 31 December 2021. The purpose of this relief is to encourage the transfer of farmland (including the farmhouse and other buildings on the farmland) to a new generation of farmers with relevant qualifications. The transfer may be by way of gift or sale.

With effect from 1 January 2019 there is an aggregate limit of €70,000 on the amount of state aid that may be granted to a young trained farmer under this relief and other income tax reliefs, including section 667B TCA 1997 (stock relief). The limit applies to the aggregate of relevant reliefs claimed in the preceding five-year period. For example, any such relief claimed in 2015 would reduce the amount of relief available in 2019, subject to the total reliefs claimed from 2015 to 2019 not exceeding €70,000.

To qualify for the relief the farmer must:

1. be less than 35 years of age on the date of execution of the deed of transfer;
2. have attained a recognised agricultural qualification; and
3. furnish a declaration to the effect that:
   (a) for a period of **five years** from the date of execution of the deed of transfer they will:
      (i) spend not less than 50% of their normal working time farming the land, and
      (ii) retain ownership of the land;
   (b) they will submit a business plan to Teagasc before the execution of the instrument concerned; and
   (c) they come within the EU Commission definition of a micro or small enterprise.

If the young farmer does not have a relevant qualification at the date of execution of the deed of transfer but acquires one within four years of that date, they will be entitled to a refund of stamp duty paid. To qualify for a refund the farmer must: submit a business plan to Teagasc; come within the EU Commission definition of a micro or small enterprise; and intend to, for five years from the date of the repayment claim, spend not less than 50% of their normal working time farming the land and to retain ownership of the land.

If the land is disposed of within five years from the date of execution of the deed of transfer and is not replaced by other land within one year of the disposal, then the exemption will be **clawed back** by way of a penalty. If only part of the land is disposed of, then any clawback will relate only to the portion disposed.

9.2.2 *Transfers of Farmland between Relations (Consanguinity Relief)*

Consanguinity relief applies to transfers between close relatives of **farmland only**, subject to certain conditions being satisfied. Farmland includes buildings on farmland used for farming purposes, but not to a farmhouse as this is considered a residential property. The relief applies to transfers by way of sale or gift.

The relief operates by applying a 1% rate of stamp duty to qualifying transfers of farmland between close relatives before 1 January 2021.

Conditions

The following conditions must be satisfied:

1. The individual to whom the land is transferred/conveyed must either:
   (a) farm the land for a period of not less than six years, or else
   (b) lease it for a period of not less than six years to someone who farms the land.

2. The person farming the land must do so on a commercial basis and with a view to the realisation of profits. The person must also spend not less than 50% of their normal working time farming land, including the land transferred, **or** be the holder of one of the agricultural qualifications set out in legislation.
3. The transfer/conveyance must be to a relative.
4. The transfer must take place on or before 31 December 2020.

The Revenue Commissioners considers that "normal working time", including on-farm and off-farm working time, is about 40 hours per week. Therefore a farmer with off-farm employment would qualify provided he/she spends a minimum average of 20 hours working on the farm per week. Farmland includes any farm buildings on that land.

(Note: there is a relief in capital acquisitions tax called agricultural relief. The conditions for this stamp duty relief also apply to CAT agricultural relief (see **Section 14.5.3**), namely: farming the land or leasing it to someone who farms it for six years; and the person having a farming qualification or farming the land for at least 50% of their time and doing so on a commercial basis. However, the tests at 3. and 4. above apply for stamp duty relief only.)

This relief applies to transfers of the **entire** beneficial interest to most relatives, i.e. where the person to whom the property is being transferred (or each of them if there is more than one transferee) is related to the transferor in one of the following ways:

- Lineal descendant (child, grandchild, etc.)
- Parent
- Grandparent
- Step-parent
- Husband, wife or civil partner
- Brother/sister of parent (i.e. aunt, uncle)
- Brother or sister
- Lineal descendant of a parent (e.g. step-brother/sister)
- Lineal descendant of a husband/wife (e.g. stepchild)
- Lineal descendant of a brother/sister (e.g. nephew/niece)
- Civil partner of a parent
- Lineal descendant of a civil partner.

Example 9.1
Ben gives his granddaughter, Jane, Irish land worth €100,000 on 4 March 2019.
The stamp duty payable on this voluntary disposition *inter vivos* would be €100,000 @ 6% = €6,000.
As there is no mention of farming, relief cannot be claimed.

Example 9.2
Peter wishes to transfer 100 acres of land valued at €1.2m to his nephew, Eoin, on 23 May 2019. What is the stamp duty payable if Eoin is a farmer?

The stamp duty will be €1.2m × 1% = €12,000.

9.2.3 Transfers between Associated Companies

Stamp duty chargeable under the "conveyances on sale" headings in Schedule 1 SDCA 1999 (deemed transfers included) can be reduced to 0% where a transaction is between "associated companies" as defined in section 79 SDCA 1999. In order for the relief to apply, the transfer must be for bona fide commercial reasons and not to avoid tax.

One company is associated with another if there is a 90% direct or indirect relationship between them in terms of:

1. ordinary share capital (ordinary shares excluding fixed rate preference shares);
2. profits available for distribution; and
3. assets available for distribution on a winding up.

Example 9.3

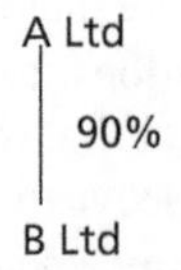

Conveyances on sale between A Ltd and B Ltd will qualify for the reduced rate of 0%.

Example 9.4

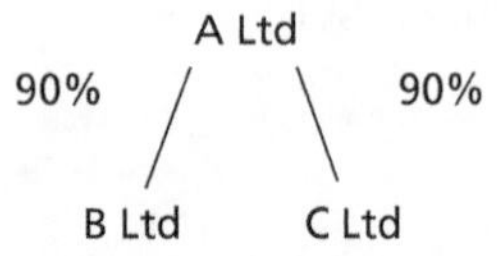

Transfers between A Ltd and B Ltd, and between B Ltd and C Ltd will qualify for the relief.

Example 9.5

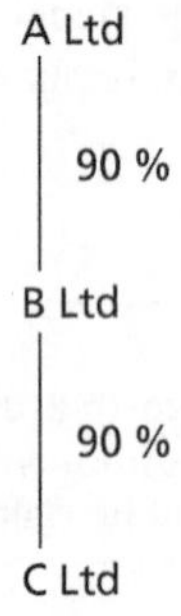

Transfers between A Ltd and C Ltd will not qualify as there is only an 81% relationship, i.e. A Ltd owns 90% of B Ltd's ownership in C Ltd, 90% of 90% = 81%.

If the companies cease to be associated within two years of the date of the conveyance or transfer, then full stamp duty will be payable. However, the relief is not clawed back where the companies cease to be associated because the transferor company is liquidated, provided the transferee continues to own the property that was transferred for at least two years.

Example 9.6
Arklow Ltd transfers freehold land worth €1 million to its 100% subsidiary, Gorey Ltd.

The transfer will qualify for the associated companies relief, therefore no stamp duty will be payable. However, if the 90% relationship is broken within two years, Gorey Ltd will have to pay €60,000 in stamp duty.

Example 9.7
Arklow Ltd grants Gorey Ltd, its 100% subsidiary, a leasehold interest in land. The premium payable is €900,000 with no annual rent.

The transaction is chargeable under the "Lease" heading and therefore associated companies relief is not available.

Stamp duty liability is 6%, i.e. €54,000.

Questions

Review Questions

(See Suggested Solutions to Review Questions at the end of this textbook.)

Question 9.1

Joseph is married to Anne and they have two sons, Alex and Shane. Joseph has decided to make the following gifts:

(a) land worth €100,000 to Alex for him to build a house;
(b) a cottage in Galway worth €500,000 to Anne;
(c) land in Mayo to an Irish charity to build a hostel for homeless people;
(d) shares in his company, XYZ Limited, worth €200,000 to Shane; and
(e) land in the UK worth €90,000 to Alex.

Requirement
Joseph would like advice regarding whether or not stamp duty is payable and, if so, the amount payable. He would also like to know the stamp duty consequences if, instead of making the gifts now, he leaves them to the same people in his will.

Question 9.2

Holdings Limited owns shares in three companies as follows:

(a) 100% of the shares in Private Limited;
(b) 85% of the shares in Free Limited; and
(c) 95% of the shares in Major Limited.

In each case, Holdings Limited is entitled to the same percentage of profits available for distribution and assets available for distribution on a winding up.

Holdings Limited is proposing to transfer the following assets:

(a) a commercial building worth €1 million to Private Limited;
(b) a residential property worth €1.5 million to Free Limited;
(c) a holding of shares in an Irish plc worth €1 million to Major Limited; and
(d) a patent worth €3 million to Free Limited.

Requirement
Advise Holdings Limited as to the stamp duty payable if these transfers are made.

10

Transfer of a Business

Learning Objectives

After studying this chapter you will be able to:

- Advise on the stamp duty arising on sale or incorporation of a business and how to minimise the liability.

10.1 Stamp Duty Consequences on Acquisition of Business Assets

Contracts for the sale of property can be deemed to be a conveyance on sale and therefore liable to stamp duty. Where a business is sold, the contract for the sale is liable to stamp duty as a deemed conveyance on sale. However, if assets are already chargeable to stamp duty (e.g. a building) or the asset is goods and merchandise of the business (e.g. inventories and machinery), then there is no deemed conveyance of those assets. In practice, this means that contracts for the sale of intangible assets such as goodwill, debtors and cash on deposit are deemed conveyances on sale.

Where a contract for the sale of property (e.g. the sale of a sole trader's business) comprises both chargeable and non-chargeable property, the consideration must be apportioned as only the chargeable property is liable to stamp duty under this rule. This will also apply where a sole trader/partnership decides to incorporate the business.

Example 10.1

X Ltd agrees to sell its business to Y Ltd for a cash sum of €300,000. It is agreed that the following assets and liabilities will be transferred to Y Ltd.

	€
Machinery	150,000
Goodwill	30,000
Receivables	250,000
Patents and designs	100,000
	530,000
Payables	(230,000)
Net worth of business	300,000

A written agreement is drawn up to evidence the sale of the business.

continued overleaf

Therefore, Y Ltd will have the following stamp duty liability (before claims for exemptions, etc.):

1. The contract for sale is stampable as a deemed conveyance on sale due to the fact that the sale of certain intangibles has been dealt with by it, i.e. goodwill, debts, patents and designs.
2. As the entire transaction has been dealt with in one agreement, the total consideration for stamp duty purposes is split between that which is liable to stamp duty and that which is not. As the machinery is not liable, stamp duty is charged on:

	€
Goodwill	30,000
Receivables	250,000
Patents and designs	100,000
Stampable consideration	380,000
Stamp duty @ 6%	22,800

10.2 Minimising Stamp Duty on Acquisition of Business Assets

From **Example 10.1** above, Y Ltd can minimise its stamp duty liability as follows:

1. Do not transfer receivables and payables to Y Ltd. Instead, let X Ltd (or Y Ltd as its agent) collect the debts and use them to pay off the payables.
2. The patents and designs – avail of exemption for intellectual property.

Therefore, only the goodwill is liable, i.e. €30,000 @ 6% = €1,800.

Questions

Review Questions

(See Suggested Solutions to Review Questions at the end of this textbook.)

Question 10.1

Jack Feeley carried on his sole trader business for many years. He has decided to incorporate the business for commercial reasons. He will transfer all of his trading assets and his trade payables to the company in return for shares in the company. The assets and liabilities of the business are as follows:

	€
Land and buildings	500,000
Machinery	30,000
Goodwill	180,000
Receivables	40,000
Inventories	120,000
Trade payables	(70,000)

Requirement

(a) Advise Jack as to whether any CGT will be payable. You are not required to calculate the CGT or base cost of the shares.

(b) What would be the stamp duty if the transaction is evidenced by a contract?

Part Three

Capital Acquisitions Tax

11

Capital Acquisitions Tax – Gifts and Inheritances

Learning Objectives

After studying this chapter you will be able to:

- Identify and discuss how and when gifts and inheritances arise, and distinguish between them.

Chartered Accountants Ireland's *Code of Ethics* applies to all aspects of a Chartered Accountant's professional life, including dealing with capital acquisitions tax issues. As outlined at the beginning of this textbook, further information regarding the principles in the *Code of Ethics* is set out in **Appendix 2.**

Students should also be aware of the issues around tax planning, tax avoidance and tax evasion, and these are discussed in **Appendix 3**.

11.1 Introduction to Capital Acquisitions Tax

Capital acquisitions tax (CAT) is a tax on the acquisition of a benefit by a person for less than full consideration. The benefit can be either a gift or an inheritance. It is an aggregable tax, i.e. when assessing an individual's exposure to CAT all benefits taken by them on or after 5 December 1991 must be included. However, gifts and inheritances up to certain values may be taken tax-free in a person's lifetime, depending on their relationship with the person providing the benefit.

The Capital Acquisitions Tax Consolidation Act 2003 determines:

- If the benefit is a gift/inheritance.
- If the benefit is within the charge to CAT (**Chapter 13**).
- How the taxable value of the benefit is computed (**Chapters 15** and **17**).
- If there are any reliefs or exemptions available (**Chapters 14** and **16**).
- How the tax is calculated (**Chapter 12**).
- The administration of the CAT system (**Chapter 18**).

11.2 Gifts and Inheritances

All benefits, be they gifts or inheritances, are taxed together. When the legislation was originally introduced there were significant differences assessing CAT on gifts and on inheritances, and the legislation was structured accordingly. However, over the years these differences have been reduced and you will find that the rules for dealing with gifts and inheritances are almost completely the same.

Broadly speaking, if an individual becomes entitled to any property or benefit, for less than full consideration, and there is no death involved, then that individual is deemed to have received a **gift**. The amount of the gift is represented by the full market value of the property or benefit taken as reduced by any consideration given, and any debts or encumbrances taken over. Where a private company makes or receives a gift, the liability to CAT is determined by looking through the company, or series of companies, to the ultimate individual shareholders and by treating the shareholders as having made or received the gift.

If the benefit or property is received as a result of a death, the beneficiary is deemed to have taken an **inheritance**. The amount of the inheritance is calculated in the same manner as for gifts.

11.2.1 Basic Elements of a Gift/Inheritance

Section 5 CATCA 2003 provides that a **gift is deemed to be taken** when:

- a **disposition** is made,
- by a **disponer**,
- whereby a **donee**,
- becomes **beneficially entitled in possession**,
- otherwise than **on a death**,
- to **any benefit**,
- otherwise than for **full consideration in money or money's worth paid by the donee**.

Section 10 CATCA 2003 provides that **an inheritance** is taken when:

- a **disposition is made**,
- by a **disponer**,
- whereby a **successor**,
- becomes **beneficially entitled in possession**,
- **on a death**,
- to any **benefit**,
- otherwise than for a full consideration in money or money's worth **paid by the successor**.

We see, therefore, that most of the basic elements constituting an inheritance correspond to those constituting a gift. These definitions contain many elements that need to be examined carefully.

Disposition

The disposition represents the **method by which the ownership of the property or benefit involved is transferred**. For every gift, there must be a disposition; but every disposition is not necessarily a gift. For example, if one sells a car at market value, this is a disposition but it is not a gift. The term is specifically defined in section 2 CATCA 2003 for the purposes of CAT. This definition is intentionally very wide and includes:

1. Any act or omission by a person as a result of which the value of that person's estate is reduced, e.g. the transfer of property otherwise than for full consideration.
2. The release of any debt or failure to exercise a right by an individual, as a result of which the value of that person's estate is reduced.

> ***Example 11.1***
> The passing of a resolution by a company that results, directly or indirectly, in one shareholder's property being increased in value at the expense of the property of any other shareholder, if that other shareholder could have prevented the passing of the resolution by voting against it.

3. Payment of money.
4. The grant or creation of any benefit.
5. The transfer of any property or benefit by will or on intestacy (intestacy means that a person dies without making a will).
6. The "disposition" may, therefore, be said to be the legal method of alienating the property in favour of a beneficiary, e.g. the deed of conveyance in respect of the transfer of a farm, the trust deeds in relation to the transfer of property to a trust fund, or the act of delivery in the case of the transfer of movable property.

Disponer

The **disponer** is the person who, directly or indirectly, is the **source of the financial benefit** comprised in the disposition. This is usually very straightforward, e.g. a parent who gifts shares to a child is the disponer. It is important to establish who the disponer is as the amount of benefit that can be taken tax-free depends on the recipient's relationship with the disponer.

Other examples of the disponer include:

- the deceased, in the case of a will or an intestacy;
- the settlor, in the case of property transferred to express or discretionary trusts;
- a person who has made a reciprocal arrangement with a third party to provide property comprised in a disposition to a second person.

> ***Example 11.2***
> Brian owes Alan €10,000. Alan agrees to waive the debt if Brian transfers shares valued at €10,000 to Alan's brother, James. The financial source of James's benefit (and therefore the disponer) is Alan, and not Brian who actually provided the property.

Donee/Successor

The **donee** is simply the person who receives the **gift**, whereas the recipient of an inheritance is known as the **successor**. In the example of a parent gifting shares to a child, the child is the donee. Alternatively, if an aunt dies leaving money to a niece, the aunt is the disponer, the niece is the successor.

Entitled in Possession

"Entitled in possession" is defined in CATCA 2003 as "**having a present right to the enjoyment of property** as opposed to having a future such right".

A gift/inheritance is not deemed to be taken until the happening of the event upon which the donee/successor (i.e. the beneficiary) becomes beneficially entitled in possession to the benefit. For example, if a father gives his solicitor €20,000 to give to his son when the son marries, the gift will only arise when the son actually gets married, as it is only at that time that the son will have a present right (as opposed to a future right) to enjoy the funds.

On a Death

Section 3 CATCA 2003 defines this term as meaning a benefit taken under any of the following circumstances:

1. Under the terms of a will (whether the benefit is taken immediately or after an interval).
2. Under an intestacy, i.e. individual dies without leaving a will.
3. Under a disposition where the disponer dies within two years of the date of the disposition. In such cases, the gift is effectively deemed to be an inheritance. Previously, the distinction was relevant as the rates of gift tax and inheritance tax differed. As both rates are now the same, the distinction is no longer significant.
4. An appointment of property from a discretionary trust where the trust was created by the will of a deceased person.
5. On the termination of a life interest by the death (or the deemed death) of the life tenant or at a definite interval after such a death. Advance termination of a limited interest is beyond the scope of this textbook.
6. On the death of a person who is a joint tenant.
7. On the happening of any event following the termination of an intervening life interest which gives rise to the benefit in question.

If a person becomes beneficially entitled in possession to any benefit on a death otherwise than for full consideration, then he is deemed to take an inheritance. A "gift", therefore, arises *otherwise* than on a death.

Benefit

For CAT purposes, a benefit refers to a gift or inheritance. Section 2 CATCA 2003 defines it to include "any estate, interest, income or right". Such a wide definition would clearly include:

- an absolute interest/ownership in property;
- a life interest in property; and
- an annuity or other periodic payment.

> ***Example 11.3***
>
> 1. Jim transfers ownership of his farm to Joe – Joe takes an absolute interest in the farm. As full ownership passed, the gift taken was equal to the full value of the farm.
> 2. Jim gives Joe a right to the use of his farm for Joe's lifetime – Joe takes a limited interest in the farm (i.e. a life interest). Obviously, the benefit taken is less than the full value of the farm as it is not full ownership of the property.

It is only the value of the actual benefit taken that is taxable and not necessarily the full value of property comprised in the gift or inheritance. Where the benefit involved does not comprise an absolute interest it is a "limited interest" and CATCA 2003 provides a statutory method of valuing the benefit. The calculation of the taxable value of a limited interest, be it an annuity or a life interest, is dealt with in **Chapter 15**.

Consideration in Money or Money's Worth Paid by the Beneficiary

There can be no gift or inheritance if full consideration in money or money's worth is paid by the recipient of the benefit. As such, it would not be subject to CAT. Payment can be non-monetary, hence the "money's worth".

Any consideration, monetary or otherwise, given by the recipient therefore reduces the value of any benefit taken for the purposes of CAT.

> ***Example 11.4***
>
> 1. Tony transfers his hotel, valued at €2,000,000, to Mary for €2,000,000 – clearly there is no gift here as full consideration has been paid.
> 2. Tony transfers the hotel to Mary for €1,200,000 – here the gift comprises the full value of the hotel reduced by the consideration paid by Mary, i.e. €2,000,000 – €1,200,000, i.e. €800,000.
> 3. Tony transfers the hotel to Mary, subject to Mary giving Colin €500,000 – this involves two gifts as follows:
>   (a) the hotel less €500,000 from Tony to Mary, i.e. Mary receives a gift of €1,500,000; and
>   (b) €500,000 from Tony to Colin.

11.2.2 CAT Differences between Gifts and Inheritances

In essence, an inheritance is distinguished from a gift in that an inheritance is taken *on a death* while a gift is taken otherwise than on a death. The recipient of a gift is known specifically as the *donee* whereas the recipient of an inheritance specifically is the *successor*. (The general term for the recipient of a benefit, be it a gift or inheritance, is "the beneficiary".)

There are some differences in the treatment of gifts and inheritances for CAT purposes. Where relevant, these will be addressed in the following chapters. However, it should be noted at this stage that the main difference between gift tax and inheritance tax is that **the first €3,000** of the total taxable value of the total **gifts taken from a single disponer in the same year is exempt from CAT** (known as the small gift exemption, see **Section 16.1**). There is no equivalent exemption for inheritances.

11.2.3 Dates of the Disposition, Gift and Inheritance

We have seen that in order to have a gift or an inheritance there must be a disposition by a disponer. It should be noted that the date of the disposition may differ from the date of the gift/inheritance. These dates are defined in the legislation.

Date of the Disposition
Section 2 CATCA 2003 defines the date of the disposition to mean:

1. the date of death of the deceased in the case of a benefit taken by will or an intestacy;
2. the date of death of the deceased in the case of benefits derived under the Succession Act 1965 (i.e. basically a widow's legal right or claims of children to a share in the estate);
3. the latest date when the disponer could have exercised the right or power which has been waived, where the disposition consisted of a failure or omission to exercise a right or power;
4. in any other case, the date of the disposition is the date on which the act or, where more than one act is involved, the last act of the disponer was done by which he provided or bound himself to provide, the property comprised in the disposition.

> ***Example 11.5***
>
> 1. If Pat leaves €200,000 to his son in his will, the date of disposition is Pat's date of death.
> 2. If Pat gives his solicitor €200,000 to give to his son when the son marries, the date of the disposition is the date of payment of the money to the solicitor.

The date of the disposition is important as it determines the tax rules that apply. This is covered in greater detail in **Chapter 13**. It is also important in determining if certain CAT exemptions apply (**Chapter 16**).

Date of the Gift

Section 2 CATCA 2003 defines the date of the gift as "the date of the happening of the event on which the donee becomes beneficially entitled in possession to the benefit". In other words, something has to happen for the donee to be in possession of the benefit, and it is only when this has happened that the donee becomes liable to CAT.

> ***Example 11.6***
> Following from Example 11.5 above, while the date of the disposition was the date Pat gave his solicitor the money, the date of the gift will be the date the son marries as it is only at that time that the son will have a present right (as opposed to a future right) to enjoy the funds.
>
> If Pat had merely given his son €200,000 on a certain day, the date of the disposition is the actual date of payment of the money and the date of the gift is the same date because the son immediately becomes entitled in possession to the benefit.

> ***Example 11.7***
> A father gives (by deed of conveyance) his son the right to use a property for a period of 10 years with absolute ownership of the property passing to his grandson after the 10-year period has expired. The deed of conveyance is the disposition.
>
> In the son's case, he receives an immediate benefit, i.e. the use of the property (though for a limited period only). In that instance, the date of the gift corresponds to the date of the disposition.
>
> The grandson is not treated as having received a gift until he becomes entitled in possession, i.e. until the 10-year period has elapsed. In his case, the date of the disposition (i.e. the date of execution of the deed) and the date of the gift are completely different. When the 10-year period has elapsed, the grandson is treated as having received the gift direct from his grandfather, and only then does he becomes entitled in possession.

The date of the gift is important as it determines the tax rates and tax-free thresholds that apply to the calculation of CAT arising on that gift. In subsequent chapters we will see that the date of the gift is also important for determining whether or not a gift is liable to CAT (**Chapter 13**) or whether the gift qualifies for certain reliefs (**Chapter 14**) or exemptions (**Chapter 16**).

Date of the Inheritance

The term "date of the inheritance" normally means the date of the death which has to occur in order for a successor to become entitled to an inheritance. An exception is where a gift becomes an inheritance because the disponer dies within two years of the date of the disposition, in which case the date of the inheritance is the date of the gift.

> ***Example 11.8***
> Jack dies on 1 February 2019. Under the terms of Jack's will, he leaves a life interest in a property to his son, Joe, and provides that the property is to pass absolutely to Joe's son, George, on Joe's death. The date of Joe's inheritance from his father is 1 February 2019. The date of George's inheritance from his grandfather will be the date of Joe's death.

The date of the inheritance is important as it determines the tax rates and tax-free thresholds that apply to that inheritance. So, if the date of inheritance is 2019, the 2019 CAT rate and tax-free group thresholds will apply – even if the successor does not receive the inheritance until a later date (when different rates or thresholds may well be in place), as is common with inheritances. As with gifts, we will see in subsequent chapters that the date of the inheritance is also important for determining whether or not an inheritance is liable to CAT (**Chapter 13**) or whether it qualifies for certain reliefs (**Chapter 14**) or exemptions (**Chapter 16**).

Questions

Review Questions

(See Suggested Solutions to Review Questions at the end of this textbook.)

Question 11.1

Mary owes John €8,000. John tells her to give €8,000 to Peter, in settlement of the debt.

Requirement
Who is the disponer for the €8,000?

Question 11.2

A mother agrees to give a farm to her daughter when she has her first child.

Requirement
When is the gift taken by the daughter?

Question 11.3

Joyce gives Paddy the family company worth €1 million, subject to Paddy giving €100,000 to Nora.

Requirement
What gifts are taken?

Question 11.4

You are a tax specialist in a firm of Chartered Accountants. The managing partner has asked you to write a memo dealing with the following CAT queries.

Requirement

(a) What is regarded as a "disposition" for CAT purposes?
(b) What is the "date of the disposition"?
(c) What does "beneficially entitled in possession" mean?
(d) Explain what is meant by "date of the gift".

12

Computation of CAT

Learning Objectives

After studying this chapter you will be able to:

- Identify and advise on the correct group threshold for any particular benefit.
- Calculate the CAT arising on taxable gifts and inheritances taken in 2019.

12.1 Introduction to the Computation of CAT

The computation of CAT depends upon a number of factors, including:

- The **relationship** between the recipient of the gift/inheritance (beneficiary) and the person from whom the gift/inheritance is taken (disponer). This relationship governs the **group threshold** to be applied.
- The **taxable value** of the gift/inheritance received.
- The **aggregate** of the taxable value of all previous benefits taken by the beneficiary from persons within the **same group threshold** on or after **5 December 1991**.
- The date on which the gift/inheritance is taken (because group threshold can change).

12.2 Group Thresholds

12.2.1 Group Thresholds 2019

The amount of the **group threshold** applicable in computing the CAT arising on receipt of a benefit depends on the relationship between the recipient of the benefit (beneficiary) and the provider of the benefit (disponer) and the year in which the benefit is taken. The group thresholds to be used when taxing a gift or inheritance taken in 2019 are:

Group A **€320,000** where the beneficiary is, on the day the gift or inheritance is taken:

- the child of the disponer; or
- the child of the civil partner of the disponer; or
- the minor child of a deceased child (see **Section 12.2.2**); or

- a parent of the disponer taking an inheritance that is not a limited interest on the death of the disponer (see **Section 12.2.2**); or
- a "favorite niece/nephew" of the disponer taking a gift/inheritance of business property (see **Section 12.2.2**).

A child includes an adopted child and a stepchild. For the purposes of the Group A threshold, it is also deemed to include a natural child who has been adopted by someone else and also a foster child, subject to certain conditions.

Group B **€32,500** where the beneficiary is, on the day the gift or inheritance is taken:

- a lineal ancestor of the disponer (some exceptions for a parent (see **Section 12.2.2**)); or
- a lineal descendant of the disponer (other than relationships as set out in Group A); or
- a brother or sister of the disponer; or
- a child of a brother or sister, or a child of a civil partner of a brother or sister of the disponer (other than relationships as set out in Group A).

Group C **€16,250** in all other cases.

Example 12.1

David gives (by deed of conveyance) his son, Nigel, the right to use a property for a period of 10 years with absolute ownership of the property passing to his grandson, Dylan, after the 10-year period has expired. David also gifts his own mother, Kate, and her sister, Mary, €20,000 each. The group thresholds that apply when assessing each beneficiary's CAT exposure are:

- Nigel is a child of the disponer, David – Group A
- Dylan is a grandchild (i.e. lineal descendant) of the disponer, David – Group B
- Kate is a parent (i.e. lineal ancestor) of the disponer, David – Group B
- Mary is David's aunt (his mother's sister). She is not a lineal ancestor, nor a lineal descendant, nor a sister, nor a child of a brother/sister of the disponer – Group C

We will see that, when computing CAT, the fact that *prior* gifts/inheritances were taken in a different year is irrelevant. **When taxing a benefit taken in 2019, use only the group threshold figures and CAT rates for 2019**. The group thresholds for earlier periods are set out in **Appendix 1** at the end of this textbook. Earlier thresholds are only relevant when computing CAT for a year earlier than 2019. Such calculations are beyond the scope of this book.

12.2.2 Group Thresholds – Special Relationships

Minor Child of Deceased Child

The Group A €320,000 threshold applies where the beneficiary is, on the day the gift or inheritance is taken:

- the minor child of a deceased child of the disponer; or
- the minor child of a deceased child of the civil partner of the disponer; or
- the minor child of the civil partner of a deceased child of the disponer; or
- the minor child of the civil partner of a deceased child of the civil partner of the disponer.

A minor child is defined in CATCA 2003 as a child who is under 18 years of age and has never been married.

> ***Example 12.2***
> Anthony and Harriet are Jim's parents. Jim is married to Nora, and they have a daughter, Emma, who is five years old. Jim died on 1 January 2019. On 2 February 2019, Anthony gave Emma €200,000. On 1 March 2019, Alan, Nora's father, gave Emma €100,000.
>
> The gift of €200,000 by Anthony to Emma will be subject to the Group A €320,000 tax-free threshold, as Emma is a minor child of a deceased child (i.e. Jim) of Anthony's.
>
> The gift by Alan to Emma is in the Group B €32,500 tax-free threshold as Alan is Emma's grandparent. Emma is not a minor child of a deceased child of Alan's and therefore the Group A threshold is not applicable.

Benefit taken by a Parent

A parent is a lineal ancestor of their child so, generally, Group B threshold applies to gifts and inheritances taken by a parent from their child unless:

1. the parent takes an inheritance from their child, on the death of that child, and the inheritance is not a limited interest, the applicable threshold is Group A for that inheritance (see **Section 12.2.1**); or
2. the parent takes an inheritance from their child, on the death of that child, and that child had taken a non-exempt gift or inheritance from either parent within five years immediately prior to the death of that child, in which case the inheritance by the parent is **exempt** from CAT (see **Chapter 16, Section 16.4)**

> ***Example 12.3***
> Tara, a wedding planner, died intestate (i.e. without a will), leaving an estate valued at €500,000. She is survived only by her mother, Colette. As Colette is inheriting absolute ownership of Tara's estate on Tara's death, the Group A threshold applies when assessing Colette's CAT liability.
>
> However, if Colette had made a non-exempt gift to Tara in the five years preceding Tara's death, Colette's inheritance from Tara would be exempt from CAT.

Benefit taken by a Spouse/Civil Partner

Gifts and inheritances taken by a spouse/civil partner from their spouse/civil partner while married are exempt from CAT – so no group threshold is necessary (see **Chapter 16, Section 16.2**).

Favourite Niece/Nephew

Schedule 2 CATCA 2003 provides that, in certain circumstances, a nephew or niece may be deemed to be the child of a disponer and, therefore, qualify for the Group A threshold of €320,000 rather than the Group B threshold of €32,500. The beneficiary must be a child of the disponer's brother or sister or a child of the civil partner of the disponer's brother or sister.

In order to qualify for the Group A threshold in respect of the benefit, the niece/nephew must have:

- **worked substantially on a full-time basis for the disponer for the relevant period** in carrying on, or assisting in carrying on, the trade, business or profession of the disponer and the benefit consists of property which was used in connection with that trade, business or profession, or
- **worked substantially on a full-time basis for a company controlled by the disponer** for the **relevant period** in carrying on, or in assisting in carrying on, the trade, business or profession of the company and the benefit consists of **shares** in that company.

The term "worked substantially on a full-time basis" requires that the beneficiary:

- works **more than 24 hours a week** for the disponer/company at a place where the business, trade or profession is carried on; or
- works **more than 15 hours a week** for the disponer/company at the place where the business, trade or profession is carried and such business, trade or profession is carried on exclusively by the disponer, the disponer's spouse/civil partner and the beneficiary.

The **"relevant period"** means:

- the period of **five years** ending on the date of the disposition; or
- in the case where, at the date of the disposition, an interest in possession is limited to the disponer under the disposition, the period of five years ending on the coming to an end of that interest.

Reasonable periods of annual or sick leave are allowed.

A **"company controlled by the disponer"** means a company that:

- is a **private trading company** (as defined in **Chapter 14, Section 14.2.2**);
- has the **disponer as one of its directors**; and
- is under the **control** of the disponer, or nominees of the disponer.

"Control" generally means holding 50% or more of the nominal value of the shares in a company or more than 50% of the voting share capital.

> ***Example 12.4***
> June leaves her farm, worth €800,000, to her niece Catherine, who had worked full-time on the farm with her for the last eight years. She also left her shares in Abbey plc worth €50,000. The group threshold in respect of the farm is Group A €320,000, as she has worked on the farm for at least five years and it is an inheritance of a trade asset. The group threshold in respect of the shares is the normal Group B threshold of €32,500.

Surviving Spouse/Civil Partner of a Deceased Person

CATCA 2003 provides a specialised relief that effectively permits the surviving spouse or civil partner of a deceased person to "stand in the shoes of the deceased person" in certain circumstances. The relief applies where:

- at the date of the gift or inheritance,
- the beneficiary is the surviving spouse or civil partner of a deceased person who at the time of their death was of a closer blood relationship to the disponer than the beneficiary.

In these circumstances, for the purposes of calculating the liability, the beneficiary is deemed to take up the same relationship to the disponer as the deceased spouse or civil partner had at the time of death. This can result in the use of a more favourable tax-free threshold for the computation of any liability due.

> ***Example 12.5***
> Jim died on 28 February 2019 and left €200,000 to his son-in-law, James. James' wife, Ann, (i.e. Jim's daughter), had died some years previously. In these circumstances, James is deemed to stand in Ann's shoes, *vis-à-vis* her blood relationship with her father and, accordingly, the €320,000 group threshold applies. If this rule did not apply, James would be treated as a stranger and a threshold of only €16,250 would apply. If James also received a gift from Ann's aunt, the group threshold would be €32,500 instead of the usual €16,250.

12.2.3 Group Thresholds – Anti-avoidance: Gift Splitting

In the absence of anti-avoidance legislation, the practice of 'connected dispositions' (i.e. gift splitting) could save substantial CAT through the utilisation of more advantageous tax-free thresholds than might otherwise be available if the gift were made directly from the original disponer to the final recipient, as shown in the following example.

> ***Example 12.6***
> Peter wishes to give his grandson, Mark, €200,000 in January 2019. If the gift is made directly to Mark, the tax-free threshold applicable is only €32,500. However, if Peter were to first gift the €200,000 to his son, John (Mark's father), the tax-free threshold applicable between father and son is €320,000. John could then subsequently gift the €200,000 to Mark without attracting CAT liability.

Section 8 CATCA 2003 is an **anti-avoidance** provision designed to prevent the avoidance of CAT by passing property through one or more intermediaries before vesting ownership in the final recipient, as suggested in **Example 12.6**. Section 8 provides that where a gift is made within three years before or three years after the original gift, then *two gifts* are deemed to have been made by the original disponer as follows:

1. a gift by the original disponer to the first recipient; and
2. a gift by the original disponer to the final recipient.

Both gifts are taxable in the normal way (including if the original disponer dies within two years of the original gift the beneficiaries will be deemed to have taken an inheritance).

> ***Example 12.7***
> (a) In 2019, Peter gives a gift to his son, John, and John subsequently gives a gift to his son, Mark, in 2020. John and Mark will be assessed to CAT as follows:
>
> - John takes a gift from Peter, his father – Group A threshold.
> - Mark is deemed to take a gift from Peter, his grandfather – Group B threshold.
>
> (b) In 2019, John borrows €100,000 from the bank and gifts it to his son, Mark. Subsequently, in 2020, Peter gives a gift of €100,000 to his son, John. John uses the gift to repay his bank loan. John and Mark will be assessed to CAT as follows:
>
> - John takes a gift from Peter, his father – Group A threshold.
> - Mark is deemed to take a gift from Peter, his grandfather – Group B threshold.

Section 8 does not apply in the following circumstances:

- Where it can be shown that the original disposition was not made with a view to enabling or facilitating the making of the subsequent disposition or with a view to facilitating the recoupment in any manner of the cost of the disposition to the final recipient.
- Section 8 only applies to gifts, and therefore will not have effect unless the original and subsequent benefits are gifts rather than inheritances, i.e. if the gift splitting occurs as a result of an **intervening death, then the provisions are not invoked**.
- Revenue will not invoke this legislation where a gift is taken by a **married child** of the disponer of a house or site for a house, and the married child has to **transfer the property into the names of that child and his/her spouse in order to get a mortgage** from a lending institution.

12.3 Aggregation

The aggregate taxable values of all taxable gifts and taxable inheritances taken **on or after 5 December 1991** by the recipient from **all disponers *within the same group threshold***, are taken into account to determine the amount of CAT payable on the current benefit. This means that in a lifetime, from 5 December 1991 an individual can currently receive taxable gifts and inheritances totaling up to €320,000 from Group A disponers, plus €32,500 from Group B disponers, plus €16,250 from Group C disponers without crystallising a CAT liability.

While all benefits from persons within the one group threshold are aggregated, there is only one group threshold (i.e. tax-free) amount. For example, if benefits are received from a brother, a sister and an aunt, all three benefits are aggregated, but the maximum tax-free group threshold that can be availed of is €32,500, i.e. one cannot get €32,500 tax-free from each person within the same group threshold.

12.4 Basic Computation

CAT payable on a gift or inheritance is calculated as follows:

Step 1: Calculate "**Aggregate A**", which is the aggregate of:

(i) the taxable value of the current gift or inheritance; PLUS
(ii) the taxable value of all previous taxable gifts and inheritances taken from persons within the **same group threshold** on or after **5 December 1991**.

Step 2: Calculate the CAT chargeable on "**Aggregate A**":

CAT on Aggregate A = (Aggregate A – Group threshold) × 33%

Step 3: Calculate "**Aggregate B**", which is:

(i) Aggregate A, i.e. the aggregate taxable value in Step 1; MINUS
(ii) the taxable value of the current gift or inheritance (i.e. (i) in Step 1. above).

Step 4: Calculate the CAT chargeable on "**Aggregate B**" (i.e. the notional amount of CAT that would arise on the prior benefits if they were received using the current tax rate and group threshold):

CAT on Aggregate B = (Aggregate B – Group Threshold) × 33%

Step 5: Calculate the **CAT on the current benefit**:

CAT on current benefit = CAT on Aggregate A – CAT on Aggregate B

It should be noted that where current group threshold exceeds Aggregate B (total prior taxable benefits), the notional tax on prior benefits (i.e. CAT on Aggregate B) will be nil, resulting in the full amount of CAT on Aggregate A being payable. Also, where total prior taxable benefits (Aggregate B) exceed the current group threshold, the CAT on the current taxable benefit will be 33% of the current benefit.

Example 12.8

On 1 February 2019, Mary O'Hagan received an inheritance with a taxable value of €350,000 from her father. Mary had previously received the following benefits:

- gift of €10,000 on 1 December 1988 from her aunt;
- inheritance of €5,000 on 20 December 2003 from her sister;
- gift of €255,000 on 1 June 2004 from her mother;
- gift of €15,000 on 1 November 2005 from her uncle.

What is Mary's CAT liability, if any, on the February 2019 inheritance from her father? (Ignore small gift exemption.)

As Mary is inheriting from a parent, Group A is the relevant threshold. Assess prior benefits for other Group A gifts and inheritances:

- gift of €10,000 on 1 December 1988 from her aunt – pre-5 Dec 1991, not applicable.
- inheritance of €5,000 on 20 December 2003 from her sister – Group B, not applicable.
- gift of €255,000 on 1 June 2004 from her mother – Group A, aggregable.
- gift of €15,000 on 1 November 2005 from her uncle – Group B, not applicable.

Computation

1. Calculate Aggregate A, i.e. total taxable gifts and inheritances taken since 5 December 1991 from persons in the Group A threshold:

Current inheritance from father	€350,000
Gift from mother 2004	€255,000
Total benefits Group A	€605,000

2. Calculate CAT on Aggregate A:

Deduct: Group A threshold	(€320,000)
Taxable	€285,000
CAT @ 33% on Aggregate A	€94,050

3. Calculate Aggregate B, i.e. total taxable gifts and inheritances taken since 5 December 1991 from persons in the Group A threshold excluding the current benefit:

Gift from mother 2004	€255,000

4. Calculate CAT on Aggregate B:

Deduct: Group A threshold	(€320,000)
Taxable	NIL
CAT @ 33% on Aggregate B	NIL

5. Calculate CAT on current benefit:

CAT on Aggregate A	€94,050
Less: CAT on Aggregate B	Nil
CAT on current benefit	€94,050

Example 12.9
On 4 April 2019, Mary Ryan received an inheritance with a taxable value of €60,000 from her uncle. She had received no other gifts or inheritances from any source since 5 December 1991. What is Mary's CAT liability on the inheritance from her uncle?

As she has no previous benefits, there is nothing to aggregate. Therefore, simply calculate CAT on the current benefit.

	€
Taxable value	60,000
Deduct: Group B threshold	(32,500)
	27,500
CAT @ 33%	9,075

Example 12.10
Louise and Ellen are civil partners. On 5 October 2019, Louise's sister Catherine gifts €30,000 to Ellen's daughter, Olivia. Olivia has received no other benefit since 5 December 1991. (Ignore small gift exemption.) What is the CAT liability, if any, on the gift taken by Olivia?

As Olivia is the daughter of Ellen, who is the civil partner of Catherine's sister, Louise, the Group B threshold applies.

As she has no previous benefits, there is nothing to aggregate. Therefore, simply calculate CAT on the current benefit.

	€
Taxable value	30,000
Deduct: Group B threshold	(32,500)
	NIL

As the taxable value is less than the Group B threshold, no liability arises.

Example 12.11
During October 2019 Michael Moran received the following gifts:

1. a gift of a rental property worth €220,000 from his father;
2. a gift of shares worth €30,000 from an aunt; and
3. a gift of €5,000 cash from a cousin.

He had previously received the following benefits:

- an inheritance of investments valued at €200,000 from his mother on 1 June 1991;
- an inheritance of shares valued at €30,000 from an uncle on 6 May 1993;
- an inheritance of a holiday cottage valued at €50,000 from a friend on 11 December 1999.

What is the CAT liability, if any, on the gifts received in 2019 (ignoring the small gift exemption)?

Computation

1. Gift of rental property from father – the only other Group A benefit is the inheritance from his mother, but as this was received before 5 December 1991 it is ignored. Therefore, no aggregation is necessary and the total taxable value of the current gift is €220,000. This is below the Group A threshold of €320,000; therefore, no CAT is payable on this gift.

continued overleaf

2. Gift of shares from aunt:

	€
Current gift	30,000
Prior gift from uncle	30,000
Aggregate A	60,000
Group threshold B	(32,500)
	27,500
CAT on Aggregate A @ 33%	9,075
Prior gift from uncle	30,000
Group B threshold	(32,500)
	NIL
CAT on Aggregate B @ 33%	NIL
CAT on Aggregate A	9,075
CAT on Aggregate B	NIL
CAT on shares from aunt*	9,075

* As the threshold exceeds previous taxable benefits CAT due equals CAT on Aggregate A.

3. Gift of cash:

	€
Current gift	5,000
Previous gift from friend	50,000
Aggregate A	55,000
Group C threshold	(16,250)
	38,750
CAT on Aggregate A @ 33%	12,787
Aggregate B, i.e. previous gift from friend	50,000
Group C threshold	(16,250)
	33,750
CAT on Aggregate B @ 33%	11,137
CAT on Aggregate A	12,787
CAT on Aggregate B	(11,137)
CAT on cash from cousin**	1,650

** As the threshold is already used, €5,000 is taxable at 33%.

4. Total CAT payable on gifts taken during 2019:

	€
Rental property from father	NIL
Shares from aunt	9,075
Cash from cousin	1,650

We will see later that these liabilities are payable by 31 October 2020 as the valuation date, in this case the date of the gift, is in October 2019.

Example 12.12
Frank and Jonathon are civil partners. On 15 April 2019, Frank died. Under the terms of his will he left property worth €500,000 to Jonathon, cash of €100,000 to his daughter, Alexa, and cash of €70,000 to Jonathon's son, Ryan. None of the beneficiaries has received a gift or inheritance since 5 December 1991, except for Ryan, who received a gift of €255,000 from his mother in May 2017.

What is the CAT liability, if any, of each beneficiary on the inheritances taken in 2019? (Ignore small gift exemption.)

Computation
As Jonathon is Frank's civil partner, he is exempt from CAT on the benefit of €500,000 which he receives from Frank.

As Alexa is Frank's daughter, the Group A threshold of €320,000 applies. As this is the first benefit she has received in Group A and the taxable value is less than the threshold, there is no tax payable on the €100,000 she receives.

As Ryan is the son of Frank's civil partner Jonathon, the Group A threshold applies. The prior gift of €255,000 from his mother must be aggregated:

	€
Current inheritance	70,000
Previous gift from mother	255,000
Aggregate A	325,000
Group A threshold	(320,000)
	5,000
CAT on Aggregate A @ 33%	1,650
CAT on Aggregate B*	NIL
CAT on cash from Frank	1,650

* Previous benefit below group threshold of €320,000.

Questions

Review Questions

(See Suggested Solutions to Review Questions at the end of this textbook.)

Question 12.1

Identify the **group threshold amounts** applicable to the following gifts/inheritances in 2019:

1. Gift of investment property by father to daughter.
2. Gift of shares by son to father.
3. Gift of 25% of shares in a private trading company by uncle to nephew. Remaining 75% of shares owned by unrelated parties. Nephew has worked for company on a full-time basis for last 10 years.
4. Gift of farmland by uncle to nephew. Nephew has worked on a full-time basis for uncle farming this land for previous 10 years.
5. Gift of shares by father-in-law to daughter-in-law, son still alive.
6. Gift of shares by grandfather to 19-year-old grandson, grandson's father is deceased.
7. Gift of cash from cousin.
8. Gift of cash from uncle to niece.
9. Gift of cash from nephew to uncle.

10. Gift of 75% of shares in trading company by aunt to niece. Remaining 25% of shares owned by two unrelated parties. Niece has worked for company on a full-time basis for last 10 years. Aunt is a director in the company.
11. Gift of farmland to sister's civil partner's son who had worked on a part-time basis farming the land for the previous 10 years.
12. Gift of cash by stepfather to stepchild.
13. Gift of investment property by grandfather to grandson's wife. Grandson is deceased.
14. Gift of 100% of shares in trading company by uncle to nephew. Nephew has worked for company on a full-time basis for previous four years.
15. An inheritance of cash from mother's civil partner.
16. Gift of shares to brother's wife. Brother is deceased.
17. Gift of antique vase by granddaughter to grandmother.
18. Gift of cash to adopted child of brother.
19. Gift of farmland to wife's nephew. Nephew has been working on a full-time basis farming the land for the previous 10 years.
20. Gift of cash by Tom to Alannah. Alannah, aged 17, is Tom's civil partner's son's civil partner's child. Tom's civil partner's son died tragically six months before the gift from Tom to Alannah.

Question 12.2

During his lifetime, Peter made the following gifts, net of small gift exemption, to his son, Edward:

(a) on 17 June 1990 he gifted €300,000 to Edward; and
(b) on 8 June 2001 he gifted €100,000 to Edward.

On 11 April 2019, Peter died and left his estate, valued at €350,000, to Edward.

The only other gifts or inheritances that Edward had received were an inheritance of €30,000 on the death of his mother on 15 May 2016 and of €40,000 on the death of his uncle Harry on 13 January 2017. All gifts are net of small gift exemption.

Requirement
Compute the CAT payable by Edward on the inheritance of €350,000 on the death of his father.

13

Territorial Scope

Learning Objectives

After studying this chapter you will be able to:

- Apply the territoriality rules for CAT as determined by the location of the asset and a person's residence, ordinary residence and domicile.

13.1 Introduction

The territorial scope of CAT must clearly be limited, as is the case for other taxes, such as income tax and CGT. CATCA 2003 therefore sets out a number of rules which determine whether or not a particular gift or inheritance is within the scope of CATCA 2003, i.e. whether a particular gift is a **"taxable gift"** or whether a particular inheritance is a **"taxable inheritance"**. A liability may not necessarily result even where these territorial rules are satisfied. For example, the particular gift or inheritance may be covered by a tax-free threshold or may be exempt altogether.

13.2 Location of Property

CATCA 2003 does not include rules for determining where property is situated. General law determines where property is located. The main rules are as follows:

1. **Land and buildings** Situated where they are physically located.
2. **Debts**
   (a) A simple contract debt is situated where the debtor resides.
   (b) A speciality debt, i.e. a debt payable under a sealed instrument, is situated where the instrument happens to be.
   (c) A judgment debt is situated where the judgment is recorded.
3. **Securities/Shares** Situated where the share register is kept, if the securities/shares are registered (Irish incorporated companies are required to maintain a register of members in Ireland). Bearer securities/shares are situated where the security/share certificate is physically located.
4. **Tangible property, e.g. cars, furniture, movable goods** Situated where they are physically located.

5. **Cash or currency of any kind** Situated where they are physically located. Bank balances are located in the country where the bank branch in which the account is located.

13.3 Taxable Gifts and Inheritances

13.3.1 Irish Property – Always Taxable

A benefit is a taxable benefit to the extent that it, or a portion of it, consists of property that is situated in the State (i.e. Republic of Ireland) at the date of the gift/inheritance.

13.3.2 Foreign Property – General Rule

The current rules apply to gifts where the date of the disposition is on or after 1 December 1999. Before this date, one looked at the domicile of the disponer.

Foreign property is taxable if:

- the disponer is resident or ordinarily resident in the State in the year of assessment in which the disposition is made; or
- the beneficiary is resident or ordinarily resident in the State in the year of assessment in which the benefit falls.

The income tax rules for determining residence, ordinary residence and domicile apply (see **Chapter 2, Section 2.1**). However, this general rule would mean that foreign-domiciled persons who were only in Ireland for a short time could trigger an Irish CAT liability. To ensure that this does not happen, there is a special five-year rule for foreign-domiciled persons.

13.3.3 Foreign Property – Foreign-domiciled Persons

For CAT purposes, foreign-domiciled persons are not treated as resident or ordinarily resident on a date unless:

- the date occurs on or after 1 December 2004;
- the person has been resident in the State for **five consecutive years of assessment immediately preceding the year of assessment in which that date falls**; *and*
- the person is either **resident or ordinarily resident** in the State on that date.

The date is:

- the date of the disposition in the case of the disponer;
- the date of the gift or the inheritance in the case of the beneficiary.

> ***Example 14.1***
> On 1 April 2019, Joe gives Ray one acre of land in Dublin. As this is Irish property it is liable to CAT. It does not matter where either of them is domiciled, resident and ordinarily resident.

> ***Example 14.2***
> On 31 August 2019, Mary, who is domiciled, resident and ordinarily resident in Ireland, gifts her villa in Spain to her friend Manuel, who is Spanish and lives in Spain. As Mary is Irish resident (or ordinarily resident) and domiciled, the gift is subject to Irish CAT, i.e. Manuel must pay CAT.

> ***Example 14.3***
> On 31 August 2019, Martin, who is domiciled, resident and ordinarily resident in Germany, gifts his shares in a German company to his cousin Joe, who is domiciled, resident and ordinarily resident in Ireland. As Joe is Irish resident (or ordinarily resident) and domiciled, the gift is subject to Irish CAT, i.e. Joe must pay CAT.

> ***Example 14.4***
> On 31 August 2019, Peter, who is domiciled, resident and ordinarily resident in France, gifts his shares in a US company to his brother Ivan, who moved to Ireland in early 2015. Ivan is French domiciled, but resident and ordinarily resident in Ireland under the income tax rules for 2019. However, as Ivan is foreign domiciled, he is only liable on foreign property if he has been resident in Ireland for the five tax years preceding the year in which he receives the gift, i.e. 2019. As he has not been so resident, he is not liable to Irish CAT.

> ***Example 14.5***
> On 31 October 2019, Joey, who is domiciled, resident and ordinarily resident in Italy, gifts his house in Rome to his brother Bart, who moved to Ireland in 2010. Bart is Italian domiciled, but resident and ordinarily resident in Ireland under the income tax rules. As Bart is foreign domiciled, he is only liable on foreign property if he has been resident in Ireland for the five tax years preceding the year in which he receives the gift, i.e. 2019. As he has been so resident, he is liable to Irish CAT on the gift of the house in Rome.

(The rules regarding benefits where the date of the disposition is before 1 December 1999 are beyond the scope of this textbook. The above definitions, and those that follow in later chapters, exclude rules regarding discretionary trusts, which are also beyond the scope of this textbook.)

Questions

Review Questions

(See Suggested Solutions to Review Questions at the end of this textbook.)

Question 13.1

A gift or inheritance of property situated in the State is within the charge to Irish CAT regardless of the domicile/residence position of the disponer or the donee/successor.

Requirement
Outline the general rules which determine where property is situated.

Question 13.2

The following gifts/inheritances were taken during the year ended 31 December 2019:

1. Donal, an Irish domiciled and resident individual, died on 19 April 2019. He left all his assets, consisting of Irish and UK property, to his son Brendan, also Irish domiciled and resident.

2. Gordon, an Irish domiciled and UK resident person, died on 11 July 2019. He left shares in a UK trading company to his Irish resident and domiciled nephew, Dermot.
3. Jonathan, a UK domiciled and resident person, died on 15 August 2019 and left land in Cork to his son John, also UK domiciled and resident.
4. Noel, a UK domiciled and resident person, died on 16 September 2019 and left a house in the UK and €20,000 in a Sterling bank account in London to his son, Nevin, also UK domiciled but resident in Ireland since 2011.
5. Michael, an Irish domiciled and resident individual, died on 1 February 2019. He left all his assets equally to his two children, David and Jane. His assets consisted of a house in Clare and €30,000 in an Irish bank account. David and Jane are both Irish domiciled; however, while David is also Irish resident, Jane has been resident in the UK for many years.
6. On 23 August 2019, Maurice, an Irish domiciled and UK resident person, gave shares valued at €10,000 in various UK companies to his nephew Darren, also Irish domiciled and UK resident. Maurice has been living in the UK since 2000. Darren only moved to the UK in June 2018. Prior to moving to the UK, Darren had always lived in Cork.
7. Jim, an Irish domiciled and resident individual, gave his daughter Brid, also Irish domiciled and resident, a rental property in the UK by deed dated 12 December 2019.
8. Jean, an individual domiciled in France but resident in Ireland since 2009, gifted her daughter Amelie, also domiciled in France and resident in Ireland since 2010 except for the year 2017 when she was non-resident, shares in an Irish trading company and shares in a French trading company on 31 December 2019.

Requirement

(a) Outline the rules for determining whether a gift or inheritance taken during the year ended 31 December 2019 is a taxable gift or inheritance.

(b) For each gift or inheritance outlined above, state whether the gift/inheritance is a taxable gift/inheritance, giving reasons for your answer.

Question 13.3

Calculate the CAT payable in respect of the gift/inheritance taken in 2019 in each of the following cases:

(a) Michael, who is Irish domiciled and resident, gave his daughter, also Irish resident and domiciled, a cash gift of €40,000 on 1 January 2019. His daughter had previously received the following benefits:

   (i) a house in Sligo valued at €80,000 inherited from her grandmother, also Irish domiciled and resident, in June 2007; and

   (ii) jewellery valued at €20,000 inherited on the death of her mother, also Irish domiciled and resident, in August 2009.

(b) Bridget, who is domiciled in the State but resident in the USA, inherited a property in the UK valued at €120,000 from an uncle, who is Irish domiciled and resident, on his death in October 2019. Bridget had previously received the following benefits:

   (i) shares in an Irish quoted company valued at €50,000 inherited on the death of an aunt, US domiciled and resident, in March 2006;

   (ii) a gift of a car valued at €15,000 from a cousin, Irish domiciled and resident, in January 1994; and

   (iii) €25,000 in an Irish bank account inherited on the death of Bridget's grandmother, Irish domiciled and resident, in September 1990.

14

Taxable Value

Learning Objectives

After studying this chapter you will be able to:

- Determine the valuation date of a gift/inheritance.
- Advise on the CAT implications of the "free use of property".
- Calculate the taxable value of a gift/inheritance.
- Explain the principles and conditions of CAT agricultural relief on receipt of a gift/inheritance of agricultural property.
- Determine and calculate the availability and impact of CAT agricultural relief on receipt of a gift/inheritance of agricultural assets.
- Explain the principles and conditions of CAT business relief on receipt of a gift/inheritance of business assets.
- Determine and calculate the availability and impact of CAT business relief on receipt of a gift/inheritance of business assets.
- Prepare CAT computations involving agricultural relief and business relief.

14.1 General Principles

We have seen that CAT is levied on the **taxable value** of the gift or inheritance concerned. The basic steps involved may be illustrated as follows:

	€
Market value	X
Less: liabilities, costs and expenses payable out of the taxable benefit	(X)
Incumbrance-free value	X
Less: market value of consideration paid by the beneficiary	(X)
Taxable Value	X

We will now examine in detail the meaning of the above terms.

14.2 Market Value

CATCA 2003 contains specific provisions setting out the method by which the market value of different types of property is to be computed.

14.2.1 Market Value – General Rule

The general rule is that the market value of any property is to be the price that, in the opinion of the Revenue Commissioners, the property would fetch if sold on the open market, **on the valuation date**, in such manner and subject to such conditions as might reasonably be expected to obtain for the vendor the best price for the property.

CATCA 2003 sets out the general market value rule and specifically states that the Revenue Commissioners will not make any reduction in the estimate of market value on the grounds that the whole property is to be placed on the market at the same time.

Revenue has the power to authorise the inspection of property by any person it considers fit at all reasonable times. If Revenue requires a professional valuation, then the cost of such valuation is to be paid for by Revenue.

For the purposes of estimating the market value of unquoted shares or securities if sold on the open market, it is to be assumed that there is available to any prospective purchaser of the shares or securities all the information a prudent prospective purchaser might reasonably require if he/she were proposing to buy them from a willing vendor at arm's length.

The meaning of the term **valuation date** is dealt with at **Section 14.3**.

14.2.2 Market Value of Shares in Certain Private Companies

A **private company** is defined to mean a body corporate (wherever incorporated) that:

1. is under the control of not more than five persons; and
2. is not a quoted company which is excluded from the corporation tax close company rules (as adjusted for CAT purposes to counter tax avoidance).

Therefore most companies in Ireland, particularly family-owned companies, are covered by the definition.

CATCA 2003 provides that the market value of each share in a private company that is (after the taking of the gift or inheritance), on the date of the gift or inheritance, a **company controlled by the beneficiary** (see **Section 14.6.3** for definition) is to be computed on a market value basis, i.e. each share is valued as if it formed an apportioned part of the market value of the shares in that company. Such apportionment, as between shares of a particular class, is by reference to nominal amount and, as between different classes of shares, is with due regard to the rights attaching to each of the different classes.

14.2.3 Valuation of Annuities

CATCA 2003 contains special provisions for calculating the value of a gift or inheritance of an annuity. The method of valuation depends on whether or not the annuity is charged/secured on any property. These are dealt with separately in detail in **Chapter 15**.

14.2.4 Market Value of a Limited Interest

CATCA 2003 contains specific provision for the valuation of limited interests (e.g. a house for life). These are dealt with separately in detail in **Chapter 15**.

14.2.5 Valuation of Free Use of Property

A charge to CAT arises where a person has the use and enjoyment of property either for no consideration or for less than full consideration. If the "free" use is ongoing, the benefit is deemed to be taken on 31 December each year. The benefit taken is deemed to be the difference between the consideration given by the person for the use, occupation or enjoyment of the property and the best price obtainable in the open market for such use, occupation or enjoyment. If the free use is of land or a house, the best price obtainable would be the market rent payable for such a property. If the free use is of cash, for example an interest-free loan, the best price obtainable would be the income from the investment of such cash, i.e. the bank deposit rate applicable to such sum and not the rate which a bank might apply to a loan. The following examples explain how the benefit is calculated.

Example 14.1 Market value of benefit in "free" use case involving a loan
Joe gives an interest-free loan of €100,000 to his nephew, John, on 1 January. The **bank deposit rate of interest is, say, 2%.** John is deemed to take a gift of €2,000 on 31 December. He is also deemed to take a gift each year, on 31 December, until the loan is repaid and each such deemed gift is taken into account for aggregation purposes. If the loan is repaid during the year, the date of the deemed gift for that year is the date of repayment. If the loan was repaid after six months, the value of the gift for that year would be €1,000.

Example 14.2 Market value of benefit in "free" use case involving accommodation
Anne gives the use of her house, worth €200,000, to her cousin, Colette. The annual market rent is €15,000. Colette pays Anne €5,000 per annum. Colette is deemed to take a gift of €10,000 on 31 December each year that she has the use of the house and each deemed gift is taken into account for aggregation purposes.

14.3 Valuation Date

14.3.1 Importance of Valuation Date

The valuation date is very important for a number of reasons:

- It is the market value of the gift/inheritance at the valuation date that is assessed to CAT.
- It is the date used to determine when the CAT is paid and the return filed. If the valuation date is from 1 January to 31 August 2019, CAT is payable and the return must be filed on or before 31 October 2019. If the valuation date is from 1 September to 31 December 2019, CAT is payable and the return must be filed on or before 31 October 2020. Where a return is filed on ROS (the Revenue Online Service), the filing date is extended to 12 November 2019.
- It is the date used to determine whether certain conditions are fulfilled for agricultural relief (**Section 14.5**) and business relief (**Section 14.6**).

For example, if a parent is considering gifting shares on 1 April 2019 but actually delays making the gift for, say, six months until 1 October 2019, then the valuation date is 1 October 2019. If the shares have increased in value by, say, 20% during that period, then the child bears a higher market value, taxable value and probably CAT. Obviously delaying the gift six months has delayed the payment of tax from 31 October 2019 to 31 October 2020, but in this case will probably have increased the amount of CAT as the market value has increased 20%.

14.3.2 Valuation Date of a Taxable Gift

CATCA 2003 sets out the rules for determining the valuation date. The valuation date is normally the **date of the gift**. The valuation date in relation to a **gift which subsequently becomes an inheritance** as a result of the death of the disponer within two years of the disposition is specifically deemed to remain the **date of the gift**.

14.3.3 Valuation Date of a Taxable Inheritance

The determination of the valuation date for inheritances is complex. The following are the main rules:

1. For cases not covered by 2. below, the valuation date of a taxable inheritance will be the **earliest** of the following dates:
   (a) the earliest date on which any person is **entitled** to retain the subject matter of the inheritance for the benefit of the successor; or
   (b) the date on which the subject matter of the inheritance **is** actually retained; or
   (c) the date of **actual delivery/payment** of the inheritance to the successor.
2. The valuation date for a gift which has become an inheritance as a result of the disponer dying within two years of the date of the disposition is deemed to be the date of the gift.

Generally speaking, the residue of an estate cannot be regarded as retained for the benefit of the beneficiary until the estate is finally administered. This is, of course, subject to the possibility of interim payments having been made to the legatee in question.

The basic principle to be applied therefore is **that the valuation date will be the date of delivery or payment** of the subject matter of the inheritance to the beneficiary, or the date of retainer on their behalf, whichever is the earliest.

The valuation date for assets passing under a will or intestacy is usually the date on which the Grant of Representation issues from the Probate Office or District Probate Registry. (The Grant of Representation is the document which allows the people distributing the assets to the beneficiaries to do so.) If assets are passing outside of the will or intestacy, the valuation date will normally be the deceased's date of death.

There can be several valuation dates where multiple benefits are taken from the same estate.

Examples of when date of death is the valuation date include where the beneficiary is in occupation of the property and where there is joint ownership of the property.

Litigation and family disputes may cause the valuation date to be put back to a later time.

Example 14.3
Jim dies in 2019. He bequeaths his farm to his wife, who lives on the farm with him, a cash legacy to his nephew and the residue of his estate to his son for life with the remainder to his grandson. The valuation dates would be as follows:

(i) the date of death in the case of the inheritance taken by the wife, as this is probably the earliest date on which the personal representatives are entitled to retain the farm for the benefit of his wife;
(ii) the valuation date in the case of a cash legacy would be the date the personal representative actually paid the legacy to the nephew;
(iii) his son has a life interest in the residue of the estate and the valuation date in this case would be the date of retention of the residue for him by the personal representative. This will be sometime after the issue of the grant of probate when the personal representatives have collected the assets and the liabilities of the estate have been established, but not necessarily paid;
(iv) the grandson's valuation date would probably be the date of the son's death, as the grandson would become beneficially entitled in possession to the benefit at that time.

> ***Example 14.4***
> On 1 November 2019, Ian, by deed, transfers property to trustees on trust for Brian for life with remainder to Conor absolutely. On creation of the trust, Brian would immediately become beneficially entitled to his benefit and the date of the gift would therefore be 1 November 2019. The valuation date in respect of this gift would be the same date.
>
> The date of Conor's inheritance is the date of Brian's death, as that is the date when Conor becomes beneficially entitled in possession to the benefit. Again, the valuation date is probably the same date.

It is clear from CATCA 2003 that different parts of the same inheritance may have different valuation dates, e.g. if interim payments are made out of a deceased's estate prior to the date of final retainer, the valuation date of each interim payment will be the date on which the advances are actually paid.

The Revenue Commissioners are entitled to determine the valuation date for a particular inheritance, but this determination is subject to an appeal by the taxpayer if he/she wishes.

Appendix 14.1 contains a summary of the definitions of the date of the disposition, date of the gift/inheritance and the valuation date.

14.4 Deduction for Liabilities, Costs, Expenses and Consideration

We have seen that the market value of the taxable benefit is reduced by any liabilities, costs and expenses that are properly payable out of the taxable gift or taxable inheritance in order to arrive at what is known as the incumbrance-free value.

Any legal or other cost associated with the transfer of property will normally fall under this heading, e.g. solicitors' fees or stamp duty.

The most common examples of expenses that are deductible in calculating CAT are debts owed by the deceased at the date of death, funeral expenses and costs of administering the estate.

Where the property transferred is charged with the payment of a liability, then that liability is properly deductible under this heading also in arriving at the incumbrance-free value.

> ***Example 14.5***
> Ann transfers a house worth €500,000 to Barbara, subject to a mortgage charged on the house on which there is an outstanding amount due of €150,000. In this case the incumbrance-free value is €500,000 less €150,000, i.e. €350,000. This assumes, of course, that Barbara takes over the property subject to the mortgage. If Barbara also paid stamp duty and solicitor's costs in connection with the transfer, such expenses would also be deducted.

> ***Example 14.6***
> Joe dies and leaves a business worth €5,000,000 to his son, Ray. The executor of Joe's will paid legal expenses of €50,000. These legal expenses are a deductible expense in calculating the taxable value of the benefit taken by Ray, i.e. €5,000,000 – €50,000 = €4,950,000.

14.4.1 Consideration Paid by Donee/Successor

CATCA 2003 permits the incumbrance-free value of the property transferred to be reduced by any "bona fide consideration in money or monies worth paid by the donee or successor" in computing the taxable value of the gift or inheritance.

Consideration is the last deduction to be made in arriving at the taxable value and is deductible in effect from the value of the interest taken by the donee, whether absolute or limited. The treatment of limited interest will be dealt with separately (**Chapter 15**).

CATCA 2003 particularly mentions that consideration will *include*:

1. Any liability of the disponer which the beneficiary undertakes to discharge as their own **personal** liability.
2. Any other liability to which the gift or inheritance is subject under the terms of the disposition under which it is paid. For example, Claire transfers property to Damien on condition that Damien pays €1,000 to Emer. The €1,000 paid by Damien to Emer would represent consideration to be deducted from the incumbrance-free value of the property taken from Claire in calculating the final taxable value.

Consideration paid by a beneficiary may take many forms:

- a part payment;
- an annuity payable to the disponer (**Chapter 15**);
- a CGT liability of the disponer arising out of the disposal, which the donee agrees to pay.

14.4.2 Deductions Specifically Prohibited in Arriving at Taxable Values

Set out below are the main deductions not allowable in arriving at taxable values.

1. Contingent liabilities: where the payment of a liability is contingent upon the happening of some future event, no deduction is permitted. If the contingent liability eventually becomes payable by the donee/successor, then an adjustment is allowed.
2. Liabilities, costs, etc. for which reimbursement can be obtained.
3. The tax, penalties or interest payable under CATCA 2003 and any costs of raising money to pay those liabilities.
4. Liabilities connected with exempt assets cannot be used to reduce the taxable value of non-exempt property.

14.5 Agricultural Relief

14.5.1 Summary: Calculation of Taxable Value where there is Agricultural Relief

The calculation of taxable value where there is agricultural relief is as follows:

Market value	X
less: agricultural relief (90%)	(X)
Agricultural value	X
less	
Proportion of liabilities, costs and expenses	(X)
equals	
Incumbrance-free value	X
less	
Proportion of consideration	(X)
equals	
Taxable value	X

14.5.2 The Relief

Provided certain conditions are fulfilled, section 89 CATCA 2003 permits the market value of specified "**agricultural property**" to be **reduced by 90%** in computing the taxable value of the gift/inheritance taken by a "**farmer**".

Example 14.7
Joe received a gift of a farm, livestock and machinery worth €1 million. The value for CAT purposes is calculated as follows:

	€
Market value of agricultural property	1,000,000
Agricultural relief (90%)	(900,000)
Agricultural value	100,000

The relief was lower in the past. Previous rules are not covered in this textbook.

14.5.3 Definitions

"**Agricultural property**" is defined as:

- agricultural land, pasture and woodlands situated in the EU;
- crops, trees and underwood growing on such land;
- such farm buildings, farm houses, and mansion houses (together with the lands occupied therewith) as are of a character appropriate to the agricultural property;
- farm machinery, livestock and bloodstock thereon;
- a payment entitlement under the EU Basic Payment Scheme to a farmer.

To qualify for the relief, the gift/inheritance must be agricultural property at the date of the gift/inheritance *and* at the valuation date.

The term "**agricultural value**" refers to the **market value of the agricultural property as reduced by 90%**.

"Farmer"
To qualify for the relief, the beneficiary must qualify as a "farmer" on the valuation date. For gifts or inheritances taken on or after 1 January 2015, there are two tests to be satisfied: an "asset test" and a "farming the land test".

1. **Asset test**
   A "**farmer**" is defined as a beneficiary who is, **on the valuation date and after taking the gift or inheritance**, an individual in respect of whom **not less than 80% of the market value** of the property to which they are beneficially entitled in possession is represented by the market value of property in the EU which consists of **agricultural property** (as defined above). The gross value of all property is used for the purposes of the 80% test, i.e. no deduction is made for mortgages, etc. except **borrowings on an off-farm principal private residence are deductible for the purpose of the 80% test** provided that the borrowings have been used to purchase, repair or improve that residence.

2. **"Farming the land" test**
   In this situation, the beneficiary must:
   (a) farm the agricultural property for a period of not less than six years commencing on the valuation date; or
   (b) lease the agricultural property to a tenant who farms the land for a period of not less than six years commencing on the valuation date.

In addition, the beneficiary (or the lessee, where relevant) must:

(c) have one of the agricultural qualifications set out in the legislation; or

(d) farm agricultural property, including the agricultural property, for not less than 50% of his or her normal working time.

Revenue will accept working 20 hours per week on average as satisfying the condition of farming for not less than 50% of his or her normal working time. The agricultural property must also be farmed on a commercial basis and with a view to the realisation of profits.

(Note: there is a stamp duty relief called consanguinity relief. The same conditions for this CAT agricultural relief also apply to stamp duty consanguinity relief (see **Chapter 9, Section 9.2.2**), namely: farming the land or leasing it to someone who farms it for six years, the person having a farming qualification or farming the land for at least 50% of their time and doing so on a commercial basis. However, the asset test applies for CAT relief only. Also, for the stamp duty relief to apply, the transferor must be related to the transferee).

14.5.4 Computation of Relief

In the computation of taxable value, the market value of the agricultural property comprised in the gift or inheritance is reduced to its agricultural value.

Example 14.8: **Gift of agricultural property**

John gives the following to his mother, Mary, who has no other assets and who intends to farm the land on a full-time basis for at least six years:

	€
Farmland	300,000
Woodland	100,000
Farm buildings	50,000
Farm machinery	20,000
Bloodstock	30,000
Total	500,000

If there were no agricultural relief, the full gift would be taxable, i.e. taxable value of €500,000. The relief would not be due, for example, if she had other assets and could not satisfy the 80% test or if the land is not farmed.

She is a "farmer" as at least 80% of her assets (in this case, 100%) are agricultural assets and she intends to farm the land. Therefore, agricultural relief is due and the taxable value is reduced. The agricultural value is calculated as follows:

	€
Market value of agricultural property	500,000
Relief @ 90%	(450,000)
Agricultural value	50,000

Example 14.9

Assume the same facts as in Example 14.8 except that Mary has other assets, as follows:

	€
Bank deposit account	10,000
Shares	20,000
Principal private residence (PPR)	300,000
Mortgage to buy PPR	250,000

Gross market value of all Mary's assets (less mortgage re off-farm PPR) is €580,000, i.e. €500,000 + €10,000 + €20,000 + €300,000 – €250,000.

Gross value of agricultural assets is €500,000.

Is Mary a farmer? $\frac{€500,000}{€580,000} = 86\%$

Yes, Mary is a farmer as she satisfies the asset and "farming the land" tests. So, agricultural relief is due and the taxable value is reduced as follows:

	€
Market value of agricultural property	500,000
Relief @ 90%	(450,000)
Agricultural value	50,000

***Example 14.10:* Inheritance of agricultural property**

Jack, who has no other assets, inherits the following from his aunt:

	€
Farmland and buildings	200,000
Crops growing on the land	30,000
Livestock and machinery	20,000
Total	250,000

He intends to farm the land for not less than six years from the valuation date.

If there were no agricultural relief, the full inheritance would be taxable, i.e. taxable value of €250,000.

Due to agricultural relief, the taxable value is reduced. The agricultural value is calculated as follows:

	€
Market value of agricultural property	250,000
Relief @ 90%	(225,000)
Agricultural value	25,000

***Example 14.11:* Client may have given incorrect information**

If, in Example 14.10, you deal with Jack's tax affairs, you know that when you filed his last return on his behalf he owned property. However, he has stated that he does not have any property in his recent correspondence to your manager.

You should advise your manager of the fact that his last tax return showed that Jack had property. Your manager can raise this with Jack to establish whether there was some other explanation, such as having sold the property to pay off debt or whether there was an error made by Jack.

14.5.5 Computation of Relief: Restriction of Deductions

CATCA 2003 also provides that the **allowance for debts, incumbrances and consideration connected with the agricultural property** which has been artificially reduced in value must be **proportionately reduced** to ensure that the final deduction is proportionate to the agricultural value of the property *vis-à-vis* its market value.

Example 14.12

Jim gives agricultural land worth €600,000 to John (who qualifies as a "farmer"). The lands are charged with a mortgage of €100,000. John is required by Jim, in consideration for the transfer, to give Stewart €50,000.

Computation of Taxable Value

		€
Market value of agricultural property, i.e. lands		600,000
Less:	agricultural relief @ 90%	(540,000)
"Agricultural value"		60,000
Less:	mortgage charged on land (as restricted):	
	€100,000 × agricultural value/market value (i.e. 10%)	
	$€100{,}000 \times \frac{60{,}000}{600{,}000}$	(10,000)
Incumbrance-free value		50,000
Less:	consideration (as restricted):	
	$€50{,}000 \times \frac{60{,}000}{600{,}000}$ (i.e. 10%)	(5,000)
Taxable value		45,000

Example 14.13

Colin died leaving agricultural land worth €100,000 to Desmond (who qualifies as a farmer). The executors of Colin's will incur legal expenses of €1,400.

Computation of Taxable Value

		€
Market value of agricultural property		100,000
Less:	agricultural relief @ 90%	(90,000)
Agricultural value		10,000
Less:	legal expenses $€1{,}400 \times \frac{10{,}000}{100{,}000}$	(140)
Taxable value		9,860

Computation where Agricultural Property and Other Property are Involved

Where the gift/inheritance comprises both agricultural and non-agricultural property, then the taxable value of each must be computed separately. This is because:

- any expenses, etc. related to agricultural property will only be 10% allowable;
- any expenses, etc. related to non-agricultural property will be fully allowable; and

- any expenses, etc. related to both agricultural and non-agricultural properties will have to be apportioned between the two, and then allowed to the extent of 10% for the agricultural one and fully for the non-agricultural.

Example 14.14

Michael transfers the following assets to his brother, Sean:

	Market Value
	€
Agricultural land	1,200,000
Shares	100,000
Total value	1,300,000

Sean, in consideration of the gift, has paid €39,000 to Michael's nephew, Jim.

Sean, who has been a salesman, intends to become a farmer. His only asset is his private residence, which is worth €160,000 (mortgage outstanding of €100,000 for the purchase of the residence).

Legal fees and other costs of the transfer amount to €13,000 and are payable out of the gift.

Computation

Is Sean a "farmer"?

Yes, as he satisfies the "farming the land" test. After accepting Michael's gift he also satisfies the asset test, i.e. more than 80% of his **gross assets** comprise agricultural property, bloodstock and farm machinery, i.e.

$$\frac{€1,200,000}{€1,360,000^*} \times 100 = 88\%$$

* €1,300,000 + €160,000 − €100,000

(a) Computation of Taxable Value of Agricultural Property

		€
Market value		1,200,000
Less: Relief: €1,200,000 @ 90%		(1,080,000)
Agricultural value		120,000
Less: Liabilities, costs, etc.		
Legal (relating to total property transferred)		
Portion applicable to agricultural property only:		
$€13,000 \times \frac{€1,200,000}{€1,300,000}$	€12,000	
Restricted for agricultural value, i.e. allow €12,000 @ 10%		(1,200)
Incumbrance-free value		118,800
Less: consideration (relates to total property)		
Portion applicable to agricultural property:		
$€39,000 \times \frac{€1,200,000}{€1,300,000}$	€36,000	
Allowable 10%		(3,600)
Taxable value of agricultural property		115,200

continued overleaf

(b) Computation of Taxable Value of Non-agricultural Property

	€
Market value	100,000
Less: Liabilities, costs, etc.	
Legal (balance €13,000 – €12,000)	(1,000)
Incumbrance-free value	99,000
Less: Consideration:	
Balance €39,000 – €36,000	(3,000)
Taxable value of non-agricultural property	96,000

(c) Computation of Total Taxable Value of Property

Taxable value of agricultural property	115,200
Taxable value of non-agricultural property	96,000
Total	211,200

Note: Sean must farm the land for not less than six years from the valuation date.

14.5.6 Other Matters

1. It should be noted that all agricultural land in the EU is within the definition of "agricultural property".
2. If a taxable gift/inheritance is taken by a beneficiary subject to the **condition that it is to be invested in agricultural property** and this condition is complied with **within two years** of the date of the benefit, then the benefit is deemed to be agricultural property. Therefore, the individual will initially pay the CAT but get a refund of any overpaid CAT, based on availing of agricultural relief. The six-year period from which the property must be farmed runs from the date the beneficiary invests in the agricultural property.
3. In the case of agricultural property which consists of **trees or underwood**, it is **not necessary for the beneficiary to satisfy the "farmer test"**.
4. Agricultural relief of 90% can be claimed in respect of **all** qualifying gifts and inheritances, i.e. there is no limit on the relief.
5. If an individual does not qualify for agricultural relief (e.g. does not satisfy the test that 80% of assets are agricultural property), the individual **may qualify for business relief** (see **Section 14.6**). The differences between agricultural relief and business relief are set out in **Appendix 14.2.**
6. The farmhouse or farm buildings qualify for agricultural relief when disposed of with the farmland. If the farmhouse or farm buildings are not received at the same time as the farmland, they will not qualify as agricultural property and therefore agricultural relief will not be due. For example, farmland, excluding the farmhouse, is given to a son. One year later the farmhouse is given to the same son. While the gift of the farmland may qualify, the gift of the farmhouse cannot qualify for agricultural relief. If the farmhouse had transferred at the same time, it would have qualified as agricultural property and agricultural relief would have been available, assuming the "farmer test" is satisfied.

Ranking of Agricultural and Business Relief

An individual does not have the option of claiming either agricultural or business relief – agricultural relief applies if the conditions are satisfied.

14.5.7 Clawback of Relief

Agricultural relief previously claimed will be recaptured if the agricultural property (other than crops, trees or underwood), or part of it, **is disposed** of or compulsorily acquired within six years from the date of the gift or inheritance, ***and*** **not replaced by other agricultural property**:

- within a year in the case of a sale; or
- within six years in the case of a compulsory acquisition.

The reinvestment does not have to be in the same type of agricultural property.

This clawback **does not apply where the beneficiary dies** before the property is sold or compulsorily acquired.

If there is **full reinvestment** of proceeds, there is **no clawback**. If there is **no reinvestment** of proceeds, there is **full clawback**.

If a proportion of the proceeds are reinvested, only a proportion of the relief is clawed back.

Example 14.15

Joe inherited a farm, with a market value of €1,000,000 on the valuation date. He qualified for agricultural relief and therefore the taxable value of the inheritance was €100,000. Joe paid CAT at the then rate of 33% on the inheritance as his tax-free threshold was fully utilised. Two years later, Joe sold the farm for €1,400,000. He reinvested none of the proceeds. What is the CAT due as a result?

The CAT payable on clawback is calculated as follows:

	€
Original relief claimed is clawed back	900,000
Additional CAT payable (at the rate that prevailed when the inheritance was received) (€900,000 @ 33%)	297,000

14.5.8 Ceasing to Farm Land within Six Years

If within six years of qualifying for agricultural relief, the beneficiary or lessee ceases to satisfy the "farming the land test" due to ceasing to farm the land or ceasing to lease it to a person who farms the land (otherwise than on the death of the beneficiary or lessee), then the benefit is treated as not being agricultural land. For example, the individual takes up full-time 'off the farm' employment and no longer spends at least 20 hours a week farming the land. Agricultural relief is clawed back and CAT is payable accordingly.

14.6 Business Relief

14.6.1 Summary: Calculation of Taxable Value where there is Business Relief

The calculation of taxable value where there is business relief is as follows:

Market value	X
less	
Liabilities, costs and expenses	(X)
equals	
Incumbrance-free value	X
less	
Consideration	(X)
equals	
Taxable value before relief	X
less	
Business relief @ 90%	(X)
equals	
Taxable value	X

14.6.2 The Relief

Provided certain conditions are fulfilled, sections 90–101 CATCA 2003 permit the taxable value of any relevant business property to be **reduced by 90%** in computing the taxable value of the gift/ inheritance taken.

In the case of sole traders and partnerships, the relief applies to the value of the net assets of the business that are used in the course of its qualifying business activities. In the case of companies, the relief applies to that proportion of the value of the shares of the company derived from qualifying business activities. Assets that are not used for the purposes of a qualifying business activity are excluded.

14.6.3 Relevant Business Property

The property that can qualify for relief is "relevant business property", which is as follows:

1. A business or an **interest in a business.**
2. **Unquoted shares** in a company subject to the condition that on the valuation date:
   (a) the **beneficiary** holds **more than 25%** of the voting rights; or
   (b) the company is **controlled by the beneficiary**. A company is controlled by a beneficiary if it is controlled by any one or more of the following:
      (i) the beneficiary;
      (ii) relatives of the beneficiary;
      (iii) civil partner or children of the civil partner of the beneficiary; and
      (iv) certain nominees and trusts.

   "Controlled" generally means holding 50% or more of the nominal value of the shares in a company or more than 50% of the voting share capital. There is no minimum ownership requirement for the beneficiary. The following are relatives of a beneficiary: his spouse, parent, child, aunt, uncle, their children and grandchildren, the spouse of any of these relatives (other than the beneficiary's own spouse or civil partner) and his grandparents. For this purpose, a company controlled by a beneficiary under the definition above is deemed to be a relative of a beneficiary; or

(c) the **beneficiary** holds at least **10%** of the issued share capital of the company **and has worked full-time** in the company (or a group company) for the **five years** prior to the date of the gift or inheritance.

In (a)–(c) the per cent ownership test is carried out **after taking the benefit.**

3. **Land, buildings, machinery and plant** owned by the disponer but **used by a company controlled** by the **disponer**, or by the disponer and his or her spouse or civil partner, or used by a partnership of which the disponer was a partner. The land, etc. must, however, be **transferred to the beneficiary at the same time as the partnership interest or the shares** or securities of the company are transferred, and the partnership interest or shares must be relevant business property. The definition of "control" for this purpose is different from the definition in 2. above. In order for a company to be controlled by the disponer, and his or her spouse or civil partner, they must hold a majority of the voting rights in the company.
4. **Quoted shares** or securities of a company only where:

   (a) they were **owned by the disponer prior** to their becoming **quoted**; and
   (b) **one of the ownership tests** set out at 2. above is satisfied.

Example 14.16
If a sole trader gifts his or her **business** to a child, this is a gift of relevant business property. If a partner in a partnership leaves the share in the partnership to a child, this is relevant business property.

If a sole trader gifts **just the premises** in which the trade is carried on (and not the trade itself) to a niece, this is **not relevant business property,** i.e. it is a gift of a premises only and not of a business.

Example 14.17
In order to qualify for business relief, the shares generally must be unquoted and **minimum ownership conditions** must be satisfied.

If a parent gifts shares in AIB plc to a child, this is not relevant business property and business relief will not apply.

If a parent owns a company and leaves it equally to the three children, then the shares are relevant business property. This is due to the fact that the beneficiary (each child) owns more than 25% of the voting rights. Alternatively, it qualifies as the company is controlled by the beneficiary and relatives.

A parent owns 30% of an unquoted company. The other 70% is owned by people who are not related to the parent. If the parent gifts these shares to a child, the child receives relevant business property – holds more than 25% of voting power.

If, alternatively, the parent wants to gift shares equally to two children, then the 15% shareholding received by each child will only be relevant property if the child has worked full-time in the company for the preceding five years.

This means that minority (non-controlling) shareholders in a company (which is not their family company), who want a beneficiary to benefit from business relief, must ensure that they give/leave shares to one person who will have:

- **more than 25% of voting rights** after receiving the shares; or
- **worked in the business** for five years and will hold **at least 10% of the shares** after receiving the shares.

Non-qualifying Property

A business or interest in a business, or shares or securities in a company, are **not qualifying property** where the business, or the business of the company, consists wholly or **mainly of dealing in currencies, securities, stocks or shares, land or buildings, or making or holding investments.** A business of "dealing in land" would not include genuine building and construction businesses or businesses which acquire land with a view to its development and disposal where most of the profit is derived from the increase in value of the land as a result of its development.

A holding company can qualify provided that its value is primarily attributable, directly or indirectly, to trading activities.

14.6.4 Minimum Period of Ownership and Use by Disponer

The minimum period of ownership by the disponer depends on the type of benefit taken and is as follows:

- in the case of an **inheritance taken on the date of death of the disponer**, the property must have been owned by the **disponer or his/her spouse or civil partner** for at least **two** years prior to the date of the inheritance; and
- in any other case (i.e. a gift, or an inheritance taken on the death of a person other than the disponer) the property must have been owned by the **disponer or his/her spouse or civil partner** for at least **five** years prior to transfer.

The two-/five-year minimum period of ownership is modified in two situations, namely replacement assets and successive benefits. These are beyond the scope of this book.

If it is to qualify for relief, an asset must have been **used** wholly or mainly for the purpose of the business concerned for the two-year period prior to the gift or inheritance. In the case of land, buildings, machinery or plant which qualifies for business relief because it has been used by a company controlled by the disponer (see **Section 14.6.3**), the period for which such assets must have been used by the company is at least five years, in the case of a gift, or two years in the case of an inheritance.

14.6.5 Valuation of Property

Value of a Business

The value of the business or an interest in a business (e.g. share in a partnership) is computed on **a net value basis**, i.e. the market value of the *assets used in the business* (including goodwill), reduced by the aggregate market value of any *liabilities incurred for the purposes of the business.*

Valuing Groups

There are specific rules for valuing groups, but these are beyond the scope of this book.

Assets Excluded in Determining the Value Attributable to Relevant Business Property

Having determined that the property is relevant business property, one must then value the property. As noted above, normal market value rules are used. However, CATCA 2003 provides that the value of **certain assets must be excluded** when determining how much of the total value of the business will actually qualify for business relief. The most important are assets used wholly or mainly for **personal use and any non-business assets**. In determining the amount of the value of a company which can qualify for relief, the value of business assets which were used wholly or mainly for the purposes of the business concerned throughout the last two years before the gift or inheritance may qualify for relief. Where an asset has been owned for less than two years, its value can qualify for relief if it has been used for the business of the company for the entire period of ownership.

Example 14.18

Harry Porter owned Hogmount Ltd since its formation in 2009 and transferred his 100% shareholding to his son, Trevor, in October 2019. The company is valued as follows:

	€
Rental property	310,000
Goodwill	300,000
Equipment	70,000
Inventories	30,000
Trade receivables	50,000
Trade payables	(60,000)
	700,000

The company operated a chain of fast-food outlets and used surplus funds to invest in rented residential property.

Trevor's CAT liability is as follows:

	Qualifying Property	**Non-qualifying Property**
	€	€
Market value	450,000	310,000
Less: liabilities		
Trade payables	(60,000)	
Taxable value before relief	390,000	310,000
Business relief 90%	(351,000)	0
Taxable value	39,000	310,000

Total taxable value is €349,000.

14.6.6 Other Matters

- The relief is deducted from taxable value, i.e. **after deduction of expenses and consideration.** *(Agricultural relief is deducted from market value with a proportionate reduction in expenses and consideration.)*
- Where agricultural relief applies, business relief does not also apply. Agricultural relief will apply, if available. Where the beneficiary does not satisfy the 80% asset test, then business relief should be considered.

14.6.7 Clawback of Relief

Disposal within Six Years

There is a clawback of the relief if at any time within six years after the gift or inheritance:

- the business concerned ceases to be a qualifying business, other than by reason of bankruptcy or a bona fide winding up on grounds of insolvency; or
- to the extent that the relevant business property is sold, leased, redeemed or compulsorily acquired within that six-year period and not replaced within one year by another qualifying business property.

Reinvestment

If there is **full reinvestment** of proceeds, there is **no clawback**. If there is **no reinvestment** of proceeds, there is **full clawback**.

If a proportion of the proceeds are reinvested, a similar proportion of the relief is clawed back.

Example 14.19

Albert inherited a business, with a market value of €1 million on the valuation date. He qualified for business relief at 90% of €900,000 and therefore the taxable value of the inheritance was €100,000. Albert paid CAT at 33% on the inheritance as his tax-free threshold was fully utilised. Two years later, Albert sold the business for €1,400,000. He did not reinvest any of the proceeds in buying another business. What is the CAT due as a result?

	€
Original relief claimed is clawed back	900,000
Additional CAT payable (€900,000 @ 33%)	297,000

Appendix 14.1: Summary Chart

Gift

Date of the disposition	■ The date the person (disponer) does something which binds them to provide the property. ■ In the case of failure to act, the latest date when the disponer could have acted.
Date of gift	■ The date the person (donee) becomes beneficially entitled in possession.
Valuation date	■ The date of the gift.

Inheritance

Date of the disposition	■ Normally the date of death. ■ Date when the person (disponer) is bound to provide the property (including situation where a gift becomes an inheritance). ■ In the case of failure to act, the latest date when the disponer could have acted.

Date of the inheritance	■ Date of latest death. ■ Date of death of life tenant. ■ Date of gift where it becomes an inheritance.
Valuation date	■ Normally it is the earliest of the following dates: ● when entitled to retain property; ● retain property; ● property is delivered. ■ Gift becomes an inheritance, date of the gift.

Appendix 14.2: Differences between Agricultural Relief and Business Relief

- There is no minimum ownership period for the disponer for agricultural relief, while there is a two-year (inheritance) or five-year (gift) minimum ownership period for business relief.
- Agricultural relief applies to the market value of property, while business relief applies to taxable value.
- Agricultural relief applies to the farmhouse, but business relief does not apply to a residential property.
- Non-agricultural assets can be used to purchase agricultural assets, in certain circumstances, and can qualify for relief. There is no such provision for business relief.
- Unsecured liabilities are apportioned pro rata between agricultural and non-agricultural assets, while in business relief only liabilities applicable to the business are deductible from the business assets and all other liabilities (as far as possible) are deductible from the non-business assets.
- There must be a farming business for business relief to apply. It is not sufficient that there is an asset that could be used for a business, e.g. property.
- There is no 80% asset test for business relief. While there is no farming the land test that has to be satisfied for agricultural relief **before** the transfer, if the farming the land test is not satisfied after the transfer, then the relief is effectively not available as it is clawed back immediately.
- A beneficiary does not have the option of claiming either agricultural or business relief. If the property is agricultural and the beneficiary qualifies as a farmer, then agricultural relief must be claimed. It is only in the event of failure to qualify for agricultural relief that business relief may be claimed on agricultural property.
- If land is disposed of because it has been compulsorily acquired and agricultural relief has been claimed, replacement land must be acquired within six years; whereas if business relief has been claimed, replacement business property must be acquired within one year.

Questions

Review Questions

(See Suggested Solutions to Review Questions at the end of this textbook.)

Question 14.1

You are a tax specialist in a firm of Chartered Accountants. The managing partner is meeting with a client who is considering gifting a substantial amount of land and farm assets to his son. The managing partner has asked you to write a memo to him outlining the conditions which would need to be satisfied if his client's son is to qualify for agricultural relief on the transfer.

Requirement
Write a memo to the partner outlining the conditions which must be satisfied if agricultural relief is to be claimed. Your memo should cover the following items:

(a) What relief is given.
(b) The definition of "agricultural property".
(c) The definition of "farmer".
(d) Withdrawal of the relief.

Question 14.2

Amy Smyth died on 1 February 2019 and her estate was administered in accordance with the terms of her will as follows:

1. To her niece, Margaret:

	Market value at 1 February 2019 and at the valuation date
	€
Holiday home in France	180,000
Quoted stocks and shares	230,000
€120,000 6% Irish Government Loan Stock	101,500

2. To her nephew, Liam:

	€
Farmland	850,000
Farm buildings	90,000
Bloodstock	100,000
Farm machinery	50,000

The farmland was charged with a mortgage of €120,000 and with the payment of farm creditors. Farm creditors amounted to €15,000 at 1 February 2019 and at the valuation date. Liam intends to farm the land on a full-time basis for at least six years from the valuation date.

3. To her daughter, Eva:

100% of the shares in Fine Arts Ltd, which were valued at €950,000. Amy owned the shares for many years. The company's net assets at the valuation date were as follows:

	€
Factory premises	130,000
Goodwill	215,000
Investment property	360,000
Plant and machinery	70,000
Inventories	180,000
Receivables	80,000
Net liabilities	(75,000)
Net assets	960,000

4. The residue of her estate, charged with the payment of funeral expenses, was also left to her nephew, Liam. The residue consisted of cash on deposit of €50,000. Amy's funeral expenses amounted to €20,000.

   Prior to his inheritance from Amy, Liam's only asset was his residence, which had a market value of €200,000 on 1 February 2019 and at the valuation date was subject to a mortgage used to buy the residence of €130,000.

   Margaret, Liam and Eva had previously received no gifts or inheritances other than the inheritance received from Amy.

   Amy, Margaret, Liam and Eva are all Irish domiciled and resident.

Requirement
Calculate the CAT payable, if any, by Margaret, Liam and Eva.

Question 14.3

Sandra and John are married with one son, James, and all are Irish domiciled, resident and ordinarily resident. On 1 June 2019, Sandra died, leaving the following estate:

	Market value at 1 June 2019 and date of retainer
	€
Investment property	520,000
Proceeds of non-exempt life policy	104,000
Bank accounts	60,000

In addition to the above assets, Sandra owned 20% of the issued share capital of the family trading company, Tyrex Ltd, which owns and operates a number of retail outlets. The total issued share capital comprised of 1,000 €1 ordinary shares which, prior to Sandra's death, were held as follows:

John	350	€1 shares
James	50	€1 shares
Sandra	200	€1 shares
Sandra's brother	400	€1 shares
	1,000	

The company has been valued at €1 million on a net assets basis. Included in the company's net assets is a house occupied by Sandra's brother as his main residence that has been valued at €300,000. There is a mortgage charged on the house of €50,000 included in the company's liabilities. This is the only non-trade asset and liability included in the company's net assets. Sandra had owned these shares since 2004.

Sandra's estate had the following liabilities:

	€
Funeral expenses	10,600
Income tax	3,800
Rates on investment property	1,600
	16,000

All these liabilities are to be met from the residue.

Sandra's will contained the following provisions:

- The investment property was left jointly to her husband, John, and son, James.
- Her 20% shareholding in the family company was left to her son, James.
- The residue was left equally to her husband, John, and her son, James.

James has received the following gifts:

- A gift of €15,000 from his aunt on 1 July 2000.
- A gift of €16,000 from his uncle, Sean, on 1 July 2007.
- A gift of 50 shares in Tyrex Ltd from his mother on 1 November 2006. For CAT purposes, the taxable value of these shares was €167,000 on that date. This figure was net of the small gift exemption.

None of the other beneficiaries has previously received gifts or inheritance from any source.

Requirement
Compute the CAT liabilities, if any, in respect of:

(a) The benefits taken by James under Sandra's will.
(b) The benefits taken by John under Sandra's will.

15

Treatment of Limited Interests

Learning Objectives

After studying this chapter you will be able to:

- Determine and calculate the taxable value of gifts/inheritances received for a limited period or where the interest is not an absolute interest, including annuities.
- Determine the appropriate deduction available where a limited interest forms part of the consideration given for a gift/inheritance.

15.1 Introduction

Section 2 CATCA 2003 defines "limited interest" as meaning:

"(a) an interest (other than a leasehold interest) for the duration of a life or lives or for a period certain, or

(b) any other interest which is not an absolute interest".

This includes an annuity (i.e. an annual fixed payment for a limited period).

Obviously a limited interest, whether a life interest or for a period certain, is less than an absolute interest and therefore the taxable value will be lower. The taxable value of a limited interest is achieved by reducing the incumbrance-free value of the benefit (i.e. the market value less expenses, costs and liabilities but before deducting consideration). The rules for ascertaining the market value of a benefit, other than an annuity, have been outlined in **Chapter 14, Section 14.2**.

15.2 Market Value of an Annuity

Section 5 CATCA 2003 contains special provisions for calculating the value of a gift or inheritance of an annuity. The method of valuation depends on whether or not the annuity is charged or secured on property.

15.2.1 Annuity Charged or Secured on Property

Where an annuity or limited interest is charged on any property, the value of the gift or inheritance is deemed to consist of the **appropriate part** of the property on which the annuity or limited interest is charged. The **appropriate part** is ascertained using the following formula:

$$\text{Entire property} \times \frac{\text{Gross annual value of benefit}}{\text{Gross annual value of entire property}}$$

> ***Example 15.1***
> Gary gives an annuity of €5,000 to his son, Stephen, and charges a specific block of investments owned by him with payment of the annuity. The investments have a capital value of €150,000 and produce an annual income of €10,000. The gift given by Gary to Stephen is deemed to consist of the appropriate part of the entire block of investments, i.e.
>
> $$€150{,}000 \times \frac{€5{,}000}{€10{,}000} = €75{,}000$$
>
> This €75,000 is used as the market value of the gift received by Stephen from his father.

15.2.2 Annuity Not Charged or Secured on Property

Where a gift or inheritance of an annuity is given that is not charged on any particular property, the value of the benefit is calculated by deeming it to be equal to the market value of a capital sum required to be invested in the latest Government security issued prior to the date of the gift, which is not redeemable within 10 years, to yield an income equal to the annuity.

> ***Example 15.2***
> Eoin covenants to pay his mother Bernadette, aged 62, €10,000 per annum. The value of the benefit taken by Bernadette is calculated as follows.
>
> Say the latest Government stock issued which was not redeemable within 10 years was a 4% Government Bond and this was quoted at €0.90 for €1 of stock.
>
> In order to produce an annual income of €10,000 by investing in this Government stock, it would be necessary to buy €250,000 of the stocks, i.e. €10,000/4%. At the current price of €0.90 per €1 of stock, it would cost €225,000 to buy €250,000 of this stock, i.e. €250,000 × 0.9. Accordingly, the market value of the benefit received by Bernadette is deemed to be €225,000.

Having ascertained the market value, deduct any liabilities, costs and expenses to give the **incumbrance-free value.**

15.3 Taxable Value of Limited Interests

The taxable value of a limited interest is achieved by reducing the incumbrance-free value of the benefit (i.e. the market value less expenses, costs and liabilities). The incumbrance-free value of the benefit is reduced by applying a factor (i.e. a figure of less than 1) as prescribed in Tables A and B of Schedule 1 Part 2 CATCA 2003 (which are reproduced in **Appendix 1**). Table A applies to the valuation of life interests (i.e. the interest is for the duration of a person's life), while Table B applies to the valuation of interests for "periods certain" (i.e. a fixed amount of time).

> ***Example 15.3: Use for remainder of life (life interest)***
> John receives a life interest in his deceased uncle's farm. If John was aged 45 at the date of his uncle's death, and the incumbrance-free value of the farm was valued at €100,000, the taxable value of his benefit would be computed as follows:
>
> €100,000 × 0.7897 = €78,970 (Table A, Column 3)

Example 15.4: Use for a fixed period of time (period certain)
If John had instead been granted the use of the farm for a period of eight years, his taxable value would have been computed as:

€100,000 × 0.4177 = €41,770 (Table B, Column 2)

Example 15.5
Following on from Example 15.2, as Bernadette has received the annuity for life, she has received a life interest in €225,000. The €225,000, assuming no deductible costs are incurred, must be multiplied by the factor in *Table A for a female aged 62, i.e. 0.6162,* to arrive at the taxable value of the benefit received. The taxable value of the gift received by Bernadette is, therefore, €138,645 (€225,000 × 0.6162).

There are special rules for valuing interests involving one or more lives and for periods not equal to a year, which are beyond the scope of this textbook.

15.4 Deduction of Limited Interests as Consideration

It is quite common for a beneficiary to be required to pay an annuity to another person, for a limited period, as a consequence of receiving a benefit. For example, a son inherits his father's estate subject to the son paying his aunt an annuity for the rest of her life. The market value of the annuity is "consideration" paid by the beneficiary for the benefit.

Example 15.6
Ann inherited an investment property valued at €1,750,000 from her father. The property yields an annual income of €125,000. The property was to be charged from the time of his death with the payment of an annuity of €25,000 to his sister, Mary, aged 60, for Mary's lifetime.

Taxable value of Mary's inheritance:

$$€1{,}750{,}000 \times \frac{25{,}000}{125{,}000} = \mathbf{€350{,}000} \times 0.6475 = €226{,}625$$

Taxable value of Ann's inheritance:

€1,750,000 − **€350,000** = €1,400,000

15.5 Cessation of an Annuity

A taxable gift or inheritance arises on the cessation of the payment of an annuity charged or secured on a property. The "slice" of the property subsequently received is taxable. The value of the "slice" is calculated by reference to the relative values at the date the annuity payments cease.

Example 15.7
Following on from Example 15.6, Mary dies when the property is valued at €2,000,000 and yields an annual income of €160,000. Therefore Ann takes a further inheritance, being Mary's "slice" of the property at Mary's date of death, the valuation date. The value of the annuity is calculated based on current values as follows:

€2,000,000 x 25,000/160,000 = €312,500

Ann will be assessed to CAT on an additional inheritance of €312,500 from her father.

Questions

Review Questions

(See Suggested Solutions to Review Questions at the end of this textbook.)

Question 15.1

Calculate the CAT payable in respect of the gift/inheritance taken in 2019 in each of the following cases:

(a) Tom, who is Irish domiciled but UK resident and ordinarily resident, executed a deed of covenant on 8 April 2019 for €10,000 per annum for life in favour of his mother, who is Irish domiciled and resident. Tom's mother is a widow aged 59. The latest Government stock issued before 8 April, which is not redeemable within 10 years, was 5% Government bonds quoted at €0.92 for €1 of stock.
Tom's mother had previously received the following benefits:

(i) assets valued at €250,000 on the death of her husband, also Irish domiciled and resident, in 2003;
(ii) €25,000 in cash on the death of her own mother, Tom's grandmother, also Irish domiciled and resident, in 1997; and
(iii) jewellery and other assets valued at €30,000 on the death of her sister, also Irish domiciled and resident, in March 2006.

(b) Martha, an Irish domiciled and resident person, died in January 2009. Under the terms of her will she left a life interest in a UK property to her brother, Jason, who is Irish domiciled and resident, and on his death absolutely to his son, Mark, also Irish resident and domiciled. Jason died on 5 September 2019, at which date the absolute ownership of the UK property reverted to Mark, then aged 56. The market value of the UK property at the date of Jason's death was €300,000.
Under the terms of Jason's will, Mark also inherited cash in a Dublin bank account of €260,000.
Apart from the above, the only previous benefit received by Mark was €190,000 worth of savings certificates inherited from his mother, also Irish domiciled and resident, on her death in June 1999, and €10,000 inherited from a nephew in May 2008.

Question 15.2

Calculate the taxable value of the following gifts/inheritances arising in the year 2019.

(a) Martin, a grocer for many years, died on 1 March 2019. He left his entire estate to his brother Dermot, aged 42, for life. His estate consisted of the following at the valuation date:

	€
Grocery business and premises	600,000
House and contents	150,000
Bank accounts	15,000

Funeral and other expenses of €8,000 were outstanding.

(b) Jack, a publican for many years, died on 2 June 2019. He left his pub premises and business, valued at €600,000, to his son, John, absolutely. The pub produces an annual income of €150,000. Jack charged the premises and business with the payment of an annuity to his sister Margaret, aged 54, of €15,000 for 10 years.

Jack also left the residue of his estate to his son John. Any liabilities are to be paid out of the residue. These were as follows at the valuation date:

	€
Residue	50,000
Income tax liabilities outstanding	20,000
Funeral expenses and expenses of administering the estate	9,000

(c) In 2013 David inherited an investment property from his father valued at €250,000. The property was charged with the payment of an annuity to David's brother, Larry, for six years of €10,000. In 2013 the property produced an annual rental income of €20,000.

The last payment was made to Larry in April 2019. In April 2019 the property was valued at €375,000 and produces an annual rental income of €30,000.

(d) On 7 August 2019, Alan executed a deed of covenant of €10,000 per annum for life in favour of his widowed mother, aged 65.

The latest Government stock issued before 7 August, which is not redeemable within 10 years, was 4% Government bonds quoted at €0.89 for €1 of stock.

(e) Tom died on 11 October 2019. He left his entire estate absolutely to his son, Fintan. His estate consisted of the following:

	€
Farmland	950,000
Farm buildings	120,000
Stocks and shares	50,000
Cash	25,000

Funeral expenses of €9,500 were also outstanding.

Under the terms of Tom's will, he charged the farmland and farm assets with the payment of an annuity of €15,000 per annum to his daughter Emer, aged 40, for life. Annual income produced by letting the farmland and farm buildings to a lessee who farms the land full-time amounts to €50,000. Fintan has no other assets. Emer's only asset is a house valued at €120,000 that she rents to a tenant.

Question 15.3

Andrew McNeill has owned and farmed land for 16 years. On 6 August 2019 he took his son, David, into partnership on a 75/25 (25% to David) basis, and at that time transferred to David 25% of the farm and farm assets. Andrew had made no previous lifetime transfers.

Andrew and David McNeill continued farming in partnership on a full-time basis until Andrew's death on 25 November 2019 when all of Andrew's remaining assets, which consisted of the remainder of the farm, other farm assets and a number of investments, passed to David. The values of the assets were as follows:

	Value at 6 August 2019	Value at 25 November 2019 and at valuation date
Assets (Farming)	€	€
300 acres of farmland	2,200 per acre	3,600 per acre
Farm buildings	28,200	33,600
Machinery	15,600	19,300
Livestock	24,400	31,700
Other investments		95,000

The transfer of the investments to David under Andrew's will was subject to and charged with the payment of an annuity of €5,000 to Andrew's sister, Rachel. The investments produce an annual income of €8,000.

During 2018, David had inherited assets valued at €120,000 from an uncle. By 6 August 2019, David had sold all these assets and had cash in the bank of €126,000. On 10 October 2019, David spent €120,000 on farmland adjoining his father's land. This land was valued at €150,000 on 25 November 2019 and at the valuation date.

Legal fees associated with Andrew's estate amounted to €25,000.

Apart from the gifts and inheritances outlined above, David had not previously received any taxable gifts or inheritances.

All persons outlined above are Irish domiciled and resident persons.

Requirement

Compute the CAT payable by David on:

(a) the gift from Andrew on 6 August 2019, assuming all available reliefs and exemptions were utilised; and

(b) Andrew's death, assuming that no lifetime transfers had been made after 6 August 2019.

You may ignore stamp duty.

Question 15.4

Peter O'Connor, a farmer aged 57, gifted farmland and farm assets located in Co. Monaghan to his son, Stephen, valued at €5 million on 18 August 2019, on condition that Stephen would pay him €30,000 per annum for the rest of his life. (The latest Government stock issued before 18 August, which is not redeemable within 10 years, was 5% Government bonds quoted at 90c for €1 of stock.)

Peter had inherited this farmland and assets from his own father in January 2001, at which time the lands were valued at €200,000. Peter had farmed this land since he'd inherited it; and Stephen will continue to farm the land on a full-time basis.

Stephen paid stamp duty and legal fees of €165,000 on the transfer of the land to him.

Stephen had previously inherited a site valued at €10,000 on the death of his mother in May 2011. At the time of his mother's death, the land had planning permission for residential development. Stephen subsequently built apartments on the site, which are now fully let.

Stephen had also previously inherited land in Co. Antrim (Northern Ireland) from an uncle, Peter's brother, in March 2008, valued at €300,000.

On 18 August 2019, Stephen's assets consisted of the following:

	€
His house (Note)	350,000
A car	20,000
Farmlands in Co. Antrim (Northern Ireland)	500,000
Site, now fully developed, inherited from mother	450,000

All the O'Connor family are Irish domiciled. Peter and his wife have always been Irish resident. Stephen's uncle was Irish domiciled and UK resident at the date of his death.

Note: in respect of the purchase of the house there was a mortgage outstanding of €100,000 on 18 August 2019.

Requirement

(a) Calculate the CGT liability, if any, arising on the transfer to Stephen on 18 August 2019.

(b) Calculate the CAT liabilities, if any, arising on the same transfer.

16

Exemptions from CAT

Learning Objectives

After studying this chapter you will be able to:

- Identify and advise on certain gifts and inheritances that are exempt from CAT, including:
  - €3,000 gift per disponer per annum;
  - between spouses/civil partners;
  - Government securities;
  - certain inheritances taken by parents;
  - certain dwelling houses;
  - gifts/inheritances taken free of tax;
  - certain receipts and insurance policies.

16.1 Exemption of Small Gifts

Under section 69 CATCA 2003, the first **€3,000** per annum in **gifts** made by any one disponer to any one donee is exempt, i.e. in computing the amount of a gift to be aggregated, the first €3,000 of total value taken from the *same disponer* in each year is disregarded. The amount of the exemption was lower for gifts taken before 1 January 2003.

The annual exemption does not apply to inheritances. However, where a gift subsequently becomes an inheritance, due to the death of the disponer within two years of the date of the gift, then the annual exemption is not recaptured.

The annual exemption applies to gifts taken during **calendar years**.

Example 16.1
John receives a gift of €10,000 from his uncle. In consideration of the gift he has to give €1,000 to his sister. John's taxable value is €10,000 − €1,000 = €9,000. The small gift exemption of €3,000 is deducted so that the final taxable value is €6,000. John's sister will have received a gift of €1,000 from her uncle. As the amount is less than the small gift exemption no CAT arises and it will not be aggregated in future.

16.2 Exemption of Gifts and Inheritances taken from a Spouse or Civil Partner and Certain Benefits taken from a Former Spouse or Civil Partner

Inheritances taken by the surviving spouse or civil partner of a deceased spouse or civil partner and gifts taken from a spouse or civil partner are exempt from CAT, and also are not aggregated for the purposes of calculating CAT payable on any other gifts or inheritances taken by that person in the future.

16.2.1 Couples who are Separated

In order for the exemption to apply, the couple must be legally married or be a party to a civil partnership registration. If they are separated but are not divorced or their civil partnership has not been dissolved, then they are still legally married or in a civil partnership and the exemption applies.

> ***Example 16.2***
> Darren and Tracey signed a deed of separation on 1 July 2019. Under the terms of the deed, Darren agreed to sign over to Tracey his interest in a house he owns. As they are still married, the gift from Darren to Tracey is a gift to a spouse and is, therefore, exempt from CAT. (Note: the transfer is exempt from stamp duty as they are married. For CGT purposes, the disposal is exempt as it is a transfer on foot of a deed of separation. If, however, in a subsequent year Darren voluntarily gives Tracey shares, while the CAT and stamp duty exemptions would be available, for CGT purposes there would be no relieving provision.)

16.2.2 Married Couples who are Divorcing or are Divorced, and Civil Partnerships that are being Dissolved or have been Dissolved

Where a couple obtains an Irish divorce or a dissolution of a civil partnership, transfers between former spouses or civil partners made on foot of an Irish court order governing the divorce or dissolution of a civil partnership are exempt from CAT. This exemption also applies to a foreign divorce or dissolution of a civil partnership that is recognised as valid under Irish law.

Once divorced or the civil partnership has been dissolved, any transfers made voluntarily between the former spouses or civil partners are not exempt and Group C would be the relevant threshold.

> ***Example 16.3***
> Grace and Ivan divorced on 1 August 2019. Under the terms of their divorce, Grace agreed to sign over her interest in the family home to Ivan. The transfer of the house from Grace to Ivan is exempt from CAT as it arises under the terms of the divorce. (Note: the transfer is exempt from stamp duty and CGT also.)
>
> If, three years later, Ivan had financial problems and Grace decided to give him €20,000, he would be liable to CAT on this receipt of a gift and the relevant group threshold would be Group C.

> ***Example 16.4***
> Leopold and Peter registered their civil partnership on 8 April 2014. Having lived apart for two of the last three years, they decided that they would separate and get the civil partnership dissolved. When they are granted the decree of dissolution, any provision made under the decree regarding transfer of property, etc. is exempt from CAT, stamp duty and CGT. If, two years after the dissolution, Leopold decided to make a gift of shares to Peter, that gift would be taxable and the Group C threshold would apply.

16.3 Exemption of Certain Government Securities

Irish assets are always liable to Irish CAT. However, to get non-Irish persons to hold Irish Government securities, **certain Government securities are exempt from CAT**, provided the following conditions are satisfied:

1. the **beneficiary** must **neither be domiciled nor ordinarily resident** in the State at the date of the gift or inheritance; and
2. the **disponer was the beneficial owner** of the securities for **15 years** prior to the date of the gift or inheritance. The period of ownership was six years for benefits taken before 24 February 2003. Where a disponer already beneficially owns the securities before 24 February 2003, the six-year rule continues to apply. This **condition does not apply** where the **disponer is neither domiciled nor ordinarily resident** in the State at the date of the disposition.

16.4 Exemption of Certain Inheritances taken by Parents

Inheritances (not gifts) taken by a **parent on the death of a child** are exempt **if the deceased child had taken a non-exempt gift or inheritance from either parent** in the **five-year period prior to the death of the child** (see **Chapter 12, Section 12.2.2**).

Example 16.5
On 1 June 2016 Frank gave a gift of €100,000 to his daughter, Joanne, which she used as part-payment to acquire an apartment. Joanne died in 2019 and Frank inherited her entire estate, which was valued at €500,000. The €500,000 inherited by Frank is exempt from CAT as Frank had given Joanne a non-exempt gift within five years before her death.

16.5 Exemption of Certain Dwelling Houses

There has been a dwelling house exemption for many years. However, the exemption was significantly changed in respect of gifts of dwelling houses taken on or after 25 December 2016. Provided conditions are satisfied, any inheritance of a dwelling house may be exempt, but gifts are only exempt if taken by a relative who is aged 65 or over or who is permanently and totally incapacitated (i.e. a dependent relative).

For **inheritances**, the conditions that must be satisfied are as follows:

1. The donor must have occupied the dwelling house as their only or main residence at their date of death. This requirement is relaxed in situations where the deceased person had to leave because of ill health, e.g. to live in a nursing home. This condition does not apply to an inheritance by a dependent relative on or after 25 December 2017.
2. The beneficiary must have occupied the dwelling house continuously as their only, or main, residence for a period of **three years** prior to the date of the inheritance. Where the dwelling house has directly or indirectly replaced other property, this condition may be satisfied where the recipient has continuously occupied both properties as their only or main residence for a total period of three out of the four years immediately prior to the date of the inheritance.

3. The beneficiary must **not**, at the date of the inheritance, be beneficially entitled to any **other dwelling house** or to any interest in any other dwelling house (including a dwelling house that is subject to a discretionary trust under, or in consequence of, a disposition made by the successor where that successor is an object of the trust).
4. The beneficiary must continue, except where the recipient was aged 65 years or more at the date of the inheritance, to **occupy** that dwelling house as their only or main residence for a period of **six years** commencing on the date of the inheritance (the **relevant period**). A period of absence while working elsewhere, due to a condition of their employment, counts as a period of occupation for this purpose, as does absence from the dwelling due to ill health.

For **gifts of dwelling houses**, conditions 2 to 4 above must be satisfied (with the relevant date being the date of the gift instead of the date of the inheritance). Condition 1 above does not have to be satisfied, however, there is an extra condition – that the **donee must be a dependent relative**. A **dependent relative** is a direct relative of the donor or of the donor's spouse or civil partner, who is permanently and totally incapacitated because of physical or mental infirmity from maintaining himself or herself, or who is aged 65 or over. (Where a gift becomes an inheritance, due to the donor dying within two years of the disposition, it continues to be a gift for the purposes of this exemption and it is therefore these conditions that must be satisfied.)

16.5.1 Definition of "Dwelling House"

A "dwelling house" means:

1. a building or part of a building which was used or suitable for use as a dwelling; and
2. grounds of up to one acre attaching to the house and, where the grounds attaching to the house exceed one acre, one acre of the total area which is most suitable for enjoyment and occupation with the dwelling house.

16.5.2 Clawback of Exemption

The exemption will cease to apply if:

1. The dwelling house is sold or otherwise disposed of before the death of the beneficiary and within the relevant period, unless the recipient was aged 65 years or more at the date of the gift or inheritance.

   If, however, the recipient sells or disposes of the dwelling house and invests some or all of the proceeds in a replacement house and continuously occupies both for a total period of six out of the seven years commencing on the date of the gift or inheritance, the clawback will be limited to the proportion of consideration not invested in the replacement dwelling house, e.g. if 90% of the proceeds are re-invested, then 90% of the exemption continues and 10% of the benefit is taxable.
2. The recipient ceases to occupy the dwelling house as their only or main residence during the relevant period, unless it is required that they cease to occupy the house as a result of any condition imposed by the employer of the beneficiary requiring them to reside elsewhere.

   There is, however, no clawback where the beneficiary ceases to occupy the dwelling house in consequence of a mental or physical infirmity. The infirmity must be certified by a doctor.

Example 16.6

Pat and Joe are two brothers, aged 45 and 47, who have lived together in the house they inherited from their parents in December 2008. The house was valued at €100,000 in December 2008. In January 2019, Pat moved out and gave his half share in the house to Joe, together with contents valued at €20,000 (in total). The house was valued at €500,000 at the date of Pat's gift. Apart from the inheritance from his parents, Joe has not previously received any other taxable gifts or inheritances.

What is Joe's CAT liability arising from his gift from Pat (ignoring small gift exemption)?

Computation

The half share in the house is valued at €250,000. This is **not exempt,** as Joe is not a dependent relative, i.e. he is neither incapacitated nor aged 65 or over.

Taxable gift	€	
House	250,000	
50% share in contents	10,000	
Taxable inheritance	260,000	€
Group threshold	32,500 @ Nil	Nil
Balance	227,500 @ 33%	75,075
CAT payable		75,075

Note: as no previous gifts or inheritances were taken from persons within the same group threshold, therefore tax on Aggregate B is nil.

If, instead, Pat had died and left his share of the house to Joe, then the inheritance of the house would be exempt as (1) the donor, Pat, occupied it as his main residence at the date of his death; and (2) the beneficiary, Joe, has lived in the house for the previous three years; and (3) owns no other dwelling house. Joe must continue to own and occupy the house (or a replacement) for six years after the inheritance to avoid a clawback. The share of the contents (€10,000) will be taxable, although no actual CAT will be payable as this is less than the threshold of €32,500.

16.6 Exemption of Certain Receipts

There are a large number of exemptions, including:

1. Gifts/inheritances taken by charities.
2. The receipt, during the **lifetime** of the disponer, by:
   (a) a minor child of the disponer or of the civil partner of the disponer; or
   (b) a child of the disponer or of the civil partner of the disponer who is older than 18 years but not older than 25 years and who is receiving full-time education at any educational establishment or undergoing training for a trade or profession for at least a two-year period; or
   (c) a child of the disponer or of the civil partner of the disponer (of any age) who is permanently incapacitated by reason of physical or mental infirmity from maintaining himself or herself; or
   (d) certain dependent relatives.

   of sums from the disponer for normal support, maintenance or education. These sums must be reasonable having regard to the financial circumstances of the disponer.
3. **Post-death** support, maintenance or education is exempt where received by a minor child or a child who is either 18 years or under, over 18 but not older than 25 and in full-time education or training or permanently incapacitated (see (a) to (c) above) and the other parent of the child

is also dead. These sums must be reasonable having regard to the financial circumstances of the deceased disponer.

4. Gift/inheritance taken exclusively for the purpose of discharging qualifying medical expenses of an individual who is permanently incapacitated by reason of physical or mental infirmity.
5. Bona fide compensation or damages for any wrong or injury suffered by the person or compensation for the death of another person.
6. Gifts or inheritances provided by the disponer to himself, e.g. from a trust created by the disponer.
7. Bona fide winnings from betting, lotteries, Sweepstakes or prizes from games.
8. Any benefit arising from the write-off of some or all of a debt under a debt relief notice, a debt settlement arrangement or a personal insolvency arrangement under the Personal Insolvency Act 2012 is not a gift or an inheritance.

16.7 Gifts and Inheritances taken Free of Tax

The law provides that where a gift or inheritance is taken by direction of the disponer free of CAT, the benefit taken is deemed to include the amount of tax chargeable on the gift or inheritance, but not the amount of tax chargeable on such tax.

Example 16.7

Brian receives a gift of €132,500, net of small gift exemption, from his sister Ann in July 2019. Ann has agreed to pay any tax due on the gift, i.e. the gift is free of tax. Brian is regarded as taking two benefits, i.e. the gift of €132,500 and the CAT on that amount. On the basis that Brian has received no previous gift or inheritance, the CAT on the gift is:

	€
Gift	132,500
Threshold amount	(32,500)
Taxable	100,000
Tax @ 33%	33,000
Tax on €33,000 @ 33%	10,890
Tax payable	43,890

Therefore the additional CAT due on the benefit as a result of it being free of CAT is €10,890. There is no further CAT due as a result of Ann paying this €10,890 of tax.

16.8 Relief in Respect of Certain Insurance Policies

There is a valuable relief under section 72 CATCA 2003 whereby the proceeds of **certain insurance policies are exempt from inheritance tax**, where the policy was taken out for the **sole purpose of paying inheritance tax** due in respect of dispositions made by the person insured. The relief, which originally applied to inheritances only, was subsequently extended and also covers ***inter vivos*** **dispositions (i.e. gifts)** provided that certain conditions are satisfied (see **Section 16.8.2**).

In the absence of this relief, the proceeds of a life insurance policy, whether taken out to pay inheritance tax or otherwise, are aggregated with the other assets of the deceased and itself subject to inheritance tax in the hands of the beneficiary. Indirectly, therefore, the insurance policy results in an increased tax liability.

16.8.1 Policies to Pay Inheritance Tax Only

To qualify for exemption, the assurance company gets its policy approved by Revenue to ensure Revenue conditions are satisfied. The premiums are payable annually. Obviously a person who is older or has an illness will find that they cannot get insurance or the premiums are too expensive. The policy can cover the life of one or both spouses/civil partners.

The **exemption available is limited to the proceeds of the insurance policy** which are **actually used to pay inheritance tax.** If, for example, the proceeds exceed the inheritance tax liability, then only the portion of the proceeds equal to the inheritance tax liability qualify for exemption. The balance of the proceeds would then become subject to inheritance tax in the normal manner.

Example 16.8

Mary died in June 2019. The inheritance tax liability of her estate amounted to €45,000. She held a qualifying life assurance policy which paid €50,000 to her estate on her death. As the proceeds exceed the inheritance tax liability, then only the portion of the proceeds equal to the inheritance tax liability of €45,000 qualifies for exemption. The balance of the proceeds, i.e. €5,000, would then become subject to inheritance tax in the normal manner.

This type of exempt policy can also be used to cover the income tax required to be deducted, in certain situations, from an approved retirement fund (commonly known as an ARF). Income tax at 30% must be deducted from assets in an ARF where the beneficiary of those assets is a child of the deceased who is aged 21 years or over.

The policy proceeds are payable on the death of the person insured. For people who are married or in a civil partnership, the policy can be taken out on the joint lives of the insured and his spouse/civil partner. In this case, the annual premiums are payable by either or both spouses/civil partners during their joint lives and the survivor of them during the life of the survivor. The proceeds of the policy are payable on the death of each survivor or the simultaneous death of both such spouses/civil partners. **Example 16.9** illustrates the operation of this exemption.

Example 16.9

Pat, a bachelor, died in November 2019 and in his will he left the following:

- a legacy of €30,000 to his housekeeper Mrs Brown, who is unrelated;
- a specific bequest of shares valued at €35,000 to his brother Bart; and
- the residue of his estate, valued at €120,000, equally between his two brothers, Bart and Cathal.

None of these three beneficiaries has taken any previous gift or inheritance since 5 December 1991.

Pat had taken out a qualifying insurance policy, the proceeds of which amounted to €20,000. Pat's will had specifically provided that all relevant CAT payable on his death was to be paid *pro rata* from this policy.

Note: the residue of €120,000 **does not** include the qualifying insurance policy.

The CAT in connection with Pat's death is calculated as follows:

continued overleaf

(i) **Housekeeper Mrs Brown**

	€		€
Tax on threshold amount of	16,250		nil
Tax on	13,750	@ 33%	4,537
Total	30,000		4,537

(ii) **Brother Bart**

Bart takes the specific bequest of €35,000 and half of the residue, which will amount to €60,000, making a total inheritance of €95,000.

Tax on €95,000 is as follows:	€		€
Tax on threshold amount of	32,500		nil
Tax on	62,500	@ 33%	20,625
Total	95,000		20,625

(iii) **Brother Cathal**

Cathal takes half the residue valued at €60,000.

	€		€
Tax on threshold amount of	32,500		nil
Tax on	27,500	@ 33%	9,075
Total	60,000		9,075

It will be noted that the total of the CAT liability of the three beneficiaries is €34,237 (€4,537 + €20,625 + €9,075). As Pat directed in his will that the proceeds of the policy of €20,000 were to be paid *pro rata*, the CAT will be paid as follows:

(i) Mrs Brown's liability is paid out of the proceeds in the proportion of:

$$\frac{€4,537 \times €20,000}{€34,237}$$ which amounts to €2,650.

She pays the balance of tax of €1,887 from her own funds.

(ii) Bart's liability is discharged out of the policy proceeds in the proportion of:

$$\frac{€20,625 \times €20,000}{€34,237}$$ which amounts to €12,049.

Thus Bart pays the balance of tax of €8,576 from his own funds.

(iii) Cathal's liability is paid out of the policy proceeds in the proportion of:

$$\frac{€9,075 \times €20,000}{€34,237}$$ which amounts to €5,301.

The balance of €3,774 is paid by Cathal out of his own funds.

16.8.2 Inter Vivos *Dispositions*

There is a similar relief under section 73 CATCA 2003 (i.e. **exempts from CAT the proceeds of a qualifying policy**) when the policy is taken out to pay CAT arising on *inter vivos* dispositions made by the insured. The CAT which may be covered by the policy is the CAT payable in respect of a disposition made by the insured **within one year after the appointed day**. The appointed day is:

- a date not earlier than **eight years** after the date on which the policy is taken out; or
- the date on which the proceeds of the policy became payable either on the critical illness or the death of the insured.

Questions

Review Questions

(See Suggested Solutions to Review Questions at the end of this textbook.)

Question 16.1

Sarah and Enda are married with one son, Patrick, and all are Irish domiciled, resident and ordinarily resident. On 1 June 2019, Sarah died leaving the following estate:

	Market value at 1 June 2019 and date of retainer
	€
€18,000 stock of 10% Irish Government National Loan Stock	14,000
€20,000 stock of 12% Irish Government National Loan Stock	16,000

Both Government securities comprised in the estate qualify for exemption from Irish income tax when beneficially owned by individuals not domiciled or ordinarily resident. Sarah has owned these securities since December 2002.

Sarah's will contained the following provisions:

- the 10% National Loan Stock was left to Patrick;
- the 12% National Loan Stock was left to Harry, Sarah's cousin, who is domiciled and resident and ordinarily resident in the United States.

Patrick has received the following gifts:

- a gift of €15,000 from his aunt on 1 July 1989;
- a gift of €16,000 from his uncle, Sean, on 1 July 1995;
- a gift of 50 shares in Xbarn Ltd from his mother on 15 May 2005. For CAT purposes, the taxable value of these shares was €477,000 on that date. This figure was net of the small gift exemption.

Requirement
Compute the CAT liabilities, if any, in respect of:

(a) the benefits taken by Patrick under Sarah's will; and
(b) the benefits taken by Harry under Sarah's will.

Question 16.2

Shane Murray, a widower, died on 30 June 2019. Under the terms of his will he provided the following bequests:

	Value at 30 June 2019 and at the valuation date
To his son John:	€
100% of the shares in Murray Developments Ltd (Note 1)	1,500,000
Two investment properties (Note 2)	850,000
To his daughter Emily:	
His house (Note 3)	950,000
To his sister Sarah:	
An annuity of €10,000 for life (Note 4)	

The residue of his estate was left equally between John and Emily and was charged with the payment of funeral and testamentary expenses. The residue consisted of €146,000 in cash and €50,000 in quoted shares.

Shane had taken out a qualifying insurance policy in 2010 for the sole purpose of paying CAT on dispositions made by him under his will. The proceeds of the policy were €1,000,000 and Shane's will provided that all inheritance tax payable by John, Emily and Sarah on his death was to be paid *pro rata* from this policy.

The Murray family are all Irish domiciled and resident. In November 2000, Shane had transferred an investment property valued at €300,000, with a mortgage of €200,000 charged on the property, to John. This transfer gave rise to a gift tax liability to John of €3,800. In 2001 Emily inherited a house from her mother valued at €200,000. Emily has since let the house.

Notes:

1. Shane Murray established Murray Developments Ltd in 1988. It carries on a trade of buying and selling land. The company has employed John for the last five years.
2. The two properties transferred to John were valued at €400,000 and €450,000 with attaching mortgages of €150,000 and €75,000, respectively.
3. Emily, who is unmarried, had been living, and has always lived, with her father in his house when he died.
4. The annuity payable to Shane's sister is charged on the property valued at €400,000 inherited by John. This property yields an annual rental income of €30,000. Sarah was 63 at the date of Shane's death.
5. Funeral expenses and legal fees associated with the administration of his estate amounted to €3,500 and €8,500, respectively.

   (Ignore small gift exemption.)

Requirement

Compute the CAT liabilities, if any, payable by John, Emily and Sarah.

Question 16.3

Jerome Nutley, a widower, died on 26 October 2019. Under the terms of his will he provided the following bequests:

	Value at 26 October 2019 and at the valuation date
	€
To his nephew Declan:	
55% of the shares in Wiggies Wholesalers Ltd (Note 1)	350,000
To his son Jonathan:	
Property let to Wiggies Wholesalers Ltd (Note 2)	500,000
To his daughter Louise:	
His house (Note 3)	750,000

The residue of his estate was left equally between Jonathan and Louise, and was charged with the payment of funeral and testamentary expenses. The residue consisted of €65,000 in cash.

Jerome had taken out a life assurance policy some years previously and had nominated Louise as the sole beneficiary of the policy. Proceeds payable on his death amounted to €360,000.

The Nutley family are all Irish domiciled and resident. Declan had not previously received any taxable gifts or inheritances. Jonathan had previously received a gift of €10,000 from an aunt, an Irish domiciled and resident person, in March 2006. Louise had previously received an inheritance of €179,500 from her father-in-law in 2008.

Notes:

1. Wiggies Wholesalers Ltd carries on the trade of electrical wholesalers. The company was established by Jerome Nutley in 1984. However, he sold 45% of the shares to an unrelated party when he retired in September 1998. Jerome is a director of Wiggies Wholesalers Ltd. Declan has been working full-time for Wiggies Wholesalers Ltd for the past 10 years.
2. The property out of which Wiggies Wholesalers Ltd operates was acquired by Jerome Nutley in 1984 and has been let to the company by him for use in its trade since then.
3. Louise Nutley, a schoolteacher aged 50, had been living with her father in the house which he left to her since her husband died in 2005. Louise has no other interests in a dwelling house.
4. Funeral expenses and legal fees associated with the administration of Jerome's estate amounted to €2,500 and €4,000, respectively.

Requirement

Compute the CAT liabilities, if any, payable by Declan, Jonathan and Louise.

17

Credit for Certain CGT Liabilities

Learning Objectives

After studying this chapter you will be able to:

- Ascertain and apply the CGT tax credit for CGT paid to reduce the CAT payable on the "same transaction".

17.1 Credit for Certain CGT Liabilities

Certain events can result in the triggering of both a CGT liability and a CAT liability.

Typically, an inheritance will not trigger a CGT liability as assets passing on a death do not trigger CGT.

Gifts frequently trigger both CGT and CAT. If the asset gifted is a capital asset, then the disponer may have a capital gain liable to CGT and the donee receives a gift that may trigger a CAT liability. For instance, the gift of a farm by a father to a son is:

- a disposal of a chargeable asset by the father that may give rise to a CGT liability, computed by reference to the market value of the land transferred; and
- a gift received by the son that may give rise to a CAT liability, by reference to the market value of the land received.

Section 104 CATCA 2003 provides that where the **same event triggers both CAT and CGT liabilities and provided the CGT liability has been paid,** the amount of CGT may be **deducted** as a ***credit*** **from the net CAT liability arising on the event.** The **maximum amount of credit** deducted is **restricted to the lower of the CGT liability or the CAT liability arising on the same event**.

Example 17.1

On 5 October 2019, Michael gives his sister, Debbie, quoted shares worth €80,000. He had bought them for €10,000 on 1 August 1997. What are their CGT and CAT positions, ignoring small gift and annual exemptions?

Under CGT rules, he is treated as disposing of the shares at their market value of €80,000. Therefore, ignoring annual exemption, Michael's CGT liability will be as follows:

continued overleaf

	€	€
Market value		80,000
Cost	10,000	
Index – 1997/98 @ 1.232		
Indexed cost		(12,320)
Gain		67,680
CGT @ 33%		22,334

Ignoring small gift exemption, Debbie's CAT liability is calculated as follows:

	€	€
Taxable value of gift		80,000
Group threshold amount		32,500
€32,500 @ Nil	Nil	
€47,500 @ 33%	15,675	
CAT liability	15,675	
Less: credit for CGT paid by Michael	(15,675)	max
CAT payable	Nil	

The maximum credit available is the lower of the CGT liability or the CAT liability, i.e. it is restricted to €15,675.

Example 17.2

Assume the same facts as the previous example except that Debbie had previously received €70,000 from Michael. Debbie's CAT liability is calculated as follows:

	€
Aggregate A	
Taxable value of gifts: €80,000 + €70,000	150,000
Group threshold amount	32,500
€32,500 @ Nil	Nil
€117,500 @ 33%	38,775
CAT on Aggregate A	38,775
Aggregate B	
Taxable value of previous gift	70,000
Group threshold amount	32,500
€32,500 @ Nil	Nil
€37,500 @ 33%	12,375
CAT on Aggregate B	12,375
CAT on current benefit = CAT on Aggregate A − CAT on Aggregate B	
= €38,775 − €12,375	26,400
Less: credit for CGT paid by Michael	(22,334)
CAT payable	4,066

A person's CAT liability is determined by their lifetime gifts and inheritances. The CAT arising on the current benefit exceeds the CGT because Michael had used his lifetime tax-free threshold when he received the prior gift of €70,000, meaning that the full amount of the current gift is taxable. As this current tax liability has arisen on an event whereby a CGT liability also arose, then credit relief is available up to a maximum of the lower of the CGT or CAT.

17.2 Clawback of CGT Credit

The credit for CGT will be clawed back if the beneficiary disposes of the property transferred within two years of the date of the gift or inheritance.

In **Examples 17.1** and **17.2**, if Debbie disposed of the shares within two years then the credit for CGT would be clawed back, i.e. she will have to pay €15,675 of CAT in **Example 17.1** and €22,334 of additional CAT in **Example 17.2.**

17.3 Identification of CAT Liabilities where more than One Asset

The same event must trigger both the CGT and CAT liability. If the CAT relates to two different capital assets, then the CAT and CGT related to each asset must be established and the lower of the two is the creditable amount.

Prior to Finance Act 2012 the law required that, where benefits were taken on the same day, the CAT arising was apportioned between each asset taken on that day. As a result of the repeal of this legislation there is no guidance in law other than in section 104(1)(b) CATCA 2003, which states that the CAT is the amount equal to the CAT "attributable to the property which is that asset, or that part of that asset". Therefore the taxpayer may choose the approach that will minimise their tax liability (i.e. maximise the CGT credit to be deducted). Depending on the facts of the case regarding the CGT relating to an asset, the taxpayer will treat a particular asset as being received before another asset or that they were all received at the same time. This is illustrated in **Example 17.3** below.

Example 17.3

On 28 July 2019 Jack gifts his son, Shane, his principal private residence and quoted shares. Shane has received no prior benefits and does not live with his father. Information regarding these assets is as follows:

	House	Shares
	€	€
Market value	600,000	100,000
Cost	80,000	20,000
Indexation factor	3	1.5

Capital Gains Tax

House	Exempt as it is his principal private residence	
		€
Shares	Market value	100,000
	Indexed cost €20,000 × 1.5	(30,000)
	Gain	70,000
	Annual exemption	(1,270)
	Taxable gain	68,730
	CGT @ 33%	**22,681**

Capital Acquisitions Tax

		€
Taxable value: €600,000 + €100,000		700,000
Small gift exemption		(3,000)
		697,000
Group threshold	320,000	

continued overleaf

€320,000 @ 0%	–
€377,000 @ 33%	124,410
Less: credit for CGT (Note)	22,681
CAT payable	101,729

Note: the CAT relates to both the shares and the house, whereas the CGT only relates to the shares. Therefore, the **CGT** credit (in respect of the shares) **can only be offset against the CAT** attributable to the gift of **the shares**.

The CAT payable of €124,410 relates to both the house and the shares.

How is the CAT of €124,410 apportioned between the house and the shares?

Option 1: Deemed to receive house first then shares

	House	Shares
	€	€
Value	600,000	100,000
Less: small gift exemption	(3,000)	
Threshold	(320,000)	
Taxable	277,000	100,000
CAT @ 33%	91,410	33,000

Option 2: Deemed to receive shares first then house

	Shares	House
	€	€
Value	100,000	600,000
Less: small gift exemption	(3,000)	
Threshold	(97,000)	(223,000)
Taxable	NIL	377,000
CAT @ 33%	NIL	124,410

Option 3: CAT apportioned between house and shares

CAT on house = €124,410 × 600,000/700,000 = €106,637
CAT on shares = €124,410 × 100,000/700,000 = €17,773

From Shane's perspective, he wishes to maximise the CAT associated with the shares as they carry a CGT credit. This is achieved by choosing the option that maximises the CAT arising on the shares (i.e. option 1). Therefore, the CAT re shares is €33,000.

The creditable CGT is the lower of:

(i) CGT on shares €22,681; or
(ii) CAT on shares €33,000

i.e. €22,681

If the shares are disposed of within two years, the CGT credit is clawed back, i.e. an additional €22,681 of CAT must be paid.

17.4 Other Matters

In certain circumstances, the entitlement to a CGT credit against a CAT liability may need to be apportioned between a number of beneficiaries and, in these circumstances, the Revenue Commissioners are empowered to make any necessary apportionments as appears to be "just and reasonable". There is, however, a right of appeal to the Tax Appeals Commission if the method of apportionment is disputed.

The **CGT must be paid** in order for a credit against CAT to be allowed. If it has not been paid by the due date for payment of the CAT, the full CAT will have to be paid and a refund of CAT sought at a later stage, when the CGT has been paid. However, where the due date for payment of CAT on a gift is before the due date for payment of CGT arising on the same event, in practice a credit may be claimed for the CGT payable.

Questions

Review Questions

(See Suggested Solutions to Review Questions at the end of this textbook.)

Question 17.1

You are a tax specialist in a firm of Chartered Accountants. A client of your firm, Mr O'Donovan, owns a substantial portfolio of investment properties. Mr O'Donovan has two daughters, Lorraine and Sheila. Mr O'Donovan is considering transferring an apartment currently valued at €350,000 to Lorraine and an apartment valued at €250,000 to Sheila.

You are given the following additional information:

1. Lorraine has been living rent-free in the apartment which her father intends to transfer to her since 1 April 2017. She intends to continue to live in the apartment. She may, however, be transferred by her employer to work in the UK for a six-month period in 2020. Her father also owns an identical apartment next to hers, which he has been letting out at €1,500 a month for the last five years. Mr O'Donovan had acquired the apartment that Lorraine occupies in November 1999 for €220,000. (Legal fees and stamp duty associated with the purchase amounted to €15,000.)
2. Sheila has been living at home with her father but intends to live in the apartment which her father has bought to give to her. A monthly rent of €1,200 could be charged if this apartment were let at arm's length to a third party. Mr O'Donovan had acquired this apartment in July 2017 for €240,000. (Legal fees and stamp duty associated with the purchase amounted to €28,000.)
3. Lorraine and Sheila had each inherited assets on the death of their mother in May 2010. Lorraine received €160,000. Sheila received €225,000. Sheila had also received a gift of Irish quoted shares valued at €20,000 from an uncle in June 2009. Apart from this, neither has previously received any taxable gifts or inheritances.
4. Neither Lorraine or Sheila has, or has ever had, any other interest in a residential property.
5. Mr O'Donovan has made no other disposals for CGT purposes during 2019.

Requirement

Write a letter to Mr O'Donovan advising him on the taxation consequences arising from the proposed property transfers to his daughters. (You should assume that the transfers take place on 1 December 2019 and that the transfers cannot be delayed and given as inheritances.) In your letter you should also advise Mr O'Donovan on any steps which might be taken by him to mitigate the tax liabilities arising. (Ignore small gift exemption.)

Question 17.2

Janet, a 58-year-old widow, made the following gifts during 2019.

1. 20 April 2019 – 100% of the shares in Fogarty Fabrics Ltd, a company involved in the manufacture of curtains and bed linen, to Janet's son, Adam. Fogarty Fabrics Ltd had been incorporated by Janet's husband in 1987 with a share capital of €100. Janet's husband died in March 1997 and Janet has been a full-time working director since then. The shares in Fogarty Fabrics Ltd were valued at €340,000 in March 1997.
   On 20 April 2019, the shares in Fogarty Fabrics Ltd were valued at €950,000. The company's net assets at 20 April 2019 were as follows:

	Market Value
	€
Factory premises	130,000
Goodwill	215,000
Investment property	350,000
Plant and machinery	70,000
Inventories	180,000
Receivables	80,000
Net liabilities	(75,000)
Net assets	950,000

   Adam has previously received a gift of €150,000 (net of small gift allowance) on 2 May 2010 from his mother.
2. 20 May 2019 – A house valued at €250,000 to her daughter, Julie, and Julie's husband, Nigel. Janet had acquired this house in December 1989 for €40,000. The house had been let by Janet since then.
   Julie has not previously received any taxable gifts or inheritances. Nigel had previously inherited Bank of Ireland shares valued at €10,000 from an aunt.
3. 30 June 2019 – An antique vase valued at €3,100 to her niece, Sally. Janet had inherited this vase from an aunt in June 1980 when it was valued at €150.
   Sally had previously inherited a house valued at €75,000 from an uncle in November 2000.
4. 30 September 2019 – Farmland valued at €1.5 million to her son, Kevin. Janet had inherited this land from her mother in August 1974, at which time the land was valued at €80,000. The land had always been leased out by Janet.
   Kevin has no other assets and has not previously received any taxable gifts or inheritances. Kevin intends to lease the land to a neighbouring farmer who will farm the land full-time.
   All persons mentioned above are Irish domiciled and Irish resident.
   Janet had capital losses forward of €10,000 at 31 December 2018.

Requirement

(a) Calculate Janet's CGT liability for 2019, assuming she made no other disposals in 2019 other than those listed above and that she has not previously disposed of any chargeable business assets.

(b) Calculate the CAT liabilities arising from each of the above gifts. You may ignore stamp duty.

Question 17.3

On 16 July 2019, on the occasion of his 56th birthday and in order to mark his early retirement, Ronnie Doyle made the following gifts:

		Market value on 16 July 2019
1.	To his sister Janet:	€
	€35,000 4.5% Government stock purchased by Ronnie in December 2002 and which is exempt from income tax where held by a foreign domiciled and ordinarily resident person	40,000
2.	To his son Jake:	
	His interest in a van rental business (Note 1)	1,280,000
	Cash	20,000
3.	To his son Brendan:	
	Two vans (Note 2): Van 1	15,000
	Van 2	25,000
	An office building (Note 2)	250,000
	Cash	50,000

Brendan and Jake had each inherited assets valued at €460,000 on the death of their mother in March 2006. Brendan had also inherited €120,000 on the death of his grandfather in 2000. Apart from this, none of the above had previously received any taxable gifts or inheritances.

Ronnie, Jake and Brendan are all Irish domiciled and resident. Janet is UK domiciled and UK resident and ordinarily resident.

Notes:

1. Ronnie purchased the van rental business as a going concern in January 2012 for €350,000. He has been involved in running the business on a full-time basis since then.
   The value of the business at the relevant dates is made up as follows:

	January 2012	July 2019
	€	€
Vans	175,000	650,000
Inventories of spare parts	30,000	150,000
Net receivables	10,000	180,000
Building	80,000	0
Goodwill	55,000	300,000
Total	350,000	1,280,000

   The cost of all vans exceeds their values outlined above. The vans given to Brendan are not included in the above figures.

2. Ronnie gave most of the assets of the business to Jake, but he gave two vans and the building to Brendan to help him establish his own office supplies business. The vans and building transferred to him had been acquired by his father for his van rental business at the following costs:

	Date of acquisition	Cost
		€
Van 1	06/05/2013	20,000
Van 2	20/08/2014	45,000
Building	11/01/2012	80,000

Requirement

(a) Calculate the CGT liability, if any, arising from the above gifts.
(b) Calculate the CAT liability, if any, arising on the above gifts.

(Small gift exemption and annual exemption and stamp duty may be ignored.) It may be assumed that Ronnie has not disposed of any chargeable business assets since 1 January 2016.

Question 17.4

You are a tax specialist in a firm of Chartered Accountants. In June 2019, the tax director to whom you report has a telephone conversation with a client to whom your firm has provided tax advice occasionally in the past.

The client, Mr Mark Murphy, owns all the shares in an unquoted company, Murphy Electrical Wholesalers Ltd, which carries on a trade as electrical wholesalers. Mr Murphy inherited the shares in Murphy Electrical Wholesalers Ltd from his brother in June 1995. Mr Murphy has many other business interests and has **only been a non-executive director of the company**. Mr Murphy's son, Jake, works on a full-time basis for the company. Mr Murphy is considering gifting his shares in Murphy Electrical Wholesalers Ltd to Jake. Murphy Electrical Wholesalers Ltd has been valued recently at €3.5 million. The shares were valued at €2 million on the date of Mr Murphy's brother's death in 1995.

Mr Murphy has asked the tax director to advise him on the tax consequences of the proposed gift to his son.

Requirement

Draft a letter in the name of the tax director advising Mr Murphy on the tax consequences of the proposed gift of shares. Your letter should outline in particular the conditions that must be satisfied if any relief from CAT is to be availed of. (Annual exemption and small gift exemption may be ignored.)

18

Administration

Learning Objectives

After studying this chapter you will be able to:

- Advise on the CAT administrative requirements of the accountable person and the implications of non-compliance.

18.1 Accountable Persons

The person accountable for payment of the CAT is the beneficiary. If a beneficiary is deceased, the CAT is recoverable from their personal representative.

18.2 Delivery of Returns

Self-assessment applies to CAT. Any return involving claiming an exemption (other than small gift exemption) or a relief must be filed on ROS. All other returns may be filed using a paper tax return, short form IT38, provided the benefit received is an absolute interest without conditions and restrictions. If a paper return is filed, the taxpayer must calculate the CAT due. There are penalties if a return is not filed by the due date.

18.2.1 Content of a Return

A person who is accountable for CAT is obliged to **deliver a return** by 31 October (see **Section 18.3**) where the aggregate taxable value of all taxable benefits taken by a beneficiary within the same group threshold exceeds 80% of the group threshold amount.

1. The return must show:
   (a) every applicable gift or inheritance;
   (b) all property comprised in such gift or inheritance;
   (c) an estimate of the market value of the property; and
   (d) such particulars as may be relevant to the assessment of CAT in respect of such gift or inheritance.
2. The taxpayer must make on the return an assessment of the amount of CAT payable to the best of their knowledge, information and belief that ought to be charged and paid.
3. Finally, the person must pay any CAT calculated as due.

18.2.2 Obligation to File Returns for Capital Acquisitions Tax

The obligation to file self-assessment returns for CAT is imposed on persons who are accountable for CAT under CATCA 2003 where the **aggregate taxable values of all taxable benefits taken within the same group threshold exceeds 80% of the group threshold amount** that applies in the computation of CAT on that aggregate. Where a taxpayer is claiming a relief, Revenue expects a return to be filed by the taxpayer even if the taxable value is less than 80% of the threshold amount.

> ***Example 18.1***
> In December 1993, €10,000 was received as a gift from a brother. In January 2019, €20,000 was received as a gift from a sister.
>
> The €32,500 group threshold applies to both of these gifts.
>
> The total aggregate is €30,000. Therefore, as the aggregate exceeds 80% of the group threshold amount, a return is required.

Even if no benefit has been received, a person is required to deliver a return if requested to do so by the Revenue Commissioners.

Forms 11 and 12 and CG50 (application for a CGT clearance certificate) all contain questions designed to act as prompts for the filing of CAT returns in relevant cases.

18.3 Payment of CAT and Interest, and Filing Returns

There is a fixed 'pay and file' date for CAT of 31 October. **All gifts and inheritances with a valuation date in the 12-month period ending on the previous 31 August will be included in the return to be filed by 31 October**. That means where:

1. the valuation date arises in the period from 1 January to 31 August, the pay and file deadline is 31 October in that year; and
2. where the valuation date arises in the period from 1 September to 31 December, the pay and file deadline is 31 October in the following year.

Similar to income tax and capital gains tax, where the taxpayer files the return and pays tax using ROS, the filing date is extended. For 2019, the date is extended to 12 November 2019.

> ***Example 18.2***
> Ann receives a gift and it has a valuation date of 21 August 2019. The CAT due is €40,222 after claiming agricultural relief. Ann must file and pay €40,222 of CAT on ROS by 12 November 2019.
>
> Terry receives an inheritance and it has a valuation date of 6 November 2019. The CAT due is €30,522. Terry is not entitled to any reliefs or exemptions.
>
> As Terry is not entitled to any reliefs or exemptions, he can file a paper return if he wishes. That return (short form IT38) and payment are due by 31 October 2020. If he files and pays on ROS, the deadline will be some date (not yet known) in mid-November 2020.

A paper return may be filed where the beneficiary is not claiming any reliefs, exemptions, etc. other than the small gift exemption and the benefit received is an absolute interest without conditions or restrictions.

Where any other relief, etc. is being claimed, the return must be filed electronically through ROS.

Provided that CAT is paid by the due date, no interest is payable. However, if the CAT is not paid by the due date, simple interest of 0.0219% per day or part of a day is charged (equivalent to an annual rate of approximately 8%) from 1 November until the date of payment.

Provision is made whereby payments on account are applied first by the Revenue Commissioners in settlement of any outstanding interest charges and only then may the balance be set against the principal due.

There is a surcharge for the late filing of a return. The surcharge is calculated as follows:

1. 5% surcharge applies, subject to a maximum of €12,695, where the return is delivered within two months of the filing date (e.g. for the year ending 31 August 2019, any date between 1 November 2019 and 31 December 2019 inclusive);
2. 10% surcharge, up to a maximum of €63,485, applies where the tax return is not delivered within two months of the filing date.

Example 18.3
Anthony receives a gift on 1 August 2019 and the CAT due is €20,000. He files his form IT38 and makes a payment of €20,000 CAT on 1 December 2019. It was due on 31 October 2019. As a result of late filing, he is subject to a surcharge of 5% of €20,000, i.e. €1,000. He will also be liable to interest on €20,000 from 1 November to 1 December and on €1,000 from 31 October to the date of payment.

A person is deemed to have failed to deliver a return before the due date and will be liable to the surcharge where:

1. the person fraudulently or negligently delivers an incorrect return before the due date and does not correct the error in the return before the due date for filing the return;
2. the person delivers an incorrect return, but does not do so fraudulently or negligently, and it comes to the person's notice that the return is incorrect, but the person fails to correct the return without unreasonable delay; or
3. the person files a return before the due date but is served with a notice by the Revenue Commissioners, by reason of their dissatisfaction with the return, to deliver further evidence and that evidence is not provided within the time specified in the notice.

The accountable person must retain records for six years from the valuation date, or the filing date if the return is filed late. However, where the taxpayer has claimed a relief with conditions that needed to be satisfied for a period greater than four years (e.g. agricultural relief), supporting documentation must be retained for four years from the length of period for which the conditions to avail of the relief need to be satisfied.

18.4 Payment of CAT by Instalments

The accountable person may elect to pay CAT in respect of a taxable gift or inheritance by means of monthly instalments over a period not exceeding five years in such manner as may be determined by the Revenue Commissioners, the first of which becomes due on 31 October following the valuation date. Interest on the unpaid tax at 0.0219% per day must, however, be added to each instalment and paid at the same time as each instalment.

This option is only open where the taxable gift/inheritance comprises either of:

1. real property, e.g. freehold land and buildings; or
2. a limited interest, e.g. a life interest or interest for a period certain.

The CAT will be regarded as paid under self-assessment where the CAT due and payable is paid in instalments, by the payment of:

1. an amount which includes any instalment that is due prior to or on the date of the self-assessment; and
2. any further instalments of such CAT on the due dates as they fall due.

If a life tenant dies before all instalments have been paid, any instalments due after death cease to become payable. This applies whether or not instalment arrangements were entered into. Accordingly, where a life tenant dies and an instalment arrangement was not entered into, any instalments which would have not yet been paid had an instalment arrangement been entered into can be reclaimed.

If the property comprising a gift or inheritance is sold at any time prior to payment of all instalments, then the balance due becomes immediately payable, unless the interest of the donee or successor is a limited interest.

18.4.1 Agricultural and Business Property

If the gift or inheritance is property that is agricultural or business property (except quoted shares), then the daily interest rate is only three-quarters of the normal daily rate, i.e. 0.0164%. Also, the instalment arrangement can continue even if the property is sold or compulsorily acquired within the instalment period, provided that the proceeds are re-invested in other qualifying property within a year of the sale or compulsory acquisition or within six years in the case of the compulsory acquisition of agricultural property.

18.5 Overpayment of CAT

If CAT has been overpaid, the Revenue Commissioners will repay the excess CAT paid if a valid claim is made within four years, commencing on 31 October in the year in which the tax was due to be paid. Interest on CAT overpaid will accrue starting 93 days after the date on which a valid claim is made. In the case where the repayment arises due to a mistaken assumption on behalf of Revenue, interest will accrue from the date of payment of the excess CAT. Interest is payable at the rate of 0.011% per day or part of a day (equivalent to an annual interest rate of approximately 4%).

18.6 Surcharge on Undervaluation of Property

There is a surcharge to **penalise accountable persons who underestimate the market value of property** in returns for CAT purposes. The surcharge can be as high as 30%.

Questions

Review Questions

(See Suggested Solutions to Review Questions at the end of this textbook.)

Question 18.1

The managing partner of your firm of Chartered Accountants has asked you, as the CAT specialist, to advise him on each of the following matters:

(a) Who is an accountable person for CAT purposes?
(b) Under what circumstances is a return required from an accountable person and what is the time frame for the submission of each return?
(c) What details must be shown on a return and what must accompany a return?
(d) What action is required of an accountable person who becomes aware that a return that has been lodged is defective in a material respect?
(e) What are the consequences for the taxpayer of having made a return where the estimated value of the gift or inheritance is materially understated?

Requirement
Write a memorandum to the managing partner setting out your reply to the queries raised by him as outlined at (a) to (e) above.

Question 18.2

Robert Doyle died suddenly on 20 April 2019 without leaving a will. Under the laws of intestacy, his estate was inherited two-thirds by his wife Sheila, from whom he had been separated for the last 10 years, and one-third by his daughters, Ruth (21) and Angela (16).

Ruth and Angela had been living with their father when he died. Ruth has a full-time job and Angela is in full-time education and has no income of her own. Robert had taken out a life insurance policy and had nominated Ruth and Angela as the beneficiaries of this policy. The proceeds from the policy amounted to €140,000.

Apart from the insurance proceeds, Robert's assets at the date of his death consisted of the following:

	Value at 20 April 2019 and at the valuation date
	€
His house	600,000
50% share in a newsagents (Note 1)	900,000
€60,000 6% Exchequer Stock purchased by Robert in Nov. 2001	66,000
Cash	45,000
Holiday home in Co. Kerry	150,000
The following debts were outstanding:	
Income tax liabilities	15,000
Mortgage on his house	60,000

Notes:
1. Robert was a 50% owner in a thriving Dublin newsagents which he had established in 2000. Robert's partner will continue to manage the Doyles' 50% share in the newsagents on their behalf.
2. Funeral expenses and legal fees associated with the administration of his estate amounted to €3,000 and €6,000, respectively.
3. Neither Sheila, Ruth nor Angela had previously received any taxable gifts or inheritances. Sheila lives in the US but is Irish domiciled. The rest of the Doyle family are Irish domiciled and resident.

Requirement
(a) Compute the CAT liabilities, if any, payable by Sheila, Ruth and Angela.
(b) If the valuation date is 19 October 2019, outline the latest date by which CAT is payable if interest charges are to be avoided.

Part Four

Corporate Taxation

19

Introduction and General Principles of Corporation Tax

Learning Objectives

After studying this chapter you will be able to:

- Determine and advise on a company's residence for tax purposes, and the Irish tax implications for resident and non-resident companies generating income and gains in the State.
- Determine and apply the appropriate rate of corporation tax for each profit source.
- Advise on and calculate corporation tax payment and reporting requirements of a company, depending on its size and its accounting period.
- Explain the principles and conditions of the three-year tax exemption for start-up companies, and determine and calculate its availability and impact for a company.

Chartered Accountants Ireland's *Code of Ethics* applies to all aspects of a Chartered Accountant's professional life, including dealing with corporation tax issues. As outlined at the beginning of this book, further information regarding the principles in the *Code of Ethics* is set out in **Appendix 2**.

Students should also be aware of the issues around tax planning, tax avoidance and tax evasion, and these are discussed in **Appendix 3**.

19.1 Overview

Under the Taxes Consolidation Act 1997 (TCA 1997), corporation tax is charged on the income and chargeable gains that together constitute the "profits" of companies. The period for which corporation tax is charged is the "accounting period" (see **Section 19.7**).

Companies produce accounts normally on an annual basis. Included in these accounts are the various sources of income and gains less the expenses incurred by the company. These profits are taxable unless there is a specific exemption. The nature of the profits earned determines under which Case of Schedule D the income is taxable. Capital gains are also liable to corporation tax (with the exception of gains arising on development land – these gains are liable to CGT).

When taxing the profits of a company, it is essential that the total profits and expenses are correctly analysed between:

Case I	Trading income
Case II	Professions – but actually treated the exact same as Case I (the only difference is when calculating the professional services surcharge – see **Chapter 26, Section 26.3.5**)
Case III	Untaxed Irish income or foreign income
Case IV	Taxed Irish income and miscellaneous
Case V	Irish rental income
Chargeable gains	Capital disposals (excluding development land)
FII	Franked investment income (i.e. distributions from Irish-resident companies), excluding Irish REITs – see **Chapter 25, Section 25.1**

The correct analysis is important because of the different treatments given to these items under Irish tax law and practice. For example:

- Profits within Cases I and II and chargeable gains are generally taxed at 12.5%.
- Profits within Cases III, IV or V are generally taxed at 25% (certain foreign dividends are taxed at 12.5%).
- Franked investment income (FII) is exempt from corporation tax.

Understanding the source and nature of the income or gain is, therefore, necessary to be able to correctly calculate the tax payable and the reliefs or exemptions that may be available.

For companies, all transactions will be included in the financial statements. Therefore, computation of corporation tax requires the analysis of those profits between the various Cases and gains.

19.2 Charge to Corporation Tax

The question of whether, and how, a company is to be charged to corporation tax depends on whether or not it is resident in the State.

19.2.1 Resident Company

In the case of a **company resident in the State**, the charge to corporation tax is imposed on **all its income and chargeable gains** (excluding gains on development land) wherever arising and whether or not they are remitted to the State. Certain tax reliefs are only available to resident companies. Gains on disposals of development land are subject to CGT.

19.2.2 Non-resident Company

A **non-resident company** is chargeable to corporation tax only if it carries on a trade in the State through a branch or agency. Such a company is chargeable to corporation tax on any **income attributable to the branch or agency** and on any **chargeable gains on the disposal of specified Irish assets** used for the purposes of the trade or **attributable to the branch or agency**.

For example, if a German resident company sets up a factory in Ireland, the German company would be liable to Irish corporation tax on any income or gains attributable to the Irish factory.

A non-resident company with Irish source income not attributable to an Irish branch (e.g. Case V income) may be subject to Irish income tax, depending on the terms of the double tax treaty, if any.

A non-resident company is liable to CGT on chargeable gains on the disposal of:

- development land used for the purpose of an Irish branch; and
- specified Irish assets not used for the purpose of an Irish branch.

19.3 Residence of Companies

The residence of a company is normally located in the place from which it is managed and controlled. However, certain Irish-incorporated companies are also regarded as resident in the State.

19.3.1 Rules to Establish Residence of a Company

The chart below summarises the rules used to establish whether a company is resident or non-resident in Ireland for tax purposes.

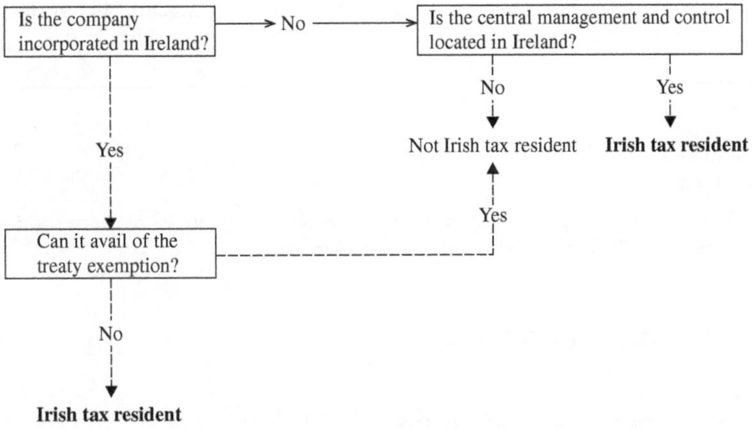

Companies Managed and Controlled in the State

The rules for determining the residence of a company have evolved from UK case law, which has been followed in Ireland. A company, irrespective of where it is incorporated, is Irish tax resident if it is "managed and controlled" in the State. Again, UK case law has provided guidance on what constitutes "managed and controlled". Based on these cases, the *key* factors that are taken into account in determining where a company is "managed and controlled" are:

- Where are the questions of important policy determined?
- Where are the directors' meetings held?
- Where do the majority of the directors reside?
- Where are the shareholders' meetings held?
- Where is the negotiation of major contracts undertaken?
- Where is the head office of the company?
- Where are the books of account and the company books (minute book, share register, etc.) kept?
- Where are the company's bank accounts?

As you can see, control is to do with where the directors hold their meetings and **"whether real decisions affecting the company are taken at those meetings"**. In each case, one needs to look at the facts of the case to determine where the company is actually managed and controlled.

Irish Incorporated Companies

As can be seen from the chart, Irish incorporated companies are tax resident in Ireland unless they can avail of the treaty exemption. In the past, certain Irish incorporated companies were not considered resident in Ireland. Certain companies can still avail of the old rules (these are beyond the scope of this textbook).

Treaty Exemption

The treaty exemption applies where the Irish incorporated company is regarded as resident in another country (generally managed and controlled in that other country) under the terms of the double taxation treaty (DTT) between Ireland and that country. The rules for determining where a company is managed and controlled are set out above.

Example 19.1

R Ltd is a UK incorporated company that manufactures clothes in England, France and Germany. It has a warehouse and offices in Ireland. All of its directors are Irish residents. All directors' and shareholders' meetings take place in Ireland. It has the following sources of income:

- UK profits;
- French profits;
- German profits;
- New Zealand deposit interest; and
- rental income in the USA.

Therefore, as its controlling body and management is located in Ireland, its place of residence is Ireland. **All** sources of profits are liable to Irish corporation tax.

19.4 Rates of Corporation Tax

19.4.1 Standard Rate of Corporation Tax

The standard rate of corporation tax is **12.5%** and applies to Schedule D Case I and II profits, capital gains as adjusted for tax and to certain foreign dividends (see **Chapter 28, Section 28.1.2**).

Example 19.2

Mary Ltd had total Case I profits of €700,000 in the year ended 31 December 2019. Corporation tax payable by Mary Ltd is €87,500 (€700,000 @ 12.5%).

19.4.2 Higher Rate of Corporation Tax

A higher rate of corporation tax of **25%** applies to the following income of companies:

1. **Case III** income, i.e. foreign income and untaxed Irish interest. (Certain foreign dividends are, however, taxable at 12.5% (see **Chapter 28, Section 28.1.2**).)
2. **Case IV** income, i.e. taxed Irish income and miscellaneous income not taxed under any other Case of Schedule D.

3. **Case V** income, i.e. Irish rental income.
4. Income from an "excepted trade" (which is beyond the scope of this textbook).

Example 19.3
John Ltd, a company involved in the construction of office buildings, has the following income for the year ended 31 December 2019:

	€
Case I – construction operations	800,000
Case III interest	20,000
Case V rental income	150,000
Total	970,000

The corporation tax payable by John Ltd is as follows:

	€
Case I: €800,000 @ 12.5%	100,000
Case III and Case V: €170,000 @ 25%	42,500
Total corporation tax payable	142,500

19.5 Dates of Payment of Corporation Tax

Corporation tax is assessed on the profits of companies for accounting periods. Accordingly, the concept of basis periods in the income tax legislation is not carried into the corporation tax system. The due dates for paying and filing corporation tax are determined by the date of the accounting period. Corporation tax includes not only the corporation tax due on profits but also any income tax payable (see **Chapter 21**) and any close company surcharge (see **Chapter 26**).

A company is required to discharge its corporation tax liability for an accounting period by paying preliminary tax before the end of the accounting period, and the balance of corporation tax when filing its corporation tax return at a date following the end of the accounting period. The number of preliminary tax instalments, and the amount to be paid at each instalment, is based on whether the company is deemed to be a large or a small company for preliminary tax purposes for that particular accounting period.

19.5.1 Preliminary Tax: Small Companies

A company is deemed to be a small company for preliminary tax purposes if its "corresponding corporation tax liability for the preceding accounting period of a year" does not exceed €200,000 (where the accounting period is less than 12 months this limit is reduced proportionately; see **Section 19.5.4**). A company's "corresponding corporation tax liability" for the preceding accounting period is its corporation tax liability for that period excluding any income tax payable.

For small companies, preliminary tax is payable in one instalment 31 days before the end of the accounting period, provided that where that day is later than day 23 of the month, the tax will be due and payable not later than day 23 of the month.

The amount of preliminary tax payable is the lower of either:

- **90% of the corporation tax liability of the company for the current accounting period;** or
- **100% of the corresponding corporation tax liability of the company for the preceding accounting period of same length.**

> ***Example 19.4***
> A Ltd's corporation tax for the year ended 31 December 2019 is expected to be €120,000. Its liability for 2018 was €90,000.
>
> As it is a small company (corporation tax in 2018 did not exceed €200,000), preliminary tax should be paid by 23 November 2019 and is calculated as the lower of:
>
> | | | |
> |---|---|---|
> | 90% current year: 2019 | €108,000 | or |
> | 100% preceding year: 2018 | €90,000 | |
>
> Pay the lower, i.e. €90,000 by 23 November 2019

The **balance of corporation tax due** is payable at the **same time** as the company is due to **file its return** (see **Section 19.6**).

Where a small company defaults in the payment of preliminary tax, does not pay sufficient preliminary tax or does not pay its preliminary tax by the due date, interest on the late payment arises at 0.0219% per day or part of a day on any underpaid corporation tax. All of the corporation tax for that accounting period is deemed to be due on the date the preliminary tax was due, but on the 21st day of the month not the 23rd day of the month.

> ***Example 19.5***
> Dimm Ltd, a small company, has a corporation tax liability of €20,000 for the year ended 31 December 2019. It paid no preliminary tax but paid its entire corporation tax liability on 23 September 2020.
>
> The company will have an interest liability as follows:
>
> €20,000 deemed due on 21 November 2019:
>
> Interest €20,000 × 0.0219% × 306 days = €1,340

19.5.2 Preliminary Tax: Large Companies

A company is deemed to be a large company for preliminary tax purposes if its "corresponding corporation tax liability for the preceding accounting period of a year" exceeds €200,000 (reduced proportionately where the accounting period is less than 12 months; see **Section 19.5.4**). In this context, a company's corresponding corporation tax liability for the preceding accounting period is calculated without taking into account income tax payable for the preceding accounting period.

For large companies, preliminary tax is payable in two instalments.

1. The **first instalment is payable in the sixth month** of the accounting period (e.g. 23 June for a company with calendar year accounts) and the amount payable is the lower of either:
   - **45% of the corporation tax liability for the current accounting period;** or
   - **50% of the corresponding corporation tax liability of the preceding accounting period of same length.**
2. The **second instalment is payable in the 11th month** of the accounting period (e.g. 23 November for a company with calendar year accounts) and the amount payable should bring the **total preliminary tax paid to 90%** of the **current** corporation tax liability.

Example 19.6

B Ltd's corporation tax for the year ended 31 December 2019 is expected to be €220,000. Its liability for 2018 was €230,000. As it is a large company (corporation tax liability in 2018 was greater than €200,000), preliminary tax should be paid in the following instalments:

	€	
1st instalment due 23 June 2019		
45% current liability (2019: €220,000 × 45%)	99,000	or
50% corresponding liability of preceding period (2018: €230,000 × 50%)	115,000	
The lower amount should be paid, i.e. €99,000		
2nd instalment due 23 November 2019		
90% of final liability for 2019 (€220,000 @ 90%)	198,000	
Minus amount paid in the 1st instalment	(99,000)	
Amount to be paid	99,000	

Where the accounting period is less than seven months, preliminary tax of 90% of the tax liability is payable in one instalment, as for small companies.

The **balance of tax due** is payable at the **same time** as the company is due to **file its return** (see **Section 19.6**).

Where a large company either defaults in the payment of preliminary tax, does not pay sufficient preliminary tax or does not pay its preliminary tax by the due date, interest on late payment arises at 0.0219% per day or part of a day. Forty-five per cent of the corporation tax liability for that accounting period is deemed to be due on the date the first instalment of its preliminary tax was due, but on the 21st day of the month not the 23rd day of the month. The remaining 55% of its corporation tax liability is deemed due on the 21st day of the month its second instalment of preliminary tax was due.

Example 19.7

E Ltd, a large company, has a corporation tax liability for the year ended 31 December 2019 of €100,000. Its corresponding corporation tax liability for the year to 31 December 2018 was €250,000. The company paid its entire liability on 31 December 2020 rather than paying €45,000 on 23 June 2019, €45,000 on 23 November 2019 and €10,000 on 23 September 2020. As a result, 45% of the full corporation tax liability of €100,000 is deemed due on 21 June 2019, and 55% due on 21 November 2019. The company will have an interest liability on the late payment of corporation tax as follows:

€45,000 (€100,000 × 45%) deemed due 21 June 2019:
Interest €45,000 @ 0.0219% × 559 days = €5,509

€55,000 deemed due on 21 November 2019:
Interest €55,000 @ 0.0219% × 406 days = €4,890

Total interest liability = €10,399

In order to minimise interest exposure where a large company in a group does not meet the 90% preliminary tax payment, any excess preliminary payments made by another large group company can be transferred to the group member who has not met the 90% rule. Both companies must jointly advise Revenue and the claimant company must have paid 100% of its tax by its tax return due date.

19.5.3 Pay and File

A company, regardless of its size, is required to pay the balance of corporation tax for an accounting period, and file the corporation tax return, by the 23rd day of the ninth month after the end of the accounting period. For example, a company with an accounting period ended 31 December 2019 must pay the balance of corporation tax and file its corporation tax return by 23 September 2020.

The corporation tax return (Form CT1) is submitted electronically using ROS (Revenue Online Service). **Section 19.6** outlines in greater detail the administrative filing requirements for a company to meet its corporation tax obligations.

19.5.4 Rules for Three Special Situations

1. Corresponding Corporation Tax

The "corresponding corporation tax" of the preceding accounting period is used by a company to determine when and how much preliminary tax it must pay in respect of the current accounting period. In this context, a company's corresponding corporation tax liability for the preceding accounting period is calculated without taking into account income tax payable for the preceding accounting period.

A company's size, for preliminary tax purposes, is determined by whether or not its corresponding corporation tax liability for the preceding accounting period of a year exceeds €200,000, regardless of the magnitude of the current corporation tax liability, or the length of the current accounting period. If the preceding accounting period is less than a year, the preceding corporation tax liability must be adjusted so that it corresponds to a year to determine whether or not the €200,000 limit is exceeded, as follows:

$$\text{Preceding corporation tax liability} \times \frac{\text{Number of days in current accounting period}}{\text{Number of days in preceding accounting period}}$$

When paying its 'first' instalment of preliminary tax, a company (large or small) can choose between the lower of a percentage of its current corporation tax liability and a percentage of the "corresponding corporation tax" liability of the preceding accounting period of the same length. The corresponding corporation tax of the preceding accounting period is the amount of the preceding corporation tax liability when the preceding accounting period equals in length the current accounting period. If the lengths of the current and preceding accounting periods differ, the corporation tax liability for the preceding accounting period must be adjusted using the formula above.

Example 19.8

K Ltd prepares accounts for six months to 31 December 2018 showing a corporation tax liability of €90,000. To check if the company qualifies as a small company in respect of the next accounting period ending 31 December 2019, the corporation tax liability must be adjusted for a year to compare with the limit for small companies (€200,000).

€90,000 × 365/184 = €178,533 = small company

K Ltd estimates its corporation tax liability for 31 December 2019 to be €210,000. Therefore K Ltd can pay the lower of 90% of the current corporation tax liability (i.e. €189,000) or 100% of the corresponding corporation tax liability of preceding accounting period (i.e. €178,533). The company must pay preliminary tax of €178,533 by 23 November 2019.

The balance of the corporation tax due, i.e. €31,467 (€210,000 – €178,533), must be paid, and the tax return filed, within nine months of the end of the accounting period, but not later than day 23, i.e. not later than 23 September 2020 in this case.

When determining a company's size for preliminary tax purposes, the limit of €200,000 is reduced proportionately where the current accounting period is less than 12 months, as follows:

$$€200{,}000 \times \frac{\text{Number of days in current accounting period}}{\text{Number of days in preceding accounting period}}$$

If the preceding and current accounting periods differ in length, and the current accounting period is less than 12 months, the corresponding corporation tax of the preceding accounting period is compared with the limit as adjusted above.

Example 19.9

Q Ltd prepares accounts to 31 December. Its corporation tax liability for the year ended 31 December 2018 is €140,000. The company changes its accounting date to 30 June and prepares a six-month set of accounts to 30 June 2019 showing a corporation tax liability of €160,000.

As it is now a six-month accounting period ending 30 June 2019, the relevant limit is reduced proportionately, i.e. €200,000 × 181/365 = €99,178.

Q Ltd's corresponding corporation tax liability for the period ended 31 December 2018 was €69,425, i.e. €140,000 × 181/365. As this does not exceed the relevant limit of €99,178, Q Ltd is considered a small company.

As a small company its preliminary tax requirement for 2019 is €69,425, to be paid by 23 May 2019.

The balance of the corporation tax due, i.e. €90,575 (€160,000 – €69,425), must be paid, and the tax return filed, within nine months of the end of the accounting period 30 June 2019, but not later than day 23, i.e. not later than 23 March 2020 in this case.

Example 19.10

M Ltd prepares accounts for the six months ending 31 December 2018 and for the year ending 31 December 2019. M Ltd's corporation tax liability for the six months ended 31 December 2018 is €120,000 and for the year ended 31 December 2019 is €300,000.

The company's corresponding corporation tax liability for the six-month accounting period ending 31 December 2018 is €238,043, i.e. €120,000 × 365/184. As this exceeds the relevant limit of €200,000 for a year, the company is a large company for preliminary tax purposes.

The company will satisfy its preliminary tax requirements for 2019 if preliminary tax is paid as follows:

1st instalment due 23 June 2019
45% of €300,000 = €135,000 or
50% of €238,043* = €119,022
The lower amount should be paid, i.e. €119,022

*Corresponding corporation tax liability for the year ended 31 December 2018.

2nd instalment due 23 November 2019	€
90% of final liability for 2019 (€300,000 @ 90%)	270,000
Deduct: amount paid in the 1st instalment	(119,022)
Amount to be paid	150,978

The balance of corporation tax, i.e. €30,000 (€300,000 – €270,000), is due to be paid when filing the corporation tax return by 23 September 2020.

2. Top-up Payments of Preliminary Tax Due to Chargeable Gain after Preliminary Tax Due
Where a chargeable gain arises after the due date for the payment of a company's preliminary tax liability, the preliminary tax may have to be amended to take into account the additional corporation tax arising on the gain.

A top-up payment will be required if the preliminary tax paid was based on paying 90% of the company's corporation tax for the current year. If the preliminary tax paid was based on 100% of the corresponding corporation tax for the preceding year, no amendment is required. If, as a result of the chargeable gain, the company's preliminary tax payment is now less than 90% of its corporation tax liability for that year, and if corporation tax due in respect of the chargeable gain were excluded the company's preliminary tax payment would not have been less than the necessary 90%, then the company may make an additional payment of preliminary tax and not incur interest on late payment of tax. This is providing that:

1. the additional payment is made within one month of the end of the accounting period; and
2. the aggregate of the additional payment and the preliminary tax paid amounts to at least 90% of the company's corporation tax liability.

If these two conditions are met, the company is deemed to have paid its preliminary corporation tax liability by the due date.

> ***Example 19.11***
> N Ltd, a large company, has a corporation tax liability for the year ended 31 December 2019 of €250,000. Of this liability, €40,000 is in respect of a chargeable gain which arose in December 2019. The company made preliminary tax payments of €189,000 up to 23 November 2019.
>
> This amounts to less than 90% of its liability for 2019. However, excluding the tax arising in respect of the chargeable gain which arose in December 2019, the preliminary tax paid would have amounted to 90% of the company's liability for 2019. If the company makes a top-up payment of preliminary tax of €36,000 (90% of €250,000 = €225,000, minus €189,000 preliminary tax paid = €36,000) by 31 January 2020, the company will have satisfied its preliminary tax requirements.
>
> The balance of the corporation tax, i.e. €25,000 (€250,000 – €225,000), must be paid, and the tax return filed, within nine months of the end of the accounting period, but not later than day 23, i.e. not later than 23 September 2020 in this case.

Where the following conditions are satisfied, a large company will be deemed to have paid sufficient preliminary tax by the due date:

1. the total of the company's first instalment and second instalment of preliminary tax amount to at least 90% of the company's corporation tax liability for the current accounting period;
2. the company's first instalment of preliminary tax amounts to not less than 45%* of the company's corporation tax liability for the current accounting period; and
3. the company's first instalment of preliminary tax is less than 45%* of the company's corporation tax liability for the current accounting period but would not have been less than 45%* of the company's corporation tax liability for the current accounting period if no amount were included in the company's profits in respect of chargeable gains arising on the disposal of assets after the due date for the payment of the company's first instalment of preliminary tax.

*If the first instalment of preliminary tax is based on 50% of the corresponding corporation tax for the preceding year, this issue does not arise.

Example 19.12
J Ltd, a large company, had a corporation tax liability for the year ended 31 December 2019 of €500,000. Of this, €100,000 is in respect of a chargeable gain that arose in August 2019.

The company had made the following preliminary tax payments:

	€	€
1st instalment 23 June 2019: 45% of €400,000		180,000
2nd instalment 23 November 2019: 90% of €500,000	450,000	
Less: 1st instalment	(180,000)	270,000
Total preliminary tax paid		450,000

The company's first instalment of preliminary tax is less than 45% of its actual corporation tax liability for the accounting period, however the amount paid would have amounted to 45% of the corporation tax liability if the gain which arose after the due date for the payment of the first instalment of preliminary tax were excluded. In addition, the total preliminary tax paid amounted to 90% of its corporation tax liability for the accounting period. Accordingly, the company is deemed to have paid a sufficient first instalment payment of preliminary tax and to have met its preliminary tax requirements.

3. Accounting Period Less than One Month and One Day
Where a company's accounting period is less than a month and a day in length, preliminary tax will be due and payable not later than the last day of the accounting period, but where that day is later than day 23 of the month, the tax will be due and payable not later than day 23 of that month.

Example 19.13
Q Ltd changes its accounting date from 30 November to 31 December. Accounts are prepared for one month to 31 December 2019. Preliminary tax for the one-month period ended 31 December 2019 will be due on or before 23 December 2019.

19.6 Filing Tax Return and Other Administration

19.6.1 Filing Requirements

Corporation Tax Return
A company must file its corporation tax return (Form CT1) electronically through the Revenue Online Service (ROS). Subject to an exception outlined below, all returns submitted after 1 October 2014 in respect of accounting periods ending on or after 31 December 2013 must be filed using iXBRL. XBRL is a computer language that allows the presentation of financial information in a computer-readable format; iXBRL is a more recent version that allows human-readable presentation of XBRL documents. Companies satisfying all of the following criteria do not have to file using iXBRL:

- the balance sheet total (i.e. aggregate assets before deduction of liabilities) of the company does not exceed €4.4 million;
- the turnover of the company does not exceed €8.8 million; and
- the average number of persons employed by the company does not exceed 50.

These criteria correspond to audit-exemption criteria.

A company's corporation tax return must include a "self-assessment", i.e. a statement that sets out the income, profits and gains of the company for the accounting period, the company's tax liability and the balance of tax payable. A Revenue online tax return automatically produces a self-assessment statement. A company must either accept the self-assessment produced by the online system or substitute it with its own self-assessment. A return cannot be filed online if a self-assessment is not included. When the return is submitted, Revenue will not issue an assessment; instead an acknowledgement of the self-assessment submitted by the company is issued.

Where a company is in doubt as regards any matter to be included in a return, the company should specify the doubt in the return and retain supporting documentation to submit to Revenue should the Inspector request it. If the company does this and the doubt is accepted as **genuine**, the company is regarded as having made a full and true return and accordingly is protected from the penalties which apply where a company fails to make a full and true return. In addition, any additional tax which becomes payable when the doubt is resolved is due within 30 days of the issue of an amended assessment, so the company is also regarded as not having underpaid its preliminary tax.

The balance of corporation tax must be paid at the same time as the return is filed. (*Note:* if the return is filed early, the payment does not have to be made at the same time, but it must be paid on or before the deadline date.)

Country-by-Country (CbC) Reporting

There is an additional filing requirement for an Irish-resident parent company of a large multinational enterprise (MNE), i.e. one where consolidated turnover exceeds €750 million in the preceding accounting period. The parent company is required to provide a country-by-country (CbC) report to Revenue within 12 months of the fiscal year end for each tax jurisdiction in which it does business.

The CbC report is based on guidance published in the OECD/G20 Action Plan on Base Erosion and Profit Shifting (BEPS). The report must contain details of the MNE's revenue, profit before income tax and income tax paid, income tax accrued, stated capital, accumulated earnings, number of employees and tangible assets in each tax jurisdiction. It also requires the tax identification numbers of all entities within the MNE, each company's tax residence and an indication of the business activities engaged in by each entity. Revenue will share the report with other tax administrations under mandatory automatic exchange of information provisions.

Revenue may impose a penalty for failure to make a return, or where an incorrect or incomplete return is filed. The penalty is €19,045, plus €2,535 for each day the failure continues.

19.6.2 Interest

If there is a default in payment of preliminary tax or the balance of tax (e.g. late payment of tax, payment is too small, or the balance of tax is paid late), interest is charged at 0.0219% per day or part of a day. Interest on late payment of tax is not tax deductible.

Example 19.14: Accounts year ended 30 September 2019

Preliminary tax paid on 20/08/2019 of €92,000
Corporation tax for year is €100,000
Corporation tax for preceding year was €150,000
Company pays balance of €8,000 on 20/06/2020

Is condition 1 satisfied? Yes – preliminary tax paid of 92% (>90%) by 23/08/2019

Is condition 2 satisfied? Yes – balance of tax paid by 23/06/2020

If tax is overpaid, it carries interest at a rate which is currently 0.011% per day. However, the date from which interest runs depends on whether the overpayment is as a result of a mistake made by Revenue or the taxpayer. Where the repayment arises because of a mistaken assumption of the law by Revenue, the interest will be calculated from the end of the accounting period to which the repayment relates or, if later, when the tax was overpaid. In all other cases, including repayments of preliminary tax, interest will run from 93 days (previously six months) after a valid claim to the date the repayment is made.

Claims for repayment of tax must be made on a timely basis, i.e. the repayment must be subject to a claim being made to Revenue within four years of the end of the period to which it relates (there was a longer time limit in the past). Revenue will only pay interest if it exceeds €10. Interest received on overpayment of tax is not taxable.

19.6.3 Annual Tax Returns and Surcharges

If the return is filed within two months after the filing date, the surcharge is 5%, subject to a maximum of €12,695. If the delay is two months or more, the surcharge is 10%, subject to a maximum of €63,485.

Example 19.15

A company had a tax-adjusted Case I profit of €500,000 for the year ended 31 December 2019. If the return is filed within nine months, i.e. by 23 September 2020, the liability is €62,500, i.e. €500,000 @ 12.5%.

	€
If it is not filed until 10/10/2020 the liability is	62,500
+5% surcharge	3,125
	65,625
If it is not filed until 01/12/2020 the liability is	62,500
+10% surcharge	6,250
	68,750

The surcharge payable is treated as part of the company's corporation tax liability for the accounting period, which may mean that as a result of having to pay a surcharge, the company may have underpaid its preliminary tax.

Example 19.16

A "large" company has a corporation tax liability of €200,000 for the year ended 31 December 2019 and €300,000 for the previous year. The company paid preliminary tax for 2019 as follows:

Preliminary tax: €90,000 paid on 23 June 2019.
Preliminary tax: €180,000 less €90,000 paid on 23 November 2019, bringing total to 90% of final corporation tax liability, i.e. €180,000.

The company filed its return for 2019 on 20 December 2020 and accordingly a surcharge of €20,000 (10%) applies. The company's total corporation tax liability for 2019 is deemed to be €220,000. Accordingly, the company has underpaid its preliminary tax (amount paid was less than 45% / 90% of €220,000). 45% of the company's corporation tax liability of €220,000 is deemed to have all been due on 21 June 2019 and the balance on 21 November 2019, and interest is charged from these dates to the actual date on which the balance of the tax was paid.

19.7 Accounting Periods

Corporation tax is assessed on the profits arising in the company's accounting period. The term "accounting period" is given a special meaning for corporation tax purposes – ordinarily it is the period for which the company makes up its accounts ("period of account"), **but for corporation tax purposes an accounting period cannot exceed 12 months.**

The **first accounting period** for corporation tax purposes of a company begins whenever the company **comes within the charge to corporation tax**. This may happen in one of several ways:

- A new company may be created and acquire a source of profits.
- A non-resident company that becomes resident in the State. Its first accounting period will start on the day it becomes resident.
- A company may acquire for the first time a source of income chargeable to corporation tax, e.g. a non-resident company may start to trade in the State. An accounting period will start on that date.

An accounting period runs for a maximum of 12 months from its start. It will end earlier if the company's own accounting date falls within the 12 months. An accounting period will end:

- after a period of 12 months;
- on the company's own accounting date if within the 12 months;
- when the company:
  - begins to trade or first comes within the charge to corporation tax in respect of a trade, or
  - when it ceases to trade or ceases to be within the charge to corporation tax in respect of its trade, or
  - if it begins or ceases to be resident in the State.

A new accounting period starts immediately at the end of the preceding accounting period (unless the company ceased trading or to be within the charge to corporation tax).

Example 19.17

Start Ltd was incorporated on 1 June 2019 when the money subscribed for share capital was put on deposit. The company commenced to trade on 1 September 2019. It prepared its first set of financial statements for the period ended 31 December 2019 and intends to prepare annual financial statements to 31 December each year thereafter.

As Start Ltd acquired a source of income on 1 June, an accounting period commenced. As it commenced to trade on 1 September, an accounting period is deemed to end, even though no actual set of financial statements are prepared. Therefore, Start Ltd has an accounting period of three months, ending on 31 August 2019. Its next accounting period is from 1 September to 31 December 2019. Thereafter it will have accounting periods ending on 31 December each year.

19.7.1 Accounting Periods of Less than 12 Months

For the purposes of corporation tax, short accounting periods, i.e. those less than 12 months, that are the result of a change in the normal accounting date, do not require any special treatment. Unlike income tax, there is no need to revise the prior period. For example, if a company has prepared 12-month accounts to 31 December 2017 followed by an eight-month set of accounts to 31 August 2018 followed by a 12-month set of accounts to 31 August 2019, then corporation tax is simply payable for each of these three accounting periods.

There are, however, some implications of short accounting periods:

- Where normal wear and tear allowances are available they must be scaled down appropriately. For example, if an accounting period is eight months long, the normal wear and tear annual allowances would be reduced to 8/12ths.
- The calculation of the **corresponding corporation tax** (see **Section 19.5.4**) of the preceding accounting period and the **carryback period for losses** will have to be reduced to reflect the fact that the company has a short accounting period.
- Preliminary tax payments are based on when an accounting period ends. A shorter than 12-month accounting period results in the earlier payment of preliminary tax.

19.7.2 Accounting Periods Exceeding 12 Months

As already noted, for corporation tax purposes the maximum length of an accounting period is 12 months, therefore, where a company prepares a set of accounts for a period exceeding 12 months, this "period of account" must be broken down into shorter periods, each a maximum of 12 months long.

> ***Example 19.18***
> X Ltd prepared a set of accounts for 18 months, ending on 30 June 2019. In these circumstances corporation tax is payable for the following "accounting periods":
> - 12-month accounting period to 31 December 2018;
> - 6-month accounting period to 30 June 2019 (remember an accounting period is terminated automatically by reference to the date to which a set of accounts is prepared).

As you can see from this example, **if the period of account is longer than 12 months, the first accounting period will always be at least 12 months long**.

In the above example, the period of account was 18 months long. As mentioned at **Section 19.1**, it will be necessary to analyse the company's income and gains, contained in the income statement, into the appropriate Cases under Schedule D for corporation tax purposes. This is achieved by preparing a tax-adjusted profit computation to identify and calculate the company's Cases I and II, Cases III and IV and Case V income and chargeable gains (see **Chapter 20**) for the 18-month period. One would then **time-apportion** the tax-adjusted **Case I** profits for this 18-month period to arrive at the relevant Case I income for each of the accounting periods mentioned above.

It should be particularly noted that only the Case I profits are apportioned. **Case III, Case IV, Case V and chargeable gains arising in the 18-month accounting period will be charged by reference to the actual accounting period in which they occur**. For example, if there was only one capital disposal in the 18-month period, say, on 1 May 2019, then the chargeable gain would be assessed and brought into the computation for the six-month accounting period ending on 30 June 2019.

In the above example, the capital allowances would have to be computed separately for each of the two accounting periods by reference to additions and disposals of assets which occurred during year ended 31 December 2018 and six months to 30 June 2019. In the case of the latter six-month period, clearly the wear and tear allowances would have to be restricted appropriately as discussed above. Therefore, in this situation, capital allowances are not allowed as a trading expense (see **Chapter 20, Section 20.7**) until after the Case I income has been time-apportioned. (The calculation of capital allowances is beyond the scope of this text book.)

19.8 Three-year Tax Exemption for Start-up Companies

19.8.1 Overview

Section 486C TCA 1997 provides **relief from corporation tax for new companies commencing to trade in the period 1 January 2009 to 31 December 2021**. The exemption is granted in respect of the profits of a new trade and chargeable gains on the disposal of any assets used for the purposes of a new trade. The exemption is granted by reducing the total corporation tax relating to the new trade to nil. **Full relief** is granted where the total amount of **corporation tax** payable by a company for a 12-month accounting period **does not exceed €40,000. Marginal relief** is granted where the total amount of corporation tax payable by a new company for a 12-month accounting period exceeds €40,000 but does not exceed €60,000. No relief applies where corporation tax payable exceeds €60,000. For accounting periods beginning on or after 1 January 2011, there is a **limit on the relief**, which is **linked to the Employers' PRSI** paid or deemed paid. While the concept is straightforward, the calculations are somewhat complex.

The exemption is available for a period of three years from the commencement of the new trade and separate exemptions are available for each new trade. However, the relief will cease if part of the trade is transferred to a connected person. Where an accounting period is less than 12 months, the limits above are proportionately reduced.

With effect for accounting periods ending on or after 1 January 2013, if a company has an excess of Employers' PRSI contributions over corporation tax payable in the first three years, the excess may be carried forward to the fourth year and claimed then or in later years, subject to having sufficient Employers' PRSI paid in that year.

19.8.2 Qualifying and Non-qualifying Trades

A qualifying trade for the purposes of this exemption means a trade which is set up and commenced by a new company in the period 1 January 2009 to 31 December 2021, **other than a trade:**

- which was previously carried on by another person. This means that where a sole trader transfers a business to a new company, the company cannot avail of this exemption on income from this trade;
- which is an excepted trade;
- a professional service company (see **Chapter 26, Section 26.3.5**);
- the activities of which are excluded due to an EU Regulation on state aid (e.g. certain fishery, agricultural, transport, coal and export activities);
- the activities of which, if carried on by an associated company of the new company, would form part of a trade carried on by that associated company (thus preventing an existing company undertaking an expansion of its existing trade from availing of the exemption by putting the expansion through a new company). A company is the new company's associated company if one controls the other or both are under the control of the same person or persons.

19.8.3 Calculation of Relief

The relief applies to:

1. corporation tax payable by the company for an accounting period in respect of income from the qualifying trade for that accounting period; and

2. corporation tax payable by the company for an accounting period in respect of chargeable gains on the disposal of qualifying assets in relation to the trade. Qualifying assets are assets (including goodwill but not investments) used for the new trade.

Corporation tax in respect of income from the qualifying trade is computed based on the "relevant corporation tax", i.e. the total corporation tax for an accounting period **apart from** corporation tax due to:

- close company surcharges (see **Chapter 26**);
- income tax which is withheld by companies (see **Chapter 21**) and paid over at the same time as corporation tax;
- the corporation tax chargeable on the profits of the company attributable to chargeable gains for that accounting period; and
- the corporation tax chargeable on the part of the company's profits which are charged to tax at 25%.

(There are some other exclusions, but these are not noted here as they relate to areas beyond the scope of this textbook.)

The profits of a company attributable to chargeable gains for an accounting period is taken to be the amount of its profits for that period on which corporation tax falls finally to be borne exclusive of the part of the profits attributable to income. The part attributable to income is taken to be the amount brought into the company's profits for that period for the purposes of corporation tax in respect of income after any deduction for charges on income, expenses of management or other amounts which can be deducted from or set against or treated as reducing profits of more than one description, i.e. charges, expenses of management, etc. are deductible from income and thereby reduce the trading income, which benefits from the tax exemption, if there is no other income against which to offset them.

Limit on Relief – Employers' PRSI

For accounting periods commencing on or after 1 January 2011, there is a limit on the relief. If the amount of qualifying Employers' PRSI paid by a company in an accounting period (i.e. total specified contributions) is less than the corporation tax on the income and gains of the new trade, the relief is restricted to the total specified contributions.

The amount of qualifying Employers' PRSI paid by a company in an accounting period in respect of each employee or director (the specified contribution), irrespective of whether the employee is an employee of the new or existing (if any) trade of the new company, is the **lower** of:

(i) the actual Employers' PRSI paid in respect of that employee or director in the accounting period; or
(ii) €5,000.

The amount in respect of each employee or director is aggregated to establish **the total of these specified contributions** for the accounting period.

Note: certain directors, who are not regarded as employees for social insurance purposes, are liable to PRSI under Class S and, therefore, there is no Employers' PRSI.

Full Corporation Tax Relief for New Trade

Provided the total specified contributions (as calculated above) paid by the company in the accounting period amount to at least €40,000 and the total corporation tax payable by the company for that accounting period in respect of income and gains from the new trade does not exceed €40,000, the corporation tax arising on the income and gains from the new trade will be reduced to nil.

Otherwise, the corporation tax on income and gains of the new trade is reduced by the lower of the total specified contributions or the corporation tax on income and gains of the new trade.

Example 19.19

Start Ltd was incorporated on 1 November 2018 and commenced to trade on 1 January 2019. Trading income from the shop for the year ended 31 December 2019 is €100,000.

The company has three employees and one director. The employers' PRSI is as follows:

	Employers' PRSI paid
Employee 1	€2,000
Employee 2	€4,000
Employee 3	€6,000
Director	0 (Class S, so no Employers' PRSI)

What is the corporation tax payable?

Solution

Corporation tax payable would be €12,500 (i.e. €100,000 × 12.5%). As this is less than €40,000 and all conditions are satisfied, the exemption is due. The amount of the exemption depends on the amount of Employers' PRSI that has been paid.

Calculation of total specified contributions

	Specified contribution
	€
Employee 1	2,000
Employee 2	4,000
Employee 3	5,000 (maximum)
Director	0
Total specified contributions	11,000
Relief due under normal rules	12,500
(i.e. corporation tax on income and gains of new trade)	
Relief due (restricted to lower amount)	11,000
Final corporation tax payable €12,500 – €11,000 =	€1,500

As Start Ltd commenced to trade on 1 January 2019, the exemption applies for 2019, 2020 and 2021. The company will not be entitled to the exemption in 2022.

Qualifying Relevant Period

The relief applies for the first three years only – the "relevant period". This commences when the company commences to trade, and ends three years later. In **Example 19.19**, as Start Ltd commenced to trade on 1 January 2019, the exemption applies for 2019, 2020 and 2021. The company will not be entitled to the exemption in 2022.

Example 19.20

Gain Ltd was incorporated on 11 November 2017 and commenced to trade on 1 January 2018. It had the following income and gain for the year ended 31 December 2019:

- trading income from distribution trade €200,000;
- gain on sale of building used for distribution trade €24,000.

It has six employees and two directors. Employers' PRSI contributions are as follows:

	Employers' PRSI paid
Employee	€4,000
Six employees	€24,000 (each contribution is less than €5,000)
Director 1	0 (Class S – no Employers' PRSI)
Director 2	€8,000

continued overleaf

What is the corporation tax payable?

Solution

Corporation tax payable would be:	€
Case I	200,000
Chargeable gain: €24,000 × 33/12.5	63,360
Profit	263,360

Corporation tax @ 12.5% = €32,920

As this is less than €40,000, all conditions are satisfied and this is qualifying trading income and gains only, the exemption is due and the corporation tax payable is nil, provided that total specified contributions are at least €32,920.

	Specified contribution
	€
Employee 1	4,000
Six employees	24,000
Director 2	5,000
Total specified contributions	33,000
Relief due under normal rules	32,920
Relief due	32,920*

Final corporation tax payable €32,920 − €32,920 = €nil

*The excess of €33,000 (total specified contributions paid) over €32,920 (relief claimed) is available to carry forward to 2021, i.e. the year after the relief ends under normal rules (see **Section 19.8.4**).

Where a company has an existing trade and commences a new trade, the corporation tax is apportioned proportionately between the income from the existing trade and the new trade. The same treatment applies for chargeable gains.

Example 19.21

Complex Ltd was incorporated on 14 June 2018, commenced to trade on 1 January 2019 and had the following income and gains for the year ended 31 December 2019.

	€
Case I – existing distribution trade transferred into company	100,000
Case I – new marketing trade	20,000
Case III – interest income	100
Adjusted chargeable gain on disposal of asset used for marketing trade	12,000
Adjusted chargeable gain on disposal of investment	8,000
Income tax withheld when paying interest to non-bank	1,200

It has the following employees and directors and Employers' PRSI contributions:

	Employers' PRSI paid
One employee	€6,000
Six employees	€27,000 (each contribution is less than €5,000)
Director	0 (class S – no Employers' PRSI)

continued overleaf

What is the corporation tax payable?

Solution	€	€
Case I – existing distribution trade transferred into company		100,000
Case I – new marketing trade		20,000
Case I – total		120,000
Case III – interest income		100
Total income		120,100
Chargeable gain – asset for marketing trade	12,000	
Chargeable gain – investment	8,000	20,000
Total profit		140,100
Corporation tax:		
€140,000 @ 12.5%		17,500
€100 @ 25%		25
Total corporation tax before relief		17,525
Less: total relief (Note 1)		(4,000)
		13,525
Add: income tax		1,200
Total payable		14,725

Notes:

1. Calculation of relief

Total corporation tax	17,525
Relevant corporation tax: €17,525 – (€100 × 25% – (12.5% of €20,000))	15,000
Corporation tax referable to income from qualifying trade:	
$\text{RCT} \times \frac{\text{Qualifying trade income}}{\text{Total income (excl. income taxed at 25\%)}} = 15{,}000 \times \frac{20{,}000}{120{,}000}$	(2,500)
Corporation tax referable to chargeable gains on qualifying assets:	
$\text{CT on gains} \times \frac{\text{Net gains on qualifying assets}}{\text{Net gains on chargeable assets}} = 2{,}500 \times \frac{12{,}000}{20{,}000}$	(1,500)
Total relief (provided sufficient Employers' PRSI is paid) (Note 1a)	(4,000)

Note 1a:

	Specified contribution
	€
One employee	5,000 (maximum allowed)
Six employees	27,000
Aggregate	32,000
Relief due under normal rules	4,000
Relief due	4,000*

* The excess of €32,000 (Employers' PRSI paid) over €4,000 (relief claimed) is available to carry forward to 2022, i.e. the year after the relief ends under normal rules (see **Section 19.8.4**).

Marginal Relief

Marginal relief can be claimed, but is beyond the scope of this textbook.

19.8.4 Carry Forward of Relief to Years After the Qualifying Relevant Period

Finance Act 2013 recognised that many companies will not have sufficient corporation tax payable in the first three years of trading to utilise the total specified contributions paid during those three years due to losses or very low trading profits.

With effect from 1 January 2013, where a company qualifies for full exemption from corporation tax on the new trade but total specified contributions exceed the relevant corporation tax, this excess can be used to reduce the company's corporation tax liability in the fourth (and subsequent) year of trading, provided sufficient Employers' PRSI has been paid in that year also.

Example 19.22

Too Little Ltd was incorporated on 25 November 2018 and commenced to trade on 1 January 2019. It had the following results for the year ended 31 December 2019:

Case I	€1,000

Too Little Ltd has eight employees and paid Employers' PRSI of €32,000 for the year. The Employers' PRSI in respect of each employee was less than €5,000.

What is the corporation tax payable? How much, if any, is available to carry forward and to which period? If the company had similar figures for Case I and Employers' PRSI for 2019 and 2020, what would be the consequences?

Solution

	€
Corporation tax @ 12.5%	125
Less: relief (Note)	(125)
Corporation tax payable	nil

Note: the corporation tax is reduced by the Employers' PRSI of €32,000. However, only €125 is required to reduce the corporation tax to €nil. The surplus specified contributions of €32,000 – €125 = €31,875 is available to carry forward. The company is entitled to the start-up exemption for three years, i.e. for 2019, 2020 and 2021. Therefore, the surplus is carried forward to when the relief no longer applies, i.e. to 2022. The €31,875 may be claimed in 2022, to offset against corporation tax of that year, provided at least €31,875 of Employers' PRSI has been paid in 2022.

If Too Little Ltd had an excess of specified contributions over the corporation tax on trading profits of 2020 and 2021, these would also be available to carry forward to 2022.

Example 19.23

Doing Fine Ltd was incorporated on 11 November 2018 and commenced its retail trade on 1 January 2019. Assume it has the following profits and qualifying Employers' PRSI:

	2019	**2020**	**2021**	**2022**	**2023**
	€	€	€	€	€
Trading profits	14,000	12,000	70,000	100,000	120,000
Qualifying Employers' PRSI	10,000	10,000	10,000	10,000	10,000

How much corporation tax will Doing Fine Ltd pay each year?

continued overleaf

Solution

	2019	2020	2021	2022	2023
	€	€	€	€	€
Trading profits	14,000	12,000	70,000	100,000	120,000
Corporation tax @ 12.5%	1,750	1,500	8,750	12,500	15,000
Relief – in first three years (Note 1)	(1,750)	(1,500)	(8,750)		
Relief – carried forward (Note 2)				(10,000)	(8,000)
Corporation tax payable	nil	nil	nil	2,500	7,000

Notes:

1. As all the conditions for the start-up exemption are satisfied and qualifying Employers' PRSI of Doing Fine Ltd is greater than the corporation tax for each of the first three years, the company has no corporation tax to pay and it has the excess Employers' PRSI to carry forward to the fourth year or later (2022 or later) as follows:

	2019	2020	2021	Total
	€	€	€	€
Qualifying Employers' PRSI	10,000	10,000	10,000	
Used to relieve corporation tax	(1,750)	(1,500)	(8,750)	
Unused amount	8,250	8,500	1,250	18,000

2. While there is €18,000 available for carry forward to 2022 and the corporation tax on trading income is €12,500, the claim in 2022 cannot exceed the qualifying Employers' PRSI of that year, i.e. €10,000. The unclaimed amount of €8,000 is carried forward to 2023. As both the corporation tax on trading income and the qualifying Employers' PRSI of that year exceed €8,000, a claim can be made for the full €8,000.

There is also a carry forward of excess Employers' PRSI where a company claims marginal relief, the calculation of which is beyond the scope of this book.

19.8.5 Other Issues

Where the accounting period is less than 12 months, all the limits are reduced proportionately.

There are special rules which limit the relief for transport and haulage companies. Also, as the law must comply with the EU *de minimis* State aid regulations, Revenue is allowed to provide details of relief claimed to other State bodies.

Questions

Review Questions

(See Suggested Solutions to Review Questions at the end of this textbook.)

Question 19.1

Lemmon Ltd, a distribution company, prepares accounts annually to 31 December. On 1 January 2019, it decided to change its accounting date to 29 February and accordingly a 14-month set of accounts was made up to 29 February 2020. Two brothers, Walter and Jack, who also own a property rental company, Rentco Ltd, own Lemmon Ltd. On 1 July 2019 Lemmon Ltd acquired all the share capital of another distribution company, Distributors Ltd.

Results for the three companies, as adjusted for tax purposes, are as follows:

	Notes	Lemmon	Rentco	Distributors
		14 months ended 29/02/2020	**Year ended 31/12/2019**	**8 months ended 29/02/2020**
		€	€	€
Schedule D Case I		308,000	–	20,000
Schedule D Case III	1.	5,000	–	–
Schedule D Case V		–	50,000	–
Chargeable gain (as adjusted for corporation tax)		5,156	–	–

Note

1. Case III income received: €3,000 on 31 December 2019, and €2,000 on 29 February 2020.

Requirement

(a) Calculate the corporation tax liabilities for all three companies for the above accounting periods.

(b) State the latest date by which all corporation tax liabilities are to be paid. (Assume all companies are small companies, but ignore the rule that allows "small companies" to base their preliminary tax on its corresponding corporation tax liability for the previous period.)

(c) State the latest date by which returns must be filed for the above periods.

20

Computation of Corporation Tax

Learning Objectives

After studying this chapter you will be able to:

- Identify and advise on the appropriate corporation tax treatment of a company's income and gains.
- Prepare a Case I and Case II adjusted profit/loss computation for corporation tax purposes for inclusion in a corporation tax computation.
- Prepare a standard corporation tax computation from a company's financial statements.
- Advise on the relief for expenditure incurred on the provision of intangible assets for trade purposes.
- Advise on and calculate relief in respect of expenditure incurred on qualifying research and development activities.

20.1 Overview

Corporation tax is charged on the total profits of a company for an accounting period, i.e. on the income and gains contained in its financial statements for the accounting period. The basic rule for the calculation of income is that, apart from certain special provisions relevant only to companies, it is to be computed in accordance with income tax principles. The computation will therefore be made for each class of income under the same Schedules and Cases as apply for income tax purposes (as covered in the CA Proficiency 1 course). CGT principles, as covered in Part One of this book, supplemented by some company-specific provisions, apply to the calculation of chargeable gains.

A pro forma corporation tax computation is set out in **Section 20.2** to provide an overview to the calculation. Case I income is the main source of income for most companies, but its computation is generally more difficult than that of other income and gains. Therefore, we will first consider the more simple computation around Cases III, IV and V and chargeable gains.

20.2 Pro Forma Corporation Tax Computation

COMPLEX COMPANY LTD

CORPORATION TAX COMPUTATION FOR THE 12-MONTH ACCOUNTING PERIOD TO 31/12/2019 (*Note 1*)

		Notes	€	€
Case I	Tax-adjusted trading profits y/e 31/12/2019	2.	X	
	Less: allowable Case I losses forward section 396(1)	7.	(X)	
	Less: section 396A(3) Case I losses	7.	(X)	
	Less: allowable trade charges paid section 243A	8.	(X)	X
Case III	Interest on Irish Government Securities	3.	X	
	Foreign bond deposit interest		X	
	Irish building society interest (received gross)		X	
	Irish commercial bank deposit interest (received gross)		X	
	Income from foreign sources		X	X
Case IV	Income subject to Irish tax at source	4.		X
Case V	Rental profit from the letting of property in the Republic of Ireland	5.		X
Chargeable Gains	(as adjusted, i.e. × 33%/12.5%)	6.		X
Total Profits				X
Deduct:	Excess Case V capital allowances	11.		(X)
				X
Deduct:	Non-trade charges paid during y/e 31/12/2019 (e.g. protected interest)	9.		(X)
Profits liable to corporation tax				(X)
Corporation tax	Cases I, II and III and chargeable gains @ 12.5%	12.	X	
	Cases III, IV and V @ 25%	12.	X	
Deduct:	Excess relevant trading charges allowed on a value basis under section 243B	10.		(X)
	Relief for trading losses allowed on a value basis under section 396B(3)	7.		(X)
Add:	Surcharge (close company)	15.	X	
	Income tax deducted by the company on annual payments	13.	X	X
Deduct:	R&D tax credit	14.		(X)
				X
Deduct:	Income tax suffered by deduction	4.		(X)
Net corporation tax liability				X

Notes

1. The computation should always have the name of the company at the top and an appropriate heading, e.g. "Corporation tax computation for the 12-month *accounting period* to..........". It is possible for a corporation tax accounting period to be less than 12 months, but it can never exceed 12 months.
2. The tax-adjusted trading profits are arrived at after making a number of adjustments (see **Sections 20.7** and **20.10**).

3. See **Section 20.3.**
4. See **Section 20.3.**
5. This is the actual Case V income arising in the accounting period net of any expenses and capital allowances (see **Section 20.4**).
6. See **Section 20.6**. Remember, gains on development land are not liable to corporation tax but to CGT.
7. See **Chapter 22, Section 22.1.**
8. See **Chapter 21, Section 21.2.**
9. See **Chapter 21, Section 21.2.3.**
10. See **Chapter 22, Section 22.2.**
11. See **Chapter 22, Section 22.7.**
12. Certain Case III foreign dividends are taxable at 12.5% (see **Chapter 28, Section 28.1.2**).
13. See **Chapter 21, Section 21.2.1.**
14. See **Section 20.12.**
15. See **Chapter 26, Section 26.3.**

20.3 Computation of Income Assessed – Cases III and IV

The following income is charged under Case III and Case IV Schedule D:

- Case III untaxed interest income and income from foreign sources.
- Case IV income which has been subject to Irish tax at source and miscellaneous income. Corporation tax is charged on the gross amount of the Case IV income. The income tax suffered by deduction may be set against the corporation tax chargeable (see proforma computation above and **Chapter 21**). Companies have the option to receive interest income **without the deduction of DIRT** by simply completing a declaration in writing and providing their Irish tax reference number to the relevant deposit taker that the company is within the charge to corporation tax and interest will be included in the profits on which it is to be charged to corporation tax.

20.3.1 Basis of Assessment

Strictly, tax is charged under Case III and Case IV on the income **received** during the accounting period. In practice, however, interest that is received gross is taxed on an accruals basis.

20.4 Computation of Income Assessed – Case V

The following income is charged under Case V Schedule D:

- rents in respect of any premises or lands in the State, i.e. offices, shops, factories, land, etc.; and
- certain premiums received for the granting of a lease.

20.4.1 Basis of Assessment

Tax is charged under Case V on the income **arising** during the accounting period. The rental income taken into account is the amount receivable in the accounting period, whether or not it is actually received.

20.4.2 Premiums on Short Leases

Many years ago, it was possible for a landlord to avoid being taxed on income from let property by letting the property at a large "once-off" premium in the first year and charging a nominal rent thereafter. This once-off premium was treated as a capital receipt and was not within the charge to income tax. Legislation was introduced so that a certain proportion of a premium on a short lease, i.e. one that does not exceed 50 years, is taxable under Case V.

Calculation of Taxable Portion of Premium

Where a landlord receives a premium on the creation of a short lease they will be treated as receiving an amount by way of rent (in addition to any actual rent) as computed by the following formula:

$$P \times \frac{51 - N}{50}$$

where: P = premium; and
N = the duration of the lease.

> ***Example 20.1***
> A Ltd lets a premises to B Ltd on 1 April 2019 for 21 years at a rent of €18,000 per annum subject to a premium of €20,000. The taxable portion of the premium is:
>
> $$P \times \frac{51 - N}{50} = €20{,}000 \times \frac{(51 - 21)}{50} = €12{,}000$$
>
> This is treated as additional rent for the purposes of calculating A Ltd's taxable rental income for 2019.

20.4.3 Allowable and Disallowable Deductions in Calculating Case V Profits

The following amounts may be deducted from the gross rental income:

- Rent payable.
- Rates (if any).
- Cost of goods or services that the landlord company is obliged to provide and for which it receives no separate consideration, e.g. gas, electricity, waste disposal, etc.
- Cost of repairs, excluding improvements and items treated as capital expenditure.
- Interest on money borrowed for the purchase, improvement or repairs to a commercial property – but interest charges incurred prior to the first letting are not deductible.
- Interest on money borrowed for the purchase, improvement or repairs to a residential property where the taxpayer has satisfied the registration requirements of the RTB (Residential Tenancies Board). Generally, interest charges incurred prior to the first letting are not deductible but, if the residential letting qualifies for relief for pre-letting expenses in respect of vacant premises introduced in Finance Act 2017, some interest incurred may be allowed as a deduction (see below).
- Accountancy fees incurred in drawing up rental accounts and keeping rental records. Strictly, such expenses are not allowable as they relate more to the management of the landlord's affairs than to the receipt of rent or the management of the premises. In practice, however, Revenue allows a deduction for such expenses as it recognises that the efficient running of a business of letting premises requires that financial accounts should be prepared.

- Mortgage protection policy premiums. Generally, financial institutions insist on a mortgage protection policy being taken out by a borrower before they will approve a loan in respect of a property. Like accountancy fees, premiums on such policies would not be strictly allowable, being more to do with the landlord's financial affairs than to the management of the property or the receipt of rent. Revenue allows a deduction for such premiums.
- Pre-letting expenses in respect of vacant premises. Expenses incurred before a property is first let are generally not deductible. However, Finance Act 2017 provides that expenditure up to €5,000 incurred on a residential premises prior to it being first let between 25 December 2017 and 31 December 2021, after being vacant for at least 12 months, is allowed as a deduction against rental income from that premises. The expenditure must have been incurred in the 12 months before the premises is let as a residential premises. The pre-letting expenditure must be expenditure that would be allowed as a Case V deduction if incurred after the letting commenced. It also includes interest on money borrowed prior to the premises being occupied, which is generally not allowable. If the person who incurs the expenditure sells the property or changes the use from rented residential premises within four years of the first letting the deduction will be clawed back in the year in which the property ceases to be let as a residential premises. The clawback will be made by deeming the deduction previously allowed to be a Case V profit or gain of the year of cessation. However, reasonable periods of vacancy to clean or upgrade the property during the four-year period should not generate a clawback.
- Wear and tear allowances. A wear and tear allowance of 12.5% per annum on a straight-line basis for eight years is available on the cost of furniture and fittings in the case of furnished lettings.
- Expenses incurred after the termination of one lease and before the commencement of another lease in respect of the property are deductible provided the following three conditions are satisfied:
    1. the expenses would otherwise be deductible;
    2. the person who was the lessor of the property does not occupy the premises during the period when the property is not let; and
    3. the property is let by the same lessor at the end of the period.

Allowable expenses are normally deducted on an accruals basis rather than on a paid basis. In order to be deductible, the expense must be incurred wholly and exclusively for the purpose of earning the rent and must be revenue, rather than capital, in nature.

Expenses **not deductible** against property income include:

- Local property tax payable by the owners of residential property.
- Expenses incurred before a lease commences on the property, other than legal or advertising expenses, and qualifying pre-letting expenditure on vacant residential property outlined above.
- Interest or rent payable before the property is first occupied by a lessee other than qualifying pre-letting expenditure on vacant residential property outlined previously.
- Expenses incurred after the termination of a lease unless followed by another lease to a new tenant, as outlined above.

Example 20.2: Rental computation

A company purchased a vacant rental residential property on 1 February 2019. The previous occupants had vacated the property in June 2018. Between the date of purchase and 30 June 2019 the company spent €25,000 refurbishing the property. On 1 July 2019 the property was leased for €1,800 per month, payable in advance.

The following expenses were incurred up to 30 June 2019:

	€
Auctioneers' and advertising fees for first tenants	1,180
Repairs and maintenance	1,300
Light and heat	450
Security and insurance	800
Interest on loan	2,750
	6,450

The following expenses were incurred in the period 1 July to 31 December 2019:

	€
Insurance	100
Management and letting fees	1,540
Interest (property was registered with RTB on 25 July 2019)	3,300
RTB registration costs	90
Local property tax (LPT)	495

Solution

	€	€
Gross rents (€1,800 × 6)		10,800
Less: qualifying expenses		
Auctioneers and advertising	1,180	
Pre-letting expenses (maximum)	5,000	
Insurance	100	
Management and letting fees	1,540	
Interest (€3,300 × 85%)	2,805	
RTB registration costs	90	(10,715)
Net Case V income		85

LPT is not deductible for tax purposes.

20.5 Irish Dividends

Irish dividends received are exempt from corporation tax when received by an Irish-resident company from an Irish-resident company, excluding dividends received from an Irish REIT (real estate investment trust, a tax-efficient property investment company, which is beyond the scope of this textbook). They are referred to as franked investment income (FII) (see **Chapter 25, Section 25.1**). No deduction is allowed for dividends paid by a company (or any item treated as a distribution of profits under corporation tax rules) when computing taxable profits.

20.6 Computation of Chargeable Gains

Chargeable gains of a company, other than those arising from disposals of development land, are subject to corporation tax rather than CGT. (Gains on disposal of development land are subject to CGT.) The gain is after deducting capital losses from the current accounting period and those brought forward for earlier periods.

CGT computation principles apply to the calculation of the gain as set out in Part One of this textbook. If the chargeable gain was subject to CGT it would be taxed at 33%, i.e. if an individual made the disposal. However, the corporation tax rate applicable to chargeable gains is only 12.5%. Therefore, to avoid inequity, the chargeable gain subject to corporation tax needs to be adjusted so that when the adjusted chargeable gain is taxed at 12.5%, the amount of the tax arising equals the amount of tax that would arise if the disposal was subject to CGT at 33%. The adjusting formula is:

$$\text{Adjusted chargeable gain} = \text{chargeable gain} \times 33\%/12.5\%$$

The adjusted chargeable gains are added to total income in the corporation tax computation as per the pro forma computation at **Section 20.2**.

Example 20.3

X Ltd prepares accounts to 31 December each year. In the year ended 31 December 2019 the tax-adjusted Case III profit was €20,000. During that year the company bought an asset for €10,000 and sold it for €15,000 in June 2019:

X Ltd
Year ended 31 December 2019

	€
Case III	20,000
Adjusted chargeable gain: €5,000 × 33%/12.5%	13,200
	33,200
Corporation tax due @ 12.5%	1,650
Corporation tax due @ 25%	5,000
Total corporation tax	6,650
Proof:	€
Case III €20,000 @ 25%	5,000
Capital gain €5,000 @ 33%	1,650
	6,650

Example 20.4

Capital Ltd had the following disposals of fixed assets in its accounts for the year ended 31 December 2019:

1. Freehold premises acquired on 12 December 1974 for €80,000
   Sold for €680,000 on 31 December 2019
2. Plant acquired on 1 May 1992 for €5,000
   Sold for €14,670 on 30 May 2019
3. Fixtures and fittings acquired on 1 February 2007 for €3,000
   Sold for €2,500 on 31 May 2019
4. Leasehold premises acquired on 1 December 2008 under a 60-year lease for €25,000
   Sold for €30,000 on 30 June 2019
5. Investments acquired on 3 January 1999 for €10,000
   Sold for €8,000 on 30 September 2019

The company also had capital losses forward of €2,000 from previous accounting periods.

What is the amount to be included in the corporation tax computation in respect of chargeable gains?

continued overleaf

Solution

The amount to be included in the corporation tax computation for the year ended 31 December 2019 would be calculated as follows:

	€	€
1. Disposal of premises		
Cost on 12/12/74	80,000	
Index factor: 7.528		602,240
Proceeds		680,000
Chargeable gain		77,760
2. Disposal of plant		
Cost on 01/05/92	5,000	
Index factor: 1.356		6,780
Proceeds		14,670
Chargeable gain		7,890
3. Sale of fixtures and fittings		
Cost on 01/02/07		3,000
Proceeds		2,500
Loss		(500)

However, no relief is available for the loss of €500 as the assets have, or could have, qualified for capital allowances.

4. Sale of Leasehold Premises

Lease is a long lease as it has more than 50 years to run. Therefore it is not a wasting asset.

	€
Cost on 01/12/08	25,000
Proceeds	30,000
Chargeable gain	5,000

No indexation due. (Indexation relief was abolished for assets acquired on or after 1 January 2003.)

5. Sale of Investments

	€	€
Cost on 03/01/99	10,000	
Index factor: 1.212		12,120
Proceeds		8,000
Loss		(4,120)
Restrict to monetary loss		
Cost	10,000	
Proceeds	8,000	
	(2,000)	

Summary of net chargeable gains for the accounting period

	€	€
Freehold premises	77,760	
Plant	7,890	
Leasehold premises	5,000	90,650
Less: losses		
Investments	(2,000)	
Loss forward	(2,000)	(4,000)
		86,650

Amount to be included in the corporation tax computation as adjusted chargeable gains:

$$€86,650 \times \frac{33\%}{12.5\%} = €228,752$$

20.7 Computation of Cases I and II Income

A company carrying on a trade or profession will prepare financial statements based on accounting principles to arrive at 'profit before tax' for a particular accounting period. However, as previously noted, the accounting profit before tax is not necessarily the taxable Case I (trading) or Case II (professional) income. The profit before tax will require adjustment to arrive at the 'tax-adjusted' Case I or Case II profits for corporation tax purposes. Many of these adjustments also apply for income tax purposes, as covered at CA Proficiency 1. In calculating Case I and Case II profits, income earned is included on an **accruals basis**. Two fundamental principles in deciding whether an item is included when calculating Cases I and II adjusted profit/loss apply:

1. If an item is of a capital nature it must be disallowed.
2. Even if an item is of a revenue nature, it may be specifically disallowed by statute.

20.8 Income and Gains not Taxable under Cases I and II

In accordance with the aforementioned fundamental principles, the following items are not taxable under Cases I and II for corporation tax purposes:

- Grants. Most employment grants and capital grants paid by State bodies are exempt from corporation tax. Such grants are deducted from profit before tax when calculating the adjusted Case I and Case II profit.
- Interest on tax overpaid is specifically exempt from corporation tax. It must be deducted when calculating the adjusted Case I and Case II profit.
- Investment income. Interest, royalties and dividends must be deducted when calculating the adjusted Case I and Case II profit. Interest, royalties and foreign dividends will be assessed under Case III or Case IV (see **Section 20.3**). Irish dividends (FII) are exempt (see **Section 20.5**).
- Rental income must be deducted when calculating the adjusted Cases I and II profit. Irish rental income is assessed under Case V (see **Section 20.4**) and foreign rental income is assessed under Case III (**Section 20.3**).
- Profits/gains on disposal of non-current assets (e.g. property or shares) are deducted when calculating the adjusted Case I and Case II profit. Chargeable gains will be assessed to corporation tax as outlined in **Section 20.6** unless they relate to the disposal of development land, in which case CGT applies.

20.9 Capital Expenditure and Losses

Capital expenditure and losses are not deductible when calculating the adjusted Case I and Case II profit. Therefore, depreciation, purchase of non-current assets and related expenses (e.g. legal fees), improvements to premises, losses on disposal of non-current assets and related expenses and finance lease interest charges (see **Section 20.11**) must be added back.

The income tax scheme of capital allowances and balancing charges is brought into the corporation tax system. However, **capital allowances** due to trading companies are **treated as trading expenses** for corporation tax purposes and not as a deduction from the assessable income as in the case of income tax. Similarly, balancing charges are treated for corporation tax purposes as trading receipts. Furthermore, the capital allowances are calculated by reference to assets in use/expenditure incurred in each accounting period. Capital allowances in respect of intangible assets (e.g. patents, trademarks) are discussed in greater detail in **Section 20.11**. The calculation of capital allowances is beyond the scope of this textbook.

20.10 Allowable and Disallowable Case I and Case II Deductions

The main statutory provision disallowing expenditure is section 81 TCA 1997 (as outlined for income tax at CA Proficiency 1). Expenditure not wholly and exclusively laid out for the purpose of the trade is disallowed, including:

- rental expenses (but may be allowed as a deduction for Case III or Case V purposes);
- political donations;
- fines, penalties and interest for late payment of tax;
- payments from which tax is deducted (e.g. patent royalties). These may be allowed as a charge (see **Chapter 21, Section 21.2**).

20.10.1 Treatment of Certain Specific Items

Bad Debts

Historically, where there was a bad debts general provision, increases in the provision were not deductible as increases in general provisions are not deductible. Under IFRS and IFRS-influenced standards, bad debts generally do not require any adjustment for tax purposes as companies assess their financial assets, including trade receivables, to see whether those financial assets are impaired and so do not make general provisions. The impairments charged to the income statement (profit and loss account) are tax deductible and, if reversed, are taxable.

Entertainment Expenses

General entertainment expenses incurred are completely disallowed, e.g. entertainment of customers and suppliers. Entertainment includes the provision of accommodation, food, drink or any other form of hospitality, including the provision of gifts.

Expenditure on bona fide staff entertainment is not subject to the foregoing restrictions provided its provision is not incidental to the provision of entertainment to third parties. Expenditure incurred in relation to capital assets used for entertainment purposes is subject to similar restrictions.

Legal Expenses

Legal expenses include:

- debt recovery – allowable;
- acquisition of assets – not allowable;
- renewal of short lease – allowable;
- product liability claims and employee actions – allowable.

Repairs

Replacement/redecoration, repairs not involving material improvements – expenditure is allowable.

Leased Motor Vehicles

In the case of a leased vehicle, the list price of which exceeds €24,000 (the specified amount) when the car is first registered, the following restriction applies for accounting periods ending in 2019.

The leasing charges are restricted by:

$$\text{Total lease hire charges} \times \frac{\text{List price} - €24{,}000^{*}}{\text{List price}}$$

* €24,000 applies for accounting periods ending on or after 1 January 2007.

The amount of lease hire charges allowed depends on the CO_2 emissions category of the car. The following chart sets out the **carbon emissions restrictions on motor vehicles** for each CO_2 emissions category:

Category	**CO_2 Emissions**	**Restriction**
A	0–120g/km	Use the specified amount regardless of cost.
B and C	121–155g/km	
D and E	156–190g/km	Two steps to calculate limit: 1. take the lower of the specified limit or cost; 2. limit is 50% of this amount.
F and G	191+g/km	No allowance available.

Example 20.5

A company, which prepares annual accounts to 31 December, leased a new car in March 2019 when its retail price was €35,000. CO_2 emissions category B.

In the annual accounts to 31 December 2019, lease hire charges of €10,000 were incurred.

Disallow:

$$€10{,}000 \times \frac{€35{,}000 - €24{,}000}{€35{,}000} = €3{,}143 \text{ add-back}$$

Example 20.6

A company, which prepares annual accounts to 31 December, leased a new car in March 2019 when its retail price was €35,000. CO_2 emissions category D.

In the annual accounts to 31 December 2019, lease hire charges of €10,000 were incurred.

Disallow:

$$€10{,}000 \times \frac{€35{,}000 - (€24{,}000/2)}{€35{,}000} = €6{,}571 \text{ add-back}$$

If, alternatively, the retail price of the car was €20,000, the add-back would be 50% × €10,000 = €5,000.

If, alternatively, this were a category F car, the full €10,000 would be added back.

Example 20.7

A company, which prepares annual accounts to 31 December, leased a new car in March 2019 when its retail price was €20,000. CO_2 emissions category B.

In the annual accounts to 31 December 2019, lease hire charges of €10,000 were incurred.

$$€10{,}000 \times \frac{€20{,}000 - (€24{,}000)}{€20{,}000} = €2{,}000 \text{ additional deduction}$$

Where a car is in categories A, B or C and its list price is less than €24,000, there will always be an additional deduction.

Accountancy/Taxation Fees

- Normal accounting, auditing and taxation compliance costs are allowable.
- Special costs associated with Appeal Hearings are likely to be disallowed following the decision of *Allen v. Farquharson Bros & Co.* (1932) where the cost of employing solicitors and counsel in connection with an appeal against income tax assessments was held to be disallowed.

Pre-trading Expenses

Pre-trading expenses, as their name indicates, are incurred before the trade is commenced. As a general rule, pre-trading expenses are not tax deductible. However, tax law was changed so that certain pre-trading expenses are deductible in calculating trading income or losses once the trade commences.

The qualifying expenses are those:

- incurred within three years prior to the commencement; and
- which would be allowed as a deduction in calculating trading profits if they had been incurred after trading commenced.

Examples of qualifying pre-trading expenses include: accountancy fees, market research, feasibility studies, salaries, advertising, preparing business plans and rent. These pre-trading expenses are deductible against income of the trade.

Example 20.8

Ray Ltd commenced to trade on 1 July 2019. It incurred the following pre-trading expenditure:

		€
December 2015	Market research	8,000
December 2018	Director's salary	30,000
January 2019	Business entertainment	5,000
May 2019	Marketing expenditure	17,000

The market research expenditure is not deductible as it was not incurred within three years before the trade commenced. The business entertainment expenditure is never allowable. The expenditure on the director's salary and marketing are allowable. Therefore, Ray Ltd incurs deductible expenses of €47,000 on 1 July 2019. These are fully deductible in calculating the Case I income of the first accounting period.

Expenditure on Scientific Research

The full amount of any non-capital expenditure on scientific research is allowable as a deduction in computing the profits of a trade. In addition, sums paid to establishments approved by the Minister for Finance to carry on scientific research and sums paid to Irish universities to enable them to carry on scientific research are also deductible. This rule applies whether or not the payments are related to the existing trade currently being carried on.

Payments for Intangibles

There are special rules regarding the deduction for payments made to acquire intangibles – see **Section 20.11**.

Redundancy Payments

Statutory redundancy payments are specifically allowable. Amounts in excess of statutory entitlements are unlikely to be deductible where a cessation of trade has taken place but would be allowed if the trade continued.

Donations

Companies are entitled to a deduction, as a trading expense, for qualifying donations to eligible charities, educational institutions, schools, churches, research foundations and other approved organisations that satisfy certain conditions. The eligible organisation can be established anywhere in the European Economic Area (EEA) or the European Free Trade Association. Similarly, donations to an approved sports body (in the State) to enable it to purchase, construct or improve facilities and/or equipment are eligible. To qualify for a tax deduction, the donation(s) to an organisation or sports body in a 12-month accounting period must amount to at least €250. If the accounting period is less than 12 months, the €250 minimum is proportionately reduced. There is no upper limit.

Finance Leases

Where a leased asset is capitalised in the balance sheet, the amounts expensed in the income statement are interest expense and depreciation. The lease payment is not expensed to the income statement. Where the burden of the wear and tear of the asset is borne by the lessor – the typical situation – the lessee is not entitled to capital allowances. Instead the lessee is entitled to a **deduction for the lease payments** made. As only the interest element of the lease payment will have been expensed to the income statement, an adjustment is required, i.e. add back interest and instead allow a deduction for the full lease payment made.

Example 20.9

X Ltd leased a machine from Bank Ltd over a five-year period. Under accounting rules, X Ltd is required to capitalise the machine in its books. Under the terms of the lease agreement, the burden of wear and tear in respect of this machine falls on Bank Ltd. Therefore, X Ltd has no right to capital allowances.

During 2019, X Ltd paid lease payments of €10,000, of which €3,000 were expensed as interest to the income statement. In preparing the corporation tax computation for 2019, there will be:

- an add-back of €3,000 in respect of interest; and
- an additional deduction allowed for the lease payments made of €10,000.

Also, if there are any upfront payments, e.g. a lump sum paid at the start of the lease, these are allowed over the period of the lease and not in the first year.

If there is a rebate (refund) of lease rentals, typically at the end of the lease, the rebate is taxable when received.

Pension Contributions

Ordinary annual contributions by an employer to a Revenue-approved pension scheme for the benefit of employees are allowable for tax purposes in the year in which they are **paid**. Thus any accruals in respect of ordinary annual pension contributions due, which have been included in arriving at profit in the financial statements, will have to be disallowed.

If an employer makes a special contribution to a Revenue-approved pension scheme and the total amount of the special contributions made in the year does not exceed the total ordinary annual contributions paid in the year, relief is given for the special contributions in the year in which they are paid. If, however, the total amount of the special contributions paid exceeds the total ordinary annual contributions paid, relief for the special contributions made is spread forward over a number of years. The number of years over which relief is given is calculated by dividing the total special contributions paid by the total ordinary contributions paid. If the factor produced by this calculation is between one and two, relief is given over two years; otherwise, the factor is rounded to the nearest whole number, subject to a maximum of five years and a minimum divisor of €6,350.

Example 20.10
An employer makes the following pension contributions in 2019:

Ordinary annual contribution	€10,000
Special contribution	€27,000

As the special contribution made exceeds the ordinary annual contribution, relief for the special contribution will be spread forward. The number of years over which relief is given is calculated as follows:

$$\frac{\text{Special contribution}}{\text{Ordinary annual contribution}} = \frac{€27{,}000}{€10{,}000} = 2.7$$

As 2.7 is between 2 and 3, relief for the special contribution will be given over three years. In the first two years, the amount of relief given will equal the amount of the ordinary annual contribution, with the balance of the relief given in the third year. Accordingly, relief for the special contribution of €27,000 made in 2019 will be given as follows:

Tax Year	Relief Given
2019	€10,000
2020	€10,000
2021	€7,000

If the special contribution of €27,000 has been expensed in the income statement in 2019, there will be an add-back of €27,000 − €10,000 = €17,000 in 2019. However, there will be an additional deduction in 2020 and 2021, as outlined above.

If the amount of the ordinary annual contribution is less than €6,350, in calculating when relief for a special contribution is due, the amount of the ordinary annual contribution may be assumed to be €6,350.

Example 20.11
An employer makes the following contributions in 2019:

Ordinary annual contribution	€5,000
Special contribution	€8,000

As the special contribution made exceeds the ordinary annual contribution, relief for the special contribution will be spread forward. As the ordinary annual contribution is less than €6,350, in calculating relief due for the special contribution the ordinary annual contribution is deemed to be €6,350. The number of years over which relief is given is calculated as follows:

$$\frac{\text{Special contribution}}{\text{Ordinary annual contribution}} = \frac{€8{,}000}{€6{,}350} = 1.26$$

As 1.26 is between 1 and 2, relief is given over two years as follows:

Tax Year	Relief Given
2019	€6,350
2020	€1,650

Keyman Insurance

Keyman insurance is insurance taken out by a company in its own favour against the death, sickness or injury of an employee (the keyman) whose services are vital to the success of the employer's business.

In general, premiums paid under policies insuring against loss of profits consequent on certain contingencies are deductible for tax purposes in the period in which they are paid. Correspondingly, all sums received by an employer under such policies are treated as trading receipts in the period in which they are received. Keyman insurance policies qualify for this treatment where the following conditions are satisfied:

- the sole relationship is that of employer and employee;
- the employee does not have a substantial proprietary interest in the business (i.e. does not control more than 15% of ordinary share capital);
- the insurance is intended to meet loss of profit resulting from the loss of the services of the employee as distinct from the loss of goodwill or other capital loss; **and**
- in the case of insurance against death, the policy is a short-term insurance providing only for a sum to be paid in the event of the death of the insured within a specified number of years. Short-term generally means five years, but, in practice, if all other conditions are satisfied and the policy cannot extend beyond the employee's likely period of service with the business (i.e. not beyond his term of contract or beyond retirement age), then a term exceeding five years is treated as short-term.

If these conditions are not satisfied, there is no tax deduction. Usually any subsequent monies paid on a claim under the policy are not taxable.

Long-term Unemployed

Under the JobsPlus scheme, where an employer employs certain long-term unemployed individuals and other conditions are satisfied, the employer receives monthly cash payments over a two-year period from the Department of Social Protection. These payments are exempt from corporation tax.

Provisions made under IAS 37/FRS 102

Provisions made under IAS 37 *Provisions, Contingent Liabilities and Contingent Assets* and FRS 102 *The Financial Reporting Standard applicable in the UK and the Republic of Ireland*, which deal with provisions, contingent liabilities and contingent assets, are generally allowable for tax purposes, provided that the provision would be allowable under general rules if it were an expense, e.g. a provision in relation to a capital item would not be deductible.

Interest

Interest is **deductible** on an accruals basis if it is **trade** related, i.e. it is treated the same as the financial statements and therefore no adjustment is required. This is the case even if the money is borrowed to buy capital assets for trade purposes, which is due to a Revenue concession.

There are anti-avoidance rules which deny an interest deduction in certain situations.

Other interest, which is **not trade related, must be disallowed in calculating Case I**, if:

- it is interest on monies borrowed for a property generating rental income, the interest will be allowed as a Case V expense (provided that it is not pre-letting interest);
- it is interest on monies borrowed to lend to, or invest in, another company, it will either qualify for relief as a non-trade charge (see **Chapter 21** regarding conditions to be satisfied and note where it is claimed in the pro forma computation) or there is no relief for the expense.

Directors: Salaries and Company Cars

Bona fide directors' salaries, fees, benefits payable for directors are deductible, unlike the drawings/salary of a self-employed person. Such income is, of course, assessable in the hands of the individual director under Schedule E. Remuneration paid to directors is tax deductible, provided that it is not excessive.

Where a director has a company car available for private use, the full amount of motor expenses (other than restricted leased motor charges discussed above) is deductible. There is no deduction for the "personal element" for corporation tax purposes, unlike the personal element of a self-employed person. Again, a director with the use of a company car for private purposes will, of course, suffer tax on the benefit in kind.

Transfer Pricing

Tax legislation sets out transfer pricing rules that apply the arm's length principle to trading transactions between associated persons. In the absence of these rules, associated companies all over the world could buy and sell goods/services from each other at prices that maximise their taxable profits in low-tax jurisdictions and minimise their profits in high-tax jurisdictions.

Companies are associated if one controls the other, or both are controlled by the same person. Transfer pricing does not apply to groups that:

- employ less than 250 employees; and
- have a turnover not exceeding €50 million; or
- total assets not exceeding €43 million.

In Ireland, the transfer pricing rules apply to trading transactions between associated companies that result in the understatement of Case I and Case II income for Irish corporation tax purposes. If the amount payable exceeds the arm's length amount, or the amount receivable is less than the arm's length amount, then the Case I and Case II profit must be adjusted to reflect the arm's length amount.

> ***Example 20.12***
> Clifden Ltd sells goods to its subsidiary, Evergreen Ltd, at a price of €250 per unit. The arm's length price would have been €380 per unit. During the accounting period ended 31 December 2019, Clifden Ltd sold 1,000 of these items to Evergreen Ltd.
>
> A transfer pricing adjustment is made on the basis that the arm's length price was received. As a result, Clifden Ltd's taxable income for corporation tax is increased by €130,000 (1,000 × €130), as its profit was originally understated for tax purposes.
>
> Evergreen Ltd can adjust its allowable expenditure, reducing its taxable profit (or increasing its allowable loss) by €130,000 to reflect the arm's length price.

It is necessary to retain records that may reasonably be required to determine whether or not an arrangement exists for transfer pricing purposes.

20.11 Intangible Assets: Capital Allowances

(**Note:** the computations for capital allowance are beyond the scope of this textbook.)

There is tax relief for capital expenditure incurred by companies on the provision of intangible assets for the purposes of a trade. In summary, the legislation provides for capital allowances against taxable income on capital expenditure incurred by companies on the provision of intangible assets for the purposes of a trade. If the expenditure is incurred before trading commences, it will be allowed when the relevant trade commences.

The scheme applies to intangible assets that are recognised as such under generally accepted accounting practice and which are included in the specified categories listed in the legislation.

An asset may be recognised as an intangible asset in a company's financial statements only if:

- the cost of the asset can be reliably measured; and
- it is probable that future economic benefits attributable to the asset will flow to the enterprise.

The list of specified intangible assets includes: patents, registered designs, trade marks, brands, copyrights, domain names, customer lists, know-how and related goodwill to the extent that it relates to these categories of intangible property.

Companies are eligible for a writing-down allowance, which reflects the standard accounting treatment of intangible assets. However, companies can opt instead for a fixed write-down period of 15 years at a rate of **7% per annum and 2% in the final year**.

The normal rules in relation to balancing allowances/charges apply on the disposal of an intangible asset, with a significant exception.

There is no clawback of allowances where an intangible asset is disposed of more than five years after the beginning of the accounting period in which the asset was first provided. If the disposal is to a connected company, then it can only claim capital allowances of the lower of what it paid and the allowances not claimed by the previous owner.

There are a number of restrictions applying to ensure that:

1. relief is targeted to business **activities** (amounting to the conduct of a **relevant trade**) in which the specified intangible assets are used;
2. the aggregate amount of capital allowances and related interest that may be claimed in any accounting period is limited to 80% of the trading income of the relevant trade where the asset is acquired on or after 11 October 2017. Where the asset was acquired before this date, the aggregate amount of capital allowances and related interest that may be claimed in any accounting period is limited to the trading income of the relevant trade. Related interest in this context is interest incurred as a trading expense on borrowings to fund expenditure on intangible assets for which capital allowances are claimed. Where the relevant trade relates to assets acquired before and after 11 October 2017, the trading income is deemed to consist of two separate income streams, with the income apportioned reasonably. This results in capital allowances on assets acquired before 11 October 2017 not being available for offset against income arising from assets acquired after 11 October 2017 and any related interest; and
3. the capital allowances may only be offset against income from a "relevant trade", i.e. a trade consisting of:
   (a) managing, developing or exploiting the intangible assets; or
   (b) activities which consist of the sale of goods or services that derive the greater part of their value from the intangible assets or whose value is increased by the use of the intangible assets.

Example 20.13

	Accounting Period 1	**Accounting Period 2**
	€	€
Income from relevant trade before allowances	10 m	15 m
Capital allowances available under scheme*	11 m	9 m
Allowances carried forward from previous accounting period	NIL	3 m
Computation of income		
Income from relevant trade before allowances	10 m	15 m
Capital allowances (max. 80%)	8 m	12 m
Income chargeable	2 m	3 m
Allowances carried forward to next accounting period	3 m	NIL

* Intangible asset acquired after 11/10/2017.

The definition for intangible assets is the same as that for stamp duty exemption for qualifying intellectual property (see **Chapter 9, Section 9.1**).

20.12 Research & Development Tax Credit

20.12.1 Overview

The research and development (R&D) tax credit is provided for by section 766 TCA 1997 and allows a qualified company engaged in qualifying R&D activities to avail of a 25% tax credit on qualifying expenditure. The various qualifying conditions are explained in detail below.

Essentially, the R&D tax credit operates by reducing the corporation tax liability in two ways:

1. by deducting qualifying expenditure when calculating the taxable income, in the normal manner; and then
2. by applying the 25% R&D tax credit to the corporation tax liability.

There is no minimum spend required and there is no maximum limit on the qualifying expenditure. The 25% credit can be used to reward key employees (excluding directors) and/or to reduce the company's corporation tax payable and possibly get a refund of corporation tax.

20.12.2 Qualified Company

The R&D tax credit is available to all companies falling within the charge to Irish corporation tax that undertake qualifying R&D activities within the European Economic Area (EEA). In addition, the legislation specifies that "qualified company" is one that:

- carries on a trade itself, **or** is a 51% subsidiary of a trading company **or** is a member of a trading group (i.e. a 51% subsidiary of a holding company of a trading company);
- carries out R&D activities;
- maintains a record of its R&D expenditure; and
- maintains separate records if it has R&D activities in separate geographical locations.

As is evident from the first list item above, the legislation is drafted in terms applicable to groups of companies, a single company being treated as a group comprising one company. **Section 20.12.6** looks at groups in more detail.

20.12.3 Qualifying R&D Activities

The legislation defines R&D activities as "systematic, investigative or experimental activities in a field of science or technology", being one or more of the following:

- basic research;
- applied research; and
- experimental development.

Each of these is defined in tax law. In addition, activities will not be R&D activities unless they:

- "seek to achieve scientific or technological advancement; and
- involve the resolution of scientific or technological uncertainty."

However, the R&D does not have to be successful. Companies claiming the R&D tax credit are not required to hold the intellectual property rights resulting from the R&D work.

20.12.4 Qualifying R&D Expenditure

In general, expenditure incurred by a company on R&D activities carried out in an EU or an EEA Member State qualifies for the R&D tax credit. However, in the case of an Irish tax-resident company, the credit is available only if the expenditure on the R&D does not otherwise qualify for a tax benefit elsewhere. Also, this law does not apply to expenditure on a building or structure – see **Section 20.12.5** for the rules on buildings used for R&D.

For expenditure to be regarded as expenditure on R&D for the purposes of the tax credit, it must qualify for tax relief in the State under one of the following:

- as an allowable deduction of a trade (e.g. payroll) or as a charge on income (see **Chapter 21, Section 21.2**) (or would be but for accounting rules) – this does not include capital allowances;
- as capital allowances on plant or machinery, or under special rules that provide for an allowance for capital expenditure on scientific research; or
- as other expenditure that qualifies for scientific research allowance.

Where plant or machinery will not be used wholly and exclusively for R&D activities, a proportionate allocation of the expenditure, as appears to be just and reasonable, will be made.

In general, the cost of subcontracting or outsourcing R&D will not qualify for the tax credit. However, monies paid to a university or institute of higher education to conduct R&D activity on behalf of a company may qualify for a restricted amount of credit. Expenditure up to €100,000 or 5% of the company's total R&D expenditure in that accounting period, whichever is the higher, will qualify. Similarly, R&D activities subcontracted to unconnected parties may qualify, up to a limit of €100,000 or 15% of the company's total R&D spend in that accounting period, whichever is higher.

Interest payments do not qualify as expenditure on R&D. Expenditure that is met by any EU or EEA grant assistance is not considered to be expenditure incurred by the company and will therefore not be eligible for the credit. Expenditure incurred under cost sharing or pooling arrangements will qualify for the tax credit only to the extent that the expenditure is incurred by the qualified company in the carrying on by it of qualifying R&D activities. If the company carrying on the R&D in Ireland receives a cost-sharing contribution from another company in the international group, this receipt is ignored, i.e. it is the gross expenditure on R&D that is taken into account. Reimbursements or sharing of costs incurred by another company in the carrying on of R&D activities would not qualify.

Documentary evidence must be maintained in respect of the credit claim. This includes details of the technical aspects of the project, the skills of the R&D team, as well as the basis for the actual costs and time incurred on the project.

20.12.5 Buildings Used for R&D

A 25% credit will also be available for capital expenditure on buildings or structures used for the purpose of carrying on an R&D activity. Such expenditure can qualify provided that at least 35% of the use of the building, over a specified four-year period, is for R&D purposes (section 766A TCA 1997). Qualifying relevant expenditure includes construction, reconstruction, repair or renewal of a building, but not the cost of the site, and expenditure qualifying for the industrial buildings allowance. The expenditure will not qualify if it qualifies for tax relief in another EEA country.

Where only part of a building is used for R&D purposes, the relevant expenditure on the building will be restricted to the proportion used for R&D purposes (i.e. specified relevant expenditure). For example, if 50% of the building is to be used for R&D activities, then only 50% of the construction expenditure will be "specified relevant expenditure".

The tax credit is utilised in the same manner as set out in **Section 20.12.8**.

Example 20.14

Rev Ltd constructed a building in Kildare in the accounting period ended 31 December 2019 at a cost of €1 million, including site cost of €240,000. The R&D activities to be carried on by the company in that building over the specified relevant period will represent 40% of all activities carried on in the building or structure. The tax credit is calculated as follows:

	€
Building costs	1,000,000
Less: site cost	(240,000)
Relevant expenditure	760,000
Specified relevant expenditure	760,000 @ 40% = €304,000
Tax credit	304,000 @ 25% = €76,000

The full amount of the tax credit of €76,000 is used to reduce the corporation tax liability in respect of the accounting period ended 31 December 2019. If any excess remains, it may be carried back to reduce the corporation tax of the preceding accounting period. A refund of any unused credits may be claimed, as outlined at **Section 20.12.8**. Unused credits may be carried forward indefinitely.

20.12.6 Groups

The definition of a group is the same as that for loss relief purposes as outlined in **Chapter 23**, except that the shareholding requirement is only 51%, i.e. a parent and its 51% subsidiaries form a group. In addition, companies are treated as being in the same group, for the purposes of this credit, if they are under common control.

Those members of a group that incur R&D expenditure in the current period may allocate the expenditure between them as they wish. Any such allocation is to be specified in writing to the Inspector of Taxes. If no allocation is made, the relief is allocated between the group members that incurred qualifying expenditure in the current period in the same proportion as the amount of total group expenditure the company incurred, i.e. if a group member incurred 50% of the group qualifying R&D expenditure in the current period, that group member will be allocated 50% of the relief available to the group.

Corporation tax of an accounting period of a company can be reduced by 25% of so much of the qualifying expenditure of the group on R&D as has been allocated to the company.

Where, in an accounting period, the amount of the credit exceeds the corporation tax against which it can be offset, the excess is to be carried back for offset against corporation tax payable in the preceding accounting period and a refund of any unused credits may be claimed, as outlined at **Section 20.12.8**. Unused credits can be carried forward indefinitely.

20.12.7 Reward Key Employees

The 25% R&D tax credit can be used to reward key employees working in the R&D activities of the company. To qualify, the employee must not be a director or own 5% or more of the company or an associated company. At least 50% of the employee's emoluments must qualify for the R&D tax credit and the employee must perform 50% or more of the duties of his or her employment in the conception or creation of new knowledge, products, processes, methods or systems. The employee can claim the R&D credit against his or her income tax payable. An employee's maximum claim is limited in that the employee's effective income tax rate cannot be reduced below 23%. Unclaimed credits can be carried forward by the individual. If the credit or some of it is given to the employee(s), then that part of the credit is not available to the company to offset against corporation tax.

Example 20.15

High Tech Ltd, a technology company, is an Irish subsidiary of a US multinational. It has had an R&D programme for a number of years. During 2019, it significantly expanded its R&D programme. Its R&D spend was as follows:

- new building, all of which is used for R&D, at a cost of €2 million, of which €200,000 was the cost of the site;
- €200,000 on new machinery; and
- €300,000 on salaries, overheads, etc.

High Tech Ltd has a cost-sharing agreement with its US parent company and fellow subsidiaries. As a result, it received a contribution of €350,000 from these companies towards the cost of its R&D programme. High Tech Ltd satisfies the conditions regarding genuine R&D (maintaining records, etc.). High Tech Ltd's corporation tax payable for the year ended 31 December 2019, before R&D credit, is €582,000.

What is the R&D tax credit due to High Tech Ltd for the year ended 31 December 2019 and what is the final corporation tax payable, assuming that €25,000 of the credits are surrendered to key employee(s) working in R&D?

Tax credit due on qualifying R&D expenditure	€
Machinery	200,000
Salaries, overheads, etc.	300,000
Qualifying for credit	500,000
R&D tax credit @ 25%	125,000
Less: surrendered to key R&D staff	25,000
Credit due against corporation tax	100,000
Tax credit due on R&D building	
Expenditure on building	2,000,000
Less: site cost	(200,000)
	1,800,000
Total credit due re. building @ 25%	450,000
Corporation tax payable	
Originally due	582,000
Less: R&D tax credits	(100,000)
R&D tax credit re. building	(450,000)
Corporation tax payable	32,000

20.12.8 Reduce Corporation Tax

Any credit not given to a key employee working in R&D can be claimed against corporation tax. Claims must be made within 12 months of the end of the accounting period.

- The credit is used to **first reduce** the liability to **corporation tax for that accounting period.**
- The company may then offset any unused portion of the credit against the corporation tax of the **preceding accounting period.**
- Where a company has offset the credit against the corporation tax of the preceding accounting period or where no corporation tax arises for that period, and an excess still remains, the company may make a claim to have the amount of that **excess paid** to it by the Revenue Commissioners in **three instalments**. The three instalments will be paid over a period of at least 33 months, from the end of the accounting period in which the expenditure was incurred.

Students are required to do a computation involving claiming the credit against corporation tax payable, but are not required to do a calculation involving a repayment of the credit.

- There is a limit on the amount of tax credits payable to a company by Revenue. The limit refers to expenditure on R&D activities and on buildings which qualify for the credit. The amount cannot exceed the greater of:
  - the corporation tax payable by the company for the 10 years prior to the accounting period preceding the period in which the expenditure was incurred, or
  - the amount of PAYE, PRSI and USC the company is required to remit in the period in which the expenditure was incurred and in the previous accounting period, as adjusted for prior claims.
- Any credit that has not been offset against corporation tax or refunded is available to offset against corporation tax of future accounting periods.

Example 20.16

In the accounting period ended 31 December 2019, PQR Ltd incurred €400,000 of qualifying expenditure on R&D. The following shows the company's corporation tax liability:

	CT Liability
12 months ended 31/12/2018	€30,000
12 months ended 31/12/2019	€10,000
12 months ended 31/12/2020	€15,000
12 months ended 31/12/2021	€10,000

R&D tax credit due in respect of the accounting period ended 31/12/2019:

€400,000 @ 25% = €100,000

Of this €100,000, €20,000 is surrendered to key employees working in R&D.

Offset remaining R&D tax credit as follows:

	CT Liability	**Order**	**Tax credit**
12 months ended 31/12/2019	€10,000	1	€10,000
12 months ended 31/12/2018	€30,000	2	€30,000

The unclaimed credit of €100,000 – €20,000 – €10,000 – €30,000 = €40,000 may be reclaimed from Revenue over the next three years or so, to the extent it has not been used to offset against corporation tax of subsequent accounting periods. This repayment assumes that the company has paid sufficient corporation tax, PAYE, PRSI and USC in 2019 and 2018.

20.12.9 Clawback

If the building or structure, expenditure on which qualified for a R&D credit, is sold or ceases to be used by the company for R&D activities or for the purpose of the same trade that was carried on by the company at the start of the "specified relevant period" within 10 years of being incurred for the purposes of R&D, no further credit is to be given and any credit given will be clawed back. The clawback is by way of a Case IV assessment of four times the credit granted, which is then taxed at 25% to equal the amount of the credit originally granted.

Legislation also provides for a clawback in the case of a claim for a repayment or surrender of credits found to be incorrect in any material particular. Again the clawback is by way of a Case IV assessment of four times the excess repayment claimed/surrendered, which is then taxed at 25% to equal the excessive amount originally claimed/surrendered. However, the clawback amount is equal to eight times the amount of the excess credit surrendered to key employees in the case of a claim that is found to be deliberately false or overstated.

Penalties and interest charges for late payment of tax will apply where a clawback occurs.

Questions

Review Questions

(See Suggested Solutions to Review Questions at the end of this textbook.)

Question 20.1

Telstar Ltd commenced trading in 2001 and makes up its accounts each year to 31 December. The income statement to 31 December 2019 is as follows:

		€	€
Gross profit			239,800
IDA grant for extension of premises			10,000
IDA employment grant			1,000
Patent royalty (net) (Note 1)			1,600
Discount received			3,300
Dividends from Irish quoted shares			1,300
Profit on sale of van (Note 2)			1,000
Profit on sale of shares (Note 3)			2,000
Bank deposit interest (paid gross)			600
			260,600
Less:	Discount given	3,000	
	Goods stolen	3,000	
	Business overdraft interest	5,800	
	Depreciation	15,149	
	Van expense	3,400	
	Motor expenses (Note 4)	6,800	
	Bad debts	2,300	
	Obsolete inventories – written off	2,600	
	Salaries and wages	95,840	
	Telephone	311	
	Entertainment (Note 5)	2,700	
	Finance lease charges (Note 6)	1,300	
	Legal fees (Note 7)	2,400	144,600
Profit before tax			116,000

Notes:

1. The patent royalty was received in December 2019.
2. Profit on sale of van – the van was acquired second-hand on 03/02/2016 for €12,000. It was sold on 05/05/2019 for €4,000. The net book value of the van at 31/12/2018 was €3,000.
3. Profit on sale of shares – these shares were acquired on 31/03/2001 for €4,000 and sold on 30/04/2019 for €6,000.

4. There are two cars:

Mercedes purchased second-hand on 30/06/2019	€
Cost	28,000
Expenses	800
Category B car leased on 01/02/2017	
Cost	25,000
Operating lease payments	6,000

5. The charge for entertainment is made up as follows:

	€
Prizes for top salesperson of the year	900
Christmas party for staff	750
Christmas gifts for suppliers	150
Reimbursement of managing director for costs incurred entertaining customers at home	350
General customer entertainment	550
	2,700

6. Finance lease charges – these relate to a machine leased in 2017, the cost of which is capitalised in the company's accounts. The lease agreement states that the burden of wear and tear remains with the lessor. Total repayments made during the year ended 31 December 2019 were €9,400, which included both capital repayments and finance charges.
7. The legal fees relate to the extension of the premises.
8. Capital allowances for the year are €7,272.
9. The company paid €80,000 of corporation tax on its 2018 profits.

Requirement
Calculate the corporation tax liability for the year ended 31 December 2019 and show the dates on which it is payable.

Question 20.2

The income statement of Zaco Ltd for the year ended 30 September 2019 is as follows:

	€	€
Sales		2,450,000
Cost of sales		(1,959,750)
Gross profit		490,250
Less: Salaries and wages	62,500	
Rent and rates	5,400	
Repairs (Note 1)	16,100	
Insurance	1,720	
Professional fees (Note 2)	1,600	
Depreciation	13,000	
Audit Fees	1,000	
Subscriptions (Note 3)	2,400	
Entertainment (Note 4)	600	
Staff award (Note 5)	1,000	

Discount allowed	320	
Bank interest	7,060	
Light and heat	12,250	(124,950)
Add: Dividends (Note 6)	3,000	
Bad debts recovered	300	
Profit on sale of investments (Note 7)	5,200	
Interest on tax overpaid	1,200	
Profit on sale of fixtures and fittings (Note 8)	4,300	14,000
Profit before tax		379,300

Notes:

1. Repairs: includes improvements to offices of €5,200.
2. Professional fees: includes debt collection fees of €200 and architect's fees re office improvements of €300.
3. Subscriptions: includes political donations of €750 and staff race sponsorship of €1,000.
4. Entertainment: made up as follows:

	€
Customer entertainment	450
Supplier entertainment	150
	600

5. Staff award: a special award of €1,000 was made to an employee who achieved first place in Ireland in his engineering examinations during the year.
6. Dividends:

   Irish dividends – cash amount €3,000

7. Sale of investments:

Irish Treasury Bonds – Irish Government Security	€	€
Cost May 2015	2,148	
Proceeds June 2019	2,800	652
Shares in quoted investment company		
Cost June 1997	1,000	
Proceeds July 2019	5,548	4,548
		5,200

8. Profit on sale of plant: cost €8,000 in August 2017 and sold for €11,100 in September 2019. Net book value was €6,800 on 30/09/2018.
9. The capital allowances (including balancing allowances and charges) are €9,846.
10. There are capital losses forward of €10,000.

Requirement
Calculate the company's corporation tax liability for the year.

Question 20.3

Overseas Limited, a distribution company that is resident in Taxland and under the control of individuals resident in Taxland, has been trading in Ireland for many years through a branch.

The company has the following income during the year ended 31 December 2019:

	€
Trading profits	900,000
(including branch trading profits of €600,000)	
Interest income from surplus funds invested by branch	20,000
(received gross)	
Dividends received from:	
Australian subsidiary	10,000

The Irish branch had chargeable gains, before adjustment, on the sales of premises out of which the branch traded of €32,000 in December 2019.

The company also owned development land in the State, not used for the purposes of the branch, which was sold in August 2019 to a manufacturer and realised a capital gain of €50,000. This land had been acquired in 1997.

Requirement
Calculate the relevant Irish tax liabilities of Overseas Limited.

21

Income Tax on Annual Payments and Charges on Income

Learning Objectives

After studying this chapter you will be able to:

- Advise on how a company must apply the appropriate treatment to income tax withheld on certain annual payments.
- Determine when certain expenses are treated as "charges" and to apply the appropriate corporation tax treatment depending on the type of "charge".

21.1 Annual Payments and Patent Royalty Payments

A company must deduct income tax at 20% when making certain annual payments and patent royalty payments. This income tax must be paid over to Revenue by the company on behalf of the payee (see next paragraph). The income tax will be treated as part of the paying company's corporation tax liability (see pro forma computation in **Chapter 20, Section 20.2**), including for preliminary tax purposes.

Where a company receives income from which Irish income tax has been deducted, such income is assessed under Case IV (see **Section 20.3**) on the gross amount. It will then be allowed a tax credit for the income tax withheld at source against its corporation tax liability (see pro forma, **Section 20.2**).

Income tax does not have to be deducted from annual interest paid to a bank in the normal course of business. Most annual payments (and any exceptions) are beyond the scope of this textbook. Those relevant for CA Proficiency 2 are:

- annual interest, including interest paid to close company directors and their associates (see **Section 26.2.2**);
- patent royalties;
- rents paid to non-residents in respect of property in the State; and
- loans to participators in close companies (see **Section 26.2**).

21.2 Charges on Income

21.2.1 General

Certain payments, such as interest, annual payments and patent royalties, rank as "charges on income" and are allowed as deductions of the accounting period in which they are **paid**. Charges on income incurred before a trade commences are treated as paid when the trade commences, i.e. are deductible as a charge in the first year of trading. If income tax is to be withheld from the payment (as outlined in **Section 21.1**), it is the **gross** amount that is deductible when calculating taxable profits for corporation tax. The income tax withheld is then added to the corporation tax liability of the accounting period in which the payment is made.

Charges on income that are relevant trade charges (i.e. wholly and exclusively for trade purposes, e.g. patent royalties) are allowed **against trading income** in the accounting period in which they are paid (relief for excess trade charges is outlined in **Chapter 22, Section 22.2**). Non-trade charges, i.e. charges other than relevant trade charges, such as "protected interest" (see **Section 21.2.3**) may be offset against total profits, including chargeable gains, in the period in which they were paid. Non-trade charges are generally offset against income, taxed at 25%, in priority to profits, taxed at 12.5%. There is no relief for excess non-trade charges.

21.2.2 Amounts Treated as Charges

For the purposes of this discussion, the following amounts, subject to the above, are treated as "charges on income":

1. Yearly interest (other than interest allowable in computing profits chargeable under Case I and Case V).
2. Patent royalties.
3. Any other interest payable in the State on an advance from a bona fide bank or a bona fide discount house or a bona fide stock exchange member in the EU.

21.2.3 Interest Qualifying as a Charge

A company may obtain relief for interest as a non-trade charge against total profits where it uses the borrowings to acquire shares in or lend money to certain companies. This type of interest, known as "protected interest", qualifies as a non-trade charge if it cannot be deducted in computing trading profits or rental income and the following conditions are satisfied:

1. The investing company uses the borrowings to:
   (a) acquire part of the ordinary share capital of a company
      (i) which exists wholly or mainly for the purpose of carrying on a trade or whose income consists wholly or mainly of rental income; or
      (ii) whose business consists wholly or mainly of holding shares in a company as described above, and, where the loan is used to subscribe for share capital, the company into which the investment is made uses the funds received for the purpose of its trade or rental business; or
   (b) lend to such a company at (a) where the money is used by the borrower, or a connected company, wholly and exclusively for the purpose of their trade or rental business; or
   (c) pay off another loan applied for the purposes of (a) or (b) above.

2. At the time the interest is paid, the investing company must have a "material interest" in the company that uses the money, i.e. owns or controls **more than 5% of the ordinary share capital of the other company**.
3. At least one **director** of the investing company must be a director of the company that uses the money throughout the period from the application of the proceeds of the loan until the interest is paid, i.e. they share a "common director".
4. During the period of the loan, there must be no recovery of capital by the investing company. An investing company is regarded as recovering capital from the company if:

   (a) the investing company sells any of its shares or the company repays any share capital;
   (b) the company or a connected company repays a loan to the investing company;
   (c) the investing company receives consideration for the assignment of any debt due to it by the company.

There are also anti-avoidance provisions in the law to stop perceived abuses of the relief.

Example 21.1
In the year ended 31 December 2019 a company had the following results:

	€
Case I	100,000
Case V	50,000
Trade charges (patent royalties paid under deduction of tax)	10,000 (gross)
Non-trade charges (interest paid under deduction of tax)	30,000 (gross)

Corporation tax computation:	€
Case I	100,000
Trade charges	(10,000)
	90,000
Case V	50,000
Total profits	140,000
Non-trade charges	(30,000)
Taxable	110,000
€90,000 @ 12.5%	11,250
(€50,000 – €30,000) = €20,000 @ 25%	5,000
	16,250
Income tax withheld from charges:	
€40,000 @ 20%	8,000
Corporation tax due	24,250

Questions

Review Questions

(See Suggested Solutions to Review Questions at the end of this textbook.)

Question 21.1

Nifty Investments Ltd had the following results for the year ended 31 March 2019:

	€
Trading profits	90,000
– After charging the following amounts:	
Depreciation	10,000
Patent royalties (paid August 2018)	8,000 (Net)
Interest paid to an Irish bank on monies borrowed to invest in a company – conditions satisfied to qualify as protected interest	9,000
– After crediting:	
Loan interest received October	6,000 (Net €4,800 actually received)
Bank interest received October	1,000 (Gross)
Chargeable gain before adjustment (January 2019)	10,000

Requirement
Compute the corporation tax payable by Nifty Investments Ltd for the year ended 31 March 2019.

Question 21.2

From the following information you are required to calculate the corporation tax liability of Alpha Ltd for the year ended 31 December 2019.

Income Statement

	Notes	€	€
Sales			3,450,000
Cost of sales			(2,850,000)
Gross profit			600,000
Less: Salaries and wages	(1)	71,300	
Rent and rates	(2)	7,600	
Repairs	(3)	18,500	
Insurance	(4)	1,350	
Loss on sale of investments	(5)	600	
Legal expenses	(6)	2,700	
Commissions		9,209	
Depreciation		13,260	

Audit fees		1,550	
Subscriptions	(7)	3,400	
Discounts allowed		900	
Bank interest	(8)	3,300	
Other interest	(9)	7,000	
Light and heat		11,234	
Motor expenses	(10)	33,126	
Sundry	(11)	3,740	
Entertainment expenses	(12)	1,191	
Finance lease charges	(13)	1,700	(191,660)
Add: Irish dividends	(14)	4,500	
Gain on sale of Irish shares	(15)	1,000	
Enterprise Ireland employment grant		240	
Interest on tax overpaid		475	
Interest on Irish treasury bonds		2,500	
Rent received		6,000	
Deposit interest (received gross)		1,500	
Bad debts		50	16,265
Profit before tax			424,605

Notes:

1. Salaries and wages include €25,000 in respect of staff bonuses relating to the year ended 31 December 2019, which were not paid until 5 January 2020.
2. Rent and rates include an amount of €1,000 relating to part of the company's premises which has been let to a sub-tenant.
3. Repairs include an amount of €15,000 for an extension to the factory premises.
4. Insurance includes an amount of €350 relating to the let premises.
5. Loss on sale of investments:

   UK shares purchased 2014

	€	€
Cost	10,000	
Proceeds		9,400

6. Legal expenses:

Debt collection	700
Extension to factory	2,000
	2,700

7. Subscriptions:

Chamber of commerce	430
Local football club	20
Trade association	1,135
Political	1,815
	3,400

8. Bank interest – includes an amount of €1,500 relating to borrowings taken out to finance the extension to the factory premises.
9. Other interest – interest on monies borrowed from bank to acquire shares in a trading subsidiary, where Alpha Ltd is represented on the board and there has been no recovery of capital. €7,000 gross was paid during the year.
10. Motor expenses – the company leased six new motor cars on 1 April 2018, CO_2 emissions category B. The retail price of each, at the time the lease contracts were entered into, was €25,000.

    The motor expenses can be analysed as follows:

	€
Leasing charges on leased cars	21,126
Running costs of leased cars	12,000
	33,126

11. Sundry:

	€
Interest on late payments of VAT	1,630
Parking fines	30
Christmas party	500
Gifts to customers	541
General office expenses	1,039
	3,740

12. Entertainment:

	€
Hotel and accommodation for overseas customers	1,191

13. Finance lease charges – these relate to new machinery leased in 2017, the cost of which is capitalised in the company's accounts. The lease agreement states that the burden of wear and tear remains with the lessor. Total repayments made during the year ended 31 December 2019 were €12,200, which included both capital repayments and finance charges.

14. Irish dividends:

	€
Dividend on quoted shares	1,500
Dividend from subsidiary	3,000
	4,500

15. Sale of Irish quoted shares:

	€
Cost (July 2014)	19,000
Proceeds (January 2019)	20,000
Gain	1,000

16. Capital allowances for the accounting period are €26,006.

22

Corporation Tax Loss Relief

Learning Objectives

After studying this chapter you will be able to:

- Implement efficient utilisation of trading losses, excess charges, non-trade losses, certain capital allowances and capital losses.
- Advise on and calculate restrictions on loss relief following a change of ownership or late submission of corporation tax returns.

22.1 Relief for Trading Losses (other than Terminal Losses)

Where a company incurs a trading loss it may obtain relief from corporation tax for the loss as follows:

1. By carry forward from an earlier accounting period against income of the same trade (section 396(1) TCA 1997).
2. By set off against relevant trading income (section 396A(3)):
   (a) in the same accounting period; and
   (b) in the immediately preceding period of the same length.
3. By claiming relief for the loss on a "value" basis (section 396B(3)):
   (a) in the same accounting period; and
   (b) in the immediately preceding period of the same length.

Each of these methods is discussed in greater detail in **Chapter 24, Sections 24.1.1–24.1.3** below. The above order reflects the order that losses are deducted in the corporation tax computation (see **Chapter 20, Section 20.2**).

A claim for loss relief under sections 396A and 396B must be made within two years of the end of the accounting period in which the loss occurs. A section 396A claim must be made before a claim can be made under section 396B. There is no time limit for claiming section 396(1) loss relief as the loss can be carried forward indefinitely.

A loss can only be claimed once. For example, a loss claimed under section 396A against other trading income is not available under section 396B (value basis) or to carry forward section 396(1).

Most trading losses that you encounter will be 'relevant trading losses'. A relevant trading loss is a loss incurred in an accounting period in a trade carried on by a company that, if it were a profit, it would be relevant trading income for corporation tax purposes. Relevant trading income is the company's trading income taxable at the 12.5% rate, excluding income from leasing or excepted trades (i.e. land dealing and developing, excluding construction operations, mining and petroleum).

Excepted trades are beyond the scope of this textbook. Accordingly, losses are assumed to be relevant trading losses unless otherwise stated.

It is recommended that a record is kept for each loss detailing each claim for relief made (i.e. a 'loss memo').

22.1.1 Carry Forward of a Trading Loss

A trading loss in an accounting period may be carried forward under section 396(1) indefinitely and set off against income from the **same trade** in succeeding accounting periods.

A loss forward must be set off against the first available income of the same trade for an earlier future accounting period in priority to a later future accounting period (i.e. a future accounting period cannot be skipped). When carried forward, a section 396(1) loss is deducted from the income from the same trade in priority to any section 396A loss relief (see **Section 22.1.2**).

Example 22.1

ABC Ltd, a distribution company, had the following results for the years ended 31 December 2018 and 2019.

	2018	2019
	€	€
Case I profit/(loss)	(50,000)	60,000
Taxable income (Case I)	Nil	60,000
Less: section 396(1) relief		(50,000)
Taxable income	Nil	10,000

22.1.2 Trading Loss Offset against Relevant Trading Income (section 396A)

Under section 396A TCA 1997, a trading loss can be offset against relevant trading income in the same accounting period. This will only arise if the company has more than one trade. If the loss cannot be fully offset against trading income in the current accounting period, the unutilised trading loss can be set against relevant trading income in the immediately preceding period of equal length to the accounting period in which the loss was incurred.

The relevant trading income of an accounting period against which a loss is to be set off is that as first reduced by losses brought forward from earlier accounting periods (see **Section 22.1.1**).

Example 22.2

DEF Ltd, a distribution company, had the following results for the years ended 31 December 2018 and 2019.

	2018	2019
	€	€
Case I profit/(loss)	30,000	(50,000)
Taxable income (Case I)	30,000	Nil
Less: section 396A(3) relief	(30,000)	
Taxable income	Nil	Nil

The unutilised loss of €20,000 may be relieved by carrying it forward for offset against profits arising from the same trade in future accounting periods (as in **Section 22.1.1**); or, if the company has a corporation tax liability in the current or preceding period of equal length, relief could be claimed for the remaining loss on a "value" basis (see **Section 22.1.3**).

If the accounting period in which the loss is incurred is shorter than the accounting period to which the loss is to be offset, then only a proportion of the relevant trading income will be available for offset.

Example 22.3: Accounting periods of different lengths
GHI Ltd, a distribution company, had the following results for the year ended 31 December 2018 and for the nine-month accounting period ended 30 September 2019.

	2018 (12 months)	2019 (9 months)
	€	€
Case I profit/(loss)	30,000	(60,000)
Taxable income (Case I)	30,000	Nil
Less: section 396A(3) relief (Note)	(22,500)	
Taxable income	7,500	Nil

Note: as the loss arose in an accounting period nine months long, it may only be offset against 9/12ths of the relevant trading income for the year ended 31 December 2018.

The remaining loss of €37,500 may be relieved by carrying it forward against future profits from the same trade, or on the "value" basis if GHI Ltd had income and gains giving rise to a corporation tax liability in the current or preceding period of equal length.

Example 22.4: Accounting periods of different lengths
MNO Ltd, a distribution company, had the following results for the year ended 31 March 2018, the nine months ended 31 December 2018 and for the year ended 31 December 2019.

	Y/E 31/3 2018 (12)	P/E 31/12 2018 (9)	Y/E 31/12 2019 (12)
	€	€	€
Case I profit/(loss)	30,000	20,000	(60,000)
Taxable income (Case I)	30,000	20,000	Nil
Less: section 396A(3) relief (Note)	(7,500)	(20,000)	
Taxable income	22,500	Nil	Nil

Note: the loss-making period was 12 months long, therefore the loss can be offset against a 12-month period. As the immediately preceding accounting period was only nine months long, relevant trading income for three months of the previous accounting period can be relieved as there are sufficient losses, i.e. against 3/12ths of Case I income for the year ended 31 March 2018.

The remaining loss of €32,500 may be relieved by carrying it forward against future profits from the same trade, or on the "value" basis if MNO Ltd has a corporation tax liability in the current or preceding period of equal length.

22.1.3 Relief for Relevant Trading Losses on a Value Basis (section 396B)

Section 396B allows relief for an unutilised trading loss against the relevant corporation tax liability of the company in the current accounting period and in the immediately preceding period of same length on a "value" basis, i.e. the relevant corporation tax liability can be reduced by the tax value of the trading loss. As relevant trading income is taxed at 12.5%, the tax value of available trading losses is 12.5% of the remaining loss. The relevant corporation tax of the company is the corporation tax liability not including any withholding taxes or close company surcharges (see **Section 26.3**).

Before a claim can be made under section 396B, a full claim must have been made under section 396A (offsetting against relevant trading income), with the 396B claim reduced by the amount that has already been offset. In fact, even if a claim for relief has not been made under section 396A, the amount of the relevant trading loss for which relief may be claimed on a value basis is reduced by the amount for which relief *could have* been claimed under section 396A.

As with section 396A claims, section 396B claims are made first, on the value basis, against the relevant corporation tax for the accounting period in which the loss occurs, and any remaining loss is then claimed, on the value basis, against the relevant corporation tax of the immediately preceding period of equal length to the current accounting period.

In calculating the loss relief that can be claimed under section 396B it is necessary to calculate the corporation tax liability of the company after claiming section 396A relief.

Example 22.5

PQR Ltd, a distribution company, had the following results for the years ended 31 December 2018 and 2019.

	2018	2019
	€	€
Case I profit/(loss)	30,000	(55,000)
Case V income	10,000	10,000

Corporation tax computation		
Case I	30,000	Nil
Less: section 396A(3) relief	(30,000)	
Taxable Case I income	Nil	Nil
Case V income	10,000	10,000
Corporation tax @ 25%	2,500	2,500
Less: section 396B relief (Note)	(625)	(2,500)
Corporation tax payable	1,875	Nil

Note

Losses available for relief on a value basis:

	€
Total loss	55,000
Offset under section 396A	(30,000)
Losses available for relief under section 396B	25,000
"Value" of losses:	
€25,000 × 12.5% = €3,125	
Tax value of losses	3,125
Section 396B 2019	(2,500)
	625
Section 396B 2018 (max. available)	(625)
Remaining tax value	NIL

Again, as with section 396A claims, if the accounting period in which the loss is incurred is shorter than the accounting period to which the loss is to be offset, then only a proportion of the relevant trading income will be available for offset.

Example 22.6: Accounting periods of different lengths

STU Ltd, a distribution company, had the following results for the year ended 31 December 2018 and for the nine-month accounting period ended 30 September 2019.

	2018	2019
	(12)	(9)
	€	€
Case I profit/(loss)	30,000	(200,000)
Case V income	20,000	20,000
Corporation tax computation		
Case I	30,000	Nil
Less: section 396A(3) relief (Note 1)	(22,500) (i)	
Taxable Case I income	7,500	Nil
Case V income	20,000	20,000
Taxable income	27,500	20,000
Corporation tax payable:		
@ 12.5%	937	Nil
@ 25%	5,000	5,000
	5,937	5,000
Less: section 396B relief (Note 2)	(4,453) (iii)	(5,000) (ii)
Corporation tax payable	1,484	Nil

(i) to (iii) show the sequence of the loss claims.

Notes:

1. As the loss arose in an accounting period nine months long, it may only be offset against 9/12ths of the relevant trading income for the year ended 31/12/2018.
2. Relief on a value basis may only be claimed against 9/12ths of the corporation tax payable for the year ended 31/12/2018. The corporation tax for the year ending on 31/12/2018 is €5,937. Therefore, the maximum relief is €5,937 × 9/12ths, i.e. €4,453.

Loss Memo

	Losses	**Tax Value**
	€	€
Total loss 2019	200,000	
Less: section 396A 2018	(22,500)	
Unused trading loss	177,500	
Tax value (i.e. €177,500 @ 12.5%)		22,188
Less: section 396B 2019	(40,000)	(5,000)
	137,500	17,188
Less: section 396B 2018 (€5,937 × 9/12ths)	(35,622)	(4,453)
Losses available for carry forward section 396(1)	101,878	12,735

Example 22.7

VWX Ltd, a distribution company, had the following results for the year ended 31 December 2018, the nine months ended 30 September 2019 and for the year ended 30 September 2020.

	Y/E 31/12 2018 (12 months)	P/E 30/9 2019 (9 months)	Y/E 30/9 2020 (12 months)
	€	€	€
Case I profit/(loss)	30,000	20,000	(250,000)
Case V	20,000	15,000	20,000
Corporation tax computation			
Case I	30,000	20,000	Nil
Less: section 396A(3) relief (Note 1)	(7,500)	(20,000)	
Taxable Case I income	22,500	Nil	Nil
Case V income	20,000	15,000	20,000
Taxable income	42,500	15,000	20,000
Corporation tax payable:			
@ 12.5%	2,812	Nil	Nil
@ 25%	5,000	3,750	5,000
	7,812	3,750	5,000
Less: section 396B relief (Note 2)	(1,953)	(3,750)	(5,000)
Corporation tax payable	5,859	Nil	Nil

Claims for loss relief are made:

- first against trading income of 2019 and 2018 (section 396A); and
- then against corporation tax, on a value basis against 2020, then 2019 and 2018 (section 396B).

Notes:

1. The loss-making period was 12 months long, therefore the loss can be offset against a 12-month period. As the immediately preceding accounting period was only nine months long, three months of the previous accounting period can be utilised, i.e. against 3/12ths of Case I income for the year ended 31 December 2018.
2. Relief may be claimed on a value basis against corporation tax arising in the nine-month period ended 30/09/2019 and against 3/12ths of corporation tax of the year ended 31/12/2018. For the year ended 31/12/2018, corporation tax of €7,812 is payable, 3/12ths = €1,953.

Loss Memo

	€	€
Total loss 30/9/2020	250,000	
Section 396A claims:		
p/e 30/09/2019	(20,000)	
y/e 31/12/2018 x 3/12ths	(7,500)	
		222,500
Tax value of losses (i.e. €222,500 @ 12.5%)	27,812	
Section 396B claims:		
y/e 30/09/2020	(5,000)	
p/e 30/09/2019	(3,750)	
y/e 31/12/2018 x 3/12ths	(1,953)	
	17,109	
Losses available for carry forward		
section 396(1), i.e. €17,109/12.5%		136,872

Section 396B loss relief on the value basis can reduce the corporation tax liability of a company, including its corporation tax liability in respect of chargeable gains. However, it cannot be used to reduce a company's CGT liability arising from disposals of development land.

Example 22.8

A company's results are as follows:

	Year ended 31/12/2018	Year ended 31/12/2019
	€	€
Relevant trading profit/(loss)	100,000	(120,000)
Chargeable gain: non-development land – adjusted	7,680	–
Chargeable gain: 01/05/2019 – development land	–	20,000
Deposit interest (received gross)	1,600	3,400

The company must first claim to have the loss of €120,000 set off as far as possible against the trading income of the accounting period to 31 December 2018 and then used on a value basis.

Accounting period 12 months to 31 December 2019

	€
Case III	3,400
Corporation tax @ 25%	850
Less: relief on a value basis	(850) (ii)
Corporation tax payable	Nil

Losses may not be offset against the chargeable gain arising on the disposal of development land, as it is liable to CGT. Therefore CGT of €20,000 × 33% = €6,600 is due.

Accounting period 12 months to 31 December 2018

	€
Case I	100,000
Less: section 396A(3)	(100,000) (i)
Case I	–
Case III	1,600
Chargeable gains	7,680
Profit	9,280
Corporation tax	
€1,600 @ 25%	400
€7,680 @ 12.5%	960
	1,360
Less: relief on a value basis	(1,360) (iii)
Corporation tax payable	Nil

(i) to (iii) show the sequence of the loss claims.

Loss Memo	€
Relevant trading loss	120,000
Utilised by way of section 396A(3) against y/e 31/12/2018	(100,000)
Utilised by way of section 396B(3) against y/e 31/12/2019	
€6,800 @ 12.5% = €850	(6,800)
Utilised by way of section 396B(3) against y/e 31/12/2018	
€10,880 @ 12.5% = €1,360	(10,880)
Section 396(1) loss forward to 2020	2,320

22.2 Relief for Excess Charges

22.2.1 Relevant Trading Charges

As outlined in **Chapter 21**, relief is given for relevant trading charges under section 243A TCA 1997 (i.e. charges paid wholly and exclusively for the purposes of a trade) by deducting the amount paid in the accounting period from the company's Case I income. Where the amount of the relevant trading charges exceeds Case I income, relief for the excess trade charges is given in two ways:

1. by claiming relief for the excess in the same accounting period on a "value" basis (section 243B); or
2. by carrying the excess forward as a trading loss (section 396(7)).

Claim for Relief on a Value Basis

Section 243B allows relief for excess trade charges against the relevant corporation tax liability of the company in the current accounting period on a value basis, i.e. the relevant corporation tax liability can be reduced by the tax value of the excess trade charges. The tax value of the excess trade charges is 12.5% of the excess. The relevant corporation tax of the company is the corporation tax liability not including any withholding taxes or close company surcharges (see **Section 26.3**).

The **sequence of claims** is:

- section 396(1), i.e. trading losses forward from earlier periods against income of the same trade;
- section 396A, i.e. trading losses against trading income;
- section 243A, i.e. trading charges against trading income;
- section 243B, i.e. trading charges against corporation tax on a value basis; and
- section 396B, i.e. trading losses against corporation tax on a value basis.

Example 22.9

YZA Ltd, a distribution company, had the following results for the years ended 31 December 2018 and 2019:

	2018	2019
	€	€
Case I profit/(loss)	30,000	(70,000)
Relevant trading charges	20,000	15,000
Case V income	15,000	20,000
Corporation tax computation		
Case I	30,000	Nil
Less: section 396A(3) relief	(30,000)	-
Taxable Case I income	Nil	Nil
Case V income	15,000	20,000
Corporation tax @ 25%	3,750	5,000
Relief on a value basis:		
Excess trading charges (section 243B) (Note 1)	(2,500)	(1,875)
Losses (section 396B) (Note 2)	(1,250)	(3,125)
Corporation tax payable	Nil	Nil

continued overleaf

Notes:

1. Excess 2018 charges are:

	€
Case I	30,000
Less: section 396A relief	(30,000)
Less: relevant charges	(20,000)
Excess charges	20,000

Tax value of excess charges: €20,000 × 12.5% = €2,500

Excess 2019 charges are €15,000 as Case I is nil.

Tax value of excess charges: €15,000 × 12.5% = €1,875

2. Section 396B relief is claimed after relief for excess charges.

"Tax Value" of 2019 losses: €70,000 – €30,000 = €40,000 × 12.5% = €5,000

Losses available to carry forward and offset against profits arising in subsequent years from the same trade are as follows:

	€
Total loss	70,000
Utilised by way of section 396A(3) relief:	
Against y/e 31/12/2018	(30,000)
Utilised by way of section 396B(3) relief:	
Against y/e 31/12/2019: €25,000 @ 12.5% = €3,125	(25,000)
Against y/e 30/12/2018: €10,000 @ 12.5% = €1,250	(10,000)
Losses available to carry forward	5,000

i.e. €5,000 – €3,125 – €1,250 = €625/12.5% = €5,000

Claim to Carry Excess Forward

If the amount of the relevant trading charges exceeds Case I income, the excess may be treated as a Case I loss to be carried forward under section 396(1) for offset against future profits from the same trade. A claim for relief for excess charges on a value basis (section 243B) is not compulsory. If, however, a claim is made for relief under section 243B, the amount of the excess charges carried forward as a Case I loss is reduced by the amount of the charges for which relief has been claimed under section 243B.

Example 22.10

BCD Ltd, a distribution company, had the following results for the years ended 31 December 2018 and 2019:

	2018	2019
	€	€
Case I profit	10,000	80,000
Relevant trade charges	40,000	25,000
Case V income	10,000	10,000

continued overleaf

	€	€
Corporation Tax Computation		
Case I	10,000	80,000
Less: section 396(1) loss (Note 2)	–	(10,000)
Less: relevant trade charges	(10,000)	(25,000)
Taxable Case I income	Nil	45,000
Case V income	10,000	10,000
Total profits	10,000	55,000
Corporation tax @ 12.5%	–	5,625
Corporation tax @ 25%	2,500	2,500
Relief on a value basis:		
Excess charges (section 243B) (Note 1)	(2,500)	–
Corporation tax payable	Nil	8,125

Notes:

1. Excess 2018 charges are:

	€
Case I	10,000
Less relevant charges	(40,000)
Excess charges	30,000

Tax value of excess charges: €30,000 × 12.5% = €3,750

2. Excess charges carried forward to 2019 as a section 396(1) loss: €3,750 – €2,500 = €1,250/12.5% = €10,000

22.2.2 Non-trade Charges

As outlined in **Chapter 21**, charges other than relevant trading charges may be offset against a company's total profits. Where non-trade charges exceed a company's total profits, no relief may be obtained for the excess. In addition, where relief is claimed for losses under section 396B (i.e. relief for losses on a value basis), in calculating trading losses available for carry forward to subsequent years, the company is deemed to have used up any additional loss relief under section 396B instead of claiming any relief for non-trade charges, expenses of management and other amounts deductible against total profits (except excess Case V capital allowances).

22.3 Pre-trading Losses

As outlined in **Chapter 20**, pre-trading expenses are deductible against income in the company's first accounting period. Should this expenditure exceed this income, the excess is only available to offset against future income of this trade. It cannot be offset against other income or gains used on a value basis or used for group relief. Therefore, the pre-trading loss and any normal trading loss arising in the first accounting period after commencement of the trade, must be separately identified; the pre-trading loss can only be offset against Case I income from the same trade, whereas any normal trading loss can be used on a value basis, grouped, etc.

22.4 Relief for Terminal Losses (section 397)

The rules for claiming relief for trading losses when a company is continuing to trade are set out in **Section 22.1**, i.e. any losses not utilised under sections 396A and 396B for the current and preceding accounting periods of same length are carried forward for offset against income from the same trade under section 396(1). Such carry forward of unutilised trading losses is not possible when a company ceases to trade.

A company ceasing to trade may claim "terminal loss relief". Any trading losses incurred in the final 12 months of trading, which have not otherwise been used (against trading income or on a value basis), can be set against trading income of the same trade for the three years preceding the final 12-month period.

The final 12-month period may include more than one accounting period. If there is a loss for both periods, the total of the two losses (for the final 12 months that have not already been used) is available for terminal loss relief. If there is a loss in only one of the periods, the loss for that specific period (time-apportioned if necessary) is available.

In calculating terminal loss relief, charges paid wholly and exclusively for the purposes of the trade (i.e. relevant trade charges) in the final 12 months of trading are included in the terminal loss claim, to the extent that they have not already been claimed. The terminal loss is to be set against income of a later period in priority to an earlier period and is not to displace relief already given for losses carried forward from earlier periods.

Example 22.11

A Ltd ceases to trade on 31 December 2019. The accounts show the following results:

	Trading Profit (loss)	Other Income
	€	€
Year to 31 December 2015	14,000	1,600
Year to 31 December 2016	12,000	3,000
Year to 31 December 2017	10,000	2,000
Year to 31 December 2018	19,000	2,560
Year to 31 December 2019	(75,000)	3,840

It will be remembered that a loss can only be utilised as a terminal loss if it has not or cannot be otherwise relieved. The loss for the year to 31 December 2019 can be relieved as follows:

		€
By set-off: against trading profits of the preceding accounting period to 31 December 2018		19,000
On a value basis 2019:		
against corporation tax – €3,840 @ 25%	= €960	
Loss used €7,680 @ 12.5%	= €960	7,680
On a value basis 2018:		
against corporation tax – €2,560 @ 25%	= €640	
Loss used €5,120 @ 12.5%	= €640	5,120
Loss used		31,800

The unrelieved loss of the accounting period is thus €43,200 (i.e. €75,000 – €31,800).

Terminal loss relief is due as follows against the trading profits of the three-year period commencing on 1 January 2016 and ending on 31 December 2018

continued overleaf

	€
1. Against trading income of the accounting period to 31 December 2018 (profits absorbed by loss carried back)	Nil
2. Against trading income of the accounting period to 31 December 2017	10,000
3. Against trading income of the accounting year to 31 December 2016	12,000
	22,000

The balance of the loss, i.e. €21,200 (€43,200 – €22,000), cannot be relieved in any way.

22.5 Disallowance of Trading Losses following a Change of Ownership

Losses carried forward are potentially valuable – a company will not pay tax on profits until all losses carried forward are utilised. This fact would mean that companies with significant trading losses carried forward could become an attractive target for other (profitable) companies to acquire. By acquiring a company with trading losses and ensuring that it becomes profitable by, for example, transferring business from another company, corporation tax on the profits could be reduced by the original losses. Such tax planning strategies are prevented by anti-avoidance measures in TCA 1997.

Provisions in TCA 1997 disallow the carry forward of trading losses incurred prior to a substantial change of ownership of a company's shares. The disallowance will apply:

1. if "a major change in the nature or conduct of a trade" and the change in ownership both occur within any period of three years; or
2. where the activities of the trade have become small or negligible and there is a change of ownership before any considerable revival of the trade.

In applying the provisions to the accounting period in which the change of ownership occurs, the part of the period occurring before the change of ownership and the part occurring after the change are treated as separate accounting periods. Apportionments are to be made on a time basis.

A "major change in the nature or conduct of a trade" includes:

1. a major change in the property dealt in, services or facilities provided, in the trade; or
2. a major change in customers, outlets or markets of the trade.

It should be noted, however, that this definition is not exhaustive. Any such change will be regarded as occurring even if it is the result of a gradual process begun outside the three-year period.

There have been a number of legal cases that have dealt with the meaning of a "major change in the conduct of the trade" and which give some guidance on the meaning of the term.

Cases where it was held that there had been **no major change** in the nature or conduct of the trade include:

- A company that had sold its products direct to customers, mainly wholesalers, then commenced to do the same through distribution companies.
- A company that ceased to slaughter pigs and manufacture meat products and, for a temporary period of 16 months, distributed the same products manufactured by its parent company. After the 16-month period, it recommenced slaughtering and manufacturing meat products.

Cases where it was held that there had been a **major change** in the nature or conduct of the trade include:

- A company that carried on a business of minting coins and medallions from precious metals, purchased its principal supplier's entire inventories of gold and then purchased gold directly from wholesalers. This resulted in substantial increases in inventory levels.
- A company that operated a retail chain of shops changed its promotional policy by discontinuing the issue of trading stamps and reducing prices. The change resulted in a substantial increase in turnover.

There are rules for determining whether there has been a change in ownership and generally these are such as to ensure that if there is a new person or persons controlling the company, then there is a change of ownership.

22.6 Case IV and Case V Losses

Case IV losses may be set off against the amount of any other income assessable to corporation tax under Case IV for the same accounting period.

Case V losses (which are defined as losses after offset against any Case V income of the accounting period) may be set against corresponding income of a preceding period of the same length. A claim for this relief in respect of a Case V loss must be made within two years after the end of the accounting period of loss.

Both Case IV and Case V losses, so far as unrelieved, may be carried forward and set against corresponding income of subsequent accounting periods.

Example 22.12

A Ltd makes up accounts to 31 December. Recent results are as follows:

	2016	2017	2018	2019
	€	€	€	€
Trading income	100,000	110,000	120,000	130,000
Interest on Government securities	10,000	11,000	12,000	13,000
Rental income (loss)	20,000	(30,000)	5,000	20,000

Starting with earliest loss:

2017

Case I		110,000
Case III		11,000
Case V		Nil
		121,000
Loss Memo – Case V	€	
2017 loss	30,000	

2016

Case I		100,000
Case III		10,000
Case V	20,000	
Less: loss 2017	(20,000)	Nil
		110,000
Loss Memo – Case V	€	
2017 loss	30,000	
Less: used 2016	(20,000)	
Losses forward	10,000	

continued overleaf

2018

	€	€
Case I		120,000
Case III		12,000
Case V	5,000	
Less: loss forward from 2017	(5,000)	Nil
		132,000

Loss Memo – Case V	€
2017 loss forward	10,000
Less: used 2018	(5,000)
Losses forward	5,000

2019

Case I		130,000
Case III		13,000
Case V	20,000	
Less: 2017 loss forward	(5,000)	15,000
		158,000

Loss Memo – Case V	€
2017 loss forward	5,000
Less: used 2019	(5,000)
Losses forward	Nil

22.7 Case V Capital Allowances

Capital allowances available to lessors of industrial buildings (Case V allowances) are to be treated primarily as deductions from the relevant income, i.e. the lease rentals. Any excess of such allowances over the relevant income may be:

- Set-off against total profits (including chargeable gains) for the same accounting period or for an immediately preceding period of the same length. A claim must be made within two years of the end of the accounting period in which the excess occurs.
- Carried forward and treated as an allowance for a later accounting period.

Excess Case V capital allowances that arise due to wear and tear allowances claimed on rented residential accommodation may only be carried forward; they may not be set-off against total profits.

Example 22.13

Takeaway Ltd has the following income and allowances:

Year Ended	Case I	Case III	Case V	Case V Capital Allowances
31 December 2018	20,000	40,000	80,000	30,000
31 December 2019	100,000	20,000	25,000	160,000

continued overleaf

Corporation Tax Year Ended 31 December 2019

	€	€
Case I		100,000
Case III		20,000
Case V	25,000	
Less: Case V allowances	(25,000)	Nil
		120,000
Less: Excess Case V allowances		(120,000)
		Nil

Balance of Case V capital allowances available for set off against 2018 profits:
€160,000 – €25,000 – €120,000 = €15,000

Corporation Tax Year Ended 31 December 2018

	€	€
Case I		20,000
Case III		40,000
Case V	80,000	
Less: Case V allowances	(30,000)	50,000
		110,000
Less: Excess Case V allowances in 2019		(15,000)
Taxable income		95,000

Corporation tax:

€20,000 @ 12.5%	€2,500
€75,000 @ 25%	€18,750
Total	€21,250

Note: the excess Case V capital allowances are offset against total profits. The taxpayer will choose to offset them against the profits taxed at the highest rate, i.e. 25%.

22.8 Capital Losses

While trading losses may be set off against trading profits and utilised on a value basis, capital losses can only be set off against current chargeable gains on other assets or carried forward against chargeable gains in subsequent accounting periods.

22.9 Restriction of Loss Relief on Late Submission of Returns

The due date for submission of a company's accounts to the Collector-General is within nine months after the end of the accounting period provided that if the last day of that period is later than day 23 of the month, the return must be filed on day 23.

If a company fails to submit its return of income for a chargeable period on or before the specified return date for the chargeable period, then claims to offset trading losses against trading income or on a value basis, or to offset excess allowances against profits or, any claim under group relief, are reduced by 50%.

The 50% restriction or reduction referred to above is subject to a maximum amount in any particular case. There is a maximum of €158,715 in each case for those restrictions or reductions. In cases where the delay in filing a return is **less than two months**, the amount of the restriction is effectively reduced from 50% to 25% subject to a maximum amount restricted of €31,740.

Example 22.14

Lana Ltd had the following results for the year ended 31 December 2019:

	€
Case I	100,000
Case V income	60,000
Case V capital allowances	80,000

If Lana Ltd files its return for the year ended 31 December 2019 on 21 October 2020, one month late, its taxable profits for the year ended 31 December 2019 will be as follows:

	€	€
Case I		100,000
Case V	60,000	
Capital allowances	(80,000)	
Excess Case V capital allowances	20,000	
Restricted to 75%		(15,000)
Taxable profits		85,000

If Lana Ltd files its return for the year ended 31 December 2019, on 21 December 2020, three months late, its taxable profits for the year ended 31 December 2019 will be as follows:

	€	€
Case I		100,000
Case V	60,000	
Capital allowances	(80,000)	
Excess Case V capital allowances	20,000	
Restricted to 50%		(10,000)
Taxable profits		90,000

Example 22.15

HIJ Limited, a distribution company, had the following results for the years ended 31 December 2018 and 2019:

	2018	2019
	€	€
Case I profit/(loss)	60,000	(100,000)
Case V income	45,000	50,000
Corporation Tax Computation		
Case I	60,000	Nil
Less: section 396A(3)	(60,000)	–
Taxable Case I income	Nil	Nil
Case V income	45,000	50,000

continued overleaf

Taxable profits	45,000	50,000
Corporation tax @ 12.5%	Nil	Nil
Corporation tax @ 25%	11,250	12,500
Relief on a value basis (section 396B) (Note)	–	(5,000)
Corporation tax payable	11,250	7,500

Note: €100,000 – €60,000 = €40,000. €40,000 @ 12.5% = €5,000

If HIJ Ltd files its return more than two months after the due date for filing its return, relief under sections 396A and 396B will be restricted as follows:

	2018	2019
	€	€
Case I profit/(loss)	60,000	(100,000)
Case V income	45,000	50,000
Corporation Tax Computation		
Case I	60,000	Nil
Less: section 396A(3) (Note 1)	(30,000)	–
Taxable Case I income	30,000	Nil
Case V income	45,000	50,000
Taxable profits	75,000	50,000
Corporation tax @ 12.5%	3,750	Nil
Corporation tax @ 25%	11,250	12,500
Relief on a value basis (section 396B) (Note 2)	–	–
Corporation tax payable	15,000	12,500

Notes:

1. Relief under section 396A: reduction in profits because of relief is restricted to 50% of the amount they would have been reduced by, i.e. €60,000 × 50% = €30,000.
2. Relief under section 396B: the trading loss is reduced by 50% (€100,000 x 50% = €50,000). Then from this must be deducted the claim which could have been made under section 396A if the return had been filed on time, i.e. €60,000. Therefore, as this amount of €60,000 exceeds €50,000, no relief may be claimed under section 396B. The loss available for carry forward to 2020 against future income of this trade is €100,000 – €30,000 = €70,000.

Questions

Review Questions

(See Suggested Solutions to Review Questions at the end of this textbook.)

Question 22.1

Using the figures shown below for Enya Ltd, show how the Case V (rents) and Case I (trade, all non-manufacturing) losses may be used. Assume a tax rate of 12.5% on trading income and 25% for Cases III and V for all years.

	Rents	Trading profits (losses)	Case III
	€	€	€
y/e 31/03/2016	5,000	60,000	10,000
y/e 31/03/2017	(4,000)	70,000	5,000
y/e 31/03/2018	6,000	(130,000)	10,000
y/e 31/03/2019	8,000	10,000	3,500

Question 22.2

Hells Bells Ltd shows the following results:

	Year ended 31 March 2019	Nine months ended 31 December 2019
	€	€
Trading profit/(loss)	167,000	(190,000)
Rents	4,000	(4,000)
Capital gains/(losses) (non-development land)	(19,000)	10,000
Case III	10,000	20,000

Requirement
Calculate the tax payable for each accounting period, claiming the earliest possible relief for losses.

Question 22.3

Monk Ltd prepares annual accounts to 31 December each year. Recent results were as follows:

	Year Ended 31/12/2018	Year Ended 31/12/2019
	€	€
Adjusted Case I profit/(loss) (Note)	340,000	(400,000)
Interest on Government stocks	5,000	30,000
Rental income	15,000	20,000
Capital gains as adjusted for CT (non-development land)	12,000	26,000
Capital gain on development land (1 June)	–	100,000

Note: Monk Ltd has an unutilised Case I loss forward from the year ended 31/12/2017 of €20,000. The company wishes to claim the loss reliefs available so as to maximise the benefit of the losses.

Requirement
Compute the corporation tax payable for each of the above years and indicate the amount (if any) of unutilised losses available for carry forward to the year ending 31 December 2020.

Question 22.4

Monaghan Limited prepares annual accounts to 30 June each year. Recent results were as follows:

	Year Ended 30 June		
	2017	2018	2019
	€	€	€
Adjusted Case I profit/(loss)	180,000	(530,000)	140,000
Trade charges paid (Note)	10,000	10,000	6,000
Interest on Government stocks	5,000	30,000	10,000
Rental income	10,500	20,000	20,000
Capital gains as adjusted for CT	10,200	40,000	50,000
Cash dividend from subsidiary	10,000	30,000	Nil
Non-trade charges paid	–	–	50,000

Monaghan Limited has an unutilised Case I loss forward from the year ended 30 June 2016 of €20,000.

Note: trade charges of €4,000 relating to the year ended 30 June 2019 were paid in July 2019 and are not included in the figures above.

Requirement
Compute the corporation tax for each of the above years and indicate the amount (if any) of unutilised losses available for carry forward to the year ending 30 June 2020.

23

Group Relief

Learning Objectives

After studying this chapter you will be able to:

- Determine when a company can make certain payments without deduction of income tax to another group company.
- Determine when a company can surrender certain losses to another group company.
- Implement efficient utilisation of trading losses, excess charges, non-trade losses, certain capital allowances and management expenses within a group of companies.

23.1 Introduction

A company is a separate legal entity for tax purposes. However, where certain conditions are met, companies can be considered to be members of a group that can then avail of reliefs that are not available to single entities. There are different definitions of groups depending on the type of relief claimed. Broadly speaking, these reliefs may be broken down under the following headings:

1. Payments relief.
2. Loss relief.
3. Relief from tax on capital gains (see **Chapter 24**).

23.2 Payments Relief

Certain payments made by companies are generally required to be made under deduction of income tax at the standard rate, including those outlined in **Chapter 21, Section 21.1**, i.e.:

- yearly interest;
- annual payments; and
- patent royalties.

A company making any of the above payments would, in the normal course of events, be required to deduct income tax at the standard rate from the gross amount due and pay this over to Revenue as part of its corporation tax payments. Under section 410 TCA 1997, such payments of interest and royalties can be made without the necessity to withhold 20% income tax, i.e. these payments can be made gross within a group provided certain conditions are satisfied.

23.2.1 Conditions to be Satisfied

1. Both the paying and the recipient company must be resident in an EU Member State or a European Economic Area (EEA) country, i.e. a relevant Member State, which has a tax treaty with Ireland.
2. There must be a 51% (direct or indirect) shareholding relationship between paying and recipient company, i.e. more than 50% of its ordinary share capital is owned. In **Example 23.1** below, A Ltd indirectly owns 54% of D Ltd, while B Ltd owns 90% of C Ltd directly. The 51% relationship is also satisfied when both companies are 51% subsidiaries of another company. Shareholdings in share-dealing companies and companies not resident in a relevant Member State cannot be used to establish the 51% relationship.
3. If the recipient company is not resident in the State, the payment must be taxable in its country of residence.

Example 23.1: 51% test

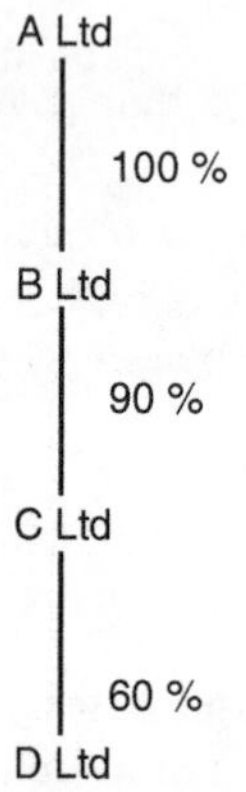

Assuming all companies are Irish resident, interest paid by D Ltd to A Ltd will qualify for relief, as there is a 54% relationship between these two companies (i.e. 100% × 90% × 60% = 54%). Equally, interest paid by D Ltd to B Ltd or C Ltd will qualify for relief, as there is at least a 51% relationship between the companies.

Example 23.2

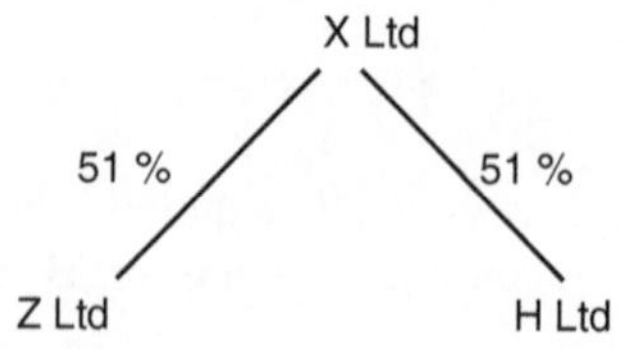

Qualifying payments from Z Ltd to H Ltd, or vice versa, would qualify for relief as both companies are 51% subsidiaries of another company, providing X Ltd, Z Ltd and H Ltd are resident in a relevant Member State and the recipient company is taxed on the interest/royalty in its country of resident.

If X Ltd is resident in, say, the USA, the conditions would not be met and relevant payments between them would be subject to 20% income tax being withheld at source.

23.3 Loss Relief

23.3.1 Introduction

We saw in **Chapter 22** how losses incurred by a company can be utilised by that company. The legislation provides that, where a loss group exists, certain losses incurred by one group company can be used by another group company (sections 411–429 TCA 1997) **during the same accounting period**. The companies and the losses must satisfy the qualifying group requirements as outlined in **Sections 23.3.2** and **23.3.3**.

A formal claim for group relief must be made by the "profit maker" within two years of the end of the accounting period in which the loss arose, Formal consent must also be given by the 'loss-maker'. Any payments to the loss maker by the profit-maker for use of the losses are ignored for corporation tax purposes provided they do not exceed the amount of the loss surrendered, i.e. no tax deduction is available to the profit-maker in respect of the payment and the receipt by the loss-maker is not taxable.

Losses that can be surrendered within a group are:

- trading losses (**Section 22.1**), excluding pre-trading losses (**Section 22.3**);
- excess charges (**Section 22.2**);
- excess management expenses (**Chapter 27**); and
- excess Case V capital allowances (**Section 22.8**).

The application of these losses for group relief purposes is outlined in **Section 23.3.4**. Losses incurred under Cases III, IV and V, capital losses, and losses from earlier or later accounting periods cannot be group relieved.

23.3.2 Qualifying Group – 75% Relationship

To avail of group loss relief, the profit-maker must be in the same "75% group" as the loss-maker. Under section 411 TCA 1997, this condition is satisfied in relation to two companies if one company holds, directly or indirectly, not less than 75% of the ordinary share capital of that company or both companies are 75% subsidiaries of a third company. In addition, the parent company must be entitled to 75% of the profits available for distribution and 75% of assets on a winding up. For the purposes of the 75% test, "ordinary share capital" is defined as meaning all the issued share capital (by whatever name called) of the company other than capital where the holders have a right to a dividend at a fixed rate but have no other right to a share in the profits of the company. It should be noted that this definition would include participating preference shares as "ordinary share capital".

In determining if one company owns 75% of another company, the following shareholdings must be ignored:

- shareholdings in share-dealing companies;
- shareholdings in companies not resident in the EU or in a country that has not signed a tax treaty with Ireland.

In addition, a company cannot be treated as a 75% subsidiary of another company unless the other company is resident in the EU or in a country that has signed a tax treaty with Ireland, or is quoted on a stock exchange in such a country or in one approved by the Minister for Finance.

A company may establish the 75% holding by aggregating any ordinary shares held directly in that company and also those held indirectly through a third company.

Example 23.3: 75% loss group

All companies are Irish tax resident unless otherwise stated.

1.The loss-maker is a 75% subsidiary of profit-maker or vice versa:

(a)

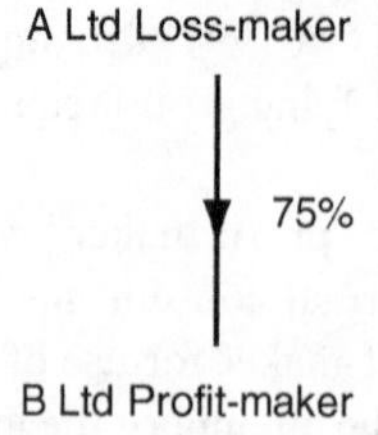

(b)

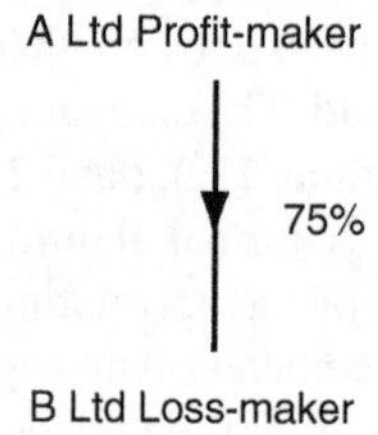

2. Both are 75% subsidiaries of a third company:

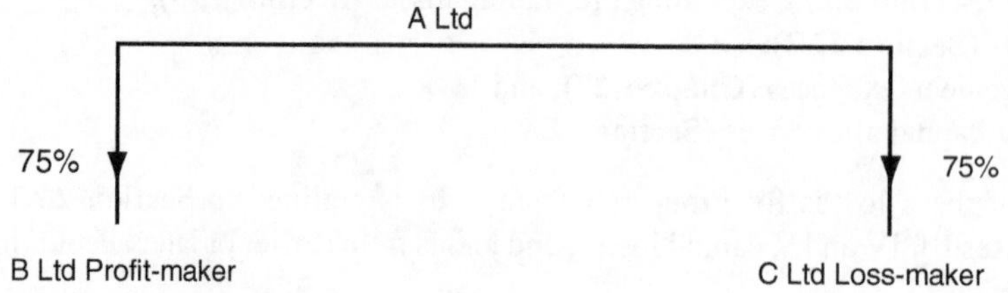

If A Ltd is resident in Germany (an EU country) or the USA (a country with which Ireland has a tax treaty), then B Ltd and C Ltd are in an Irish loss group.

If A Ltd is resident in Bolivia, a country with which Ireland does not have a tax treaty, then for a group to exist, A Ltd must be quoted on a recognised stock exchange in the EU or a country which has signed a tax treaty with Ireland, or a stock exchange which is approved by the Minister for Finance.

3. Establishing a 75% relationship through a third company:

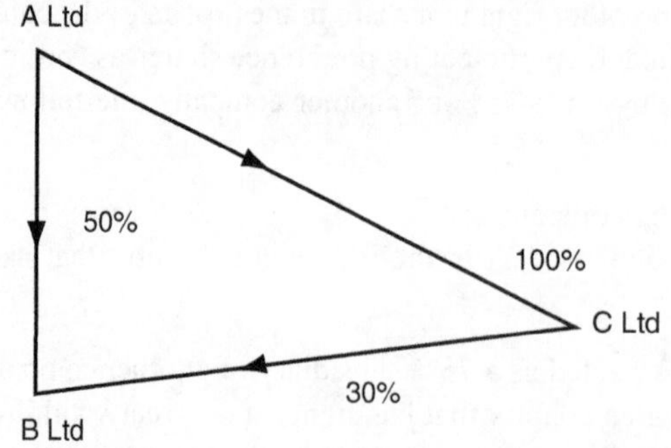

A, B and C Ltd are all members of the same 75% loss group.

continued overleaf

4. Non-qualifying group

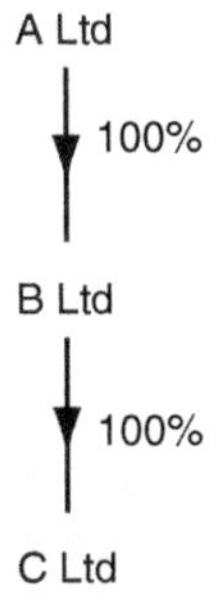

A Ltd is an Irish unquoted company. A Ltd and C Ltd are Irish resident. B Ltd, an unquoted company, is resident in Peru (which does not have a tax treaty with Ireland). A Ltd and C Ltd are not in a group for loss relief purposes as A Ltd:

- does not hold the shares in C Ltd directly; and
- does not hold the shares indirectly through a company resident in the EU or a country with which Ireland has signed a tax treaty.

23.3.3 Qualifying Group – Non-resident Company Losses

In the past, all members of the group had to be Irish tax resident. Therefore, only Irish companies could be used to establish the 75% relationship and the loss must have been incurred by an Irish resident company and only surrendered for group relief to another Irish resident group company.

This rule was changed as a result of the decision of the European Court of Justice (ECJ) in 1998 in the case of *Imperial Chemical Industries plc v. Colmer* (Case C-264/96). As a result of this and subsequent legislation, Irish tax law was amended to provide that companies resident in an EU Member State or EEA State that has a tax treaty with Ireland (i.e. a relevant Member State) can be taken into account in:

- determining if the group relationship exists, i.e. 75% relationship (**Section 23.3.2**); and
- to allow losses to be surrendered between the Irish resident company and the Irish branch of a company resident in a relevant Member State.

While the TCA now provides that companies resident in a treaty country (excluding relevant Member States detailed above) or quoted on a recognised stock exchange can be used to establish the 75% relationship, losses of these companies may not be offset against Irish profits.

Following the ECJ decision in the *Marks & Spencer plc v. Halsey* (2005) (Case C-446/03) case, Irish law was amended to provide that trading losses incurred by its non-Irish subsidiaries resident in a relevant Member State can be group-relieved against profits of the Irish parent. It must be proven that the loss cannot be otherwise used by the foreign subsidiary, the 75% relationship must exist between the companies and the claim must be made within two years.

23.3.4 Application of Losses for Group Relief

In a qualifying group, qualifying losses may be passed upwards, downwards or sideways so that any qualifying company (or Irish branch) in the 75% group may use the losses. Some or all of the loss may be used regardless of the percentage relationship. For example, even if A Ltd only owns 80% of B Ltd, all of B Ltd's loss may be used by A Ltd. In addition, two or more profit-makers can claim relief from any one loss-making company. However, before claiming group relief, the profit-maker must claim all its own losses, charges and capital allowances (except set off of losses for a subsequent accounting period and terminal loss relief). As outlined in **Chapter 22, Section 22.9**, any claim for group relief will be restricted if the company fails to submit its corporation tax return by the due date. As with single entities, separate rules apply for each type of loss to be claimed under group relief:

1. **Trading losses** – the provisions for a company to claim relief for its own trading losses under section 396A and section 396B are explained in **Chapter 22, Section 22.1**. For group relief purposes, trading losses in the current accounting period incurred by a group company, excluding trade losses attributable to pre-trading expenses, can be offset against the trading income (section 420A), or reduce the corporation tax liability on a value basis (section 420B), of another group company in the same accounting period. There are other restrictions, but these arise infrequently.

Example 23.4

Parent Ltd has a trading profit of €100,000. Subsidiary Ltd is in a group for loss relief purposes with Parent Ltd. Subsidiary Ltd has a trading loss of €60,000. The trading loss of Subsidiary Ltd can be grouped against the trading profits of Parent Ltd, reducing Parent Ltd's taxable trading income to €40,000.

Example 23.5

New Company Ltd incurs qualifying pre-trading expenses of €50,000. It commenced to trade and earned income of €10,000. New Company Ltd's tax computation would show a Case I loss of €40,000 (i.e. €10,000 – €50,000). If New Company Ltd is a member of a group, that loss of €40,000 cannot be grouped, it can only be carried forward and offset against future trading income of New Company Ltd.

As mentioned in **Section 22.1**, when a company incurs a trading loss it must make a section 396A claim before it can make a claim under section 396B. A similar rule applies for group relief, whereby a claim must be made under section 420A before a claim can be made under section 420B.

Also, the company incurring the trading loss must make a claim for loss relief under section 396A in the current accounting period, if possible, before it surrenders it to another company under section 420B (i.e. use the surrendered loss on a value basis to reduce corporation tax of another group company). The company that incurred the trading loss does not have to claim relief under section 396B (i.e. reduce its own corporation tax on a value basis in the current accounting period or preceding period of same length) before it surrenders it to another company under section 420A (i.e. offset the surrendered loss against trading income of another group company) or section 420B.

Example 23.6
A Ltd owns 80% of B Ltd. The following are the results for the year ended 31 December 2019:

	A Ltd	B Ltd
	€	€
Relevant trading income/(loss)	10,000	(25,000)
Case III	8,000	6,400

Computation
B Ltd

Case I	–	
Case III	6,400	
Corporation tax @ 25%	1,600	
Section 396B: relief on a value basis	(1,600)	
Corporation tax payable	Nil	

A Ltd

Case I	10,000	
Group relief section 420A	(10,000)	
Case I	Nil	
Case III	8,000	
Corporation tax:		
€8,000 @ 25%	2,000	
Section 420B: group relief on a value basis	(275)	
Corporation tax payable	1,725	

Loss Memo

Relevant trading loss for y/e 31/12/2019	25,000
Utilised by way of:	
section 396B(3) against corporation tax of B Ltd	
€12,800 × 12.5% = €1,600	(12,800)
Utilised by way of:	
section 420A against trading income of A Ltd	(10,000)
section 420B against corporation tax of A Ltd	
€2,200 × 12.5% = €275	(2,200)
Loss forward to 2020	Nil

A claim must be made under section 420A (trading losses) against relevant trading income of A Ltd before a claim can be made under section 420B on a value basis.

A claim does not have to be made by B Ltd under section 396B before a claim can be made by A Ltd under section 420A or section 420B. However, a claim must be made by B Ltd under section 396A, if possible, before A Ltd can make a claim under section 420B.

2. **Excess charges paid** (see **Chapter 22, Section 22.2**) comprise:

   (a) ***Relevant trading charges paid*** (e.g. patent royalties). **Chapter 22, Section 22.2** details the relief given for a company's excess trade charges against its own corporation tax liability (section 243B). A group company can surrender its excess trade charges to another group company for offset against relevant trading income of another group member (section 420A) or claim against relevant corporation tax on a value basis (section 420B). Again, section 420A relief must be claimed against relevant trading income before a claim under section 420B against corporation tax on a value basis.

(b) ***Non-trade charges paid*** (e.g. protected interest) in an accounting period that are in excess of that period's total profits (before any deduction has been made in arriving at those total profits for losses, capital allowances or management expenses of other accounting periods) may be surrendered and set against the total profits of another group company under section 420.

Example 23.7

T Ltd owns 80% of Q Ltd. The following are the results for the year ended 31 December 2019:

	T Ltd	Q Ltd
	€	€
Case I	10,000	200,000
Adjusted chargeable gain	-	40,000
Trade charges paid	50,000	
Non-trade charges paid	8,000	

Computation: T Ltd

Case I	10,000
Deduct: section 243A trade charges paid	(10,000)
Taxable profits	NIL

Computation: Q Ltd

Case I	200,000
Deduct: section 420A group relief	(40,000)
	160,000
Chargeable gains	40,000
Total profits	200,000
Deduct: non-trade charges group relief	(8,000)
Taxable profits	192,000
Corporation tax @ 12.5%	24,000

Excess Trade Charges Memo

	€
Relevant trading charges paid for y/e 31/12/2019	50,000
Utilised by way of section 243A by T Ltd	(10,000)
Available to surrender to group	40,000
Utilised by way of section 420A against trading income of Q Ltd	(40,000)
Excess forward to 2020	NIL

Excess Non-trade Charges Memo

	€
Non-trade charges paid for y/e 31/12/2019	8,000
Utilised by group relief by Q Ltd	(8,000)
Excess forward to 2020	NIL

3. **Excess management expenses** (see **Chapter 27**) of the current accounting period (excluding those of a previous accounting period which have been carried forward and are deemed to be management expenses of the current accounting period) may be grouped against total profits of the other group company. It is not necessary for the other group company to be an investment company for group relief to be claimed.

4. **Excess Case V capital allowances** (see **Chapter 22, Section 22.7**) – can be used to reduce the total profits of another group company.

Example 23.8

C Ltd owns 90% of D Ltd. The following are the results for the year ended 31 December 2019:

	C Ltd	**D Ltd**
	€	€
Relevant trading income/(loss)	(10,000)	30,000
Case III	5,000	6,000
Case V	8,000	
Case V capital allowances	15,000	

Computation

C Ltd

	€
Case I	–
Case III	5,000
Case V	–
Income	5,000
Excess Case V capital allowances (Note)	(5,000)
Taxable	nil

Note:	Case V	8,000
	Capital allowances	(15,000)
	Excess Case V capital allowances	7,000
	Utilised by C Ltd	(5,000)
	Available for grouping	2,000

D Ltd

	€
Case I	30,000
Section 420A	(10,000)
	20,000
Case III	6,000
	26,000
Excess Case V capital allowances from C Ltd	(2,000)
Taxable	24,000

Corporation tax:	€
€20,000 @ 12.5%	2,500
€4,000 (Note) @ 25%	1,000
Corporation tax payable	3,500

Note: the excess Case V capital allowances are claimed against the profits taxable at the highest rate, i.e. Case III at 25%.

It should be noted that the excess allowances available for group relief are those claimed for the current accounting period in excess of the Case V income for that period **before any reduction of that income for previous periods' capital allowances or losses forward.**

Example 23.9

Jammy Dodger Ltd is owned 100% by Biscuits Ltd. Its results for the year ended 31 December 2019 are below. Calculate the excess Case V capital allowances available for surrender to Biscuits Ltd for the year ended 31 December 2019.

	€
Current period Case V income	20,000
Current period Case V capital allowances	50,000

continued overleaf

Current period Case V balancing charge	5,000
Case V capital allowances forward	7,000
Case V losses forward from previous period	3,000
Computation	
Case V tax-adjusted income (current period)	20,000
Add: Case V balancing charge (current period)	5,000
	25,000
Deduct: current period Case V capital allowances	(50,000)
Excess Case V capital allowances available for group relief:	(25,000)

Excess Case V capital allowances which arise due to wear and tear allowances claimed on rented residential accommodation may not be surrendered by way of group relief.

23.3.5 Corresponding Accounting Periods

Group relief is only available where the accounting period of both the loss-maker and profit-maker corresponds wholly or partly. Where they correspond partly, the relief is restricted on a time apportionment basis.

Example 23.10

Group Limited has a wholly owned subsidiary, Sub Limited. In the year ended 31 December 2019, Group Limited incurs a Case I loss of €240,000. In the year ended 30 September 2019, Sub Limited has Case I income of €120,000.

The corresponding accounting period is the period 1 January 2019 to 30 September 2019, i.e. nine months. Therefore, the maximum group relief available is the lower of:

- loss of €240,000 × 9/12 = €180,000:
- profit of €120,000 × 9/12 = €90,000.

Sub Limited can make a claim to utilise €90,000 of the losses incurred by Group Limited, thereby reducing its taxable income in the year ended 30 September 2019 to €30,000. Group Limited will have unused losses of €240,000 less €90,000 = €150,000 and some of these losses may be available for group relief against Sub Ltd's trading income for the year ended 30 September 2020, i.e. the period 1 October to 31 December 2019.

Group relief is only given if the surrendering company and the claimant company are members of the same group throughout the whole of the surrendering company's accounting period and the claimant company's corresponding accounting period. Where a company joins or leaves a group, all of the companies in the group are deemed to end an accounting period at that date for the purposes of establishing any group relief due. The corresponding accounting period rules referred to above apply.

Example 23.11

Owner Limited acquired 100% of the share capital of Acquired Limited on 30 June 2019. Both companies make up their financial statements to 31 December. In the year ended 31 December 2019, Owner Limited has Case I income of €100,000, while Acquired Limited has a Case I loss of €60,000. Only losses incurred since 1 July 2019 may be grouped, i.e. the corresponding accounting period is the period 1 July 2019 to 31 December 2019, i.e. six months. Therefore, the maximum group relief available is the *lower* of:

- profit of €100,000 × 6/12 = €50,000;
- loss of €60,000 × 6/12 = €30,000.

Owner Limited can make a claim to have €30,000 of the losses incurred by Acquired Limited to be offset against its trading income, thereby reducing its taxable income for the year ended 31 December 2019 from €100,000 to €70,000. Acquired Limited will have unused losses of €60,000 less €30,000 = €30,000.

Example 23.12

A Ltd owns 80% of B Ltd. The following are the results for each company:

	A Ltd	**B Ltd**
	y/e 31/12/2019	**y/e 30/06/2019**
	€	€
Relevant trading income/(loss)	10,000	(50,000)
Case III	8,000	6,400

Computation

B Ltd

	€
Case I	–
Case III	6,400
Corporation tax @ 25%	1,600
Less: section 396B relief	(1,600)(1)
Corporation tax payable	Nil

A Ltd

	€
Case I	10,000
Less: group relief section 420A	(5,000)(2)
Case I	5,000
Case III	8,000
	13,000
Corporation tax:	
€5,000 @ 12.5%	625
€8,000 @ 25%	2,000
Less: section 420B group relief	(1,000)(3)
Corporation tax payable	1,625

Loss Memo

Relevant trading loss for y/e 30/06/2019	50,000
1 Utilised by way of section 396B against corporation tax of B Ltd (Note 1) €12,800 @ 12.5% = €1,600	(12,800)(1)
2 Utilised by way of section 420A against trading income of A Ltd (Note 2)	(5,000)(2)

continued overleaf

3 Utilised by way of section 420B against corporation tax of A Ltd (Note 3) €8,000 @ 12.5% = €1,000	(8,000)(3)
Loss forward to 2020	24,200

Notes:

1. Typically a company will make a claim under section 396B. However, there is no legal requirement to make a claim under section 396B for B Ltd before surrendering the loss to A Ltd to use under section 420A against relevant trading income of A Ltd. A claim must be made under section 420A against relevant trading income of A Ltd before a claim can be made under section 420B on a value basis.
2. Section 420A claim is for lower of:
   - trading loss of surrendering company for overlap period, i.e. 6/12 × (€50,000) = (€25,000); or
   - trading income of claimant for overlap period, i.e. 6/12 × €10,000 = €5,000.

   Therefore, claim €5,000.
3. Section 420B claim – the unclaimed loss of the overlap period on a value basis – the unclaimed loss is €25,000 – €5,000 = €20,000; its value is €20,000 × 12.5% = €2,500. Relief may be claimed against the corporation tax on profits of the overlap period which have not already been relieved. All the Case I of the overlap period has been relieved, so it is the corporation tax on the Case III income of the overlap period (6/12 × €8,000 × 25% = €1,000).

Questions

Review Questions

(See Suggested Solutions to Review Questions at the end of this textbook.)

Question 23.1

B Ltd has the following results for the year ended 31 December 2019:

	€
Tax-adjusted trading profits (i.e. after current year capital allowance claim)	180,000
Interest on Government stocks (Case III)	4,000
Profit rent (Case V)	20,000

Unutilised trading losses forward from the year ended 31 December 2018 amount to €16,000.

Z Ltd is a 100% trading subsidiary of B Ltd. During the year ended 31 December 2019 it incurred tax-adjusted trading losses of €96,000. It also had taxable Case III income of €20,000.

Requirement

Compute B Ltd's corporation tax liability for the year ended 31 December 2019, after allowing for any group relief for losses of Z Ltd.

Question 23.2

A Ltd owns 80% of B Ltd's issued share capital and 75% of C Ltd's issued share capital. Results for the year ended 31 March 2019 were:

	A Ltd	B Ltd	C Ltd
	€	€	€
Tax-adjusted Case I profit/(loss)	(90,000)	56,000	48,000
Case III income	1,000	2,000	3,000
Case V income	20,000	25,000	2,000
Case I trading losses forward	(4,000)	–	(26,000)

A Ltd wishes to arrange its affairs to ensure that it pays no corporation tax, if possible, before it surrenders any loss relief to its subsidiaries.

Requirement
Calculate the tax payable by each company for the year ended 31 March 2019.

Question 23.3

Queen Ltd has two wholly owned subsidiaries, Pawn Ltd and Rook Ltd. All three companies are trading companies. Accounts for the year to 31 December 2019 show the following results:

	Queen Ltd	Pawn Ltd	Rook Ltd
	€	€	€
Gross operating profit	297,463	81,000	47,437
Less: depreciation	12,000	10,000	16,000
Entertaining (customers)	1,350	1,200	1,650
Administration	73,650	61,110	107,373
Interest	11,150	10,720	3,000
Capital grant release	(3,000)	–	–
	95,150	83,030	128,023
Net profit/(loss) before investment income	202,313	(2,030)	(80,586)

Additional information:

1. Rook Ltd was incorporated and commenced to trade on 1 January 2019.
2. (i) Interest is analysed as follows:

	Queen Ltd	Pawn Ltd	Rook Ltd
	€	€	€
Accrued 1 January 2019	(1,250)	–	–
Paid	10,000	9,000	2,750
Accrued 31 December 2019	2,000	1,750	250
Interest on overdue tax	400	–	–
	11,150	10,720	3,000

(ii) Pawn Ltd has used its loan to purchase 7% of the share capital of Bridge Ltd, whose income consists mainly of rental income from commercial properties. None of the directors of Bridge Ltd is also a director of Pawn Ltd. Interest incurred by Queen Ltd and Rook Ltd were in respect of borrowings taken out for the purpose of their trades.

3. (i) Queen Ltd received dividends of €7,500 from other Irish resident companies. These dividends have not been included in the profit figures above.

   (ii) Queen Ltd also received deposit interest of €23,846, which was not subject to DIRT.

4. Capital allowances:

	Queen Ltd	**Pawn Ltd**	**Rook Ltd**
	€	€	€
Capital allowances	7,375	3,000	5,627

5. Pawn Ltd had trade losses brought forward of €80,000 at 1 January 2019.
6. The companies paid the following corporation tax on 2018 profits of:

	Queen Ltd	**Pawn Ltd**
	€	€
Corporation tax	55,000	10,000

Requirement

(a) Compute the corporation tax liabilities (if any) of each of the three companies for the year ended 31 December 2019, on the assumption that all available reliefs are claimed to the benefit of the group as a whole.

(b) State the amount of any losses available to carry forward at 1 January 2020 for each company.

(c) State the due date of payment of any tax payable.

24

Company Capital Gains

Learning Objectives

After studying this chapter you will be able to:

- Determine and calculate a company's exposure to corporation tax or CGT on disposal of chargeable assets.
- Determine and calculate the availability and impact of the participation exemption on disposal of certain shareholdings by a company.
- Determine when a company is a member of a group for capital transaction purposes.
- Advise on and calculate the tax implications of capital transactions within a group.
- Advise on the conditions and tax implications of certain anti-avoidance measures, including:
  - treatment of pre-entry losses;
  - treatment of a company leaving a group.

Companies can be liable to Irish tax on capital gains. In this chapter we will look at the rules that determine if the gain is actually liable, and whether it is liable to corporation tax (most commonly) or CGT. We also look at reliefs from tax on capital gains that are applicable to companies only. Note that a gain is either liable or not liable. There is no remittance basis for companies.

The tax residence status of a company is determined by where the **central management and control of the company is exercised**. However, certain Irish **incorporated** companies may be resident in the State even if the central management and control of the company is exercised abroad. See **Chapter 19, Sections 19.2** and **19.3** for a more detailed consideration of the concept of corporate residence.

24.1 Capital Gains Liable to Corporation Tax

24.1.1 Irish Resident Companies

Such companies are liable to corporation tax in respect of **all** capital gains wherever arising, excluding disposals of development land. Thus gains on disposal of foreign assets by an Irish resident company are liable to Irish corporation tax.

24.1.2 Non-resident Companies

A non-resident company is only liable to corporation tax on its capital gains if it is trading in the State through a branch or agency and it disposes of a specified Irish asset (see **Chapter 2, Section 2.3.1**), which it acquired for the purpose of its trade in the State.

Therefore, non-resident companies are not liable to corporation tax on most disposals, e.g. disposals of foreign assets, non-specified Irish assets.

24.2 Capital Gains Liable to Capital Gains Tax

24.2.1 Irish Resident Companies

Irish resident companies are liable to CGT on the disposal of development land only (see **Chapter 1, Section 1.13**).

24.2.2 Non-resident Companies

Non-resident companies are liable to CGT on the following disposals:

1. disposals of development land; and
2. disposals of specified Irish assets not used for the purpose of branch or agency in the State.

24.3 Exemption from Tax on Disposal of Certain Shareholdings (Participation Exemption)

Section 626B TCA 1997 provides for an exemption from corporation tax in certain circumstances, in the case of gains from the disposal of shareholdings by parent companies. While any such gains are not taxable, if there is a loss on disposal, there is no relief for the loss. A number of conditions must be met before a gain can be exempt:

- The company disposing of the shares, i.e. the investor company, must be a 'parent' company at the time of disposal, or had been a parent company not less than two years prior to the time of disposal. A 'parent' company must have a **minimum shareholding of at least 5% in the investee company**. That is:
  - it must hold not less than 5% of the company's ordinary share capital;
  - it must be beneficially entitled to not less than 5% of the profits available for distribution to equity holders of the company; **and**
  - on a winding up, it must be beneficially entitled to not less than 5% of the assets available for distribution to equity holders.
- The investor is required to have the minimum holding in the investee company for a **continuous period of at least 12 months.**
- The **investee company must carry on a trade**, or the business of the investor company, its investee company and their "5%" investee companies, taken as a whole, must consist wholly or mainly of the carrying on of a **trade** or trades.
- Finally, at the time of the disposal the **investee** company must be resident in a **Member State of the EU or a country** with which **Ireland has a tax treaty**.

The exemption continues to apply for two years after the parent company's minimum shareholding is no longer satisfied. **The exemption does not apply where the shares derive the greater part of their value from specified Irish assets.** A similar exemption applies to assets related to shares, e.g. options, but this is beyond the scope of this textbook.

> ***Example 24.1***
> Owner Ltd owns 100% of Irish Ltd, a trading company, for the last 10 years. Acquisition Ltd wishes to acquire Irish Ltd. The disposal by Owner Ltd will generate a profit of €5 million. Due to the exemption, Owner Ltd will pay no tax on this gain.
>
> If Owner Ltd disposed of 99% of its shareholding in Irish Ltd in 2019 and the remaining 1% in 2020, both disposals would qualify for the exemption – because even though Owner Ltd did not own 5% at the time it disposed of its 1% interest, it was not more than two years since it had been a parent company.
>
> If the facts were the same except that it is shares in French Ltd, a French resident company, the exemption would be available also to Owner Ltd. However, if it were a disposal of shares in a Jersey company, then the gain would be fully taxable as the investee company is not resident in a Member State of the EU or a country with which Ireland has a tax treaty.

24.4 Method of Taxation

The rules for calculating the chargeable gain, as set out in **Chapter 1, Section 1.6**, apply regardless of whether a company is assessed to corporation tax or to CGT on a capital gain.

Where the disposal is subject to corporation tax, the gain, net of any allowable losses, is adjusted for inclusion in the corporation tax computation (as detailed in **Chapter 20, Section 20.6**). The adjusted gain, and any tax attaching, may be further reduced for corporation tax purposes if the company has other reliefs available (e.g. excess Case V allowances; losses on a value basis) as shown in the pro forma corporation tax computation (**Section 20.2**). Any liability forms part of the company's corporation tax liability and is paid and filed in accordance with the rules detailed in **Chapter 19**.

Where the disposal is subject to CGT, normal rules regarding the rate of tax and dates for paying and filing the CGT return apply (see **Section 1.5**). Capital losses and other reliefs that are subject to corporation tax (e.g. excess Case V allowances) cannot be offset against gains subject to CGT.

> ***Example 24.2***
> X Ltd prepares accounts to 31 December each year. Its corporation tax liability for the year ended 31 December 2018 was €3,000. In the year ended 31 December 2019 the tax-adjusted Case I profit was €20,000. During that year the company bought an asset for €10,000 and sold it for €17,000 in October 2019. The company had a capital loss forward of €1,000. It also sold a site for €155,000. The current use value of the site was €55,000 at date of disposal, 10 May 2019. It had acquired the site in July 2011 for €60,000.

	Year ended 31 December 2019
	€
Schedule D Case I	20,000
Chargeable gain:	
current year €7,000	
loss forward (€1,000)	
Chargeable gain = €6,000 × 33/12.5%	15,840
	35,840
Corporation tax due €35,840 @ 12.5%	4,480

> X Ltd will pay preliminary tax of €3,000 at 23 November 2019 and the balance of corporation tax, €1,480, when it submits its corporation tax return by 23 September 2020.

continued overleaf

2019 CGT Computation

	€
Sales proceeds	155,000
Deduct: cost of acquisition 2011	(60,000)
Gain	95,000
CGT @ 33%	31,350

X Ltd will pay €31,350 CGT by 15 December 2019 and will include details of the gain in its corporation tax return (Form CT1) for the year ended 31 December 2019.

You have done this tax computation for X Ltd and are satisfied that you have done the calculations correctly. However, you are uncomfortable as you know that your father bought a property for €80,000 from X Ltd on 1 February 2019, and there is no mention of this disposal in the information that was sent to your manager by the client. What should you do?

You should advise your manager of this purchase by your father and, therefore, disposal by the client, so that your manager can raise it with the client.

24.5 Capital Gains Group

A company may be part of a group for CGT purposes. This provides important benefits to companies within the group, namely assets can be transferred from one group company to another without triggering a capital gain.

24.5.1 Definition of a Capital Gains Group

Section 616 TCA 1997 provides that a **principal company and its effective 75% subsidiaries form a capital gains group and, where a principal company itself is a member of a group (as being itself an effective 75% subsidiary), that group comprises all of its effective 75% subsidiaries.** In this, CGT groups differ from loss groups, as illustrated in **Example 24.3** below.

A principal company means a company of which another company is an effective 75% subsidiary (directly or indirectly). A company is an effective 75% subsidiary of another company, the parent, if:

1. the company is a 75% subsidiary of the parent, i.e. the parent owns, directly or indirectly, not less than 75% of its ordinary share capital;
2. the parent is beneficially entitled to not less than 75% of any profits available for distribution; and
3. the parent would be beneficially entitled to not less than 75% of the assets of the company available for distribution on a winding up.

The definition of "company" above means a company resident in an EU Member State or resident in a country that has a tax treaty with Ireland. Accordingly, both Irish and non-Irish companies may be part of a capital gains group.

(In the examples that follow, it should be assumed that a company is entitled to the same % of profits and assets as its shareholding %, e.g. where the example indicates 75% shareholding, it should be assumed that there is an entitlement to 75% of profits and assets also.)

The distinction between a group for loss relief purposes and for CGT purposes is that where a principal company is itself an effective 75% subsidiary, it and all its effective 75% subsidiaries will be part of the same capital gains group as its parent.

Example 24.3

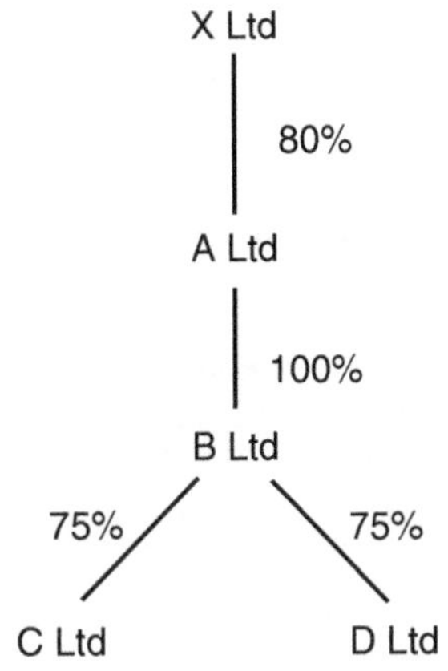

While X does not directly or indirectly own 75% of the ordinary share capital of C or D Ltd, all the companies, X, A, B, C and D, are members of the one capital gains group. This is because B, C or D are clearly 75% subsidiaries of A, and A itself is an effective 75% subsidiary of X.

All of the above companies do not form a single group for loss relief purposes, i.e. X, A, B and A, B, C, D groups form separate groups for loss relief purposes, as X does not have a 75% (direct or indirect) relationship with C or D.

Groups Incorporating Non-resident Companies

For many years the capital gains relief (transfer of assets without triggering a chargeable gain) for groups only applied to Irish resident companies.

The relief can also apply to an Irish branch of an EU resident company or of a company resident in a country that has a tax treaty with Ireland if it is a member of a group and the asset is used by the Irish branch, i.e. it is a chargeable asset. Therefore, any transfers between the branch and group members qualify for relief.

Example 24.4

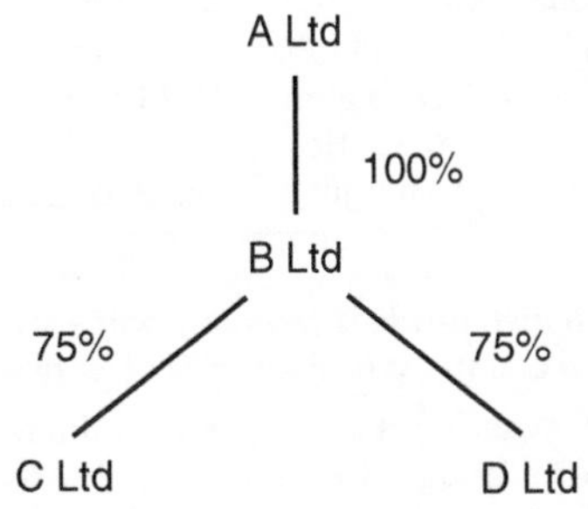

A,B,C,D form a capital gains group.

If A, C and D are Irish resident and B is resident in the UK (but has no branch in Ireland), A, B, C and D still form a capital gains group but the reliefs applying on transfer of assets between group members only apply to transfers between A, C and D. However, if B had an Irish branch and if the asset were used by the Irish branch, then a transfer of the asset between B and A,C or D would qualify.

If A, C and D are Irish resident and B is resident in the USA, A, B, C and D still form a capital gains group, i.e. B can be taken into account to determine whether C or D are effective 75% subsidiaries of A, but not for actually claiming any relief in its own right, unless it has an Irish branch.

> ***Example 24.5***
>
> 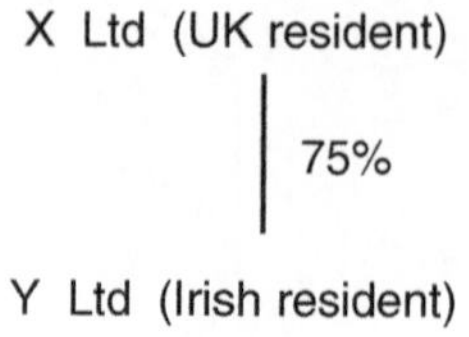
>
>
> A group structure exists.
>
> If the UK resident company has an Irish branch operation, capital assets can be transferred between Y Ltd and the Irish branch of X Ltd without triggering a gain. However, if an asset was transferred by Y Ltd to the head office of X Ltd in the UK, then Y Ltd is liable to corporation tax on the gain.

> ***Example 24.6***
>
> 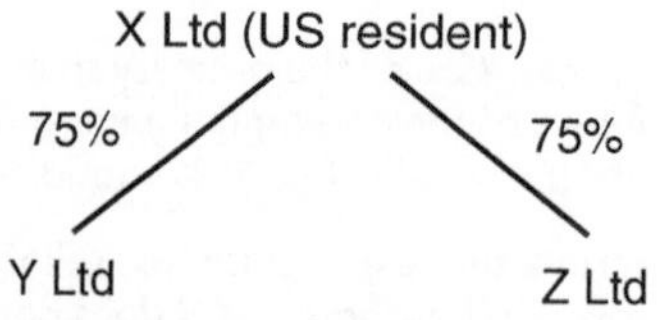
>
>
> While X Ltd, Y Ltd and Z Ltd constitute a capital gains group, only transfers between Y Ltd and Z Ltd will qualify for relief, unless X Ltd has an Irish branch.

24.5.2 Disposal of Capital Assets within a Group

In general, a transfer of an asset from one member of the group to another is deemed to be for a consideration of such amount that neither a gain nor a loss accrues.

The group is effectively treated as one taxpayer so that a chargeable gain does not arise until the asset is sold outside the group or the company holding the asset leaves the group.

> ***Example 24.7: Irish resident companies***
> X Ltd owns a building which it bought for €1 million, nine months ago. It disposes of it to its parent, Y Ltd, when it is worth €1.25 million. Therefore, a gain of €0.25 million arose. Normally this gain would be adjusted and included in the profits of X Ltd. However, this rule ensures that the asset moves at no gain/no loss, i.e. €1 million. So X Ltd has no chargeable gain and Y Ltd's base cost is €1 million.

> ***Example 24.8: Transfers between an Irish resident company and an Irish branch of an EU resident company or a company resident in a country which has a tax treaty with Ireland***
> A Ltd, an Irish resident company, is owned by B Ltd, a French resident company that has a branch in Ireland. A Ltd owns a building which it bought for €1 million, nine months ago. It disposes of it to the Irish branch of its parent, B Ltd, when it is worth €1.25 million. Therefore, a gain of €0.25 million arose. Normally, this gain would be adjusted and included in the profits of A Ltd.
>
> However, as the asset is being transferred to an Irish branch of an EU resident company and is, in any event, a specified asset, the asset continues to be a chargeable asset and, again, the rule ensures that the asset moves at no gain/no loss, i.e. €1 million. So A Ltd has no chargeable gain and B Ltd's base cost is €1 million.
>
> If the sale were from the Irish branch of B Ltd to A Ltd, again the sale would be at no gain/no loss.

The same rule applies to transfers of capital assets between Irish branches of companies resident in the EU or in a country with which Ireland has a tax treaty. **Relief for sales between group companies is granted automatically and is compulsory**. There are no provisions for making elections or time limits.

Capital Losses

There are no provisions for transferring chargeable losses between group companies.

Planning: If one member of a group has a capital loss that it is unable to utilise, and another company in the group wishes to sell an asset (to a non-group company) which will realise a gain, then to utilise the loss the asset must first be sold to the group company holding the loss and then sold by that company to the non-group company.

Example 24.9

A Ltd has a capital loss of €100,000. L Ltd, its subsidiary, wishes to sell quoted shares in November 2019 which will generate a gain of €50,000. If L Ltd just sells the shares, it must pay tax on the gain of €132,000 @12.5%, i.e. include a chargeable gain of €50,000 × 33/12.5% in its corporation tax computation.

Alternatively, if L Ltd sold the shares to A Ltd, which then sold them to the third party:

- L Ltd would have no gain as it sold the shares to A Ltd, a member of the group; and
- A Ltd would have a gain of €50,000, but it would have a loss of €100,000 to offset. Therefore, it would have no gain and a reduced loss forward of €50,000.

Inventories

An asset may be held as a capital asset by one company and as inventory by another, e.g. a property could be held as an investment or as inventory by a property dealer. Because of this, there are special rules which apply where an asset is transferred within a group and one company holds it as a capital asset and the other holds it as inventory. These rules are beyond the scope of this textbook.

24.5.3 Disposal of Capital Assets Outside the Group

If there is a disposal of an asset by a member of a group to a person outside the group, and the asset had been acquired by the company making the disposal from another group member, then **the period of ownership for the purpose of both indexation relief and determining the appropriate rate of tax to be applied to the gain (currently there is only one rate) is arrived at by reference to the length of time the asset had been owned by the group as a whole**. Of course, if the asset had originally been acquired prior to 6 April 1974, then the market value at that date will form the base cost for indexation purposes from 6 April 1974 to the date of sale.

Example 24.10

A Ltd and Y Ltd are Irish resident members of a capital gains group. Both companies prepare accounts to 31 December each year. Y Ltd acquired an asset on 13 February 1981 at a cost of €20,000 and transferred it to A Ltd in August 1999. On 31 December 2019 A Ltd sold the asset to a non-group company for €200,000. When the asset was disposed of by Y Ltd to A Ltd in 1999, no gain arose to Y Ltd.

A Ltd has a disposal in y/e 31 December 2019 of an asset with a base cost of €20,000, i.e. cost to Y Ltd on 13 February 1981.

continued overleaf

Computation of A Ltd's liability	€
Proceeds	200,000
Base cost €20,000	
Indexed at 3.240	(64,800)
Gain	135,200

Re-gross to include in corporation tax computation:

$€135,200 \times \frac{33}{12.5} = €356,928$

24.5.4 Company Leaving Group – Anti-avoidance Measure

Where a company ceases to be a member of a group of companies (otherwise than because of a genuine liquidation), the CGT deferred on any **asset transferred** between the companies since 6 April 1974 and **within 10 years of the company ceasing to be a member of the group** shall become payable.

In effect, the asset is treated as sold and immediately re-acquired by the company leaving the group, at its market value at the time of its original acquisition from the other member of the group, i.e. **the gain arising on the original transfer between the group members is triggered.** Indexation relief is applied by reference to that date and not by reference to the date the company actually leaves the group. It should be particularly noted that the gain and corresponding **liability is that of the company leaving the group** and is included as part of the corporation tax due for the accounting period in which the company leaves the group. The cost of future disposals of the assets in question by the company leaving the group will, of course, be the market value attributed to the earlier transfer.

If the asset was acquired by the company more than 10 years prior to the date the company leaves the group, this anti-avoidance rule is not triggered.

Example 24.11

Groups Ltd has owned the €2 issued share capital of Feeley Ltd since its incorporation on 3 January 1999. Both are Irish resident companies. Feeley Ltd commenced to trade on 1 February 1999. On 1 March 2009, Groups Ltd sold Feeley Ltd its warehouse for €9,000.

Groups Ltd had purchased the warehouse for €1,000 on 3 January 1999. The market value of the warehouse at 1 March 2009 was €10,000.

On 3 January 2019, Groups Ltd sold its shareholding in Feeley Ltd for €100,000.

What are the chargeable gains arising in respect of the above transactions?

Groups Ltd

2009: no chargeable gain arises on the sale of the warehouse as it is sold to another group member.

2019: if Feeley Ltd is a trading company or the business of Groups Ltd and its 5% subsidiaries taken as a whole consists of trading, then the gain on the sale of the shares may be exempt, if all other conditions are satisfied, including that the shares do not derive the greater part of their value from land (which includes buildings) in the State.

Feeley Ltd

2009: acquired asset on a no gain/no loss basis.

continued overleaf

2019: Feeley Ltd is leaving the group and, therefore, is treated as having sold and immediately re-acquired the warehouse at the market value at the time of its acquisition from Group Ltd.

	€	€
Market value on transfer at 1 March 2009		10,000
Cost 03/01/1999	1,000	
Index	1.212	
Indexed cost		(1,212)
Gain		8,788

Notes:

1. This would be taxable at the relevant rate in 2009.
2. When Feeley Ltd sells the warehouse, its base cost will be €10,000.
3. If Groups Ltd did not sell its shares in Feeley Ltd until March 2019, then no gain would arise on Feeley Ltd, as it would have held the warehouse for 10 years and, therefore, would be exempt from the anti-avoidance provisions.

24.5.5 Pre-entry Losses – Anti-avoidance Measure

In the past, companies who anticipated a future gain on the disposal of an asset would acquire a company with capital losses forward. The asset with the gain would be transferred intra-group at no gain/no loss to the company with the losses forward. This company would then sell the asset, realise the gain and the losses forward could be used to shelter the gain. The term "pre-entry losses" refers to losses accruing to the company before entry to the group as well as losses on the sale of assets brought in. Anti-avoidance provisions were introduced to prevent use of such pre-entry losses. While the provision ensures that these losses cannot be used subsequently by a group which had no previous commercial connection with the company when those losses accrued, that company will be allowed to use those losses itself in the same way that it could have had it never entered the group.

What is a Pre-entry Loss?
The term applies to:

- losses that have arisen in a company prior to it becoming a member of the group; and
- the pre-entry proportion of a loss arising on an asset held at the date a company became a member of a group (even though the loss is crystallised after it became a member).

Calculation of the Pre-entry Loss
The pre-entry loss is the smaller of:

- a loss calculated with reference to the market value at the date on which the company became a member of the group; or
- the amount of the loss which arose on disposal.

Pre-entry Loss before Joining Group: Gains from which it is Deductible
Pre-entry losses which actually accrued to the company before it joined the group can be set against:

- gains on assets disposed of after entry but which were held by the company before entry; or
- a gain arising on the disposal of an asset that was acquired from a non-group member and which has been used for the purpose of the company's trade.

Loss on Pre-entry Asset: Gains from which it is Deductible
The loss on a pre-entry asset must be split as between that which is pre-entry and can only be offset against the gains specified in the previous paragraph and that part which is post-entry and can be offset under the normal rules.

Questions

Review Questions

(See Suggested Solutions to Review Questions at the end of this textbook.)

Question 24.1

A client of yours, VC Holdings Ltd, has sent you an email seeking tax advice before closing the sale of one of its subsidiaries. The client hasn't involved you in the transaction to date, but now seeks your opinion in respect of any relevant tax matters. You have been tax advisor to the VC Holdings group for a number of years, and are familiar with most of the group's key tax issues.

VC Holdings Ltd owns two 100% subsidiaries – Irish Cable Installations Ltd and Fibre Optic Developments Ltd – both of which are Irish resident companies and have been owned by VC Holdings Ltd since they were incorporated.

Irish Cable will be sold for €20 million in the coming weeks to a third-party investor. The company has a successful cable trade, and also operates out of a high-specification factory unit based in Celbridge. The shares in Irish Cable are the subject matter of the sale. When Irish Cable was established in January 2017, VC Holdings Ltd contributed €500,000 for all its share capital.

Irish Cable took ownership of the factory premises in November 2017 from its previous owner, Fibre Optic. The value of the property in November 2017 was €4 million and all possible reliefs were claimed at that time. The property was originally purchased by Fibre Optic in 2014 at a cost of €3 million. It is currently valued at circa €4.5 million.

It is now 10 December 2019 and the sale of Irish Cable will close before 31 December. The group prepares its accounts annually to 31 December.

Requirement
Draft an email reply to VC Holdings Ltd addressing the tax implications of a sale of Irish Cable Installations Ltd before 31 December 2019 for it and/or its subsidiaries. Your email should consider CGT and stamp duty.

25

Distributions and Dividend Withholding Tax

Learning Objectives

After studying this chapter you will be able to:

- Identify and advise on company distributions and the dividend witholding tax implications for persons making or receiving distributions.

25.1 Distributions

The following constitute distributions:

- dividends paid by a company, including a capital dividend;
- scrip dividends – where a shareholder in a quoted resident company opts to take shares instead of a cash dividend;
- redemption of bonus securities;
- any distribution out of assets in respect of shares, except any part of it that represents a repayment of capital;
- sale of assets by a company at undervalue, or purchase of assets by a company at overvalue, from a shareholder;
- certain interest paid to non-resident parent companies;
- interest paid to certain directors of close companies that exceeds a prescribed limit (see **Chapter 26**); and
- certain expenses, incurred by a close company in the provision of benefits for a participator (see **Chapter 26**).

Distributions paid by an Irish resident company are not an allowable deduction when calculating corporation tax and may be subject to dividend withholding tax (see **Section 25.2**).

Distributions received by an Irish resident company from an Irish resident company are exempt from corporation tax (unless they are dividends from an Irish REIT). Distributions received by an Irish resident individual from an Irish resident company are assessed under Schedule F for income tax purposes. Distributions received by an Irish resident person from a non-resident company are assessed to tax under Schedule D Case III.

25.2 Dividend Withholding Tax

Dividend withholding tax (DWT) is payable in respect of all "relevant" distributions made by an Irish resident company, with certain exceptions. The standard rate of DWT is currently 20% on the distribution made. DWT is deducted at source by the company and paid over to Revenue on behalf of the shareholder. DWT due must be paid to Revenue and a DWT return filed within 14 days of the end of the month in which the distribution is made. The shareholder can claim a tax credit for the DWT against their tax liability.

Example 25.1
ABC Ltd, an Irish resident company, is owned by three Irish resident individuals. ABC Ltd is to make an interim dividend payment of €10,000 on 1 October 2019 to each of its shareholders for the year ended 31 December 2019. ABC Ltd must deduct DWT of €2,000 from each of the dividend payments made. Each shareholder will receive a net payment of €8,000.

As the dividends were paid in October 2019 the DWT is due to be paid and filed by 14 November 2019.

ABC Ltd must pay €6,000 DWT (€2,000 × 3) by 14 November 2019.

25.2.1 "Relevant" Distributions

DWT applies to all "relevant" distributions made by an Irish resident company. Relevant distributions are all dividends and distributions made by a company, including:

1. cash dividends;
2. any non-cash distributions;
3. expenses incurred by close companies in providing certain benefits for a participator in the company (see **Chapter 26**); and
4. interest in excess of a specified amount paid by close companies to directors (see **Chapter 26**).

The amount of the relevant distribution to which the DWT applies is the cash amount, where a cash payment is made, or the market value of the distribution where a non-cash distribution is made.

Example 25.2
DEF Ltd, which is owned by three Irish resident individuals, owns shares in another company, XYZ Ltd. DEF Ltd distributes all its shares in XYZ Ltd to its own shareholders. At the time the shares in XYZ Ltd are distributed, they have a market value of €90,000. DEF Ltd is required to pay **DWT of €18,000** (€90,000 × 20%) to Revenue. DEF Ltd is entitled to recover the DWT of €18,000 from its shareholders.

If DEF Ltd does not recover the DWT from its shareholders, the distribution will have to be grossed up (see **Section 26.2.1**).

25.2.2 Exemptions from DWT

Although DWT applies to all distributions outlined in **Section 25.1**, distributions made to persons not subject to tax on the distribution are exempt from DWT. These include:

1. an Irish resident company (unless a dividend paid from property income of an Irish REIT);
2. a pension scheme, approved minimum retirement fund and approved retirement fund;
3. a charity; and
4. certain non-resident persons (beyond the scope of this textbook); and
5. dividends paid out of exempt profits (beyond the scope of this textbook).

In order to qualify for exemption from DWT, the persons listed at 1. to 3. above must make a declaration of entitlement to relief to the company making the distribution, confirming that the declarer is beneficially entitled to the distribution and is entitled to exemption. The declaration remains valid until the person ceases to qualify as an excluded person.

However, in the case where an Irish resident company makes a distribution to its Irish resident parent (i.e. it is a 51% subsidiary), then a declaration is not required.

Questions

Review Questions

(See Suggested Solutions to Review Questions at the end of this textbook.)

Question 25.1

Lance Investments Ltd, an Irish resident company, is to pay a dividend of €500,000 on 1 November 2019. Its shareholders are as follows:

	Number of Ordinary Shares
Mr C (resident in the State)	3,000
Skeleton Investments Ltd (resident in the State)	18,000
Irish registered charity	1,000
Arrow Investments Ltd (resident in the State)	3,000
Total share capital	25,000

Requirement

(a) Compute the DWT payable by Lance Investments Ltd assuming all declarations necessary to obtain exemption are given.

(b) Indicate when the DWT is payable assuming the dividend is paid on 1 November 2019.

(c) Indicate the declarations to be made and the certificates to be provided by shareholders of Lance Investments Ltd in order to obtain exemption from DWT.

26

Close Companies

Learning Objectives

After studying this chapter you will be able to:

- Determine and advise on close company status for corporation tax purposes.
- Advise on and calculate the tax implications in respect of:
  - expenses of participators and their associates;
  - interest paid to directors and their associates;
  - loans to participators and their associates; and
  - repayment/write-off of loans to participators.
- Calculate the surcharge on undistributed estate and investment income of a trading company that is a close company.
- Calculate the surcharge on undistributed professional, estate and investment income of a professional service company that is a close company.
- Determine and advise on the tax implications of an election for a distribution not to be a distribution for close company surcharge purposes.

26.1 Meaning of Close Company

Most Irish private companies are close companies, whereas almost all publicly quoted companies are not close companies. Essentially, close company legislation is anti-avoidance legislation formulated to prevent a close company taking decisions so as to minimise tax in a way that would not be feasible for a publicly quoted company. The legislation is very widely defined to deter people finding a loophole and avoiding the rules.

Under section 430 TCA 1997, a **close company** is one that is resident in the State and:

- is under the control of:
  - five or fewer participators, or
  - participators who are directors; or
- if, on a full distribution of its income, more than 50% of it would be paid to:
  - five or fewer participators, or
  - participators who are directors.

26.1.1 "Participator"

A participator is a person having a share or interest in the capital or income of the company. The most common example would be a shareholder. However, the definition is very widely drafted so that a participator includes any person having a present or future share or interest in the capital, assets or income of the company; it also includes a "loan creditor" of the company, i.e. a creditor of the company, e.g. a debenture holder. Ordinary trade creditors are not included in the definition. A person carrying on a business of banking who has lent money to the company in the ordinary course of business is also not treated as a loan creditor.

26.1.2 "Control"

Under section 432 TCA 1997, a person is regarded as having control of a company if "such person exercises, or is able to exercise or is entitled to acquire, control, whether direct or indirect, over the company's affairs". The definition continues by making particular reference to whether "such person possesses or is entitled to acquire" more than 50% of the company's share capital, income if it were distributed, or assets in a winding up.

Importantly, in determining whether an individual satisfies any of these conditions, the rights and powers of such person's "associates", and any company over which they or their associates have control are also attributed to the individual.

26.1.3 "Associate"

An associate of a participator means:

1. a relative of the participator (i.e. spouse, civil partner, ancestor, lineal descendant, brother or sister), but it does not include an aunt, or uncle, or cousin;
2. a business partner of the participator; or
3. a trustee of a settlement established by the participator or a relative.

26.1.4 "Director"

In order to be regarded as a director, a person need not actually have the title of director. Section 433 TCA 1997 gives the meaning of "director" as:

"(a) any person occupying the position of director by whatever name called,
(b) any person in accordance with whose directions or instructions the directors are accustomed to act, and
(c) any person—
  (i) who is a manager of the company or otherwise concerned in the management of the company's trade or business and
  (ii) who is, either on his or her own or with one or more associates, the beneficial owner of, or able, directly or through the medium of other companies or by any other indirect means, to control **20 per cent or more** of the ordinary share capital of the company." (emphasis added)

Example 26.1

Shares in Alphabet Limited, an Irish resident company, are held as follows:

	Shareholding
Mr A (Director of company)	10%
Mrs A	2%
Mrs C (Mr A's aunt)	2%
Mrs B	10%
B Ltd (Shares in B Ltd held 50% each by Mr and Mrs B)	5%
Mr J (Mrs B's cousin)	4%
Mr D (Director of company)	10%
Mrs D	2%
Ms D (Mr and Mrs D's daughter)	2%
Mrs E (Mr D's sister)	2%
Mr F	6%
Mr G	5%
Other shareholdings (Unrelated parties all holding <5%)	40%
	100%

Is Alphabet Limited under the control of five or fewer participators?

Shares held by Mr A and his associates:		
Mr A	10%	
Mrs A	2%	12%
Shares held by Mrs B and her associates:		
Mrs B	10%	
B Ltd	5%	15%
Shares held by Mr D and his associates:		
Mr D	10%	
Mrs D	2%	
Ms D	2%	
Mrs E	2%	16%
Shares held by Mr F		6%
Shares held by Mr G		5%
		54%

In determining the shares controlled by each participator, shares held by associates are included. Spouses, civil partners, children, siblings and parents are included as associates; however, shares held by cousins or aunts/uncles are not included.

Alphabet Limited is under the control of "five or fewer participators" and is, therefore, a close company.

26.2 Consequences of Close Company Status

As a close company is controlled by relatively few persons, it could be perceived to be relatively easy for controlling participators to influence a company's decisions and so minimise their own, and the company's, tax liability. For example, the shareholders could choose to fund the company with loans rather than share capital, unlike a publicly quoted company with many shareholders where it would be quite infeasible. In the absence of the anti-avoidance rules applying to close companies, it would be more tax-efficient to pay shareholders interest, which is tax deductible for the company, rather than dividends, which are not tax deductible. However, close companies are subject to special anti-avoidance rules which have negative tax consequences for the company and/or its shareholders:

- Certain **expenses** for participators and their associates are treated as distributions, i.e. they are not tax deductible and are subject to DWT (**Section 26.2.1**).
- **Interest** paid to certain directors and their associates, which exceeds a prescribed limit, is treated as a distribution (**Section 26.2.2**).
- There is a tax penalty for close companies making **loans** to participators or their associates (**Section 26.2.3**).
- Loans to participators or their associates which are subsequently **written off** will be assessable to income tax in their hands (**Section 26.2.4**).
- A **surcharge** of **20%** is levied on the **distributable estate and investment income** of close companies, to the extent that it is not distributed (**Section 26.3**).
- In the case of **certain** closely held **service companies**, a **surcharge** of **15%/20%** is levied on:
  - 50% of the distributable trading income; and
  - 100% of the distributable estate and investment income (**Section 26.3.5**).

Obviously a publicly quoted company which is not a closely held company is not subject to these rules.

26.2.1 Certain Expenses for Participators and their Associates

Any expenses incurred by a close company in providing benefits or facilities of any kind for a participator or an associate of the participator will be treated as a distribution.

Where an item is treated as a distribution, there are three consequences:

1. the **expense** will be **disallowed** to the company, and is therefore added back when calculating corporation tax;
2. the company will have a dividend withholding tax (DWT) liability equal to 20% of the market value of the distribution. The company can recover this tax from the participator and, accordingly, the DWT is a cost to the participator. If the participator does not repay the DWT, the expense must be grossed up (the deemed distribution) when calculating corporation tax and DWT; and
3. the recipient will be **assessed** under **Schedule F** on the distribution, i.e. liable to income tax at the marginal rate (most likely 40%), liable to the Universal Social Charge (USC) at the marginal rate (up to 11%) and liable to PRSI at 4%.

The following expense payments are **not** treated as distributions:

- any expense repaid to the company by the participator;
- any expense incurred in providing benefits or facilities to directors or employees – as such expenses are already assessable as benefits in kind under Schedule E; and
- any expense incurred in connection with the provision for the spouse, civil partner, children or dependants or children of a civil partner of any director or employee of any pension, annuity, lump sum or gratuity to be given on his or her death or retirement.

The legislation also contains anti-avoidance measures to counter two or more close companies from arranging to make payments to one another's participators.

Example 26.2
Mr A holds 2% of the ordinary share capital of X Ltd, a close company. Mr A is not an employee or director of X Ltd.

X Ltd pays the rent on Mr A's house of €3,000 per annum. The amount is charged each year in X Ltd's accounts under rental expenses.

As X Ltd is a close company and Mr A is a participator, the expense will be treated as a distribution. Accordingly, the €3,000 will be disallowed to X Ltd in arriving at its profits assessable to corporation tax.

X Ltd will be required to pay DWT of €600 (€3,000 × 20%) to Revenue within 14 days of the end of the month in which the rent is paid. X Ltd can recover this €600 from Mr A.

Mr A will be assessed under Schedule F on €3,000, with a credit of €600 given against his total tax liability.

However, if Mr A is not going to repay the DWT, the deemed distribution of €3,000 is grossed up, i.e. €3,000 is a receipt net of DWT at 20%. Therefore, the gross amount is €3,000/0.8 = €3,750. X Ltd will have to pay DWT of €3,750 × 20% = €750. Mr A will be taxable under Schedule F on €3,750, with credit for the DWT of €750.

Whether or not Mr A repays the DWT due, he will be liable to income tax under Schedule F at his marginal rate – most likely 40%. He will also be liable to the USC, typically at 8% but up to 11% for self-employed taxpayers and others whose non-PAYE income is greater than €100,000, as well as to PRSI at 4%.

26.2.2 Interest Paid to Directors and their Associates

Generally, interest is an allowable deduction for corporation tax purposes if it is trade related (see **Chapter 20, Section 20.9.1**). The company may be obliged to withhold income tax at the standard rate (20%) from the interest payment and pay it over to Revenue on behalf of the lender (see **Chapter 21, Section 21.1**). The lender will be assessed to tax on the gross amount (Schedule D, Case IV) and will receive a tax credit for the income tax withheld.

However, close company anti-avoidance legislation restricts the amount of interest deductible by a close company where that interest is paid to a director, or associate of a director, of the close company or of any company that controls or is controlled by the close company, and who has a "material interest" in the close company or, where the company is controlled by another company, in that other company. The legislation is concerned with interest on loans in excess of a prescribed limit.

A person has a material interest if he, either on his own or with any one or more of his associates, or if any associate(s) of his with or without any such other associates, is the beneficial owner of, or is able to control, directly or indirectly, **more than 5%** of the ordinary share capital.

The prescribed limit is calculated in the first instance as an overall limit. The overall limit is then apportioned between the various directors affected according to the amounts of interest paid to them.

The overall limit is **13%** per annum on the **lower** of:

1. the total of all **loans** on which interest to directors (or their associates) with a "material interest" was paid by the company in the accounting period. Where the total of the loans was different at different times in the accounting period, the average total is to be taken; or
2. the **nominal** amount of the issued **share capital** of the company plus the amount of any **share premium** account at the **beginning of the accounting period**.

If the total amount of interest paid to a director in the accounting period exceeds this limit, the excess will be treated as a distribution. This excess is added back for corporation tax purposes and the company will have a DWT liability equal to 20% of the distribution (the excess interest payment). The director (or associate) will be **assessed** under **Schedule F** on the distribution at the marginal rate, with a tax credit for the DWT paid by the company.

Example 26.3
Zoey Ltd has an issued share capital of €100. It has two shareholders who are both directors and who each loaned the company €10,000 at an interest rate of 10% per annum.

The interest expense is €10,000 × 10% × 2 = €2,000. As both are directors with a material interest, then the limit on this interest is the *lower* of:

(a) 13% × €20,000 = €2,600; or
(b) 13% × €100 = €13.

Therefore, only €13 is a deductible expense to the company. As €2,000 has been expensed, €1,987 must be added back in the tax computation.

Zoey Ltd will be required to deduct DWT of €397 (€1,987 × 20%) from the interest paid and pay this amount to Revenue within 14 days of the end of the month in which the interest is paid. Also, assuming that the interest is annual interest, Zoey Ltd will have to withhold income tax from the interest, i.e. withhold €13 × 20% = €3.

From each director's perspective, they will be taxed on a gross distribution of 1/2 × €1,987, under Schedule F, and on interest income liable under Case IV of 1/2 × €13, with a credit for DWT of 1/2 × €397, and for income tax of 1/2 × €3, against his income tax liability.

Each will be liable to income tax at their mariginal rate – most likely 40%. Each will also be liable to the USC, typically at 8% but as high as 11%, and to PRSI at 4%.

Not all interest payments by a close company to its directors (and their associates) are restricted; only those interest payments to directors with a "material interest", i.e. directors (including their associates), controlling more than 5% of the ordinary share capital.

Example 26.4
XYZ Ltd has an issued share capital of €30,000. The shares are held as follows:

	€
Mr A (Director)	3,000
Mr B (Director)	1,200
Mrs B	400
Mr C (Director)	1,500
Mr D (Director)	4,000
Mr E (Director)	3,500
Mr F (Director)	1,500
Mr G	1,000
15 unrelated shareholders each holding less than 1,000 shares	13,900
	30,000

The following loans were made to the company:

Mr A €8,000 @ 20% per annum

Mr B €7,000 @ 10% per annum for the first six months increased to €9,000 @ 10% per annum for the last six months of the year

continued overleaf

Mr C	€6,000 @ 15% per annum
Mr E	€5,000 @ 12% per annum for the first six months and @ 16% per annum for the last six months
Mr F	€5,000 @ 15% per annum
Mr G	€2,000 @ 15% per annum

The interest charge in XYZ Ltd's profit and loss account was made up as follows:

		€	€
Mr A	€8,000 @ 20%		1,600
Mr B	€7,000 @ 10% × 1/2	350	
	€9,000 @ 10% × 1/2	450	800
Mr C	€6,000 @ 15%		900
Mr E	€5,000 @ 12% × 1/2	300	
	€5,000 @ 16% × 1/2	400	700
Mr F	€5,000 @ 15%		750
Mr G	€2,000 @ 15%		300
			5,050

The share capital of the company was the same at the start of the year. There was no share premium account.

1. **Is the company close?**

   Yes, it is under the control of participators who are directors, i.e.:

	€	€
Mr A		3,000
Mr B	1,200	
Mrs B	400	1,600
Mr C		1,500
Mr D		4,000
Mr E		3,500
Mr F		1,500
		15,100

2. Identify **directors** who made loans to the company and who, together with their associates, **own more than 5%** of the shares.

	€
Mr A	3,000 (10%)
Mr B	1,600 (5.33%)
Mr E	3,500 (11.67%)

3. **Calculate the overall limit**

   The lower of:

   (a) 13% of share capital, i.e. 13% × €30,000 = €3,900; or

   (b) 13% × loans from directors with material interest.

continued overleaf

	€
Mr A	8,000
Mr B (average)	8,000
Mr E	5,000
	21,000

13% × €21,000 = €2,730
The overall limit is €2,730.

4. **Apportion limit** to relevant directors by reference to interest paid.

	Interest Paid	Limit	Excess treated as a Distribution
Mr A	€1,600	$\frac{€1,600}{€3,100}$ × €2,730 = €1,409	€191
Mr B	€800	$\frac{€800}{€3,100}$ × €2,730 = €705	€95
Mr E	€700	$\frac{€700}{€3,100}$ × €2,730 = €616	€84
	€3,100	€2,730	€370

€370 will be disallowed to XYZ Ltd in computing its profits for corporation tax. DWT @ 20% must be deducted from the portion of the interest treated as a distribution. Each of the directors will be assessed under Schedule F to income tax, USC and PRSI on the proportion of the excess referable to him with a credit given against their total tax liability for the DWT deducted.

5. The company paid €5,050 of interest, of which €370 is treated as distribution. The balance of the interest, i.e. €4,680, is deductible. However, as with any other annual payment, the company must deduct tax at the standard income tax rate when paying this interest and remit this tax to Revenue. Each of the directors will be assessed under Schedule D Case IV to income tax, USC and PRSI on the proportion of the €4,680 referable to them with a credit given against their total tax liability for the income tax deducted.

26.2.3 Loans to Participators and their Associates

In the absence of the close company anti-avoidance rules, companies would lend money to shareholders rather than pay a dividend – such a loan would not be income in the hands of the shareholder so, therefore, it would not be taxable. To prevent this type of planning, a close company is subject to a tax penalty if it makes a loan to a participator.

Where a close company makes a loan to an **individual** who is a participator or an associate of a participator, the company will be required to pay income tax in respect of the amount of the loan grossed up at the standard rate (i.e. 20%) as if that grossed-up amount were an annual payment. A close company is to be regarded as making a loan to any person who incurs a debt to the company or where a debt due from a person to a third party is assigned to the company. As outlined in **Chapter 21, Section 21.1**, the income tax is paid to Revenue as part of the corporation tax payment for the accounting period. The deemed annual payment will not be a charge on the company's income for the purposes of corporation tax so that the company will not be entitled to a deduction for the net or gross amount.

There are **three exceptions** to the above, which means that the following are not treated as loans to participators:

1. Where the business of the company is, or includes, the lending of money and the loan is made in the ordinary course of that business.

2. Where a debt is incurred for the supply of goods or services in the ordinary course of the business of the close company, unless the credit given exceeds six months or is longer than the period normally given to the company's customers.
3. Loans made to directors or employees of the company (or an associated company) if:

   (a) the amount of the loan, together with all other loans outstanding made by the company (or its associated companies) to the borrower (or their spouse or civil partner), does not exceed €19,050;
   (b) the borrower works full-time for the company; and
   (c) the borrower does **not** have a "material interest" in the company or an associated company – a person has a material interest if, either on their own or with any one or more of their associates, or if any associate(s) with or without any such other associates, is the beneficial owner of, or is able to control, directly or indirectly, **more than 5%** of the ordinary share capital.

It should be noted that, in relation to 3(c), if the borrower subsequently acquires a material interest, the company will be required to pay income tax in respect of all the loans outstanding from the borrower at that time.

When the loan, or part of the loan, is repaid by the participator (or associate), the tax, or a proportionate part of it, will be refunded to the company provided a claim is made within four years of the year of assessment in which the loan is repaid. However, the tax will not be refunded with interest.

Example 26.5

ABC Ltd, a close company, made interest-free loans to the following shareholders in the accounting period to 31 March 2019.

	€
Mr A (full-time working director owning 10% of the share capital)	16,000
Mr B (full-time working director owning 4% of the share capital)	10,000
Mr C	8,000

What are the tax consequences for the company assuming that no other loans had been made to the three individuals in the past?

Solution

The company will be required to pay income tax in respect of the loans to Mr A and Mr C grossed up at the standard rate as if the grossed-up amount were an annual payment.

The tax penalty for the company is calculated as follows:

	€	
Mr A	16,000	
Mr C	8,000	
	24,000	× 20/80ths = €6,000

The loan to Mr B is not subject to the annual payment as Mr B:

(i) is a director who works full-time;
(ii) does not have a "material interest" in the company; and
(iii) the loan is less than €19,050.

This tax of €6,000 is added to the corporation tax on profits and must be paid over to the Collector General at the same time as the corporation tax on profits, i.e. preliminary tax due on/before 23 February 2019 and the balance due on/before 23 December 2019.

Revenue have confirmed that for the purposes of satisfying a company's preliminary tax obligations for an accounting period, Revenue will not require the company to take account of the income tax on loans to participators and their associates in circumstances where the participator or associate **repays the loan by the due date for filing of the company's corporation tax return**, i.e. within nine months of the end of the accounting period in which the loan was made.

The loan concerned must be undertaken in good faith and for purposes other than tax avoidance. The practice will not apply in the case of "bed and breakfast"-type arrangements where a new loan is taken out on, or shortly after, repayment of an existing loan. In such cases Revenue will insist that the income tax be taken into account for preliminary tax purposes. However, in circumstances where it is the practice of a director to operate a current account with the company and this account is cleared annually from the director's own resources (e.g. the director's remuneration), then such an arrangement will not be regarded as a "bed and breakfast" arrangement.

26.2.4 Write-off of Loans to Participators

Where a company makes a loan to a participator and subsequently releases or writes it off, the shareholder receives income at the time of writing off the loan, i.e. a debt is released. The participator will be assessed to tax on the amount released or written off grossed up at the standard rate of income tax. It is taxable under Case IV. The tax paid by the company can be claimed as a tax credit by the participator against their tax liability, but it can never generate a tax refund.

Example 26.6

Assume that in the previous example Mr A repays his loan of €16,000 on 31 December 2019 and at the same time the company writes off the loan to Mr C.

What are the tax consequences for the company and the shareholder?

Company

The company will be refunded the tax on Mr A's loan, i.e. €4,000 (20/80 × €16,000).
However, it will lose the tax paid on Mr C's loan, i.e. €2,000 (20/80 × €8,000).

Shareholders

There are no tax consequences for Mr A.

Mr C, however, will be assessed to tax under Case IV Schedule D on the grossed-up amount of the loan, i.e. €10,000 (8,000 × 100/80).

Assume Mr C has other income of €30,000, is liable to PRSI under Class A, has personal tax credits of €3,300, is single and the tax bands are as outlined below. The grossed-up loan of €10,000 would be taxed at current rates of tax as follows:

	€
Other income	30,000
Case IV loan	10,000
Taxable income	40,000
Tax: €35,300 @ 20%	7,060
€4,700 @ 40%	1,880
	8,940
Less: personal tax credits	(3,300)
	5,640
Less: €10,000 @ 20%	(2,000)
Tax payable (before PRSI and USC)	3,640

continued overleaf

USC:		
€12,012 @ 0.5%	= €60	
€7,682 @ 2%	= €157	
€20,126 @ 5%	= €906	1,123
PRSI €40,000 @ 4%		1,600

26.3 Close Company Surcharge

26.3.1 Introduction

Where a company has cash surplus to its trading requirements, it can invest the cash itself or dividend it to the shareholders. If the company invests the cash itself, it will be liable to corporation tax at 25% on most investment income. If, instead, it pays a dividend to its shareholders, the shareholder must pay tax – up to 55% (i.e. 40% income tax, plus up to 11% USC, plus 4% PRSI) – on the dividend and can only invest the dividend net of tax. Therefore, unless the shareholder needs the cash, it would generally be left in the company to avoid shareholder tax. The close company anti-avoidance rule, known as the surcharge, reduces some of the benefit of leaving cash in a company.

A surcharge of 20% is levied on a close company that does not distribute its after-tax estate (rental) and investment income. There is no surcharge on Case I trading income, but there is a surcharge of 15% on half the after-tax Case II income of professional services companies (see **Section 26.3.5**.)

Close company distributions (i.e. expenses for participators and associates and excess interest to directors and associates) can be taken into account to reduce the amount on which the surcharge is levied. The surcharge will not apply to any income that a company is by law precluded from distributing. If the amount liable to the surcharge is more than the accumulated undistributed income at the end of the accounting period, then the surcharge is levied on the lower accumulated undistributed income.

There will be no surcharge if the excess distributable income over the distributions is €2,000 or less. There will be marginal relief where the excess over the distributions is slightly in excess of €2,000, restricting the surcharge to four-fifths of the excess over €2,000. Where the accounting period is less than 12 months, the €2,000 will be reduced proportionately. If there are associated companies, the €2,000 will be reduced by dividing it by one plus the number of associated companies.

26.3.2 7.5% Trading Deduction

Revenue appreciates that a certain amount of undistributed income may be required within a company. Accordingly, trading and professional service companies are entitled to a 7.5% trading deduction when calculating "distributable estate and investment income" for close company surcharge purposes. This 7.5% trading deduction is not available to an investment company (see **Chapter 27**).

26.3.3 Trading Company: Basic Surcharge Calculation

In essence, the surcharge applies to after-tax non-trading income that has not been distributed to shareholders. It is a surcharge on undistributed estate and investment income, i.e. not trading income and not gains. However, it includes dividends received from Irish companies (franked investment income) that are exempt from corporation tax. The basic calculation of the surcharge for a trading company that has no trading losses, Case V losses, relevant trading charges or relevant charges is given below.

COMPUTATION – CLOSE COMPANY SURCHARGE

		€
Case III		X
Case IV		X
Case V (before capital allowances)		X
'Passive income'		Y
Franked investment income (FII)		X
Estate and investment income		X
Less: corporation tax (usually @ 25%) on 'passive income' ("Y")		(X)
After-tax estate and investment income		Z
Less: 7.5% trading deduction of "Z"		(X)
Distributable Estate and Investment Income (DEII)		X
Less:		
Dividends declared for or in respect of the accounting period and paid during or within 18 months of the end of the accounting period	X	
All distributions made in the accounting period (other than dividends)	X	(X)
Liable to surcharge		X
Surcharge @ 20%		X

Example 26.7

Shop Ltd, a close company, runs a shop in Dublin. It doesn't pay any dividends and had the following income in the year ended 31 December 2019:

Case I	€100,000
Case III	€2,000
Case V	€6,000

The close company surcharge is payable on distributable estate and investment income, to the extent that it is not distributed. Therefore:

	€
Estate and investment income (Note)	8,000
Corporation tax @ 25%	(2,000)
	6,000
Trading deduction 7.5%	(450)
DEII	5,550
Less: dividends paid/payable within 18 months	Nil
Liable to surcharge	5,550
Surcharge @ 20%	1,110

Note: as there are no dividends received from Irish companies (FII), 'passive income' in this example is the same as 'estate and investment income', i.e. Case III plus Case V (€2,000 + €6,000).

26.3.4 Trading Company Surcharge Calculation: Losses and Charges on Income

There is no deduction allowed for losses arising outside the current accounting period. Losses carried forward or back from other accounting periods are ignored.

Example 26.8

Trumps Ltd, a close company, has the following results for the year ended 31 December 2019:

	€
Trade income	480,000
Deposit interest	2,000
Rental income	40,000
Rental loss forward from 2018	(10,000)

Notes

1. The company had a loss forward relating to the trade of €20,000.
2. The company had chargeable gains in the accounting period of €2,000, after adjustment.
3. A cash dividend of €700 was received from another Irish company in the accounting period.
4. An interim dividend of €14,000 in respect of the accounting period was paid on 1 October 2020. A final dividend of €9,580 will be paid on 10 October 2021.

What is the amount of the close company surcharge (if any) arising in respect of the accounting period ended 31 December 2019?

Calculation of distributable estate and investment income

	€
Case III	2,000
Case V	40,000
Passive income	42,000
FII	700
Estate and investment income	42,700
Less: corporation tax @ 25% on €42,000	(10,500)
	32,200
Less: 7.5% × €32,200	(2,415)
Distributable estate and investment income	29,785

Note: any non-estate and investment income (e.g. Case I) and any losses forward and chargeable gains are ignored (i.e. only estate and investment income of the current accounting period is relevant).

Calculate amount on which surcharge is levied

	€
Distributable estate and investment income	29,785
Less: dividends paid within 18 months (Note)	(14,000)
Liable to surcharge	15,785
Surcharge @ 20% = €3,157	

Note: the final dividend of €9,580, paid at 10 October 2021, is not deducted as it was paid more than 18 months after the end of the accounting period.

If the final dividend were paid on, say, 30 June 2021, the surcharge could have been as follows:

	€
DEII	29,785
Less: dividends paid within 18 months (€14,000 + €9,580)	(23,580)
Liable to surcharge	6,205
Surcharge @ 20%	1,241

When a company incurs trading and investment losses in an accounting period, such losses must be deducted when calculating the distributable income for close company surcharge purposes. Similarly, relevant trade charges (see **Chapter 21, Section 21.2**) and relevant charges (i.e. non-trade charges – **Section 21.2.3**) paid in an accounting period reduce the amount of income available to be distributed by a company and must be deducted in calculating the amount liable to the surcharge. Therefore a more complex pro forma surcharge computation is required.

COMPUTATION – TRADING COMPANY
WITH LOSSES AND/OR CHARGES ON INCOME SURCHARGE

Step 1: Identify income for the accounting period

Income (i.e. Cases I, III, IV & V)	X
Less:	
current-year losses	(X)
current-year relevant trade charges	(X)
Income for accounting period	X

Step 2: Calculate 'passive income' (i.e. estate and investment income subject to corporation tax)

$$\text{Income for accounting period (from Step 1)} \times \frac{\text{(Total Cases III, IV and V)}}{\text{Income as per Step 1}}$$

Step 3: Calculate distributable estate and investment income

Passive income (from Step 2)	X
Less: relevant (non-trade) charges	(X)*
Net passive income	X
FII	X*
Estate and investment income	X
Less: CT on net passive income	(X)
	X
Less: 7.5% trading deduction	(X)
DEII	X

Step 4: Calculate surcharge

DEII (from Step 3)	X
Less: distributions paid/payable within 18 months of the accounting period	(X)
Liable to surcharge	X
Surcharge @ 20%	X

* If relevant charges exceed passive income, deduct excess from FII.

Example 26.9: Trading loss

Loss Limited, a close company, runs a garage in Dublin. It pays no dividends and had the following income in the year ended 31 December 2019:

	€
Case I	(10,000)
Case III	2,000
Case V	16,000
FII	5,000

Close company surcharge calculation

1. Calculate income for accounting period:

	€
Case III	2,000
Case V	16,000
Income	18,000
Less: Case I current year	(10,000)
Income for AP	8,000

2. Calculate 'passive income':

€8,000 × €18,000/€18,000	8,000

3. Calculate DEII:

Passive income	8,000
FII	5,000
Estate and investment income	13,000
Less: CT @ 25% on passive income (€8,000)	(2,000)
	11,000
Less: 7.5% trading deduction	(825)
DEII	10,175

4. Calculate surcharge:

DEII	10,175
Less: dividends paid/payable within 18 months	NIL
Liable to surcharge	10,175
Surcharge @ 20%	2,035

Example 26.10: Trade charge

Patent Ltd, a close company, runs a manufacturing business in Dublin. It had the following income and charges in the year ended 31 December 2019:

	€
Case I	10,000
Trade charges paid	600
Case III	2,000
FII	17,000

On 9 January 2020, the company pays a dividend of €10,000 in respect of the year. How much close company surcharge is due?

Close company surcharge calculation

1. Calculate income for accounting period:

	€
Case I	10,000
Case III	2,000
Income	12,000
Less: trade charges	(600)
Income for AP	11,400

continued overleaf

2. Calculate 'passive income':	
€11,400 × €2,000/€12,000	1,900
3. Calculate DEII:	
Passive income	1,900
FII	17,000
Estate and investment income	18,900
Less: CT @ 25% on €1,900	(475)
	18,425
Less: 7.5% trading deduction	(1,382)
DEII	17,043
4. Calculate surcharge:	
DEII	17,043
Less: dividends paid	(10,000)
Liable to surcharge	7,043
Surcharge @ 20%	1,409

Example 26.11: Non-trade charge

Interesting Limited, a close company, has a business in Dublin. It pays no dividend and had the following income and charges in the year ended 31 December 2019:

	€
Case I	100,000
Case III	2,000
Case V	16,000
FII	5,000
Non-trade charge paid	4,000

Close company surcharge calculation

1. Calculate income for accounting period:

	€
Case I	100,000
Case III	2,000
Case V	16,000
Income	118,000

2. Calculate 'passive income':

€118,000 × €18,000/€118,000	18,000

3. Calculate DEII:

Passive income	18,000
Less: non-trade charge	(4,000)
Net passive income	14,000
FII	5,000
Estate and investment income	19,000
Less: CT @ 25% on €14,000	(3,500)
	15,500
Less: 7.5% trading deduction	(1,163)
DEII	14,337

continued overleaf

4. Calculate surcharge:	
DEII	14,337
Less: dividends paid/payable within 18 months	NIL
Liable to surcharge	14,337
Surcharge @ 20%	2,867

26.3.5 Service Company Surcharge

A service company is a close company, the principal part of whose income chargeable under Cases I and II of Schedule D and Schedule E is derived from:

1. carrying on directly a profession or providing professional services or the having, or exercising, of an office or employment; or
2. providing services or facilities of any nature;
   (a) to a company within 1. above;
   (b) to an individual or partnership carrying on a profession;
   (c) to a person who holds or exercises an office or employment; or
   (d) to a person or partnership connected with any person in (a) to (c) above.

Services provided to an unconnected person or partnership are, however, ignored.

For a service company to be liable to the surcharge under this legislation, the main part of its income must come from a profession, provision of professional services, an employment or provision of the services or facilities to a connected person. Therefore, it is important to understand what is a profession. There is no definition in the law as to what is a profession. The UK case of *CIR v. Maxse* (1919) sets out the determining factors to be taken into account. A profession involves the idea of an occupation requiring either purely intellectual skill or of a manual skill controlled by the intellectual skill of the operator, e.g. painting or sculpture or surgery. This is distinguished from an occupation that is substantially the production or sale, or arrangement for the production or sale, of commodities, which would not be a profession.

The issue of whether an activity is a profession has been considered in a number of cases, particularly in the UK. Revenue has set out what, in its view, are and are not professions, taking into account case law. Activities considered as professions are:

- Accountant
- Actor
- Actuary
- Archaeologist
- Architect
- Auctioneer/estate agent
- Barrister
- Computer programmer
- Dentist
- Doctor
- Engineer
- Journalist
- Management consultant
- Optician
- Private school
- Quantity surveyor
- Solicitor
- Veterinary surgeon.

Revenue's guidance lists the following activities as, generally, **not considered** to be the carrying on of a **profession**:

- Advertising agent
- Auctioneers of livestock in a cattle mart
- Insurance brokers
- Operation of a retail pharmacy
- Public relations company
- Stockbrokers
- Bookkeeping.

The differences between this surcharge and the surcharge on trading companies is that **half the after-tax Case I/II income** is also liable to surcharge, but **a rate of only 15%** applies to this part of the income, in addition to the 20% surcharge applicable to distributable estate and investment income (net of 7.5%).

As with trading companies, there is no deduction for losses arising outside the current accounting period or for Case V capital allowances. Losses incurred in the accounting period, relevant trade charges and relevant charges paid in an accounting period must be deducted when calculating the distributable income for close company surcharge purposes. The computation is more complex as income from the trade is liable to a separate surcharge at a lower rate (15%). The distributable trading income must be identified and the distributions paid/payable must be allocated to minimise the surcharge payable. Hence, a more complex pro forma surcharge computation is required.

COMPUTATION – SERVICE COMPANY
WITH LOSSES AND/OR CHARGES ON INCOME SURCHARGE

Step 1: Identify income for the accounting period

Income (i.e. Cases II, III, IV & V)	X
Less:	
current-year losses	(X)
current-year relevant trade charges	(X)
Income for accounting period	X

Step 2: Calculate 'passive income' (i.e. estate and investment income subject to corporation tax)

Income for accounting period (from Step 1) × $\frac{\text{(Total Cases III, IV and V)}}{\text{Income as per Step 1}}$

Step 3: Calculate distributable estate and investment income

Passive income (from Step 2)	X
Less: relevant charges	(X)*
Net passive income	X
FII	X
Estate and investment income	X
Less: CT on net passive income	(X)
	X
Less: 7.5% trading deduction	(X)
DEII	X

Step 4: Calculate distributable trading income (DTI)

Income for accounting period (from Step 1)	X
Less: passive income (from Step 2)	(X)
Trading income	X*
Less: CT on trading income 12.5%	(X)
Distributable trading income	X

Step 5: Calculate amount liable to surcharge

DEII (from Step 3)	X
DTI (from Step 4) × 50%	X
	X
Less: distributions paid/payable within 18 months of the accounting period	(X)
Liable to surcharge	X

Step 6: Calculate surcharge

As DEII is taxed at 20% and DTI at 15%, the amount calculated at Step 5 needs to be divided between DTI and DEII. All distributions are treated as first offset against DEII.

DEII (from Step 3)	X
Less: distributions paid/payable within 18 months of the accounting period	(X)**
DEII liable to surcharge	X
Surcharge @ 20%	X
Liable to surcharge (from Step 5)	X
Less: DEII liable to surcharge	(X)
	X**
Surcharge @ 15%	X
Total Surcharge:	
Surcharge @ 20%	X
Surcharge @ 15%	X
Total surcharge	X

* If relevant charges (non-trade charges) exceed passive income, deduct the excess from trading income.

** If distributions paid/payable within 18 months exceed DEII, use excess to reduce the amount liable to surcharge at 15%.

Example 26.12

Good Advice Ltd, a closely held firm of management consultants, had the following income for the year ended 31 December 2019:

	€
Professional income	100,000
Interest on Government securities	30,000
Rental income	20,000
Irish dividend received (cash amount)	14,000

The company declared and paid an interim dividend of €50,000 for the accounting period on 6 July 2019.

As the principal part of the company's income is derived from carrying on a profession, the company is a service company.

continued overleaf

The amount on which the surcharge is levied is calculated as follows:

1. Calculate income for accounting period:

	€
Case II professional income	100,000
Case III interest	30,000
Case V rent	20,000
Income for AP	150,000

2. Calculate 'passive income':

$$€150,000 \times \frac{(€30,000+€20,000)}{€150,000}$$

	50,000

3. Calculate DEII:

Passive income	50,000
FII	14,000
Estate and investment income	64,000
Less: CT @ 25% on €50,000	(12,500)
	51,500
Less: 7.5% trading deduction	(3,863)
DEII	47,637

4. Calculate DTI:

Income for AP	150,000
Less: passive income	(50,000)
Trading income	100,000
Less: CT @ 12.5%	(12,500)
DTI	(87,500)

5. Liable to surcharge:

DEII	47,637
DTI × 50%	43,750
Less: dividend paid	(50,000)
Liable to surcharge	41,387

6. Calculate surcharge:

DEII	47,637
Less: dividend paid	(50,000)
Excess	2,363
Surcharge @ 20%	NIL
DTI × 50%	43,750
Less: excess dividend	(2,363)
Liable to surcharge	41,387
Surcharge @ 15%	6,208
Total surcharge	6,208

26.4 Other Matters

26.4.1 Case III Income

Foreign dividends are generally taxable under Case III. In relation to foreign dividends, there are two key points:

1. If the dividends are paid by a foreign company, a gain on disposal of whose shares would qualify for exemption (see **Section 24.3**), then that dividend is exempt from the surcharge and will not be included in Case III income for the surcharge calculation.
2. Case III income is generally taxed at 25%. However, many foreign dividends are taxable at 12.5% (see **Chapter 28, Section 28.1.2**) and, therefore, for any such Case III income, the tax rate used in the surcharge computation will be 12.5%.

26.4.2 Election – Not a Distribution for Surcharge

A company making a distribution (e.g. dividend) and a company receiving a distribution may jointly elect that the distribution will not be treated as a distribution for the purposes of the surcharge calculation.

As a result, an Irish holding company and an Irish subsidiary that pays or makes a distribution to the holding company can elect not to treat the distribution as coming under the close company surcharge provisions. Where such an election is made, the distribution will be treated as not being a distribution received by the holding company and as not being a distribution made by the subsidiary.

Example 26.13: Impact on company receiving FII

Using the information provided in Example 26.11, the company agreed with its subsidiary to treat the FII as not a distribution for surcharge purposes. Therefore, the company does not include it when calculating DEII. The surcharge will be reduced as follows:

Calculate DEII:

	€
Passive income	18,000
Less: non-trade charge	(4,000)
Net passive income	14,000
FII	n/a
Estate and investment income	14,000
Less: CT @ 25% on €14,000	(3,500)
	10,500
Less: 7.5% trading deduction	(788)
DEII	9,712
Surcharge @ 20%	1,942

Example 26.14: Impact on company paying FII

Using the information provided in Example 26.12, the company agreed with its parent to treat the dividend paid by Good Advice Ltd as not a distribution for surcharge purposes. Therefore, it is not deducted when calculating the amount liable to the surcharge. The surcharge will increase as follows:

5. Liable to surcharge:

	€
DEII	47,637
DTI × 50%	43,750
	91,387
Less: dividend paid	–
Liable to surcharge	91,387

continued overleaf

6. Surcharge:	
DEII	47,637
Less: dividend paid	–
Liable to surcharge	47,637
Surcharge @ 20%	9,527
DTI × 50%	43,750
Less: excess dividend	–
Liable to surcharge	43,750
Surcharge @ 15%	6,563
Total surcharge:	
Surcharge @ 20%	9,527
Surcharge @ 15%	6,563
Total	16,090

Such an election is beneficial where a company with only Case I income is required to pay a dividend to its parent company.

26.4.3 Payment of Surcharge

The surcharge is treated as corporation tax for the earliest accounting period that ends on or after a day which is 12 months after the end of the accounting period in which the investment or rental income arises.

Example 26.15

Again, using the information from Example 26.12. The accounting period to which the surcharge relates is the year ended 31 December 2019. If the company prepares the next accounts to 31 December 2020, the earliest accounting period that ends on a day which is 12 months after the year ended 31 December 2019 is the year ended 31 December 2020, so the surcharge of €6,208 will be added to the corporation tax liability for the year ended 31 December 2020. It will be included when calculating the preliminary tax payment(s) and the balance of tax for the year ended 31 December 2020.

However, if the company prepares the next accounts for the nine-month period ending 30 September 2020, this is not more than 12 months after the ending of the accounting period to which the surcharge relates. Therefore, the surcharge will not be added to the corporation tax liability for the period ended 30 September 2020. It will be added to the corporation tax liability for the first accounting period ending 31 December 2020 or later.

Questions

Review Questions

(See Suggested Solutions to Review Questions at the end of this textbook.)

Question 26.1

(a) State the tax effect on a close company arising out of a loan made to a participator in that company. Indicate the circumstances in which the loan would have no tax consequences for the company.

(b) Size Ltd is a close company and has the following adjusted profits for the year ended 31 December 2019:

	€
Trading profits	500,000
Rents	30,000
Deposit interest	3,000
	533,000

It has declared the following dividends payable out of the year ended 31 December 2019 profits and payable on the dates shown:

	€
30/01/2020	6,300
30/09/2020	3,000
10/07/2021	4,000

Requirement
Show Size Ltd's corporation tax liability for the year ended 31 December 2019 and the additional corporation tax payable for the year ended 31 December 2020 due to the surcharge.

Question 26.2

Close Ltd is a family-owned distribution company with no associated companies. Results to 31 December 2019 are as follows:

	€	€
Gross profit	50,000	
Other income	10,000	
		60,000
Depreciation	15,000	
Salaries	10,000	
Rent and rates	1,000	
Sundry	1,100	(27,100)
Net profit		32,900

The directors do not recommend the payment of a dividend.

Other Income	€
Interest on Government securities	8,500
Capital grants	1,500
	10,000

Sundry	
Miscellaneous office expenses	300
Expenses of majority shareholder's brother Y, who does not work for Close Ltd, paid to him on 01/07/2019	800
	1,100

Capital allowances due are €4,000.

Requirement

(a) Compute corporation tax payable.
(b) Compute surcharge arising.
(c) Indicate treatment of specific items.

Question 26.3

Maxi Ltd is a family-owned company with no associated companies, dealing in farm machinery. The results for the year ended 31 December 2019 were as follows:

	€	€
Sales		6,300,000
Opening inventories	1,100,000	
Purchases	5,650,000	
	6,750,000	
Closing inventories	1,450,000	
		(5,300,000)
		1,000,000
Less: expenses		
Administration	220,000	
Financial	200,000	
Distribution and sales (Note 1)	270,000	
Depreciation	100,000	(790,000)
Trading profit		210,000
Loss on sale of plant (Note 5)	(20,000)	
Profit on sale of building (Note 2)	1,480,000	
Rents (Note 3)	200,000	
		1,660,000
Net profit		1,870,000

Notes:

1. The following items were included in distribution and sales:

(a) Entertainment

	€
Entertaining customers	6,000
Entertaining suppliers	5,000
Staff Christmas party	10,000
Christmas gifts for suppliers	900
Cost of MD attending trade fair in London	850
	22,750

(b) Lease payments

The company leases equipment, the cost of which is capitalised in the company's accounts. The lease agreement states that the burden of wear and tear remains with the lessor. Total repayments made during the year ended 31 December 2019 were €15,000, which included both capital repayments and finance charges.

The company also leases two vans, the cost of which are not capitalised in the company's accounts. Total repayments made during the year ended 31 December 2019 were €10,000, which included both capital repayments and finance charges.

Total amounts included in distribution and sales in respect of these items were as follows:

	€
Equipment – finance charges	2,000
Vans – lease payments	10,000
	12,000

2. The building, which was sold in October 2019, had been acquired in May 1974 for €50,000. The building was located on a site on which planning permission had been granted for the construction of a shopping centre. Proceeds received for the building were €1.5 million. The current use value of the building at the time of sale was €750,000. Legal fees of €18,000 were incurred in connection with the disposal. The company acquired a new site in November 2019 for €200,000 on which it intends to build a replacement factory during 2020. €15,000 in respect of architect's fees for drawings for the new factory have been included in distribution expenses above.
3. On 1 June 2019, the company re-let its investment property under a 20-year lease. A premium of €50,000 was received on the sub-letting. This premium is included in rental income in the income statement.
4. In June 2019, the managing director (and principal shareholder) borrowed €550,000 from the proceeds from the sale of the building to purchase a new residence for himself in his own name.
5. 100% capital allowances had been claimed in respect of the plant sold. Total capital allowances, including balancing allowances and charges, for the year were €50,000.
6. Maxi Ltd has €210,000 of trading losses forward at 31 December 2018.

Requirement

Calculate in respect of Maxi Ltd:

(a) the corporation tax payable;
(b) the CGT liability, if any; and
(c) any surcharge which might become payable.

Note: the CGT consequences arising from the granting of the lease may be ignored.

Question 26.4

Servisco Ltd, a closely held company trading as management consultants, had the following income for the year ended 31 December 2019:

	€
Professional income	430,000
Rental income	100,000
Interest on Government stocks	50,000
Chargeable gains before adjustment (October 2019)	54,000

The company had a loss forward of €9,000 on its professional activities from the year ended 31 December 2018.

In the year ended 31 December 2020, the company sustained a loss on its professional activities of €10,000, all of which was claimed for set off against the 2019 income.

The company received Irish dividends of €7,500.

Dividends of €70,000 were paid within 18 months.

Requirement

Compute the company's corporation tax liability for the year ended 31 December 2019 and the surcharge that will be payable as part of the corporation tax liability for the year ended 31 December 2020.

Question 26.5

Machinery Ltd was incorporated in the Republic of Ireland on 1 June 2001 and since that date has been engaged in providing machinery to companies. The founder members of the company were Mr V. Duffy and his wife, Fanny. The company was formed to take over their existing business, which they had previously conducted in partnership. Mr and Mrs Duffy have actively encouraged members of their immediate family and other relatives to take up employment within the company and have endeavoured to ensure that the control of the company remains, as far as possible, within the family. The company's income statement for the year ended 31 December 2019 showed the following results:

	€	€
Sales		1,660,000
Inventories at 31/12/2019	450,000	
Inventories at 01/01/2019	360,000	90,000
		1,750,000
Purchases		(805,000)
		945,000
Less:		
Depreciation	59,790	
Rent	79,710	
Light and heat	17,500	
Distribution costs	39,000	
Bank and loan interest	65,000	
Motor expenses (all vans)	44,000	
Sundry expenses	13,000	(318,000)
Net profit from trading		627,000
Add:		
Bank deposit interest	10,000	
Rents from let property		
(after allowable deductions)	50,000	60,000
Profit for year		687,000

The shareholdings in, and loans made to, the company as at 31 December 2019 were:

	Ordinary €1 shares	Loans Made	Interest Paid
Mr V. Duffy (Director)	3,000	€4,000 @ 15%	€600
Mrs V. Duffy (Director)	1,250	€5,000 @ 12%	€600
G. Duffy (mother of V. Duffy)	2,900	€5,000 @ 15%	€750
S. Duffy (father of V. Duffy)	2,000	€5,000 @ 15%	€750
D. O'Connell (Director)	2,750	€5,000 @ 15%	€750
Mrs K. Moran (aunt of V. Duffy)	500	–	–
L.T. Smith (Director)	2,100	€10,000 @ 13.21%	€1,321
Louise Hare (Company Secretary and sister of Paul Hare)	3,000	€3,000 @ 12%	€360
Paul Hare (husband of V. Duffy's sister)	2,500	€3,000 @ 9.3%	€279
	20,000		€5,410

Notes:

1. The loan interest was paid in addition to bank interest of €59,590, thus reconciling with the amount shown in the income statement.
2. For the accounting period ended 31 December 2019, capital allowances were €10,700.
3. None of the shareholders is related, other than as shown above.
4. The share capital at 1 January 2019 was the same as at 31 December 2019.

Requirement
Compute the corporation tax liability of the company for the accounting year ended 31 December 2019 and the surcharge that will be payable as part of the corporation tax liability for the year ended 31 December 2020.

Question 26.6

Tax Advisors Ltd, a professional services company, had the following sources of income and charges for the year ended 31 December 2019:

	€
Case II income	100,000
Case III income	100,000
Trade charges paid during 2019	(60,000)
Non-trade charges paid during 2019	(50,000)

Tax Advisors Ltd paid an interim dividend on 1 December 2019 of €30,000.

Requirement
Calculate the surcharge payable by Tax Advisors Ltd in respect of the above figures.

27

Investment Companies

Learning Objectives

After studying this chapter you will be able to:

- Advise on investment companies and the treatment of management expenses.
- Prepare a corporation tax computation for an investment company.

27.1 Introduction

After studying this chapter you will have developed the competency to understand that, up to now, we have dealt with companies that just held shares in another company, i.e. a holding company, and companies that carried on a trade.

A holding company does not trade and therefore is not entitled to claim the type of expense deductions that a trading company could. By its nature, a holding company merely holds investments.

This is in contrast to a subsidiary of, say, a bank, which actively trades shares and securities daily so as to derive a profit from share dealing. Such a company carries on a trade and, therefore, is entitled to a deduction for its trading expenses.

An "investment company", in practice, lies somewhere between a holding company and a share-dealing company.

An investment company can have Cases III, IV and V income as well as chargeable gains, but would be unlikely to have Cases I or II income. Franked investment income (FII), other than dividends from an Irish REIT, is exempt. Chargeable gains are grossed up in the usual manner. Investment companies are often established by individuals. By establishing an investment company, expenses, i.e. management expenses, which would not otherwise be deductible for an individual are deductible for a company.

27.1.1 Definition

Under section 83 TCA 1997, an "investment company" is any company:

- whose business consists wholly or mainly in the **making** of investments; and
- the principal part of whose income is derived therefrom; and includes a savings bank.

The key issue is that there is active involvement by the company in making investments. To ensure that a company is an investment company, a company should have more than one investment.

A certain level of activity on the company's part is required, as opposed to a single, once-off investment. A company that acquires a property and manages that property is not considered to be an investment company as it is not actively making investments.

There is no specific guideline as to what level of activity a company needs to engage in to establish its "investment company" status. One would, however, expect an "investment company" to have **regular meetings to review existing investments** and decide on possible new investments.

27.1.2 Relief for Management Expenses

An "investment company" resident in the State is entitled to deduct its expenses of management in computing its total profits (including chargeable gains) for corporation tax purposes.

27.2 Management Expenses

The term "management expenses" is not defined in law. The law allows a deduction for "… any sums disbursed as expenses of management … except any such expenses as are deductible in computing income for the purposes of Case V…".

The courts have either taken the broad view or the narrow view of what are "expenses of management". The **broad** view is that *any* expenses **incurred by** management are deductible, whereas the **narrow** view is that only **expenses of management** are deductible, i.e. only the expenses of management in shaping policy and in other matters of managerial decision.

In the most recent Irish ruling on the matter, the case of *Hibernian Insurance Company Ltd v. MacUimis* (2000), the Supreme Court supported the narrower view. The judge held that the very substantial costs incurred by the group in getting advisors to evaluate three investment opportunities did not constitute "expenses of management". He held that the expenditure was capital in nature and, therefore, was not management expenses. Therefore, monies spent on evaluating new investment opportunities are not deductible as management expenses. A more recent UK case, *Camas plc v. Atkinson* (2004) decided in favour of the broader view (i.e. all costs up to the time a company makes a definitive decision to acquire a business are allowable "expenses of management"), although this decision is not binding in Ireland as it is not an Irish ruling.

The list set out below mainly reflects case law and practice. Management expenses:

1. include lump sums paid under the Redundancy Payments Act 1967 or an employer's contribution under an approved superannuation scheme;
2. do not include expenses which are deductible in computing income from rents, etc. under Case V;
3. are to be reduced by any income not subject to tax other than FII (such income is relatively rare);
4. include rent, rates, interest on loans to finance day-to-day running of the company, stationery, accountancy, secretarial and audit fees;
5. include stockbrokers' fees, but not fees spent on new investments, as these would relate to capital expenditure;
6. include directors' fees subject to the limit outlined below (Revenue practice); and
7. include donations to charities, etc. and approved sports bodies, where the donation to the charity/sports body is at least €250 (for a 12-month accounting period).

27.2.1 Directors' Remuneration

Directors' remuneration is only deductible for corporation tax purposes to the extent that it is commensurate with the services provided. In practice, Revenue permit a deduction for directors' remuneration up to 10% of the company's gross income, including FII. The maximum allowable deduction is increased to 15% gross rental income plus 10% other income, including FII where the investment company has rental income and the directors devote a substantial part of their time to the management of those properties and there is not a separate management charge.

Example 27.1

Thornton Properties Limited is an investment company. It has been established that its directors devote a substantial part of their time to the management of the company's properties. The company's income is as follows:

		€
Gross rents		400,000
Loan interest		25,000
Deposit interest, received gross		15,000
Irish dividends		35,000
Chargeable gains		6,000
Maximum deduction for directors' remuneration:		
Gross rents	€400,000 @ 15%	60,000
Other income:		
Loan interest	25,000	
Deposit interest, received gross	15,000	
Irish dividends	35,000	
	75,000 @ 10%	7,500
Maximum deduction for directors' remuneration		67,500

If the actual amount paid to directors were only €59,000, then only €59,000 would be deductible.

27.2.2 Carry Forward of Unutilised Management Expenses

If the management expenses of an accounting period, together with any charges on income paid in the period wholly and exclusively for the purpose of the company's business, cannot be wholly allowed by way of a deduction in that period, the balance may be carried forward to the succeeding period and treated as management expenses of that period, qualifying for allowance in that period or, if needs be, in subsequent periods. The balance cannot be carried back, but it is available for group relief (see **Chapter 23, Section 23.3.4**).

SUMMARY CHART OF OFFSET OF MANAGEMENT EXPENSES

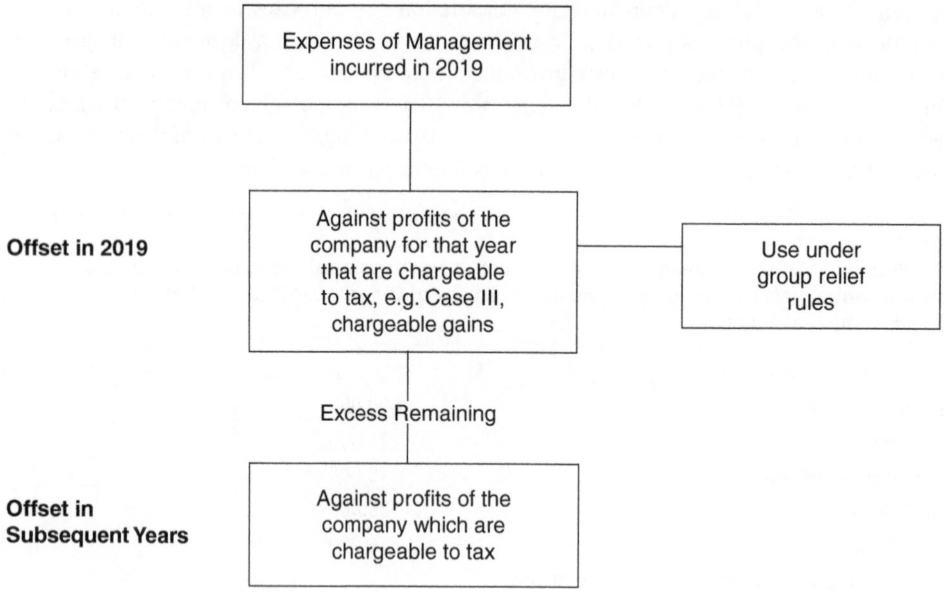

Questions

Review Questions

(See Suggested Solutions to Review Questions at the end of this textbook.)

Question 27.1

Equities Ltd, a company whose business is the making of investments, had the following income statement for the year ended 31 December 2019:

Income:		€
	Dividends from other Irish companies	140,000
	Interest on Irish Government security	15,100
		155,100
Expenditure:		
	Accounting fees	1,000
	Secretarial fees	2,000
	Auditors' remuneration	6,000
	Directors' remuneration	20,000
	Stockbroker's charges for advice	3,000
		(32,000)
Net income		123,100

Requirement
Calculate the corporation tax liability for the period, claiming all possible reliefs.

28

Double Taxation Relief

Learning Objectives

After studying this chapter you will be able to:

- Determine, advise on and calculate the Irish double taxation relief implications for Irish resident companies incurring foreign tax liabilities on income and gains generated outside the State via:
  - relief by deduction;
  - credit relief; and
  - relief by exemption.
- Advise on Ireland's attractiveness as a holding company location, the EU Parent–Subsidiary Directive and double taxation treaties in general.

28.1 Introduction to Double Taxation Relief and Rate of Tax

28.1.1 Introduction

It is common for the laws of two countries to levy tax on the same income and capital. This arises because a resident company is normally taxed on its worldwide profits and a non-resident company is taxed on its profits in that country only.

Example 28.1
An Irish resident company carries on business through a branch in a foreign country. The branch profits would be subject to corporation tax in Ireland as a resident company is liable to tax on its worldwide profits. The branch profits would also be subject to tax in the foreign country as the income arises in the foreign country.

If the foreign income is earned by an Irish tax resident company, then that income is liable to Irish tax. It may also be liable to tax in the foreign country in which it arises. This depends on the laws of that foreign country and the tax treaty between Ireland and the foreign country.

continued overleaf

Alternatively, the Irish company may establish a wholly owned subsidiary in the foreign country or make an investment (e.g. 20% shareholding) in a foreign company. In this case, the foreign company typically will not be managed and controlled in Ireland and will not have Irish source income. Therefore, the foreign company has no Irish tax liability. The Irish parent or investor company will not receive any income from this foreign company until a dividend is paid to it. Therefore, the Irish parent/investor company does not have an Irish tax liability until it receives a dividend. Generally, this dividend will have been paid out of profits which have suffered foreign tax. When the dividend is actually paid, it may also suffer withholding tax in the foreign country.

When the Irish company receives the dividend, the dividend is taxable in Ireland. Generally there is a credit for foreign tax suffered, be it the withholding tax and/or an appropriate share of the tax on profits of the foreign company. Sometimes there is only relief by deduction – see **Section 28.2.1.**

28.1.2 Foreign Income: Rate of Corporation Tax

Trading or Professional Services Income

If the foreign income is trading income from a foreign branch of the Irish company, then provided the trade is not carried out wholly abroad – and, generally, this is the case – this income is assessed as Case I or Case II income and taxable at 12.5%.

If the trade is carried out wholly abroad, it is regarded as a foreign trade and the income therefrom is Case III income, subject to corporation tax at 25%.

Interest or Rental Income

If the income is interest or rental income from a foreign deposit or property, the income is taxable at 25%.

Dividends

Foreign dividends are assessed as Case III income. Previously, all foreign dividends were taxable at 25%. Currently, certain foreign dividends are taxable at 12.5%.

The 12.5% corporation tax rate will apply where an Irish company receives a dividend from a company resident in:

- an EU Member State;
- a country with which Ireland has signed a tax treaty;
- a company quoted on any stock exchange in the EU or a tax treaty country;

and either:

- the dividend is paid out of the trading profits of the non-resident company; or
- the dividend is received by a company that is a **portfolio investor** (i.e. holds no more than **5%** of the dividend-paying company).

However, if the dividend is partly paid out of the trading profits of the non-resident company, apportionment is required unless:

- 75% of its profits are trading profits (or dividends received from trading companies resident in EU or treaty countries); and
- 75% of the assets of the group must be trading assets.

All other foreign dividends are taxable at 25%.

28.2 Methods of Relief

Relief is given for double taxation in one of the following ways:

1. deduction;
2. credit; or
3. exemption.

In the absence of a double tax treaty (DTT) the deduction method will apply. If there is a DTT with the foreign country, then either the credit or exemption method will apply.

28.2.1 Deduction Method

If no other double tax relief (i.e. credit relief or an exemption) applies, under general Irish tax law foreign profits are reduced by the foreign tax borne on these profits for corporation tax purposes.

The deduction method applies, for example, in the case of other income (e.g. interest, rental income) if there is **no** DTT with the foreign country. There is no DTT with Argentina. The list of countries with which Ireland has a DTT is outlined in **Section 28.4**.

Example 28.2

X Ltd, an Irish resident company, was in receipt of the following income for the year ended 31 December 2019:

	€	€
Irish trading profits		500,000
Argentinian bank deposit interest	10,000	
Less: Argentinian withholding tax	(1,000)	9,000

There is no tax treaty between Ireland and Argentina, therefore the foreign income of €10,000 is reduced by the foreign tax of €1,000 for corporation tax purposes.

Corporation Tax Computation

		€
Schedule D Case I		500,000
Schedule D Case III		9,000
		509,000
Corporation tax		
€500,000 @ 12.5% =	€62,500	
€9,000 @ 25% =	€2,250	
Corporation tax due		64,750

The effective rate of tax suffered on the Argentinian interest is:
(€1,000 + €2,250)/ €10,000 = 32.50%

28.2.2 Credit Method

Credit relief is allowed either because it is provided for **under a tax treaty** between Ireland and another country, or because Irish domestic tax law allows it (known as **unilateral credit relief**).

Example 28.3: Operation of credit relief

Ladder Ltd has a branch in a country with which Ireland has a tax treaty. In the year ended 31 December 2019, the branch had profits of €120,000 on which tax was paid at 10%. Ladder Ltd's total Case I profits, including the branch profit, for the year ended 31 December 2019 were €400,000.

	€
Irish corporation tax	
Schedule D Case I	400,000
Corporation tax @ 12.5%	50,000
Less: credit relief €120,000 @ 10%	(12,000)
Tax due	38,000

Irish effective rate of tax $\frac{50,000}{400,000} \times 100 = 12.5\%$

Note: branch profits are taxable under Case I rather than Case III where the trade is not carried out "wholly" abroad.

Credit relief is far more beneficial than relief by deduction as it can fully relieve any liability to Irish tax, e.g. if the foreign tax rate had been 12.5% or higher, then no Irish tax would have been payable on the foreign income. Under credit relief, the Irish company will suffer the higher of the Irish and the foreign rate.

If the foreign income is a dividend, credit relief is normally available not only for any foreign withholding tax but also in respect of **tax paid on the profits out of which the dividend has been paid (underlying tax)**. Under many of Ireland's tax treaties, there is a minimum shareholding requirement as a condition of obtaining credit relief for underlying tax on dividends. However, unilateral credit relief rules also apply and can be more beneficial in the case of dividends. (There is a formula for the calculation of underlying tax, but this is beyond the scope of this textbook.) The Irish corporation tax liability will be on the aggregate of the dividend received and the amount of credit relief.

There are other issues that arise when dealing with the credit for foreign tax, including unilateral credit relief, limit on credit relief and special provisions for dividends from EU and EEA countries with a tax treaty with Ireland. These issues are beyond the scope of this textbook.

28.2.3 Exemption Method

This simply exempts the profits from tax in one of the two countries. The most common example is that under many DTTs **interest is not liable to tax in the country of origin**, only in the country of residence.

Example 28.4

A Ltd, an Irish resident company, was in receipt of the following income for the year ended 31 December 2019:

	€
Irish trading profits	800,000
UK deposit interest	10,000

Under the terms of the Irish/UK DTT, UK deposit interest earned by an Irish resident company is only taxable in Ireland.

continued overleaf

	€
Schedule D Case I	800,000
Schedule D Case III	10,000
	810,000
€800,000 @ 12.5%	100,000
€10,000 @ 25%	2,500
Corporation tax due	102,500

No UK tax paid as exempt in UK under Ireland–UK DTT.

28.3 Ireland as a Holding Company Location

Irish tax law contains provisions designed to make Ireland an attractive location for holding companies and, thereby, attract holding companies and the related headquarter activities to Ireland.

- There is the very low holding of 5% to avail of unilateral credit relief.
- There is on-shore pooling of excess foreign tax credits in relation to qualifying foreign dividends. This topic is beyond the scope of this textbook.
- There is the exemption from tax in the case of capital gains from the disposal of holdings in "subsidiaries" – this is dealt with in **Chapter 24, Section 24.3** on company capital gains.
- There is an exemption from the close company surcharge on dividends from these shareholdings, but only where they are shares in a foreign company. This is dealt with in **Chapter 26**.

28.4 Double Taxation Treaties

Ireland has concluded double taxation treaties with the following countries.

Albania
Armenia
Australia
Austria
Bahrain
Belarus
Belgium
Bosnia & Herzegovina
Botswana
Bulgaria
Canada
Chile
China
Croatia
Cyprus
Czech Rep.
Denmark
Egypt
Estonia
Ethiopia
Finland
France
Georgia
Germany
Greece
Hong Kong
Hungary
Iceland
India
Israel
Italy
Japan
Kazakhstan
Korea (Rep. of)
Kuwait
Latvia
Lithuania
Luxembourg
Macedonia
Malaysia
Malta
Mexico
Moldova
Montenegro
Morocco
Netherlands
New Zealand
Norway
Pakistan
Panama
Poland
Portugal
Qatar
Romania
Russia
Saudi Arabia
Serbia
Singapore
Slovak Rep.
Slovenia
South Africa
Spain
Sweden
Switzerland
Thailand
Turkey
Ukraine
United Arab Emirates
United Kingdom
United States of America
Uzbekistan
Vietnam
Zambia

Given the possibility of delay in bringing treaties into force with relevant foreign countries, the treaty requirement has been relaxed to mere signing of the treaty, i.e. once the treaty has been signed with the country, companies dealing with that country may avail of its provisions as they impact on Irish tax.

For countries outside the EU, it is normal practice to advise a student in an exam as to whether Ireland has a treaty with a particular country.

Questions

Review Questions

(See Suggested Solutions to Review Questions at the end of this textbook.)

Question 28.1

Foreign Income Limited is in receipt of the following sources of income for the year ended 31 December 2019:

	€
Trading income	800,000
Dividend from Treaty Ltd (Note 1)	88,000
Dividend from Non-treaty Ltd (Note 2)	80,000
Dividend from Irish Maniacs Ltd (Note 3)	75,000

Notes:

1. The dividend of €88,000 was received from its 100% subsidiary in a country with which Ireland has a tax treaty and the dividend was paid out of trading profits.
2. The dividend of €80,000 was received from an unquoted company in a country with which Ireland does not have a tax treaty.
3. Irish Maniacs Ltd is an Irish tax resident company.

Foreign Income Ltd paid a dividend of €54,000 in total to its three shareholders, all of whom are Irish resident individuals, on 1 February 2019.

Requirement

(a) Calculate the corporation tax payable for the accounts year ended 31 December 2019.
(b) Explain the taxation consequences arising from the dividend payment in February 2019 for Foreign Income Limited.

29

Appeals, Revenue Audits and Qualifying Disclosures

Learning Objectives

After studying this chapter you will be able to:

- Advise on the operation of tax appeals and assessments.
- Advise on Revenue audits, including qualifying disclosures and mitigation of penalties.

29.1 Appeals and Assessments

A company is subject to self-assessment and must file a corporation tax return (known as Form CT1) within nine months (subject to the 23-day rule) of the end of its accounting period. Returns must include a self-assessment made by the company. Revenue will not, therefore, generally issue an assessment in respect of such returns. It will, however, issue an assessment where a return has not been filed, where it is not satisfied with the return or where it believes it is not a full and true return.

If a company does not agree with a Revenue assessment raised, it can lodge an appeal against the assessment, provided that it has filed a return for the period covered by the assessment, has paid any tax, including any interest and penalties that would be payable if an assessment were raised and which is in agreement with the return that has been filed.

The initial appeal is made by a company to the Tax Appeals Commission and heard by one or more of its Appeal Commissioners. If either party is aggrieved by the decision of the Appeal Commissioners, it may make a further appeal to the High Court, but only if the matter under dispute is on a point of law. Either party aggrieved by the decision of the High Court has a right of appeal to the Supreme Court.

The Taxes Consolidation Act 1997 (TCA 1997) sets out time limits within which the various appeals must be made, the contents of a notice of appeal, the power of the Appeal Commissioners to issue requests for further information or to summon witnesses and the requirement to issue notices regarding the timing of the hearing.

29.2 Revenue Audits, Penalties and Qualifying Disclosures

29.2.1 Introduction to Revenue Audit

Revenue's *Code of Practice for Revenue Audit and other Compliance Interventions* (to be found at www.revenue.ie) sets out the guidelines to be followed by Revenue, taxpayers and tax practitioners, in the carrying out of Revenue Compliance Interventions. Under law, Revenue is entitled to make enquiries or investigations and take such actions as it considers necessary to satisfy itself as to the accuracy or otherwise of any statement or other particular contained in any return, list, statement or other particulars.

Generally taxpayers are selected for compliance intervention based on the presence of various risk indicators. Cases are selected in a number of ways, including the use of REAP (Revenue's electronic risk analysis system) and through the use of analytics. The REAP system allows for the screening of all tax returns against sectoral and business norms and provides a selection basis for checks or audits. In more recent times, Revenue use e-auditing, which allows the Revenue auditor to use computer-assisted audit techniques on a taxpayer's data as part of its audit process.

In addition to Revenue's risk-based selection approach, it also operates a random audit programme and a re-audit programme. Compliance interventions by Revenue include non-audit compliance interventions (e.g. aspect queries/assurance checks where a taxpayer is contacted for further information or explanations about a particular item in a return), revenue audits (including risk-selected audits, random audits and re-audits) and Revenue investigations (generally where Revenue believes serious tax evasion has taken place).

The *Code* defines a Revenue audit as an examination of:

- a tax return;
- a declaration of liability or a repayment claim;
- a statement of liability to stamp duty;
- the compliance of a person with tax and duty legislation.

An examination may involve looking at all the risks in a particular case or may focus on a single issue or tax-head.

Audit at Company's Place of Business

Where a business is involved, most audits, whether comprehensive or single tax-head, include **visits** to the business premises. The length of such visits depends on the number and complexity of the points at issue. Notice is generally given in such cases to both the company and its agent. In certain exceptional circumstances (e.g. where it is suspected that records are likely to be removed or altered), a visit may take place unannounced.

Desk Audit

Certain audits (mainly verification of specific claims to expenses, allowances or reliefs) are conducted by letter (post, fax or e-mail), or by telephone where straightforward issues are involved. This type of audit, known as a desk audit, may also arise in a review of a director's tax affairs or where a company has unearned income. Similarly, CAT and stamp duty audits are normally desk audits. Taxpayers will be informed of the issues being examined in the course of a desk audit.

It should be noted that a desk audit may subsequently involve fieldwork, if this is deemed necessary, including visits to the company's premises to examine records.

Audit Notification

Twenty-one days' notice of a Revenue audit is generally given to both the taxpayer and their agent. Where an audit is to be scheduled, the letter issued will include the wording 'Notification of a Revenue Audit' and will show the date the audit will start. All audit notification letters issued to a taxpayer and agent must indicate the nature of the Revenue intervention. The scope of the audit will also be set out, and will range from a single tax-head (e.g. corporation tax, VAT, etc.) or single issue for a specific period or year, to a comprehensive audit for a number of years. The Revenue auditor is confined to examining the issues as notified and cannot extend the audit without good reason at the time of the visit. The potential use of e-auditing techniques is noted in all audit notification letters.

29.2.2 Tax, Interest and Penalties

Tax

Any tax due as a result of the Revenue audit must be paid.

Interest

Interest is always charged if a failure to pay is identified. Interest **cannot** be mitigated (i.e. reduced).

Application of Penalties

Penalties will apply if, in the course of the audit, tax defaults are identified. Penalties are "tax-geared", which means that the penalty is expressed as a **percentage of the tax** (but not the interest) in question. Penalties can be mitigated. Penalties will apply in circumstances where there has been:

- careless behaviour; **or**
- careless behaviour with significant consequences; **or**
- deliberate behaviour.

Careless Behaviour without Significant Consequences

The tax-geared penalty for careless behaviour without significant consequences is **20%**. Careless behaviour will arise if a person of ordinary skill and knowledge, properly advised, would have foreseen as a reasonable probability or likelihood the prospect that an act (or omission) would cause a tax underpayment, having regard to all the circumstances but, nevertheless, the act or omission occurred. There is also a **materiality test** to determine if the careless behaviour is without significant consequences. The tax shortfall must be **less than 15%** of the tax liability ultimately due in respect of the particular tax.

Careless Behaviour with Significant Consequences

The tax-geared penalty for this category is **40%**. Careless behaviour with significant consequences is the lack of **due care** with the result that tax liabilities or repayment claims are **substantially incorrect** and pass the 15% test described above. Careless behaviour with significant consequences is distinguished from "deliberate behaviour" by the **absence** of indicators consistent with intent on the part of the company.

Deliberate Behaviour

The tax-geared penalty for deliberate default is **100%**. Deliberate default has indicators consistent with **intent** and includes tax evasion and the non-operation of fiduciary taxes, such as PAYE.

Innocent Error

A penalty will not be payable in respect of a tax default if the tax default was not deliberate and was not attributable in any way to the failure to take reasonable care to comply with a company's tax obligations. Factors which will be taken into account in deciding whether a penalty should not be imposed include:

- Whether the auditor concludes that the company has provided for, and implemented, the keeping of proper books and records so as to fulfil tax obligations.
- The frequency with which the "innocent error" occurs. Repeatedly making such errors could indicate lack of appropriate care which could put the error into the "careless behaviour without significant consequences" category or higher.
- The previous compliance record of the company.
- Where the error being corrected is immaterial.

Interest will, however, be charged even if no penalty is charged.

Technical Adjustments

"Technical adjustments" are adjustments to a tax liability that arise from differences in interpretation or the application of the legislation.

A technical adjustment will not give rise to a penalty where:

- due care has been exercised by the company;
- the treatment concerned was based on an interpretation of law that could reasonably have been considered to be correct.

Interest will, however, be charged even if no penalty is charged.

Self-correction

This category arises outside of the audit or enquiry process. A return may be self-corrected **without** penalty where:

- Revenue is notified in writing of the adjustments to be made, and the circumstances under which the errors arose;
- a computation of the correct tax and statutory interest payable is provided, along with a payment in settlement.

Time Limits for Self-correction

Income Tax	Within 12 months of the due date for filing the return.
Corporation Tax	Within 12 months of the due date for filing the return.
Capital Gains Tax	Within 12 months of the due date for filing the return.
VAT	Before the due date of the IT or CT return for the period in which the VAT period ends, e.g. a self-correction of the Jan/Feb 2019 VAT3 for a company with a December year-end must occur before 23 September 2020. (For bi-monthly/quarterly/half-yearly remitters of VAT, if the net VAT underpayment is less than €6,000, the amount of tax can be included, without interest, as an adjustment in the next VAT return and there is no requirement to notify Revenue.)
PAYE/PRSI	Within 12 months of the due date for filing the annual return.
Relevant Contracts Tax	Within 12 months of the due date for filing the annual return.

The benefit of self-correction does not apply if Revenue had notified a taxpayer of an audit or started to make enquiries in relation to the return in question or if the correction relates to an instance of deliberate behaviour which also featured in a previous period.

29.2.3 Qualifying Disclosures and Reduction of Penalties

Penalties are mitigated where:

- there is **full co-operation** by the company;
- a "**qualifying disclosure**" is made by the company.

Full Co-operation

Full co-operation includes the following:

- having all books, records, and linking papers available for the auditor at the commencement of the audit;
- having appropriate personnel available at the time of the audit;
- responding promptly to all requests for information and explanations;
- responding promptly to all correspondence;
- prompt payment of the audit settlement liability.

Qualifying Disclosures

The company may elect to carry out a review of its own tax affairs and identify where mistakes were made **prior** to their discovery by the Revenue auditor. A company may make a qualifying disclosure, i.e. a disclosure of all information in relation to, and full particulars of, all matters occasioning a liability to tax that gives rise to a penalty. It must be in writing and signed by or on behalf of the taxpayer. It should be accompanied by a declaration that all matters contained in the disclosure are correct and complete, along with full payment of the tax plus any interest incurred on late payment of that tax. There are incentives for companies that wish to make qualifying disclosures. A qualifying disclosure results in the following:

- non-publication of the tax settlement in the list of tax defaulters published by Revenue;
- no prosecution;
- further mitigation of penalties.

With effect from 1 May 2017, any disclosure made by a company that relates directly or indirectly to foreign income or gains will not be treated as a qualifying disclosure.

Qualifying disclosures can be either **"unprompted"** or **"prompted"**. An "unprompted" disclosure is a disclosure that is made **before** the company is notified of an audit, **or** contacted by Revenue regarding an inquiry or investigation relating to its tax affairs. Revenue often carries out what are described as "non-audit compliance interventions". A non-audit compliance intervention includes contact made by Revenue with a company, either by phone, email or letter, with queries on a particular matter. It is important to remember that the company is still entitled to make an unprompted disclosure after there has been a compliance intervention; it is only when it has received notification of an audit, inquiry or investigation that it can no longer make an unprompted disclosure.

A "prompted" disclosure is a disclosure made **after** an audit notice has issued but **before** an examination of the books and records or other documentation has begun.

However, in cases not involving deliberate default, if Revenue draws the attention of the taxpayer to issues not within the initial scope of the revenue audit without formally extending the audit, the taxpayer will have the benefit of an unprompted disclosure in respect of any liabilities disclosed.

Period to Prepare a Qualifying Disclosure

In order for the company to secure an agreed 60-day period of time in which to prepare and make a qualifying disclosure, **notice of the intention** to make a disclosure must be given.

In the case of an **unprompted disclosure**, the notice of the intention to make a disclosure must be given **before**:

- a notice of audit is issued; **or**
- the company has been contacted by Revenue regarding an enquiry or investigation relating to its tax affairs.

In the case of a **prompted disclosure**, the majority of these will be submitted in the period between the date of the notification of the audit and the commencement of the audit. In the case of a prompted qualifying disclosure, if the company wishes to be given an additional 60 days to prepare the disclosure, the notice of intention to make a disclosure must be given **within 14 days** of the day of issue of the notification of audit.

A person who has given notice within the time allowed of his or her intention to make a qualifying disclosure will be given 60 days in which to quantify the shortfall and to make the relevant payment. This period of 60 days will begin from the day on which the notice of intention to make a qualifying disclosure was given and will be communicated to the taxpayer in writing by Revenue. The 60-day period allows the company or its agent to contact Revenue to discuss any matters arising, including the category of default on which the mitigated penalty is to be based.

Format of the Qualifying Disclosure

The following conditions must be satisfied for a disclosure to be a **qualifying disclosure** for the purpose of mitigation of penalties:

- The disclosure must be made in writing and signed by or on behalf of the company.
- It must be accompanied by a declaration, to the best of that person's knowledge, information and belief, that all matters contained in the disclosure are correct and complete.
- The disclosure must, whether prompted or unprompted, state the amounts of all liabilities to tax, interest and penalties, as respects all tax heads and periods, which were liabilities previously undisclosed by reason of *deliberate behaviour* by the company.
- In the case of a **prompted** disclosure, it must also state the amounts of any liabilities previously undisclosed, for any reason other than *deliberate behaviour*, which are liabilities to tax, interest and penalties within the scope of the proposed audit or audit enquiry.
- In the case of an **unprompted** disclosure, it must state the amounts of any liabilities previously undisclosed, for any reason other than deliberate behaviour, which are liabilities to tax, interest and penalties in respect of the tax types and periods which are covered by the unprompted qualifying disclosure.
- The disclosure must be accompanied by a payment of the total liability arising in respect of the tax and interest in respect of that tax. The qualifying disclosure does not need to make reference to the penalty due.

On receipt of the qualifying disclosure the auditor will agree the penalties with the company and will obtain payment at that stage. Where the company is unable to pay the full settlement amount at this stage, a real, genuine and acceptable proposal to pay the amount due in accordance with the Revenue instalment arrangement procedures will satisfy the payment requirement. If, however, the company fails to honour the instalment arrangements, the company will be regarded as not having made a qualifying disclosure.

Reduction of Penalties

The amount of the reduction available is determined by whether a qualifying disclosure was made in the previous five years. There are three different tables and the table for the first qualifying disclosure is shown below:

Category of Tax Default	Penalty as a % of Tax Underpaid	Net Penalty after Reduction where there is: Co-operation Only	Co-operation AND a Prompted Qualifying Disclosure	Co-operation AND an Unprompted Qualifying Disclosure
Deliberate behaviour	100%	75%	50%	10%
Careless behaviour **with** significant consequences	40%	30%	20%	5%
Other careless behaviour	20%	15%	10%	3%

It is important to be aware of the different types of default and that the penalty applicable is reduced depending on whether there is co-operation or not and a prompted or unprompted disclosure (although in practice it is not expected that the exact percentages are known).

Where a second or subsequent qualifying disclosure is made within five years of a first qualifying disclosure, there is still a reduction in penalties. However, the reduction in penalties where the category of tax default falls under "deliberate behaviour" or "careless behaviour with significant consequences" is less than the reduction in penalties for the first qualifying disclosure. The same reduction in penalties applies where the tax default is in the category of "careless behaviour without significant consequences". Where a subsequent qualifying disclosure is made more than five years after a first qualifying disclosure was made, the same reduction in penalties applies as if it were a first disclosure.

If a company deliberately or carelessly files an incorrect return before the due date for filing the return, it is deemed to have filed the return late unless the errors in the return are corrected without unreasonable delay. As the company is deemed to have filed its return late, a surcharge is payable. If such a company is also liable to the penalties above, it is not also liable to a surcharge for the late filing of a return (see **Chapter 19, Section 19.6.3**). If, however, a company files its return after the filing deadline and becomes liable to one of the penalties above, the surcharge for the late filing of a return is payable in addition to the tax-geared penalty.

29.2.4 Conduct of a Revenue Audit

On arrival at the place of audit, the auditor will provide identification and authorisation and explain the purpose of the audit. It is Revenue policy not to disclose the precise reason a company has been selected for audit.

The company is informed about Revenue practice on charging interest and penalties and is offered the opportunity to make a prompted qualifying disclosure.

Some of the key points pertaining to the conduct of an audit are as follows:

- The audit will generally take place at the company's place of business.
- The auditor will try not to retain any records for longer than a month. If more time is required the company will be advised of this.
- The taxpayer (or his/her information technology supplier) will be required to provide the necessary data downloads.
- A receipt is given for any records removed from the premises.
- Issues may arise during the course of the audit that require the auditor to consider opening earlier or later years. If deliberate default/deliberate behaviour is not involved, Revenue may informally draw the company's attention to these issues and the company has the opportunity to make an unprompted qualifying disclosure in relation to these other years.
- If the auditor decides to extend the scope of the audit to other taxes or years not referred to in the audit notice, the company will be given the opportunity to make a prompted qualifying disclosure in respect of those other taxes or years.

Finalisation of Audit

At the conclusion of the audit, the Revenue auditor will:

1. Outline the findings of the audit.
2. Quantify the tax, interest and penalties due.
3. Invite the company to make a written settlement offer.
4. If necessary, require the company to confirm that any issues identified have been rectified.

When a settlement has been agreed, a final letter will be issued by the Revenue audit setting out:

- the details of the settlement;
- any inadequacies in the company's records or tax treatments;
- noting the company's confirmation that any inadequacies have been rectified.

Right to a Review

A company has the right to request a review of the conduct of an audit, in particular in relation to:

- proposed adjustments to receipts or profits figures, claims for reliefs or allowances or to tax computations;
- penalties to be charged;

The initial review is carried out by the local Revenue office; however, if the company is not satisfied with the outcome of this review, it may request a review by an "external reviewer".

Appendices

Appendix 1

Taxation Reference Material for Tax Year 2019

Table of Contents

Table 1 INCOME TAX RATES AND INCOME TAX CREDITS 2019

Rates

Single/Widowed/ Surviving Civil Partner with Qualifying Children	Rate	Single/Widowed/ Surviving Civil Partner without Qualifying Children	Rate	Married Couple/ Civil Partners	Rate
First €39,300	20%	First €35,300	20%	First €44,300/€70,600[1]	20%
Balance	40%	Balance	40%	Balance	40%

[1] Depending on personal circumstances of married couple/civil partners.

Non-refundable Tax Credits

	Tax Credit
	€
Single person	1,650
Married couple/civil partners	3,300
Widowed person/surviving civil partner (year of bereavement)	3,300
Widowed person/surviving civil partner tax credit – no dependent children	2,190
Widowed person/surviving civil partner tax credit – with dependent children	1,650
Single Person Child Carer Credit (additional)	1,650
Widowed parent/surviving civil partner tax credit – with dependent children	
Year 1 after the year of bereavement	3,600
Year 2 after the year of bereavement	3,150
Year 3 after the year of bereavement	2,700
Year 4 after the year of bereavement	2,250
Year 5 after the year of bereavement	1,800
Employee tax credit	1,650
Earned Income Tax Credit	1,350
Age tax credit – single/widowed/surviving civil partner	245
Age tax credit – married/civil partners	490
Incapacitated child tax credit	3,300
Dependent relative – income limit €15,060	70
Home carer's credit – income limit €7,200 (lower)/ €10,200 (upper)	1,500
Blind person	1,650
Both spouses/civil partners blind	3,300
Third-level education fees[1]:	
Full-time course	800
Part-time course	1,100

[1] There is a maximum level of qualifying fees, per academic year, of €7,000 per student, per course, subject to the first €3,000 (full-time) or €1,500 (part-time) being disallowed (per claim, not per course). Relief is at the standard rate of tax on the amount of the qualifying fees.

Table 2 INCOME TAX ALLOWANCES AND RELIEFS 2019

Deduction for employed person taking care of incapacitated person (maximum)	– €75,000
Provision of childcare services	– income limit €15,000
Rent-a-Room relief (maximum)	– €14,000

Table 3 INCOME TAX EXEMPTION LIMITS FOR PERSONS AGED 65 AND OVER 2019

	€
Single/widowed/surviving civil partner	18,000[1]
Married/civil partners	36,000[1]

[1] Dependent children: increase exemption by €575 for each of first two, and by €830 for each additional child.

Table 4 MORTGAGE INTEREST RELIEF 2019

Interest threshold and rate of relief for first-time buyers for tax year 2019

Year loan taken out	Status	2019 threshold × % reduction	Rate of relief
2012	Single person Married/widowed/civil partner	€10,000 × 50% €20,000 × 50%	20% 20%
2009–2011	Single person Married/widowed/civil partner	€3,000 × 50% €6,000 × 50%	15% 15%
2004–2008	Single person Married/widowed/civil partner	€3,000 × 50% €6,000 × 50%	30% 30%

Interest threshold and rate of relief for non-first-time buyers for tax year 2019

Year loan taken out	Status	2019 threshold × % reduction	Rate of relief
2004–2012	Single person Married/widowed/civil partner	€3,000 × 50% €6,000 × 50%	15% 15%

Table 5 PENSION CONTRIBUTIONS

The maximum amount on which tax relief may be claimed in 2019 in respect of qualifying premiums is as follows:

Age	% of Net Relevant Earnings[1]
Under 30 years of age	15%
30 to 39 years of age	20%
40 to 49 years of age	25%
50 to 54 years of age	30%
55 to 59 years of age	35%
60 years and over	40%

[1] The earnings cap for 2019 on net relevant earnings is €115,000.

Table 6 PREFERENTIAL LOANS

The specified rates for 2019 are:

- 4% in respect of qualifying home loans;
- 13.5% in respect of all other loans.

Table 7 MOTOR CAR BENEFIT IN KIND SCALE 2019

Annual Business Kilometres	Cash Equivalent (% of OMV)
24,000 or less	30%
24,001–32,000	24%
32,001–40,000	18%
40,001–48,000	12%
48,001 and over	6%

Table 8 MOTOR VEHICLE CATEGORY BASED ON CO_2 EMISSIONS

Vehicle Category	CO_2 Emissions (CO_2 g/km)
A, B and C	0g/km up to and including 155g/km
D and E	156g/km up to and including 190g/km
F and G	191g/km and upwards

Table 9 CIVIL SERVICE MILEAGE AND SUBSISTENCE RATES

Motor Car Travel Rates (effective from 1 April 2017)

Official Motor Travel in a calendar year	Engine Capacity		
	Up to 1,200cc	1,201cc–1,500cc	1,501cc and over
0–1,500km	37.95 cent per km	39.86 cent per km	44.79 cent per km
1,501–5,500km	70.00 cent per km	73.21 cent per km	83.53 cent per km
5,501–25,000km	27.55 cent per km	29.03 cent per km	32.21 cent per km
Over 25,001km	21.36 cent per km	22.23 cent per km	25.85 cent per km

Motor Cycle Travel Rates (effective from 5 March 2009)

Official Motor Travel in a calendar year	Engine Capacity			
	Up to 150cc	151cc to 250cc	251cc to 600cc	601cc and over
Up to 6,437km	14.48 cent per km	20.10 cent per km	23.72 cent per km	28.59 cent per km
Over 6,437km	9.37 cent per km	13.31 cent per km	15.29 cent per km	17.60 cent per km

Subsistence Rates (effective from 1 April 2018)

Overnight Allowances [1]			Day Allowances [2]	
Normal rate (up to 14 nights)	Reduced rate (next 14 nights)	Detention rate (next 28 nights)	10 hours or more	5 hours (but less than 10 hours)
€147.00	€132.30	€73.50	€33.61	€14.01

[1] Night allowance: the employee is at least 100km away from their home or place of work and covers a period of up to 24 hours from the time of departure, and any further period not exceeding five hours.
[2] Day allowance: the employee is at least 8km away from their home or normal place of work.

Table 10 LOCAL PROPERTY TAX VALUATION TABLE

Valuation Band Number	Valuation Band €	Mid-point of Valuation Band €	LPT in 2019 (full-year charge) €
01	0 to 100,000	50,000	90
02	100,001 to 150,000	125,000	225
03	150,001 to 200,000	175,000	315
04	200,001 to 250,000	225,000	405
05	250,001 to 300,000	275,000	495
06	300,001 to 350,000	325,000	585
07	350,001 to 400,000	375,000	675
08	400,001 to 450,000	425,000	765
09	450,001 to 500,000	475,000	855
10	500,001 to 550,000	525,000	945
11	550,001 to 600,000	575,000	1,035
12	600,001 to 650,000	625,000	1,125
13	650,001 to 700,000	675,000	1,215
14	700,001 to 750,000	725,000	1,305
15	750,001 to 800,000	775,000	1,395
16	800,001 to 850,000	825,000	1,485
17	850,001 to 900,000	875,000	1,575
18	900,001 to 950,000	925,000	1,665
19	950,001 to 1,000,000*	975,000	1,755

*Residential properties valued over €1 million will be assessed at the actual value at 0.18% on the first €1 million in value and 0.25% on the portion of the value above €1 million (no banding will apply).

LPT Local Adjustment Factors: 2019

The local adjustment factor (LAF) increasing or decreasing the basic LPT rate in operation for 2019:

Local Authority	LPT Rate Adjustment
Dublin City Council	15% decrease
Dún Laoghaire/Rathdown County Council	15% decrease
Fingal County Council	10% decrease
Laois County Council	10% increase
Limerick City and County Council	7.5% increase
Longford County Council	15% increase
South Dublin County Council	15% decrease
Waterford County Council	2.5% increase
Wexford County Council	10% increase

Table 11 UNIVERSAL SOCIAL CHARGE (USC) 2019

Employment Income

The rates of USC (where gross income is greater than €13,000 per annum) are:

Rate of USC	Annual Income	Monthly Income	Weekly Income
0.5%	First €12,012	First €1,001	First €231
2.0%	€12,013–€19,874	€1,002–€1,656	€232–€382
4.5%[1,2]	€19,875–€70,044	€1,657–€5,837	€383–€1,347
8.0%[1,2]	Balance	Balance	Balance

[1] Persons aged 70 years and over with income of €60,000 or less are not liable at the 4.5% or 8% rates but instead pay at 2.0%.
[2] Persons who hold a full medical card and with income of €60,000 or less not liable at the 4.5% or 8% rates but instead pay at 2.0%.

Exempt Categories

- Where an individual's total income for a year does not exceed €13,000.
- All Department of Social Protection payments.
- Income already subjected to DIRT.

Self-assessed Individuals

The rates of USC (where gross income is greater than €13,000 per annum) are:

	Aged under 70/Aged 70 and over with income >€60,000/Full medical card holder with income >€60,000	Aged 70 and over with income of €60,000 or less/Full medical card holder with income of €60,000 or less
First €12,012	0.5%	0.5%
Next €7,862	2.0%	2.0%
Next €50,170	4.5%	2.0% (max. €40,126)
Balance[1]	8.0%	N/A

[1] An additional USC charge of 3% is payable by individuals on self-assessed income (excluding employment income) in excess of €100,000 in a year, regardless of age.

Surcharge on Use of Property Incentives

There is also an additional USC surcharge of 5% on investors with gross income greater than €100,000 where certain property tax reliefs have been used to shelter taxable income.

Table 12 PRSI 2019

Employees' and Employers' Rates

Employee's income	Employee rate	Employers' rate
Income of €38–€352 per week	Nil	8.7%
Income of €352–€386 per week	4%	8.7%
Income greater than €386 per week	4%	10.95%

Employee PRSI Credit

An employee PRSI credit of a maximum of €12 per week is available to Class A employees with gross earnings between €352.01 and €424 per week. The credit is reduced by one-sixth of gross earnings in excess of €352 per week. The reduced credit is then deducted from the employee PRSI liability calculated at 4% of gross weekly earnings.

Self-employed

Individuals in receipt of income of €5,000 or less in 2019 will not be subject to PRSI. Where income is greater than €5,000, PRSI at 4% is payable subject to a minimum contribution of €500. For those with an annual self-employed income of in excess of €5,000 but who have no net liability to tax, the minimum contribution is €310 for 2019.

Table 13 CAPITAL ALLOWANCES AND RESTRICTED COST FOR MOTOR LEASE EXPENSES 2019

Restricted Cost of Passenger Motor Vehicle for Capital Allowances and Motor Leases Expenses Restriction Purposes

Specified Limit	€
From 1 January 2007	24,000

Restricted Cost for Motor Vehicles bought on/after 1 July 2008

Category	CO_2 Emissions	Restriction
A	0–120g/km	Use the specified amount regardless of cost.
B and C	121–155g/km	
D and E	156–190g/km	Two steps to calculate limit: 1. take the lower of the specified limit or cost; 2. limit is 50% of this amount.
F and G	191+g/km	No allowance available.

Plant and Machinery

Expenditure incurred on or after 4 December 2002:

Plant and machinery	12.5% straight-line
Cars other than those used as a taxi or in car hire business	12.5% straight-line

Industrial Buildings

Expenditure incurred on or after 1 April 1992	4% straight-line

Table 14 VAT RATES 2019

Standard	23.0%
Reduced rate	13.5%
Second reduced rate	9.0%
Flat rate for farmers	5.4%
Livestock	4.8%

VAT Rate	Examples
Exempt	■ Medical, dental and optical services ■ Insurance services ■ Certain banking services ■ Educational services ■ Funeral services ■ Gambling and lotteries ■ Transport of passengers (and their baggage) ■ Certain lettings of immovable goods
Zero rate	■ Supply of most foodstuffs (excluding those specifically liable at the standard rate) ■ Printed books and booklets (excluding stationery, brochures, etc.) ■ Most clothing and footwear for children under 11 years of age ■ Oral medicine ■ Exported goods (i.e. despatched outside the EU) ■ Sea-going ships (more than 15 tonnes) ■ Fertilizer ■ Animal feed, other than pet food
Standard rate (23%)	All goods and services that are not exempt or zero-rated, or are not liable at the other specific rates. Includes: ■ Alcohol, soft drinks, bottled drinking water, juices ■ Chocolate and confectionery, biscuits, crisps, ice cream and similar ■ Adult clothing and footwear ■ Office equipment and stationery
Reduced rate (13.5%)	■ Fuel for power and heating (coal, peat, etc.) ■ Supply of electricity and gas ■ Waste disposal services ■ Non-residential immovable goods, including supply and development ■ Supply of concrete and concrete goods ■ Repair and maintenance of movable goods ■ General agricultural and veterinary services ■ Short-term hire of cars, boats, caravans, etc. ■ Driving instruction ■ Supply of hot food, including take-away food ■ Hotel/holiday accommodation, including caravan parks and camping sites ■ Admission to cinemas, theatres, certain musical performances, museums and fairground amusements ■ Supply and hire of live horses and greyhounds
Second reduced rate (9%)	■ Subscriptions for certain sporting activities ■ Printed newspapers, e-newspapers and e-books
Farmer flat-rate addition (5.4%)	Supply of agricultural products and services by non-VAT-registered farmers to VAT-registered customers
Livestock rate (4.8%)	■ Supply of livestock ■ Supply of horses intended for foodstuffs

Table 15 STAMP DUTY RATES 2019

	Rate
Shares	1%
Residential Property:	
Consideration up to €1m	1%
Excess over €1m	2%
Non-residential Property	6%

Table 16 CAPITAL GAINS TAX RATES AND ANNUAL EXEMPTION

	Rate
Disposals on or after 6 December 2012	33%
Disposals on or after 7 December 2011 and before 6 December 2012	30%
Disposals on or after 8 April 2009 and before 7 December 2011	25%

Annual exempt amount for 2019 is €1,270

Where revised entrepreneur relief applies:

Disposals on or after 1 January 2017	10%
Disposals on or after 1 January 2016 and before 1 January 2017	20%

Table 17 CAPITAL GAINS TAX INDEXATION FACTORS

Year of Assessment in which Expenditure Incurred	*Multiplier for Disposal in Period Ended*							
	5 April 1997	*5 April 1998*	*5 April 1999*	*5 April 2000*	*5 April 2001*	*31 Dec 2001*	*31 Dec 2002*	*31 Dec 2003 et seq.*
1974/75	6.017	6.112	6.215	6.313	6.582	6.930	7.180	7.528
1975/76	4.860	4.936	5.020	5.099	5.316	5.597	5.799	6.080
1976/77	4.187	4.253	4.325	4.393	4.580	4.822	4.996	5.238
1977/78	3.589	3.646	3.707	3.766	3.926	4.133	4.283	4.490
1978/79	3.316	3.368	3.425	3.479	3.627	3.819	3.956	4.148
1979/80	2.992	3.039	3.090	3.139	3.272	3.445	3.570	3.742
1980/81	2.590	2.631	2.675	2.718	2.833	2.983	3.091	3.240
1981/82	2.141	2.174	2.211	2.246	2.342	2.465	2.554	2.678
1982/83	1.801	1.829	1.860	1.890	1.970	2.074	2.149	2.253
1983/84	1.601	1.627	1.654	1.680	1.752	1.844	1.911	2.003
1984/85	1.454	1.477	1.502	1.525	1.590	1.674	1.735	1.819
1985/86	1.369	1.390	1.414	1.436	1.497	1.577	1.633	1.713
1986/87	1.309	1.330	1.352	1.373	1.432	1.507	1.562	1.637
1987/88	1.266	1.285	1.307	1.328	1.384	1.457	1.510	1.583
1988/89	1.242	1.261	1.282	1.303	1.358	1.430	1.481	1.553
1989/90	1.202	1.221	1.241	1.261	1.314	1.384	1.434	1.503
1990/91	1.153	1.171	1.191	1.210	1.261	1.328	1.376	1.442

Year of Assessment in which Expenditure Incurred	*Multiplier for Disposal in Period Ended*							
	5 April 1997	*5 April 1998*	*5 April 1999*	*5 April 2000*	*5 April 2001*	*31 Dec 2001*	*31 Dec 2002*	*31 Dec 2003 et seq.*
1991/92	1.124	1.142	1.161	1.179	1.229	1.294	1.341	1.406
1992/93	1.084	1.101	1.120	1.138	1.186	1.249	1.294	1.356
1993/94	1.064	1.081	1.099	1.117	1.164	1.226	1.270	1.331
1994/95	1.046	1.063	1.081	1.098	1.144	1.205	1.248	1.309
1995/96	1.021	1.037	1.054	1.071	1.116	1.175	1.218	1.277
1996/97	-	1.016	1.033	1.050	1.094	1.152	1.194	1.251
1997/98	-	-	1.017	1.033	1.077	1.134	1.175	1.232
1998/99	-	-	-	1.016	1.059	1.115	1.156	1.212
1999/00	-	-	-	-	1.043	1.098	1.138	1.193
2000/01	-	-	-	-	-	1.053	1.091	1.144
2001	-	-	-	-	-	-	1.037	1.087
2002	-	-	-	-	-	-	-	1.049
2003 et seq.	-	-	-	-	-	-	-	1.000

Table 18 CAPITAL ACQUISITIONS TAX RATES AND EXEMPTION THRESHOLDS

Rates

	Rate
Benefits taken on or after 6 December 2012	33%
Benefits taken on or after 7 December 2011 and before 6 December 2012	30%
Benefits taken on or after 8 April 2009 and before 7 December 2011	25%

Exemption Thresholds

	Group Threshold		
	A	**B**	**C**
Benefits taken on or after 10 October 2018	320,000	32,500	16,250
Benefits taken on or after 12 October 2016	310,000	32,500	16,250
Benefits taken on or after 14 October 2015 and before 12 October 2016	280,000	30,150	15,075
Benefits taken on or after 6 December 2012 and before 14 October 2015	225,000	30,150	15,075
Benefits taken on or after 7 December 2011 and before 6 December 2012	250,000	33,500	16,750
Benefits taken on or after 8 December 2010 and before 7 December 2011	332,084	33,208	16,604

Table 19 CAPITAL ACQUISITIONS TAX LIMITED INTEREST FACTORS

Table A

1	2	3	4
Years of Age	Joint Factor	Value of an interest in a capital of €1 for a **male** life aged as in Column 1	Value of an interest in a capital of €1 for a **female** life aged as in Column 1
0	.99	.9519	.9624
1	.99	.9767	.9817
2	.99	.9767	.9819
3	.99	.9762	.9817
4	.99	.9753	.9811
5	.99	.9742	.9805
6	.99	.9730	.9797
7	.99	.9717	.9787
8	.99	.9703	.9777
9	.99	.9688	.9765
10	.99	.9671	.9753
11	.98	.9653	.9740
12	.98	.9634	.9726
13	.98	.9614	.9710
14	.98	.9592	.9693
15	.98	.9569	.9676
16	.98	.9546	.9657
17	.98	.9522	.9638
18	.98	.9497	.9617
19	.98	.9471	.9596
20	.97	.9444	.9572
21	.97	.9416	.9547
22	.97	.9387	.9521
23	.97	.9356	.9493
24	.97	.9323	.9464
25	.97	.9288	.9432
26	.97	.9250	.9399
27	.97	.9209	.9364
28	.97	.9165	.9328
29	.97	.9119	.9289
30	.96	.9068	.9248

1	2	3	4
Years of Age	Joint Factor	Value of an interest in a capital of €1 for a **male** life aged as in Column 1	Value of an interest in a capital of €1 for a **female** life aged as in Column 1
31	.96	.9015	.9205
32	.96	.8958	.9159
33	.96	.8899	.9111
34	.96	.8836	.9059
35	.96	.8770	.9005
36	.96	.8699	.8947
37	.96	.8626	.8886
38	.95	.8549	.8821
39	.95	.8469	.8753
40	.95	.8384	.8683
41	.95	.8296	.8610
42	.95	.8204	.8534
43	.95	.8107	.8454
44	.94	.8005	.8370
45	.94	.7897	.8283
46	.94	.7783	.8192
47	.94	.7663	.8096
48	.93	.7541	.7997
49	.93	.7415	.7896
50	.92	.7287	.7791
51	.91	.7156	.7683
52	.90	.7024	.7572
53	.89	.6887	.7456
54	.89	.6745	.7335
55	.88	.6598	.7206
56	.88	.6445	.7069
57	.88	.6288	.6926
58	.87	.6129	.6778
59	.86	.5969	.6628
60	.86	.5809	.6475
61	.86	.5650	.6320
62	.86	.5492	.6162

1	2	3	4
Years of Age	Joint Factor	Value of an interest in a capital of €1 for a **male** life aged as in Column 1	Value of an interest in a capital of €1 for a **female** life aged as in Column 1
63	.85	.5332	.6000
64	.85	.5171	.5830
65	.85	.5007	.5650
66	.85	.4841	.5462
67	.84	.4673	.5266
68	.84	.4506	.5070
69	.84	.4339	.4873
70	.83	.4173	.4679
71	.83	.4009	.4488
72	.82	.3846	.4301
73	.82	.3683	.4114
74	.81	.3519	.3928
75	.80	.3352	.3743
76	.79	.3181	.3559
77	.78	.3009	.3377
78	.76	.2838	.3198
79	.74	.2671	.3023
80	.72	.2509	.2855
81	.71	.2353	.2693
82	.70	.2203	.2538
83	.69	.2057	.2387
84	.68	.1916	.2242
85	.67	.1783	.2104
86	.66	.1657	.1973
87	.65	.1537	.1849
88	.64	.1423	.1730
89	.62	.1315	.1616
90	.60	.1212	.1509
91	.58	.1116	.1407
92	.56	.1025	.1310
93	.54	.0939	.1218
94	.52	.0858	.1132

1	2	3	4
Years of Age	Joint Factor	Value of an interest in a capital of €1 for a **male** life aged as in Column 1	Value of an interest in a capital of €1 for a **female** life aged as in Column 1
95	.50	.0781	.1050
96	.49	.0710	.0972
97	.48	.0642	.0898
98	.47	.0578	.0828
99	.45	.0517	.0762
100 or over	.43	.0458	.0698

Table B

(Column 2 shows the value of an interest in a capital of €1 for the number of years shown in Column 1.)

1	2	1	2
Number of years	Value	Number of years	Value
1	.0654	26	.8263
2	.1265	27	.8375
3	.1836	28	.8480
4	.2370	29	.8578
5	.2869	30	.8669
6	.3335	31	.8754
7	.3770	32	.8834
8	.4177	33	.8908
9	.4557	34	.8978
10	.4913	35	.9043
11	.5245	36	.9100
12	.5555	37	.9165
13	.5845	38	.9230
14	.6116	39	.9295
15	.6369	40	.9360
16	.6605	41	.9425
17	.6826	42	.9490
18	.7032	43	.9555
19	.7225	44	.9620
20	.7405	45	.9685
21	.7574	46	.9750
22	.7731	47	.9815
23	.7878	48	.9880
24	.8015	49	.9945
25	.8144	50 and over	1.000

Appendix 2

Chartered Accountants Ireland *Code of Ethics*

Under Chartered Accountants Ireland's *Code of Ethics*, a Chartered Accountant shall comply with the following fundamental principles:

(a) **Integrity** – to be straightforward and honest in all professional and business relationships.
(b) **Objectivity** – to not allow bias, conflict of interest or undue influence of others to override professional or business judgements.
(c) **Professional Competence and Due Care** – to maintain professional knowledge and skill at the level required to ensure that a client or employer receives competent professional services based on current developments in practice, legislation and techniques and act diligently and in accordance with applicable technical and professional standards.
(d) **Confidentiality** – to respect the confidentiality of information acquired as a result of professional and business relationships and, therefore, not disclose any such information to third parties without proper and specific authority, unless there is a legal or professional right or duty to disclose, nor use the information for the personal advantage of the professional accountant or third parties.
(e) **Professional Behaviour** – to comply with relevant laws and regulations and avoid any action that discredits the profession.

The Institute's "Five Fundamental Principles, Five Practical Steps" is a useful resource for members and students and is available at www.charteredaccountants.ie. As a Chartered Accountant, you will have to ensure that your dealings with the tax aspects of your professional life are also in compliance with these fundamental principles. You may be asked to define or list the principles and also be able to identify where these ethical issues might arise and how you would deal with them.

Examples of situations that could arise where these principles are challenged in the context of tax are outlined below:

Example 1
You are working in the Tax Department of ABC & Co and your manager is Jack Wilson. He comes over to your desk after his meeting with Peter Foley. He gives you all the papers that Peter has left with him. He asks you to draft Peter's tax return. You know who Peter is as you are now living in a house that your friend, Ann, leased from Peter. As you complete the return, you note that there is no information regarding rental income. What should you do?

Action
As a person with integrity, you should explain to your manager, Jack, that your friend, Ann, has leased property from Peter and that he has forgotten to send details of his rental income and expenses. As Peter sent the information to Jack, it is appropriate for Jack to contact Peter for details regarding rental income and related expenses.

Example 2

You are working in the Tax Department of the Irish subsidiary of a US-owned multinational. You are preparing the corporation tax computation, including the R&D tax credit due. You have not received some information from your colleagues dealing with R&D and cannot finalise the claim for R&D tax credit until you receive this information. Your manager is under pressure and tells you to just file the claim on the basis of what will maximise the claim. He says, "It is self-assessment, and the chance of this ever being audited or enquired into is zero." What should you do?

Action

You should act in a professional and objective manner. This means that you cannot do as your manager wants. You should explain to him that you will contact the person in R&D again and finalise the claim as quickly as possible.

Example 3

Anna O'Shea, Financial Controller of Great Client Ltd, rings you regarding a VAT issue. You have great respect for Anna and are delighted that she is ringing you directly instead of your manager. She says that it is a very straightforward query. However, as you listen to her, you realise that you are pretty sure of the answer but would need to check a point before answering. What should you do?

Action

Where you do not know the answer, it is professionally competent to explain that you need to check a point before you give an answer. If you like, you can explain which aspect you need to check. Your client will appreciate you acting professionally rather than giving incorrect information or advice.

Example 4

The phone rings, and it is Darren O'Brien, your best friend, who works for Just-do-it Ltd. After discussing the match you both watched on the television last night, Darren explains why he is ringing you. He has heard that Success Ltd, a client of your Tax Department, has made R&D tax credit claims. Therefore, you must have details regarding its R&D. Darren's relationship with his boss is not great at present, and he knows that if he could get certain data about Success Ltd, his relationship with his boss would improve. He explains that he does not want any financial information, just some small details regarding R&D. What should you do?

Action

You should not give him the information. No matter how good a friend he is, it is unethical to give confidential information about your client to him.

Example 5

It is the Friday morning before a bank holiday weekend and you are due to travel from Dublin to west Cork, after work, for the weekend. Your manager has been on annual leave for the last week. He left you work to do for the week, including researching a tax issue for a client. He advised you that you were to have an answer to the issue, no matter how long it took. It actually took you a very short time and you have it all documented for him.

Your friend who is travelling with you asks if you could leave at 11am to beat the traffic and have a longer weekend. You have no annual leave left, so you cannot take leave. You know that if you leave, nobody will notice, but you have to complete a timesheet. Your friend reminds you that the research for the client could have taken a lot longer and that you could code the five hours to the client. What should you do?

Action

It would be unprofessional behaviour and would show a lack of integrity if you were to charge your client for those five hours.

Appendix 3

Tax Planning, Tax Avoidance and Tax Evasion

The global financial and economic crash of 2008 and the ensuing worldwide recession led to a fall in tax collected by many governments and moved tax and tax transparency higher up the agenda. Recent global developments and initiatives have further increased the focus and attention of governments and the wider public on both tax avoidance and evasion of taxes. The revelations in the Paradise Papers and the Panama Papers, the EU's state aid decision against Ireland and Apple Inc., coupled with the 'tax-shaming' of many multinational brand names and famous people has led to tax, and tax ethics, appearing in media headlines almost on a daily basis. As a result, a number of international and domestic initiatives have dramatically changed the tax planning and tax compliance landscape and brought tax transparency to the fore in many businesses and boardrooms.

The tax liability of an individual, partnership, trust or company can be reduced by tax planning, tax avoidance or tax evasion. Although the overriding objective of each is to reduce the taxpayer's tax bill, the method each adopts to do so is different. Each is also vastly different from an ethical and technical perspective.

Tax receipts are used to fund public services such as education, hospitals and roads. Individuals and businesses in a country benefit from these services directly and indirectly and it is therefore seen as a social and ethical responsibility for them to pay their fair share of taxes. Evading or avoiding paying your taxes is viewed as unacceptable as a result.

Tax Planning

Tax planning is used by taxpayers to reduce their tax bill by making use of provisions within domestic tax legislation. For example, any company with good tax governance will seek to minimise its tax liability by using the tools and mechanisms – allowances, deductions, reliefs and exemptions for example – made available to them by the government.

Planning can also take the form of simple decisions, such as delaying disposal of an asset when a fall in the rate of capital gains tax is expected so that the person pays a lower rate of tax on its taxable profits. Or a taxpayer may consider what type of assets to buy to maximise capital allowances. Any tax planning decision should work, not just from a tax planning and legislative perspective, but it should also be commercially feasible.

The Irish government accepts that all taxpayers are entitled to organise their affairs in such a way as to mitigate their tax liability – as long as they do so within the law and within the spirit in which government intended when setting the law. Tax planning is both legally and ethically acceptable.

Tax Avoidance

Tax avoidance is often viewed as a grey area because it is regularly confused with tax planning. Tax avoidance is the use of loopholes within tax legislation to reduce the taxpayer's tax liability. Although tax avoidance may seem similar to tax planning, as the taxpayer is using tax law to reduce their overall tax burden, the taxpayer is using tax legislation in a way not intended, or anticipated, by government.

TCA 1997 section 811C provides general anti-avoidance legislation. A transaction shall be a tax avoidance transaction if it would be reasonable to consider that the transaction gives rise to a tax advantage and it was not undertaken primarily for purposes other than to give rise to a tax advantage. These provisions are designed to counteract certain transactions which have little or no commercial reality but are carried out primarily to create an artificial tax deduction or to avoid or reduce a tax charge.

In addition, TCA 1997 sections 817D–817T provide mandatory disclosure of certain transactions that could result in a tax advantage. The regime seeks to force advisors, promoters and taxpayers who implement schemes designed to procure a tax advantage, to inform Revenue of the details of such schemes. The mandatory disclosure regime also has penalties for advisers who do not comply. The users of such schemes are also required to notify Revenue that they have used a particular scheme by including the scheme notification number on the relevant tax return or submission.

While tax avoidance is arguably legal, it is generally viewed as ethically unacceptable behaviour. Tax avoidance behaviour that is successfully challenged by Revenue will lead to the original tax saving being paid, in addition to interest and penalties.

Tax Evasion

At the extreme end of the spectrum is tax evasion. Tax evasion involves breaking the law deliberately and either not paying any of the taxes that fall due or underpaying the taxes that fall due when the law clearly states that they must be paid. Tax evaders intend to deliberately break rules surrounding their tax position in order to avoid paying the correct amount of tax they owe.

A tax evader illegally reduces their tax burden, either by a misrepresentation to Revenue or by not filing tax returns at all, thereby concealing the true state of their tax affairs. Tax evasion can include onshore (within the State) and offshore deliberate behaviour.

Examples of tax evasion include, *inter alia*:

- failure to file a tax return and pay the relevant tax arising;
- failure to declare the correct income;
- deliberately inflating expenses, which reduces taxable profits or increases a loss;
- hiding taxable assets;
- wrongly claiming a tax refund or repayment by being dishonest;
- not telling Revenue about a source of income;
- not operating a PAYE scheme for employees/pensioners;
- not registering for VAT when required to do so; and
- deliberate submission of incorrect or false information.

In all cases the Exchequer suffers a loss of tax. This is known as tax fraud. Tax evasion, and the tax fraud that flows from this behavior, is a criminal offence prosecutable by Revenue. It is viewed as ethically unacceptable behaviour. The error will generally fall into the "deliberate behavior" resulting in the original tax saving being paid, in addition to interest and penalties.

Suggested Solutions to Review Questions

Chapter 1

Question 1.1

1. **Maurice – Capital Gains Tax Computation 2019**

	€	€
Sale proceeds		80,000
Less: legal costs on disposal		(750)
Net sale proceeds		79,250
Deduct: Allowable cost		
House	20,000	
Legal costs	600	
	20,600	
Indexed @ 1.819		(37,471)
		41,779
Deduct: Annual exemption		(1,270)
		40,509
CGT @ 33%		13,368

2. **Vincent – Capital Gains Tax Computation 2019**

	€	€
Sale proceeds		9,300
Deduct: allowable cost	1,200	
Indexed @ 1.406		(1,687)
		7,613
Less: annual exemption		(1,270)
Taxable gain		6,343
CGT @ 33%		2,093

3(a) John – Capital Asset Sold

		€
Cost June 2001		7,600
Sale December 2019		7,800
Actual profit		200

Computation of Capital Gains 2019

		€
Sale proceeds		7,800
Cost June 2001: €7,600	indexed @ 1.087	(8,261)
"Loss"		(461)

Therefore, no gain/no loss

Note: indexation cannot create a loss where there is an actual monetary gain.

3(b) Philip – Capital Asset Sold

	€
Cost July 1980	3,000
Sale proceeds December 2019	2,700
Actual loss – maximum allowable	(300)

Computation of Capital Gains 2019

	€
Sale proceeds	2,700
Cost: €3,000 indexed @ 3.240	(9,720)
"Loss"	(7,020)
Restricted to maximum allowable loss	(300)

Note: indexation cannot create an allowable loss greater than the actual monetary loss.

3(c) Paul – Capital Asset Sold

	€
Cost June 1973	5,700
Sale proceeds December 2019	5,500
Actual loss	(200)

Computation of Capital Gains 2019

	€
Sale proceeds	5,500
Market value April 1974: €5,800 indexed @ 7.528	(43,662)
"Loss"	(38,162)
Restricted to maximum allowable loss	(200)

3(d) Oliver – Capital Asset Sold

	€
Cost July 1980	15,000
Sale proceeds	18,000
Actual gain	3,000

Computation of Capital Gains 2019

Sale proceeds	18,000
Cost €15,000 indexed @ 3.240	(48,600)
"Loss"	(30,600)
Therefore, no gain/no loss.	

Note: indexation cannot operate so as to turn an actual monetary gain into an allowable loss.

Question 1.2

1. James – CGT Computation 2019

	€
Sale proceeds	650,000
Deduct: allowable costs	
Acquisition cost €260,000 − €10,000 = €250,000	
Indexed @ 1.356	(339,000)
Enhancement expenditure:	
August 2001 – not capital expenditure	0
May 2005	(90,000)
Chargeable gain	221,000
Annual exemption	(1,270)
	219,730
CGT due @ 33%	72,511

2. Declan – CGT Computation 2019

	€	€
Sale proceeds		400,000
Deduct: allowable costs		
1. 6 April 1998 €85,000 @ 1.212	103,020	
2. Expenditure August 2001 €20,000 @ 1.087	21,740	
3. Expenditure February 2004 €39,250 @ 1.0	39,250	(164,010)
"Gain"		235,990
Deduct: annual exemption		(1,270)
		234,720
CGT @ 33%		77,458

Question 1.3

2019 – nil assessment (net loss €5,800).
Relief for the €5,800 loss will be given as follows:

		€	
(1st)	2018	1,370	(€100 + Exemption €1,270)
(2nd)	2017	1,420	(€150 + Exemption €1,270)
(3rd)	2016	1,520	(€250 + Exemption €1,270)
	Restricted total relief	4,310	

Note: it should be noted that for each of the three years, no effective loss relief has been received for the first €1,270 of losses used, as that amount of the loss merely replaced the annual exemption. CGT paid for 2016, 2017 and 2018 will be refunded.

Question 1.4

	€
Courtaulds Plc shares: proceeds	1,162
Market value 06/11/1974: €888 @ 7.528	(6,685)
Indexed loss	(5,523)
Monetary gain	274
Therefore, no gain/no loss	
Box Plc shares: proceeds	1,662
Cost €1,732 @ 2.678	(4,638)
Indexed loss	(2,976)
Restrict to monetary loss	(70)
Cox Plc shares: proceeds	16,000
Cost €1,693 @ 1.331	(2,253)
Chargeable gain	13,747
Nox Plc shares: proceeds	1,305
Cost	(623)
Chargeable gain	682

		€
Summary	Chargeable gain	13,747
	Chargeable gain	682
	Allowable loss	(70)
		14,359
Annual exemption		(1,270)
		13,089
CGT due @ 33%		4,319

Question 1.5

			€	€
1.	12-Jan-2019	Sold – market value		50,000
	31-Jan-2000	Value at date of inheritance	8,000	
		Indexed @ 1.193		(9,544)
		Gain		40,456
2.	05-Feb-2019	Sale of Florida home		320,000
	30-Oct-1999	Cost	110,000	
		Indexed @ 1.193		(131,230)
		Gain		188,770
3.	05-May-2019	Sale of shares in Plc		30,000
	30-Apr-2002	Cost price	50,000	
		Indexed @ 1.049		(52,450)
				(22,450)
		Limited to monetary loss (€50,000 − €30,000)		(20,000)
4.	10-Dec-2019	Sale of house		2,000,000
	31-Dec-1992	Purchase price	300,000	
		Less: cost used (see Note)	(100,000)	
			200,000	
		Indexed @ 1.356		(271,200)
		Gain		1,728,800

Note: cost attributable to 2001 disposal is:

$$€300,000 \times \frac{€500,000}{€500,000 + €1,000,000} = €100,000$$

5.	21-Dec-2019	Deemed sale price of chair		3,500
	03-Dec-2001	Cost	2,600	
		Indexed @ 1.087		(2,826)
				674

Summary

Tax payable on 15 December 2019

1.	Sale of shares	40,456
2.	Sale of holiday home	188,770
3.	Sale of shares	(20,000)
		209,226
	Less: exemption	(1,270)
	Taxable	207,956
	CGT @ 33%	68,625

Tax payable on 31 January 2020

1.	Sale of shares	40,456
2.	Sale of holiday home	188,770
3.	Sale of shares	(20,000)

continued overleaf

4.	Sale of house	1,728,800
5.	Sale of chair	674
		1,938,700
	Exemption	(1,270)
	Taxable	1,937,430
	CGT @ 33%	639,352
Total liability for year		639,352
Less: paid 15 December 2019		(68,625)
Due 31 January 2020		570,727

Chapter 2

Question 2.1

(a) Disposal of shares in French company

Gain is taxable when remitted.

Gain

	€	€
Proceeds		65,000
Cost 1994/95:		
$\frac{8{,}000}{16{,}000} \times €60{,}000$	30,000	
Indexation factor 1994/95: 1.309		
Indexed cost		(39,270)
"Gain"		25,730

Proceeds remitted to Ireland = portion of gain taxable in 2019, i.e. €10,000. Gain is deemed to be remitted first.

(b) Sale of UK rental property

	€
Proceeds	200,000
Cost	(180,000)
Renovations	(30,000)
Loss	(10,000)

Note: no indexation as there is a monetary loss. UK property is taxed on a remittance basis and losses are not allowable.

(c) Sale of H Plc shares

	€	€
Proceeds		24,000
Cost	8,025	
Indexation factor 1998/99: 1.212		
Indexed cost		(9,726)
Gain		14,274

Jacques' Capital Gains Tax Liability 2019

	€
Gain on disposal of shares – amount remitted	10,000
Gain on disposal of H Plc shares	14,274
Total	24,274
Annual exemption	(1,270)
Taxable gains	23,004
CGT @ 33%	7,591

Note: no relief is available for the loss incurred in 2018 as the loss arose on the disposal of an asset only liable on the remittance basis.

Chapter 3

Question 3.1

	Shareholding	Cost
		€
July 2004	4,000	6,000
October 2004	2,000	–
	6,000	6,000

	€
Proceeds	15,000
Cost:	
$6{,}000 \times \frac{5{,}000}{6{,}000}$	(5,000)
Gain	10,000
Less: exemption	(1,270)
	8,730

€8,730 @ 33% = €2,881 CGT due

Note: no indexation as acquired after 1 January 2003.

Question 3.2

	Shareholding	Cost	
		€	
Acquired 01/07/1972	6,000	1,320	(MV 06/04/1974)
Rights issue 01/11/1983	12,000	4,080	
	18,000		

	€
Deemed proceeds	16,800

continued overleaf

Less:

$$1{,}320 \times \frac{10{,}000}{18{,}000} = 733 \times 7.528 = 5{,}518$$

$$4{,}080 \times \frac{10{,}000}{18{,}000} = 2{,}267 \times 2.003 = 4{,}541 \qquad (10{,}059)$$

Gain	6,741
Less: exemption	(1,270)
	5,471

€5,471 @ 33% = €1,805 CGT due

Question 3.3

	Shareholding	Cost	
		€	
Acquired May 1973	4,000	3,000	(market value 06/04/1974)
Rights issue 06/01/1988	2,000	6,000	
	6,000		

Sale to Orla

No CGT due on inter-spouse transactions.

Sale to Gerry

	€
Deemed proceeds	9,000

Less:

$$3{,}000 \times \frac{900}{6{,}000} \times 7.528 = 3{,}388$$

$$6{,}000 \times \frac{900}{6{,}000} \times 1.583 = 1{,}425 \qquad (4{,}813)$$

Gain	4,187

Sale on open market

	€
Less proceeds:	43,200

$$3{,}000 \times \frac{3{,}600}{6{,}000} \times 7.528 = 13{,}550$$

$$6{,}000 \times \frac{3{,}600}{6{,}000} \times 1.583 = 5{,}699 \qquad (19{,}249)$$

Gain	23,951

Summary

	€
Sale to Orla	-
Sale to Gerry	4,187
Sale on open market	23,951
	28,138
Less: exemption	(1,270)

26,868 @ 33% = €8,866 CGT due

Chapter 4

Question 4.1

	€
1. Gift to wife	
No gain/loss	Nil
2. Gift to John	
Market value (connected persons) at 01/09/2019	200,000
Deduct:	
CUV €3,000 @ 2.253	(6,759)
Development premium €2,000 @ 1	(2,000)
Gain	191,241
3. Sale of farm	
Sale proceeds	260,000
Less: €32,000 indexed @ 1.442	(46,144)
Gain	213,856
4. Sale of National Loan Stock	
Exempt Government Security	Nil
5. Sale of antique necklace	
Exempt – non-wasting tangible movable property sold for less than €2,540	Nil
6. Sale of painting	
No loss relief available. (Loss arose on the disposal of tangible movable property for less than €2,540; consideration deemed to be €2,540 and so no loss deemed to arise.)	Nil
7. Gift of commercial property	
Market value on disposal	875,000
Less: allowable costs	
January 1983 – €50,000 indexed @ 2.253	(112,650)
June 1989 – €60,000 indexed @ 1.503	(90,180)
March 2008 – €50,000 indexed @ 1	(50,000)
Gain	622,170
8. Sale of development land	
Sale proceeds	18,000
Less: allowable cost	
No indexation – acquired after 01/01/03	(10,000)
Gain	8,000

9. Sale of vase		
Exempt – non-wasting tangible movable property for less than €2,540		Nil

Computation of CGT payable

		Dev. Land
Rate of CGT	33%	33%
	€	€
2. Gift to John		191,241
3. Sale of farm	213,856	
7. Gift to mother	622,170	
8. Sale of development land	–	8,000
	836,026	199,241
Deduct:		
Unrelated to development land losses	(6,000)	
	830,026	830,026
Development land losses		(1,500)
Development land losses may be set off against all gains		1,027,767
Annual exemption		(1,270)
Taxable		1,026,497
CGT @ 33%		338,744

Question 4.2

(a) Chargeable gain on sale of property	€	€
Proceeds		1,585,000
Less: Selling costs		
Legal costs	12,500	
Agent's commissions	7,000	
		(19,500)
		1,565,500
Deemed cost of property €60,000 @ 7.528	451,680	
Enhancement in 1994/95 €162,000 @ 1.309	212,058	(663,738)
Chargeable gain		901,762

(b) Tax on sale of development land		
Proceeds		1,800,000
Deemed cost: current use value of property €12,500 @ 7.528	94,100	
Deemed cost: development value of property (€25,000 − €12,500) = €12,500 × 1	12,500	(106,600)
Gain		1,693,400
CGT @ 33%		558,822

Question 4.3

Capital Gains Tax Computation 2019	€	€
Proceeds		1,680,000
Costs of disposal		(18,000)
		1,662,000
Cost: 06/04/1986 €75,000 (all current use value)		
Indexed @ 1.637	122,775	
Incidental costs: €4,251 (all attributable to current use)		
Indexed @ 1.637	6,959	(129,734)
Gross gain		1,532,266
Exempt portion of gain – private residence		
Current use value at date of disposal		800,000
Costs of disposal attributable to private residence: $\frac{€800,000}{€1,680,000} \times €18,000$		(8,571)
		791,429
Indexed cost of acquisition – as above		(129,734)
Exempt gain		661,695
Chargeable gain = gross gain − exempt gain = €1,532,266 − €661,695		870,571

Alternative Calculation	
Excess of proceeds over current use value	€
(Development premium): €1,680,000 − €800,000	880,000
Costs attributable to development premium €880,000/€1,680,000 × €18,000	(9,429)
Taxable gain	870,571

Question 4.4

Shop premises

	€
Sale proceeds	695,000
Cost of disposal	(7,000)
	688,000
Value at 06/04/1974 as indexed: €10,000 @ 7.528	(75,280)
Enhancement expenditure as indexed: €12,000 @ 1.406	(16,872)
	595,848
Personal exemption	(1,270)
Capital gain	594,578
CGT @ 33%	196,211

Holiday cottage

Sale proceeds (deemed to be market value)	(Note 1)	20,000
Cost		(25,000)
Loss	(Note 2)	(5,000)

Notes:
1. In this situation market value is substituted for the sale proceeds.
2. This loss can only be set against future gains made on transactions with his nephew as this is a disposal to a connected person.

Question 4.5

1. Disposal of shop

	€
Proceeds	224,000
Less: related costs	(3,100)
Cost €63,000 @ 1.406	(88,578)
Chargeable gain	132,322

2. Shares

	Shareholding	Cost
		€
March 1995	1,500	6,800
July 1997	300	1,050
January 1998	900	–
	2,700	

	€
Proceeds	9,000
Less:	
$€6{,}800 \times \frac{2{,}000}{2{,}700} = 5{,}037$ @ 1.309	(6,593)
$€1{,}050 \times \frac{2{,}000}{2{,}700} = 777$ @ 1.232	(958)
Chargeable gain	1,449

3. Disposal of painting

	€
Proceeds	2,600
Cost	(1,900)
	700
Potential CGT due: €700 @ 33%	231
Max. CGT: €2,600 – €2,540 @ 50%	30

Summary

1. Disposal of shop	132,322
2. DIsposal of shares	1,449
	133,771
Annual exemption	(1,270)
	132,501
CGT @ 33%	43,725
Plus CGT for disposal of painting	30
Total	43,755

Chapter 5

Question 5.1

(a) 2019 CGT Liability

The transfer of a business to a company is treated as a disposal for CGT purposes. However, if the business is transferred as a going concern together with all the assets, other than cash, in exchange for shares in the new company, then the gain may be rolled over against the cost of the shares issued. Only partial rollover relief is available where the consideration is only partly satisfied by shares, as in this case.

Chargeable gains arising

(i) Incorporation of Business

	€	€
Warehouse (Working 1)		78,640
Goodwill		130,000
Gain		208,640
Deferred (Working 2)		178,834
Chargeable in tax year 2019		29,806

(ii) Disposal of Vase

Sale proceeds		88,000
Cost: market value 06/04/1974	10,000	
Indexation factor: 7.528		
Indexed cost		75,280
Chargeable gain		12,720

(iii) Disposal of Shares

Sale proceeds	5,000
Cost (no indexation as there is a monetary loss)	(10,000)
Loss	(5,000)

(iv) Capital Gains Tax

Initial period to 30 November:	
Incorporation of business	29,806

continued overleaf

Less: loss relief – loss forward	(10,000)
Less: annual exemption	(1,270)
	18,536
CGT @ 10% (Note 1)	1,853
Later period:	
Incorporation of business	29,806
Disposal of vase	12,720
	42,526
Less: loss relief re shares	(5,000)
Less: loss relief – loss forward	(10,000)
Less: annual exemption	(1,270)
	26,256
CGT @ 10% (Note 2)	2,626
Less: paid re initial period	1,853
CGT	773

Notes:

1. The conditions for revised entrepreneur relief are satisfied, therefore CGT is payable at 10% on the gain.
2. The losses and annual exemption are offset first against the gain taxable at 33%. As they exceed that gain, they are then offset against the gain taxable at 10%.

(b) CGT Payable

The CGT of €1,853 is payable by 15 December 2019. The CGT of €773 is payable by 31 January 2020.

(c) Base Cost of Shares

The base cost of shares in O'Dowd Ltd for a future disposal is:

	€
Cost of shares	630,000
Less: deferred gain	178,834
	451,166

Workings

1. Chargeable gains

	€	€
Warehouse		
Market value		400,000
Cost – May 1981	120,000	
Indexation factor: 2.678		
Indexed cost		321,360
Chargeable gain		78,640
Goodwill		
Market value		130,000
Cost		Nil
Chargeable gain		130,000

Plant and Machinery – no capital loss can arise in respect of the plant and machinery as capital allowances will have been claimed on this expenditure.

Inventories and receivables are not chargeable assets.

2. Deferred gain

The amount deferred is restricted as follows:

$$\text{Maximum deferred} = \text{chargeable gains} \times \frac{\text{value of shares received}}{\text{value of total consideration}}$$

Value of Total Consideration	€
Warehouse	400,000
Plant and machinery	40,000
Goodwill	130,000
Inventories	48,000
Receivables	117,000
Total consideration	735,000
Less: Loan	(50,000)
Payables	(55,000)
Value of shares	630,000

Deferred gain:

$$(€78{,}640 + €130{,}000) \times \frac{630{,}000}{735{,}000} \qquad 178{,}834$$

Chapter 6

Question 6.1

(a) CGT Computation (August 2019)

	€	
Disposal of shares in family company on 1 August 2019:		
Proceeds (market value)	800,000	
Market value 01/12/1984 = €40,000 indexed @ 1.819		
	(72,760)	
	727,240	@ 10%* = €72,724

*Qualifies for revised entrepreneur relief.

No CGT is payable on this gain on the assumption that it is a "family company", as defined for the purposes of the relief, and that no restriction in the relief arises out of the underlying assets of the company.

(b) CGT Computation December 2019

	€
Sale of shares by Paul	900,000
Cost (deemed – market value)	(800,000)
	100,000
Annual exemption	(1,270)
	98,730
CGT @ 33%	32,581

In addition, Paul has to pay the tax relieved on the transfer of the shares to him – €25,000. This is calculated as follows:

The additional CGT payable by Paul is the CGT which would have been payable by his father if he had not qualified for full relief from CGT on a disposal to his son.

If his father had not qualified for this relief, he could have qualified for the relief available for a disposal of qualifying assets to **a person other than a "child"**.

If the proceeds had been less than €750,000, the father would have qualified for full relief, so no additional CGT would have been payable by Paul on the subsequent sale. He would only have paid the €32,581. In this case, as the proceeds on the disposal by the father exceeded €750,000, his father would only have qualified for marginal relief. Marginal relief in this case would have restricted his father's liability to €25,000, i.e. €800,000 − €750,000 = €50,000 × 50%, which would have been the amount payable by Paul in addition to the €32,581.

Total CGT payable by Paul for 2019 = €32,581 + €25,000 = €57,581.

Question 6.2

(a) Eligibility for Retirement Relief

Sean should qualify for retirement relief on the disposal of his shares in Tara Foods Limited as he meets the conditions as follows:

- he has reached the age of 55 years, but not 66 years;
- the shares are in Sean's trading "family" company and are held for at least 10 years;
- Sean has been a working director of the company for at least 10 years, during which period he has been a full-time working director for at least five years.

However, full relief is not available to Sean as his shares derive some of their value from quoted investments, which are not chargeable business assets.

The amount qualifying for retirement relief is determined by the formula:

$$\frac{\text{Chargeable Business Assets}}{\text{Total Chargeable Assets}}$$

$$\frac{(600{,}000 + 50{,}000)}{(600{,}000 + 50{,}000 + 120{,}000)} = \frac{650{,}000}{770{,}000}$$

Note: inventory and trade receivables are not chargeable assets.

The premises qualifies for retirement relief as it falls within the definition of "qualifying assets" for the purposes of the relief, i.e. a building which the individual has owned for a period of not less than 10 years ending with the disposal and which was used throughout that period for the purposes of the company's trade and is disposed of at the same time and to the same person as the shares in the family company.

(b) Capital Gains Tax Computation

	€	€
Deemed sale proceeds		800,000
Cost 1987/88	100	
Index factor: 1.583		
Indexed cost		(158)
Gain		799,842
Exempt portion:		
€799,842 × 650,000/770,000		(675,191)
Chargeable gain		124,651
CGT @ 10% (Note)		12,465

Note: The 10% rate of CGT applies as the conditions for revised entrepreneur relief (see **Section 4.8**) are also satisfied.

Premises

The gain on the premises is not taxable.
No annual exemption is due.

(c) Retirement Relief Withdrawn?

The retirement relief claimed at (b) in respect of the shares will be clawed back if the shares in Tara Foods Limited are disposed of by Michael within six years of the date of transfer by Sean, and the retirement relief claimed at (b) in respect of the property will be clawed back if the property is sold by Michael within six years of the date of transfer by Sean. The relief granted to Sean will, in effect, be withdrawn.

(d) Revenue's CGT Recovery

The relief is withdrawn not from Sean, who had the benefit of the relief, but by way of Michael paying the CGT relieved, i.e. Michael will have to pay the difference between the CGT already paid and the amount which would have been payable by Sean if the retirement relief were not available.

Question 6.3

(a) Disposal of shares in Crawford Sportswear Ltd

This disposal does not qualify for retirement relief as **Colin did not own the shares for at least 10 years.** The period of ownership of the trade prior to its transfer to the company is not taken into account, as **Colin would not have qualified for relief on transfer of a business to a company.** Relief on transfer of a business to a company would not have applied, as **not all of the assets of the business were transferred to the company**, i.e. the premises were not transferred.

The **premises let to the company does not qualify for retirement relief**, as it was not used for the purposes of the **company's business for 10 years.**

The cost of the shares for CGT purposes is their market value at 1 January 2010, i.e. the market value of the net assets taken over. Net assets transferred were:

		Market Value
	€	€
Fixtures and fittings		50,000
Goodwill		80,000
Inventories		120,000

continued overleaf

Receivables		25,000
Payables		(110,000)
Net assets transferred		165,000
Gain on disposal of shares:		
Market value		500,000
Market value January 2010		(165,000)
Gain		335,000
Gain on disposal of premises:		
Market value		250,000
Cost June 1980	20,000	
Indexation factor 1980/81: 3.240		
Indexed cost		(64,800)
Gain		185,200

(b) Disposal of holiday cottage

	€	€
Market value		120,000
Market value 10 October 1983	25,000	
Indexation factor 1983/84: 2.003		
Indexed cost		(50,075)
Gain		69,925

(c) Disposal of brooch

	€
Market value	3,000
Market value 1 December 2005 (Note)	(2,400)
Gain	600

Note: no indexation as acquired post-2002. Also, marginal relief does not apply. (50% × (€3,000 − €2,540)) > 33% × €600, i.e. €230 > €198.

Colin's CGT Liability 2019

	€
Gains:	
Shares	335,000
Premises	185,200
Holiday cottage	69,925
Brooch	600
	590,725
Annual exemption	(1,270)
	589,455
CGT @ 10% of €335,000 (Note)	33,500
CGT @ 33% on balance	83,970
Total CGT payable	117,470

Note: The 10% rate of CGT applies to the sale of the shares as the conditions for revised entrepreneur relief are also satisfied.

Chapter 7

Question 7.1

(a) When an Irish resident company redeems its own shares at a premium, in this case €590,000, the premium is, on first principles, liable to income tax under Schedule F.

However, if it can be shown that:

(i) the company is a trading or holding company;
(ii) the vendor is resident (and ordinarily resident in the case of an individual) in the State;
(iii) the buyback is not part of a scheme or arrangement the purpose of which is to enable the shareholder to participate in the profits of the company;
(iv) the share redemption benefits the trade of the company;
(v) the shares have been held for five years;
(vi) the shareholding is substantially reduced; and
(vii) the shareholder, post-redemption, is no longer connected with the company (shareholding less than 30%).

Therefore the proceeds of €600,000 can be regarded as a capital receipt.

(b) Provided all tests are met, Alan's liability to CGT is as follows:

	€
Proceeds	600,000
Cost €10,000 @ 1.442	(14,420)
Gain	585,580
Less: annual exemption	(1,270)
Taxable	584,310
CGT @ 33%	192,822

Alan may qualify for retirement relief, but we do not have sufficient information to establish whether he does. In addition, if Alan has worked full-time in a managerial or technical capacity for at least three continuous years in the five years before the buyback of his shares and has not disposed of any chargeable business assets giving rise to gains in excess of €414,420 (i.e. €1,000,000 – €585,580) since 1 January 2016, revised entrepreneur relief would apply so that the relevant rate of CGT would be 10%.

(c) If Alan fails the tests, he will be liable to income tax under Schedule F.

	€
Schedule F	590,000
@ 40%	236,000

The company will be obliged to deduct DWT of 20% from the payment, and Alan will be entitled to a credit for the DWT. Alan will also be liable to the USC and PRSI.

Chapter 8

Question 8.1

(a) Purchase of shares in an Irish Plc is liable to Irish stamp duty at 1%. Therefore, stamp duty payable is €30,000 × 1% = €300.
(b) Purchase of shares in a US Plc is not liable to Irish stamp duty. (Shares in a company not registered in the State and not related to property situated in the State.)

(c) The purchase of land in Galway will be liable to Irish stamp duty at 6%. Therefore, stamp duty payable is €80,000 × 6% = €4,800.
(d) The purchase of an apartment in Kilkenny will be liable to Irish stamp duty at 1% (less than €1m). Therefore, stamp duty payable is €120,000 × 1% = €1,200.

Question 8.2

(a) The purchase of an apartment is liable to stamp duty at 1%, if the value does not exceed €1 million. Therefore, stamp duty payable is €200,000 × 1% = €2,000. This is due within 44 days of 1 September, i.e. by 14 October 2019, and will be payable by Ann Murphy.
(b) A transfer by way of gift is chargeable the same way as a transfer on sale, with the market value of the shares being substituted for the consideration. Shares are liable to stamp duty at a rate of 1%. Therefore, stamp duty payable is €300,000 × 1% = €3,000. This is due within 44 days of 5 September, i.e. by 18 October 2019, and will be payable by either Frank Gibbons or his brother, depending on what has been agreed between them.
(c) Where VAT is included in the consideration, it should be deducted before calculating the charge or rate of stamp duty. Therefore, the consideration for stamp duty purposes is €567,500 × 100/113.5 = €500,000. The purchase of a house is liable to stamp duty at 1%, as the value does not exceed €1 million. Therefore, stamp duty payable is €500,000 × 1% = €5,000. This is due within 44 days of 11 September, i.e. by 24 October 2019, and will be payable by Ciara Cawley.

Chapter 9

Question 9.1

(a) Gift of Irish land is liable to Irish stamp duty at 6%. Therefore, stamp duty payable is €100,000 × 6% = €6,000.
(b) A transfer of property between spouses is exempt.
(c) Gift of Irish land would normally be liable to stamp duty at 6%. However, the recipient is a charity, so it is exempt.
(d) Gift of shares in a private Irish company is liable to stamp duty at 1%. Therefore, stamp duty payable is €200,000 × 1% = €2,000.
(e) Gift of UK land is not liable to Irish stamp duty (not related to property situated in the State and normally the transfer would not be executed in the State).

If, alternatively, he does not gift these assets and leaves them under his will, no stamp duty will arise as transfers under a will are exempt from stamp duty.

Question 9.2

Transactions between "associated companies" are taxed at 0% stamp duty. In order to be an associated company, there must be a 90% relationship, direct or indirect, between the two companies. Holdings Limited has that relationship with Private Limited (100%) and Major Limited (95%). Therefore, no stamp duty arises on the transfers to those companies. However, if either of them ceases to be a 90% subsidiary of Holdings Limited within two years, the stamp duty becomes payable, i.e. €1 million × 6% = €60,000 for Private Limited, and €1 million × 1% = €10,000 for Major Limited.

There is stamp duty due on the residential property worth €1.5 million transferred to Free Limited.

First €1,000,000 @ 1%	€10,000
Balance of €500,000 @ 2%	€10,000
Stamp duty payable	€20,000

The patent worth €3 million transferred to Free Limited is exempt from stamp duty as it is intellectual property.

Chapter 10

Question 10.1

The transfer of the business from Jack to the company will not trigger any CGT. He can claim transfer of a business to a company relief as he satisfies the conditions, i.e. he is transferring all of the assets of the business to the company. All of the CGT can be deferred as he is only receiving shares and having the trade payables taken over.

If there is a contract, stamp duty is payable by the new company on the assets which are conveyed (land and buildings) and also those that pass under the contract, but excluding the assets which are goods and merchandise, i.e. machinery and inventories are not liable but goodwill and receivables are liable.

The new company will be liable to stamp duty as follows:

	€
Land and buildings	500,000
Goodwill	180,000
Receivables	40,000
Total subject to stamp duty	720,000
Stamp duty @ 6%	43,200

If there is no contract, only the land and buildings will be liable to stamp duty. Therefore the stamp duty will be €500,000 @ 6% = €30,000.

Chapter 11

Question 11.1

John is the disponer as he instructs Mary to make the payment to Peter (the beneficiary).

Question 11.2

The date of the disposition is when the mother agrees to the future transfer. The beneficiary (daughter) does not become beneficially entitled in possession until she has her first child and this will be the date of the gift.

Question 11.3

Paddy gets a gift of €1,000,000, less consideration of €100,000, and Nora gets a gift of €100,000, both from Joyce.

Question 11.4

Memorandum

To :
From :
Date :
Re : **Capital Acquisitions Tax Queries**

I refer to the matters recently raised by you.

(a) Disposition

For capital acquisitions tax (CAT) purposes, a gift or inheritance is deemed to be taken where a disposition is made by a person, the disponer, as a result of which another person, the donee, becomes beneficially entitled in possession, see (c) below, to any benefit otherwise than for full consideration.

"Disposition" is the method by which ownership of the benefit provided is transferred. A simple example of a disposition is where a person transfers a property to another person. The deed of transfer in this case is the disposition.

The term disposition is very broadly defined in CATCA 2003 and includes the following:

(1) Any act by a person as a result of which the value of his estate is reduced, e.g. the transfer of property otherwise than for full consideration.
(2) Any trust, covenant, agreement or arrangement.
(3) An omission or failure to act by an individual, as a result of which the value of his estate is reduced.

Example:
This includes the passing of a resolution by a company which results directly or indirectly in one shareholder's property being increased in value at the expense of the property of any other shareholder, if that other shareholder could have prevented the passing of the resolution by voting against it.

(4) The payment of money.
(5) The allotment of shares in a company.
(6) The grant or creation of any benefit.
(7) The transfer of any property or benefit by will or on an intestacy.

(b) Date of the disposition

CATCA 2003 defines the date of the disposition as:

(1) The date of death of the deceased in the case of a benefit taken by will or on an intestacy.
(2) The date of the death of the deceased in the case of benefits derived under the Succession Act 1965.
(3) The latest date when the disponer could have exercised the right or power which has been waived, where the disposition consisted of a failure or omission to exercise a right of power.
(4) In any other case, the date of the disposition is the date on which the act or, where more than one act is involved, the last act of the disponer was done by which he provided, or bound himself to provide, the property comprised in the disposition.

(c) Beneficially entitled in possession

"Entitled in possession" is defined in CATCA 2003 as meaning, "having a present right to the enjoyment of property as opposed to having a future such right". CAT only arises where a person obtains the current enjoyment of a property as opposed to being entitled to enjoyment of the property at some time in the future.

A person has a "beneficial interest" in property if he is entitled to the benefits arising from a property without necessarily having legal ownership of the property. For example, X by deed appoints Y, his son, as trustee of a fund of investments the income from which is to be paid to X's wife, Mrs X, for the duration of her life. After Mrs X's death the fund is to be transferred into the ownership of X's son. Y is the legal owner of the investments. However, as the income from the investments is paid to Mrs X for her life, as soon as the deed is executed giving her the life interest, she is said to have a beneficial interest in the investments. Y also has a beneficial interest in the fund as he is entitled to the benefits from the fund in the future. Mrs X is said to be beneficially entitled in possession to the fund. However, her son Y, while having a beneficial interest in the fund, is not "entitled in possession" as he has a future interest rather than a current interest.

(d) Date of the gift

The date of the gift is defined as the date upon which the recipient of the gift becomes beneficially entitled in possession to the benefit (i.e. the date the recipient receives an immediate benefit).

Signed:

Chapter 12

Question 12.1

1.	Group A	€320,000
2.	Group B	€32,500
3.	Group B €32,500. Group A €310,000 does not apply as uncle did not control company.	
4.	Group A – favourite nephew/niece	€320,000
5.	Group C	€16,250
6.	Group B – although father is deceased, grandson is not a minor, so Group A does not apply.	€32,500
7.	Group C	€16,250
8.	Group B	€32,500
9.	Group C	€16,250
10.	Group A – favourite nephew/niece	€320,000
11.	Group B	€32,500
12.	Group A – "child" includes stepchild	€320,000
13.	Group B	€32,500
14.	Group B – not favourite nephew/niece as did not work for previous five years	€32,500
15.	Group A	€320,000

16.	Group B	€32,500
17.	Group B	€32,500
18.	Group B – "child" of brother, includes adopted child	€32,500
19.	Group C not a child of a brother or sister	€16,250
20.	Group A	€320,000

Question 12.2

Aggregate A		€
Inheritance from father		350,000
Previous gift from father		100,000
Previous inheritance from mother		30,000
Total gifts and inheritances (Note)		480,000
Less: tax-free threshold (Group A)		(320,000)
Taxable		160,000
CAT @ 33%		52,800
Aggregate B		
Previous benefits €100,000 + €30,000	€130,000	
Less: tax-free threshold (Group A)	€320,000	

Therefore, no tax on Aggregate B as benefits received are less than threshold.

CAT payable:

Tax on Aggregate A – Tax on Aggregate B = €52,800 – €nil 52,800

Note: the gift from his father in 1990 is not aggregated as it is pre-5 December 1991. The inheritance from his uncle is ignored as it is a Group B benefit.

Chapter 13

Question 13.1

CATCA 2003 does not include rules for determining where property is situated. General law determines where property is located. The main rules are as follows:

1. *Land and buildings*
   Situated where they are physically located.
2. *Debts*
   (i) A simple contract debt is situated where the debtor resides.
   (ii) A speciality debt, i.e. a debt payable under a sealed instrument, is situated where the instrument happens to be.
   (iii) A judgment debt is situated where the judgment is recorded.

3. *Securities/shares*
   Situated where the share register is kept, if the securities/shares are registered. Bearer securities/shares are situated where the security/share certificate is physically located.
4. *Tangible property, e.g. cars, furniture, moveable goods*
   Situated where they are physically located.
5. *Cash or currency of any kind*
   Situated where they are physically located. Bank balances are located in the country of the bank branch at which the account is kept.

Question 13.2

(a) A gift or inheritance taken during the year ended 31 December 2019 will be a taxable gift or inheritance if:

(1) Regardless of whether the gift or inheritance consists of Irish or foreign property,

(i) the date of the disposition is on or after 01/12/1999 and the **disponer** is resident or ordinarily resident in the State at the date of the disposition; or

(ii) the date of the disposition is on or after 01/12/1999 and the **donee/successor** is resident or ordinarily resident in the State at the date of the gift/ inheritance,

provided that, in the case of a non-Irish domiciled person, such a person will only be regarded as resident or ordinarily resident in the State on the relevant date if he has been resident in the State for the previous five tax years and is resident or ordinarily resident on the relevant date, i.e. date of the disposition for the disponer and the date of the gift/ inheritance in the case of the beneficiary.

(2) The gift or inheritance consists of Irish property (even though none of the rules under 1 above is satisfied).

(b) (1) As the disponer is Irish domiciled and Irish resident, both the Irish and the UK property are taxable inheritances. Rule (1)(i) above applies. (In any event, as the donee is also Irish domiciled and resident at the date of the inheritance, it would be a taxable inheritance even if the disponer had not been Irish domiciled and resident.)

(2) The date of the disposition, i.e. the date of Gordon's death, is after 01/12/1999. The property inherited is not Irish property. As the successor, Dermot, is Irish resident and domiciled at the date of the inheritance, the inheritance is a taxable inheritance. Rule (1)(ii) above applies.

(3) Neither the disponer nor the successor is Irish resident or ordinarily resident at the relevant dates. The property inherited is Irish property. The inheritance is a taxable inheritance. Rule (a)(2) above applies.

(4) The property inherited is not Irish property. The disponer is neither resident nor ordinarily resident in the State at the date of the disposition and the successor, Nevin, although Irish resident, is not Irish domiciled. Therefore, he is only taxable if he has been resident in the State for the preceding five tax years and resident or ordinarily resident on 16/09/2019. As he is, the inheritance is a taxable inheritance.

(5) The disponer is Irish domiciled and resident in the State at the date of the disposition. This is, therefore, a taxable inheritance. Rule (1)(i) above applies. It is irrelevant that one of the successors is not resident in the State. (In any event, as the entire property consists of Irish property, even if neither the disponer nor the successors were Irish resident at the relevant dates, the inheritance would still be a taxable inheritance.)

(6) As the donee, Darren, is Irish domiciled and is ordinarily resident in the State (he only ceased to be resident in Ireland in 2018 and, therefore, is still ordinarily resident), the gift is a taxable gift. Rule (1)(ii) above applies.

(7) As the disponer is Irish domiciled and Irish resident at the date of the disposition, the gift is a taxable gift. Rule (1)(i) above applies. (In any event, the donee is also Irish domiciled and Irish resident at the date of the gift, which means that even if Rule (1)(i) was not satisfied, the gift would be a taxable gift by virtue of Rule (1)(ii).)

(8) The disponer is Irish resident and ordinarily resident but not Irish domiciled. For Rule (1)(i) to apply, however, Jean must also have been resident for the last five years and be resident/ordinarily resident, as she is foreign domiciled. Since Jean is so resident and ordinarily resident, the gift of both the Irish and the foreign shares is taxable. (Had Jean not triggered a liability, Amelie would not be taxable on the French shares as she has not been resident for the last five years. Clearly, she would be taxable on the Irish shares.)

Question 13.3

(a) Michael

This is a taxable gift as the disponer, Michael, is Irish domiciled and resident. The relevant group threshold is €320,000 – gift from parent to a child.

Total gifts/inheritances received from persons within the same group threshold:

	€
Gift from father on 01/01/2019	40,000
Less: small gift exemption	(3,000)
Jewellery inherited from mother	20,000
Total	57,000

As this is less than the group threshold of €320,000, no CAT is payable.

(b) Bridget

This is a taxable inheritance as the disponer, Bridget's uncle, was Irish domiciled and resident at the date of his death.

Gifts and inheritances previously received from persons within the same group threshold include the inheritance from an aunt in March 2006 and the inheritance from Bridget's grandmother in September 1990. The inheritance in 1990 is ignored as it was taken before 5 December 1991. Accordingly, the only taxable gift/inheritance taken into account in calculating the CAT on the current inheritance is the inheritance of Irish quoted shares.

		€
CAT on Aggregate A:		
UK property		120,000
Irish quoted shares		50,000
		170,000
Group threshold: €32,500 @ Nil		
Balance:	€137,500 @ 33%	45,375
CAT on "Aggregate A"		45,375
CAT on Aggregate B:		
Irish quoted shares		50,000

Group threshold:	€32,500 @ Nil	
Balance:	€17,500 @ 33%	5,775
CAT on "Aggregate B"		5,775

CAT on Aggregate A − CAT on Aggregate B = €45,375 − €5,775

CAT payable in respect of inheritance of UK property	€39,600

Chapter 14

Question 14.1

Memorandum

To :
From :
Date :
Re : **Capital Acquisitions Tax Agricultural Relief**

I refer to your recent query regarding the relief from CAT available on the transfer of land by a client to his son.

(a) Nature of the Relief

Where an individual qualifies for agricultural relief in respect of a gift of agricultural property, the value of the property is reduced by 90% for CAT purposes.

The taxable value of a gift is calculated by deducting from the market value of the property comprised in the gift any consideration given and any liabilities, costs and expenses payable out of the gift. Where an individual qualifies for agricultural relief in respect of a gift of property, the amount of any consideration given or liabilities, costs and expenses payable are also reduced by 90%.

For example, a father gifts land valued at €1 million to his son. The land is subject to a mortgage of €20,000, which is taken over by the son. Normally stamp duty would be payable at 6%. However, if the son intends to farm the land for at least six years and either has an agricultural qualification as specified in the legislation or will spend at least 20 hours a week farming the land, stamp duty at 1% of the value of the land, i.e. €10,000, will be payable on the transfer. If the son does not satisfy these conditions, stamp duty at 6%, i.e. €60,000, will be payable. The son may also qualify for the reduced rate of stamp duty if he intends to lease the farm to a person who will farm the land and satisfy the qualifications/working time requirements. (Also, if the son qualified for the young trained farmer stamp duty relief, he would be exempt from stamp duty. In this solution, it is assumed that stamp duty is paid at 1%.)

If the gift qualifies for agricultural relief, the taxable value of the gift received will be as follows:

	€
Market value	1,000,000
Agricultural relief (90%)	(900,000)
Agricultural value	100,000
Stamp duty €10,000 @ 10%	(1,000)
Mortgage €20,000 @ 10%	(2,000)
Taxable value	97,000

(b) Agricultural Property

Agricultural relief applies to gifts or inheritances of "agricultural property". Agricultural property is:

"Agricultural land, pasture and woodland in the EU, including crops, trees, and underwood growing on such land and including such farm buildings, farm houses and mansion houses as are of a character appropriate to the property, and farm machinery, livestock and bloodstock thereon and entitlements under the EU Single Farm Payment Scheme."

(c) Definition of "Farmer"

In order for a gift to qualify for agricultural relief, the recipient of the gift must be a "farmer" on the "valuation date".

"Farmer" is defined by the legislation as an individual who satisfies the "asset test" and the "farming the land" test, as explained below.

Asset test – where an individual in respect of whom not less than **80% of the market value of all property to which he is beneficially entitled in possession (taking the current gift or inheritance into account) is represented by the market value of agricultural property in the EU**. In this context, an individual is deemed to be beneficially entitled in possession to any assets which are the subject of a discretionary trust of which he is a settlor and an object, and also to any future interests in property to which the individual is currently entitled.

For the purpose of the 80% test, the gross value of assets are taken, ignoring any liabilities or charges. There is one exception, i.e. borrowings used to purchase, repair or improve an off-farm principal private residence are deductible for the 80% test.

Continuing with the example at (a) above, if, after the gift, the son's only other asset consists of a house valued at €120,000 with a mortgage of €100,000 attaching to it and a car valued at €20,000, the son will qualify as a "farmer" as after taking the gift his assets will be made up as follows:

	€	%
Agricultural property	1,000,000	96
House (net of mortgage)	20,000	2
Car	20,000	2
Total assets	1,040,000	100

"Farming the land" test – for gifts or inheritances taken on or after 1 January 2015, the beneficiary must:

- farm the agricultural property for a period of not less than six years commencing on the valuation date; or
- lease the agricultural property for a period of not less than six years commencing on the valuation date.

In addition, the beneficiary (or the lessee, where relevant) must either:

- have one of the agricultural qualifications set out in tax legislation; or
- farm the agricultural property for not less than 50% of his or her normal working time.

Revenue will accept working 20 hours per week on average as satisfying the condition of farming for not less than 50% of his or her normal working time. The agricultural property must also be farmed on a commercial basis and with a view to the realisation of profits.

The farmer test does not have to be satisfied to the extent that the gift consists of trees or underwood.

(d) Withdrawal of the Relief

The agricultural relief will be withdrawn if, within six years after the date of gift or inheritance, the property is sold or compulsorily acquired and is not replaced with other agricultural property within a year, in the case of a sale, or within six years in the case of a compulsory acquisition.

If part of the proceeds on the disposal of agricultural property are reinvested, then a similar fraction of the relief is clawed back.

There is no withdrawal of the relief to the extent that the property which qualified for agricultural relief consists of crops, trees or underwood.

If the agricultural property is development land and it is disposed of in the period commencing six years after the date of the gift or inheritance and ending 10 years after that date, then the CAT will be recomputed. Agricultural relief will only be given in respect of the current use value of the property, i.e. there will be no relief given in respect of the development value, and CAT is recalculated and payable accordingly.

Where a donee, successor or lessee ceases to satisfy the "farming the land" test (otherwise than on death) within the period of six years commencing on the valuation date of the gift or inheritance, the agricultural relief granted will be clawed back.

Signed:

Question 14.2

Inheritances:

	Margaret	Liam	Eva
	€	€	€
Holiday home	180,000		
Stocks and shares	230,000		
Irish Government stock	101,500		
Shares in Fine Arts Ltd			960,000
Agricultural property		1,090,000	
Cash		50,000	
Mortgage		(120,000)	
Creditors		(15,000)	
Funeral expenses		(20,000)	
	511,500	985,000	960,000

Inheritance Tax

Margaret:

		€
Taxable value of inheritance		511,500
CAT payable:		
Group threshold:	€32,500 @ Nil	Nil
Balance:	€479,000 @ 33%	
CAT payable		158,070

Liam:

		€
Taxable value of inheritance (Working 1)		125,500
Tax payable:		
Group threshold:	€32,500 @ Nil	Nil
Balance:	€93,000 @ 33%	30,690

Eva:

Market value of shares	960,000
Value attributed to investment property	(360,000)
Value excluding investment property	600,000
Business relief	(540,000)
	60,000
Value attributed to investment property	360,000
Taxable value	420,000
Group threshold @ Nil	(320,000)
Balance	100,000
CAT @ 33%	33,000

Working 1 – Taxable value of inheritance

	€	€
Market value of agricultural property		1,090,000
Less: agricultural relief at 90%		(981,000)
		109,000
Less: mortgage €120,000 @ 10%		(12,000)
Less: farm creditors €15,000 @ 10%		(1,500)
Taxable value of agricultural property		95,500
Cash	50,000	
Funeral expenses	(20,000)	30,000
Taxable value of total property inherited by Liam		125,500
Clearly Liam qualifies as a "farmer".		
Value of agricultural property		€1,090,000
Value of total property		
(€1,090,000 + €30,000* + €200,000 – €130,000)		€1,190,000

Agricultural property as percentage of total property = 92% (greater than the required 80%).

He also satisfies the farming the land test as he intends to spend not less than 50% of his normal working time farming the land for at least six years.

*As the funeral expenses will have been paid by the valuation date, the residue will be €50,000 – €20,000 = €30,000.

Question 14.3

(a) James

	€
Assets inherited:	
Investment property: €520,000 @ 50%	260,000
Shares: €1 million @ 20% (Note 1)	200,000
Business relief relating to shares (Note 2)	(135,000)
Share of residue (Note 3)	74,000
Taxable	399,000
Aggregate A	
Current benefit	399,000
Gift from mother in 2003	167,000
	566,000
Group threshold: €320,000 @ nil	Nil
€246,000 @ 33%	81,180
Tax on Aggregate A	81,180
Aggregate B	
Gift from mother in 2006	167,000

Tax on Aggregate B = nil as €167,000 is less than the group threshold amount of €320,000.

Tax on Aggregate A – Tax on Aggregate B = Tax on inheritance
Tax on inheritance is therefore €81,180

(b) John

As the inheritance was taken from his wife, the benefits under the will are exempt from inheritance tax **and** are not taken into account (for aggregation purposes) in calculating CAT on later gifts or inheritances from other sources.

Notes:

1. Tyrex Ltd is a private company, which after the receipt of the shares by James is under the control of his relatives. Therefore, the value of the 20% shareholding in Tyrex Ltd inherited by James is valued as if it were part of a controlling holding, i.e. the value of a 20% shareholding is taken to be 20% of the market value of the company as a whole. No discount is given for the fact that a 20% interest is a minority (non-controlling) interest.

2. Business relief

	€	€
Total value of Tyrex Ltd		1,000,000
Value attributable to non-business assets:		
House	300,000	
Less: mortgage	(50,000)	
		(250,000)
Value attributable to relevant business property (balance)		750,000

Accordingly, 75% of the value of the shares in Tyrex Ltd is attributable to relevant business property.

	€
Value of shares inherited by James	200,000
Value attributable to relevant business property (75%)	150,000
Business relief @ 90%	135,000

3. Residue

	€
Bank accounts	60,000
Policy	104,000
Expenses	(16,000)
	148,000
50% share to James	74,000

Chapter 15

Question 15.1

(a) Tom

This is a taxable gift as the donee, Tom's mother, is Irish domiciled and resident.

Value of the annuity

In order to produce an annual income of €10,000, €200,000 of the 5% Government bond would have to be purchased, i.e. €10,000/5%. At 92c per €1 of stock, €200,000 of this stock would cost €184,000. The value of a life interest in €184,000 received by a 59-year-old woman is €121,955, i.e. €184,000 × 0.6628.

The relevant group threshold is €32,500, a gift from a lineal descendant. Tom's mother previously received an inheritance of €30,000, from her sister, also within the €32,500 group threshold.

CAT payable in respect of the current gift is therefore:

CAT on Aggregate A:	€
Value of gift	121,955
Less: small gift exemption	(3,000)
	118,955
Inheritance from sister	30,000
	148,955
Group threshold: €32,500 @ Nil	
Balance: €116,455 @ 33%	
CAT on Aggregate A	38,430

CAT on Aggregate B:

Inheritance from sister: €30,000	
Group threshold: €32,500	
CAT on Aggregate B	Nil
CAT on Aggregate A – CAT on Aggregate B = €38,430 – €Nil	
CAT payable in respect of gift of annuity from Tom	38,430

(b) Jason/Mark

UK Property

The inheritance of the UK property is a taxable inheritance. Although it is foreign property, it is taxable because the disponer, Martha, was Irish resident.

The relevant group threshold is €32,500. Although the property passes to Mark on the death of his father, the disponer is Martha, his aunt. Jason has not previously received any taxable gifts or inheritances from a person within the €32,500 group threshold (an inheritance from a nephew belongs to the €16,250 group threshold).

CAT payable in respect of the UK property is, accordingly:

		€
Value of inheritance		300,000
Group threshold:	€32,500 @ Nil	
Balance:	€267,500 @ 33%	
CAT liability		88,275

Cash

This is a taxable inheritance as both the disponer and successor are Irish resident and, in any event, consists of Irish property.

The relevant group threshold is €320,000. As Mark has previously received a taxable inheritance from a person within this group threshold, i.e. his mother, his CAT liability on the current inheritance is as set out below.

CAT payable in respect of the inheritance:

		€
Cash		260,000
Savings certificates from mother		190,000
		450,000
Group threshold:	€320,000 @ Nil	
Balance:	€130,000 @ 33%	
CAT liability		42,900

As the previous inheritance received was less than the Group A threshold of €320,000, €42,900 is now payable in respect of the inheritance of the cash and shares.

Total CAT payable by Mark:

	€
CAT on UK property	88,275
CAT on Irish cash	42,900
Total CAT payable	131,175

Question 15.2

(a) Martin

Taxable value of Dermot's inheritance:	€
Grocery business and premises	600,000
Business relief (90%) (assumed owned two years)	(540,000)
	60,000
House and contents	150,000
Bank accounts	15,000
Funeral costs	(8,000)
Incumbrance-free value	217,000
Discount factor for life interest: 0.8204	
Taxable value of life interest €217,000 × 0.8204	178,027

(b) Jack

Taxable value of Margaret's inheritance:

	€
"Slice" of premises and business:	
$€600,000 \times \frac{€15,000}{€150,000}$	60,000
Less: business relief (90%)	(54,000)
	6,000
Discount factor for 10-year interest: 0.4913	
Taxable value of 10-year interest €6,000 × 0.4913	2,948

Taxable value of John's inheritance:

	€
Premises and business	600,000
Less: Margaret's "slice"	(60,000)
	540,000
Business relief (90%)	(486,000)
	54,000
Residue	50,000
Costs: €20,000 + €9,000	(29,000)
Taxable value	75,000

(c) David

A taxable gift arises on the cessation of the payment of the annuity to Larry. David is taxable on the "slice" of the property returned to him.

The value of the "slice" is calculated by reference to the relative values at the date the payments cease, i.e. April 2019.

$$\text{Taxable value} = \text{“Slice”} = €375{,}000 \times \frac{€10{,}000}{€30{,}000} = €125{,}000$$

(d) Alan

Taxable value of gift of covenant = capitalised value of the annuity × discount factor for life interest of 65-year-old woman.

The capitalised value of the annuity is reached by calculating the amount which would have to be invested in the most recently issued Government bond, not redeemable within 10 years, in order to produce an annual income equal to the annuity. In order to produce an annual income of €10,000, €250,000 of a 4% Government bond would have to be purchased, i.e. €10,000/4%. At 89c per €1 of stock, €250,000 of this stock would cost €222,500 = capitalised value of annuity.

Discount factor for life interest of 65-year-old woman = 0.565.

Taxable value of annuity = 0.565 × €222,500 = €125,712.

(e) Tom

Taxable value of Emer's inheritance:

	€
"Slice" of farmland and farm assets:	
$€1{,}070{,}000 \times \frac{€15{,}000}{€50{,}000}$	321,000
Discount factor for life interest: 0.8683	
Taxable value of life interest €321,000 × 0.8683	278,724

Note: Emer is not entitled to agricultural relief in respect of her "slice" as she fails the asset test to qualify as a farmer, i.e. €321,000/€321,000 + €120,000 = 73%.

Taxable value of Fintan's inheritance:

	€
Market value of farmland and assets	1,070,000
Agricultural value (Note) @ 10%	107,000
Less: Emer's "slice" × 10%, i.e. €321,000 × 10%	(32,100)
Less: proportion of costs:	

$$€9{,}500 \times \frac{€1{,}070{,}000 - €321{,}000}{€1{,}145{,}000 - €321{,}000} = €8{,}635$$

Reduced for agricultural relief, i.e. €8,635 × 10%	(863)
	74,037
Stocks and shares	50,000
Cash	25,000
Remainder of costs: €9,500 – €8,635	(865)
Taxable value of Fintan's inheritance	148,172

Note: Fintan's agricultural asset percentage is calculated on the valuation date after receiving the inheritance (net of funeral expenses). As Fintan had no assets before the inheritance, the calculation is as follows:

$$\frac{€950{,}000 + €120{,}000}{€950{,}000 + €120{,}000 + €50{,}000 + €25{,}000 - €9{,}500} \times 100 = 94\%$$

The land is leased to a full-time farmer. Therefore Fintan is a farmer for agricultural relief. The agricultural relief will be clawed back if the farm is not leased to a full-time farmer or farmed full-time by Fintan for six years from the valuation date.

Question 15.3

(a) Gift 6 August 2019

	Total	25%
	€	€
300 acres	660,000	165,000
Farm buildings	28,200	7,050
Machinery	15,600	3,900
Livestock	24,400	6,100
Agricultural property		182,050
Cash in bank		126,000
Total assets		308,050

As agricultural property accounts for less than 80% of David's assets, he does not qualify as a farmer and so does not qualify for agricultural relief. However, business relief does apply.

	€
Market value of property gifted	182,050
Less: business relief @ 90%	(163,845)
	18,205
Small gift exemption	(3,000)
Taxable value	15,205

Group threshold amount of €320,000. Therefore, no tax payable.

(b) Inheritance 25 November 2019

	€
Farmland	1,080,000
Buildings	33,600
Machinery	19,300
Livestock	31,700
Total agricultural property	1,164,600
Agricultural property inherited 75%	873,450
Own agricultural property (25% previously received from father)	291,150
Agricultural property purchased	150,000
Total agricultural property	1,314,600
Other assets – investments	95,000
Total assets	1,409,600

As David's agricultural property accounts for in excess of 80% of the value of his total assets (i.e. 93.3%), and he is a full-time farmer, he qualifies as a farmer and so qualifies for agricultural relief.

Inheritance Tax computation

	€	€
Agricultural property: 10% × €873,450		87,345
Less: costs × 10% × €25,000 × $\frac{€873,450}{€968,450}$ (Note 1)		(2,255)
Taxable value of property		85,090
Investments	95,000	
Less: costs × €25,000 × $\frac{€95,000}{€968,450}$	(2,452)	
Less: annuity (Note 2)	(59,375)	
Taxable value of investments		33,173
		118,263

Group threshold = €320,000.

The total benefits received by David from persons belonging to this group threshold amounts to €133,468, i.e. €15,205 + €118,263 = €133,468. Therefore, no CAT is payable on the inheritance from his father.

Notes:

		€
1.	Agricultural property	873,450
	Other property	95,000
	Total inheritance	968,450

2. Deduction for annuity payable out of income from investments.

Total value of investments	€95,000
Appropriate part inherited by Rachel:	
$€95,000 \times \frac{€5,000}{€8,000}$	€59,375

Note: do not apply table factor!

Question 15.4

(a) CGT liability

No CGT liability arises on the transfer to Stephen as the conditions necessary for Peter to qualify for retirement relief are satisfied.

(b) CAT liability

(i) Is Stephen entitled to agricultural relief?

Farmer test:

	Agricultural Property	**Other Property**	**Total**
	€'000	€'000	€'000
Farmland gifted	5,000		5,000
House (less mortgage)		250	250
Car		20	20
Farmlands in Antrim	500		500
Site inherited from mother		450	450
Total	5,500	720	6,220

5,500/6,220 = 88.42%. As Stephen satisfies the asset and the farming the land tests, he is a farmer and is entitled to agricultural relief.

(ii) Taxable value of gift

	€
Agricultural value of property: €5m @ 10%	500,000
Less: stamp duty and legal fees: €165,000 @ 10%	(16,500)
Less: annuity payable: €540,000 @ 10% (Note)	(54,000)
Taxable value	429,500

Note: calculation of value of annuity

The capitalised value of the annuity is reached by calculating the amount which would have to be invested in the most recently issued Government bond, not redeemable within 10 years, in order to produce an annual income equal to the annuity. In order to produce an annual income of €30,000, €600,000 of 5% Government bond would have to be purchased, i.e. €30,000/5%. At 90c per €1 of stock, €600,000 of this stock would cost €540,000.

(iii) CAT payable

Relevant threshold is Group A €320,000. Previous gifts/inheritances received from persons within this group include the site inherited from Stephen's mother. (The farmland inherited from Stephen's uncle is Group B.)

	€
Aggregate A	
Current benefit	429,500
Small gift exemption	(3,000)
	426,500
Inheritance from mother	10,000
Cumulative gifts/inheritances within Group A threshold	436,500
Group threshold taxed @ Nil	(320,000)
Balance taxable	116,500
CAT @ 33% on Aggregate A	38,445
Aggregate B	
Inheritance from mother	10,000
CAT on Aggregate B	nil

Tax on current benefit = tax on Aggregate A – tax on Aggregate B, i.e.:
CAT payable on transfer to Stephen = €38,445

Chapter 16

Question 16.1

(a) Patrick

		€
Assets inherited:		
Government stock		14,000
Aggregate A		
Current benefit		14,000
Gift from mother in 2005		477,000
		491,000
Group threshold:	€320,000 @ nil	Nil
	€171,000 @ 33%	56,430
Tax on Aggregate A		56,430
Aggregate B		
Gift from mother in 2005		477,000
Group threshold:	€320,000 @ nil	Nil
	€157,000 @ 33%	51,810
Tax on Aggregate B		51,810

Tax on Aggregate A – Tax on Aggregate B = Tax on inheritance

Tax on inheritance is therefore €56,430 – €51,810	4,620

(b) Harry

The inheritance received by Harry is exempt because:

(i) he was not domiciled or ordinarily resident at the date of the inheritance; and
(ii) the inheritance comprised of Irish Government securities, which qualify for exemption from Irish income tax when beneficially owned by persons who are not domiciled or ordinarily resident in the State; and,
(iii) Sarah owned the securities at 24 February 2003, accordingly she was only required to have owned the securities for six years. (In any event, she has also owned them for more than 15 years.)

Question 16.2

John's CAT liability

Inheritance from father – CAT payable:

	€
Shares in Murray Developments	1,500,000
Investment properties	850,000
Part of investment property attributable to Sarah (Note 2)	(133,333)
Mortgages charged on properties	(225,000)
Residue (Note 3)	92,000
Taxable value of inheritance	2,083,667
Previous gift within same group threshold (Note 4)	100,000
Cumulative gifts/inheritances within Group A threshold	2,183,667
Group threshold taxed @ Nil	(320,000)
Balance taxable	1,863,667
CAT payable @ 33% (Note 5)	615,010

Notes:

1. Business relief does not apply as the trade is buying and selling land.
2. The inheritance received by Sarah is the "appropriate part" of the entire investment property on which the annuity payable to her is charged, i.e.:

$$\text{Entire property} \times \frac{\text{Gross annual value of annuity}}{\text{Gross annual value of property}}$$

$$€400{,}000 \times \frac{€10{,}000}{€30{,}000} = 133{,}333$$

3. Residue:

	€
Cash	146,000
Shares	50,000
Funeral expenses	(3,500)
Legal expenses	(8,500)
	184,000
50% each	92,000

4. Previous gift of property:

	€
Gross value	300,000
Less mortgage	(200,000)
Total	100,000

5. Previous gift is less than Group A threshold for 2019, so no CAT is attributed to this gift.

Emily's CAT liability

	€
House (Note 1)	950,000
Residue	92,000
Taxable value of inheritance	1,042,000
Previous inheritance with same group threshold	200,000
Cumulative gifts/inheritances within Group A threshold	1,242,000
Group threshold taxed @ Nil	(320,000)
Balance taxable	922,000
CAT @ 33%	304,260
CAT attributed to previous gift (Note 2)	Nil
CAT payable	304,260

Notes:

1. Emily does not qualify for exemption in respect of the house as she had an interest in another dwelling house at the date of the inheritance.
2. Previous gift was less than Group A threshold, so no CAT is attributed to this gift.

Sarah's CAT liability

	€
Value of inheritance (see Note 2 under John)	133,333
Factor for life interest for 63-year-old: 0.6	
Taxable value	80,000
Relevant group threshold @ Nil	(32,500)
Balance taxable	47,500
CAT payable @ 33%	15,675

Qualifying insurance proceeds (section 72 policy)

Total CAT payable:

	€
CAT – John	615,010
CAT – Sarah	15,675
CAT – Emily	304,260
Total	934,945
Proceeds from policy	1,000,000
Excess subject to CAT	65,055

Excess falls into the residue and is split evenly between John and Emily.

	Total	John	Emily
	€	€	€
Excess	65,055	32,527	32,527
CAT @ 33%	21,468	10,734	10,734

Proceeds of policy are used to pay €934,945 above. Balance of €21,468 payable separately.

Question 16.3

Declan's CAT liabilities

Declan qualifies for business relief in respect of the shares inherited from Jerome, as he satisfies the necessary share ownership requirements after receiving the inheritance. (The company is also a trading company and Jerome had owned the shares for at least two years prior to the date of the inheritance.)

The relevant group threshold is Group A €320,000 as Declan qualifies as a "favourite nephew", i.e. the inheritance is of shares in a private trading company controlled by the disponer (Jerome having held at least 50% of the shares). Jerome was a director and Declan has worked on a full-time basis for the company for the last five years.

	€
Market value of shares	350,000
Less: business relief (90%)	(315,000)
Revised taxable value	35,000

As the revised taxable value of the inheritance is less than the relevant group threshold and Declan had not previously received any taxable gifts or inheritances, no CAT is payable.

Jonathan's CAT liabilities

Jonathan does not qualify for business relief in respect of the property owned by his father and let to Wiggies Wholesalers as he only got the property and did not get any shares. In order for the property to qualify for business relief, the property and the disponer's interest in the company would have had to be given to the same beneficiary.

	€
Property	500,000
Residue (Note)	29,250
Taxable value of inheritance	529,250
Group A threshold taxed @ Nil	(320,000)
Balance taxable	209,250
CAT payable @ 33%	69,052

Note:

Residue: €65,000 – €2,500 – €4,000 = €58,500 × 50% = €29,250.

Previous gift from aunt is ignored as it belongs to the Group B €32,500 threshold.

Louise's CAT liabilities

The house is exempt from CAT, as the donor, Jerome, lived in the house at the date of death and Louise has lived in the house for at least three years prior to the date of the inheritance and owns no other dwelling house.

	€
Life insurance proceeds	360,000
Residue	29,250
Taxable value of inheritance	389,250
Previous inheritance with same group threshold (Note 1)	179,500
Cumulative gifts/inheritances within Group A threshold	568,750
Group threshold taxed @ Nil	(320,000)
Balance taxable	248,750
CAT @ 33%	82,087
CAT attributable to previous gift (Note 2)	Nil
CAT payable	82,087

Note:

1. €179,500. The €320,000 Group A threshold applies to this inheritance as Louise's husband was dead at the time of the inheritance to her from her father-in-law.
2. As the previous inheritance is less than the group threshold, no CAT attributed to this inheritance.

Chapter 17

Question 17.1

ABC & Co.
Chartered Accountants

17 November 2019

Mr O'Donovan
3 New Street
Dublin

Re: Proposed Property Transfers

Dear Mr O'Donovan,

You asked me to advise you on the taxation consequences of the proposed property transfers to your daughters on 1 December next.

Stamp Duty

Lorraine and Sheila will have the following stamp duty liabilities:
Lorraine: €350,000 @ 1% = €3,500
Sheila: €250,000 @ 1% = €2,500

Capital Gains Tax

You will be treated as disposing of both properties at market value for CGT purposes. Stamp duty and other legal fees incurred in connection with the properties are deductible in calculating the taxable gains. Accordingly, although the property to be transferred to Sheila has increased in value since you acquired it, taking account of your stamp duty and legal fees, overall a capital loss arises.

I have estimated, however, that a CGT liability of approximately €22,564 will arise on the deemed disposal of the property to Lorraine (see Appendix 1).

Capital Acquisitions Tax

Both your daughters will be treated as receiving a taxable gift from you equal to the market value of the property transferred to them. An individual may receive gifts or inheritances up to a total value of €320,000 from parents over his lifetime (since 5 December 1991) without giving rise to any CAT liability. Total gifts and inheritances in excess of €320,000 are subject to CAT at 33%.

I understand both Lorraine and Sheila have previously inherited assets valued at €160,000 and €225,000, respectively, from their mother in 2010. (Sheila also previously received a gift of shares from an uncle, however this is ignored for the purposes of this calculation.) In addition, as Lorraine has been living rent-free in an apartment owned by you for the last few years, she is treated as receiving a taxable gift from you each year equal to the market rent that would have been payable by her in respect of the apartment.

Taking account of the above, I have estimated that the transfer will give rise to a CAT liability of approximately €77,385 for Lorraine and €50,325 for Sheila (see Appendix 2). Your CGT liability of approximately €22,564 relates to the disposal of the property to Lorraine and therefore may be offset against Lorraine's CAT liability, thereby reducing the CAT payable by Lorraine to approximately €54,821. However, if Lorraine disposes of the apartment within two years, the CGT credit will be clawed back.

There is an exemption from CAT for gifts or inheritances of residential property provided certain conditions are met. A key condition for gifts is not met as neither of your daughters is a dependent relative.

If you have any queries on the above or wish to discuss further any of the issues raised, please do not hesitate to give me a call.

Yours sincerely,

Appendix 1

Capital Gains Tax Liability on Transfer of Properties

Transfer to Lorraine O'Donovan

	€	€
Market value of property		350,000
Cost in November 1999	220,000	
Legal fees and stamp duty	15,000	
Total cost	235,000	
Indexation factor: 1.193		
Indexed cost of property		(280,355)

Capital gain		69,645
Annual exemption		(1,270)
Taxable gain		68,375
CGT @ 33%		22,564

Transfer to Sheila O'Donovan

	€	€
Market value of property		250,000
Cost in July 2017	240,000	
Legal fees and stamp duty	28,000	
Total cost		(268,000)
Capital loss		(18,000)

The loss arising on the property transferred to Sheila may not be offset against the gain arising on the transfer of the property to Lorraine as the loss arose on a **disposal to a connected person**.

APPENDIX 2
Capital Acquisitions Tax Liability on Transfer of Properties

Transfer to Lorraine O'Donovan

	€	€
Cumulative gifts/inheritances received from parents:		
Inheritance from mother		160,000
Gift of rent-free apartment from father:		
2017 €1,500 × 9 months	13,500	
2018 €1,500 × 12 months	18,000	
2019 €1,500 × 11 months	16,500	48,000
Gift of property from father:		
Market value	350,000	
Less: stamp duty	3,500	346,500
Total		554,500
Tax-free amount		(320,000)
Taxable		234,500
CAT @ 33%		77,385
Less: CGT credit		(22,564)
CAT payable		54,821

Transfer to Sheila O'Donovan

	€	€
Cumulative gifts/inheritances received from parents:		
Inheritance from mother		225,000

Gift of property from father:		
Market value	250,000	
Less: stamp duty	(2,500)	247,500
Total		472,500
Tax-free amount		(320,000)
Taxable		152,500
CAT @ 33%		50,325

Question 17.2

(a) Janet's CGT liability 2019

1. Shares in Fogarty Fabrics Ltd

	€	€
Market value		950,000
Cost – market value March 1997	340,000	
Indexation factor: 1.251		
Indexed cost		(425,340)
Gain		524,660

Exempt due to retirement relief:

$$\text{Proportion} = \frac{\text{Chargeable business assets}}{\text{Chargeable assets}}$$

$$= \frac{€130,000 + €215,000 + €70,000}{€130,000 + €215,000 + €70,000 + €350,000} = 54.25\%$$

Exempt portion of gain €524,660 × 54.25%		(284,628)
Taxable gain		240,032

As the conditions for revised entrepreneur relief have been satisfied, this gain is taxable at 10% (assuming Janet has not disposed of any other chargeable business assets on or after 1 January 2016).

2. House

	€	€
Market value		250,000
Cost	40,000	
Indexation factor: 1.503		
Indexed cost		(60,120)
Gain		189,880

3. Vase

	€	€
Market value		3,100

Cost – market value June 1980	150	
Indexation factor: 3.240		
Indexed cost		(486)
Gain		2,614

4. Farmland

	€	€
Market value		1,500,000
Market value August 1974	80,000	
Indexation factor	7.528	
Indexed cost		(602,240)
Gain		897,760

CGT liability for Janet 2019

	€
Shares	240,032
House	189,880
Farmland	897,760
Total	1,327,672
Losses forward	(10,000)
Taxable gain	1,317,672
CGT @ 10%/33%:	
€240,032 @ 10%	24,003
€1,317,672 – €240,032 = €1,077,640 @ 33%	355,621
CGT on vase (marginal relief):	
(€3,100 – €2,540) @ 50%	280
Janet's CGT liability 2019	379,904

Note: no annual exemption is available as retirement relief applied.

(b) CAT liabilities

1. Shares in Fogarty Fabric Ltd (received by Adam)

	€
Market value of shares	950,000
Value attributed to investment property	(350,000)
Value excluding investment property	600,000
Business relief	(540,000)
	60,000
Value attributed to investment property	350,000
Taxable value	410,000
Small gift exemption	(3,000)
	407,000

Previous gift from mother	150,000
	557,000
Group threshold @ Nil	(320,000)
Balance	237,000
CAT @ 33%	78,210
CGT attributable to gift of shares:	
Less: CGT credit re shares	(24,003)
Adam's CAT liability	54,207

2. House

	€
Received by Julie €250,000 @ 50%	125,000
Received by Nigel €250,000 @ 50%	125,000

Julie

Taxable value	125,000
Less: small gift exemption	(3,000)
Taxable	122,000

Julie has not previously received any taxable gifts or inheritances and, as the taxable gift less annual exemption is less than the Group A threshold of €320,000, no CAT liability arises in respect of the gift to her.

Nigel	€
Market value of gift	125,000
Small gift exemption	(3,000)
	122,000
Group C threshold @ Nil	(16,250)
Balance	105,750
CAT @ 33%	34,897
CGT attributable to gift of half-share in house:	
$€355,621 \times \frac{€189,880}{€1,077,640} = €62,660 \times 50\%$	(31,330)
Nigel's CAT liability	3,567

Note: the previous gift from his aunt is ignored as the Group B, €32,500, threshold applies.

3. Vase

	€
Market value of gift	3,100
Small gift exemption	(3,000)
Taxable	100
Previous inheritance	75,000
	75,100

Group threshold @ Nil	(32,500)
Balance	42,600
CAT @ 33%	14,058
CAT attributable to previous inheritance:	
Inheritance	75,000
Group threshold @ Nil	(32,500)
Balance	42,500
CAT @ 33%	14,025
CAT attributable to current gift: €14,058 – €14,025	33
Less: CGT payable by Janet (max.)	(33)
Sally's CAT liability	nil

4. Farmland

	€
Market value	1,500,000
Agricultural relief (90%)	(1,350,000)
Taxable value	150,000
Less: small gift exemption	(3,000)
Taxable	147,000

He satisfies the asset test (100% agricultural property) and the "farming the land" test (lease to a full-time farmer), so he qualifies for agricultural relief. He must lease the land or farm it himself for at least six years to avoid a clawback.

Kevin has not previously received any taxable gifts or inheritances and, as the taxable gift is less than the Group A threshold of €320,000, no CAT liability arises in respect of the gift to him.

Note: the credit for CGT will be clawed back on any beneficiary who disposes of the asset within two years of the date of the gift.

Question 17.3

(a) CGT liability

Disposal to Janet

Government stock – exempt from CGT.

Disposal of business to Jake

Van rental business – no capital gain (loss relieved via capital allowance system).

Inventories, receivables – non-chargeable asset.

Goodwill:

	€
Market value 16/07/2019	300,000
Cost January 2012	(55,000)
Gain	245,000

Disposals to Brendan

Vans – no capital gain (loss relieved via capital allowance system).

Building

	€
Market value 16/07/2019	250,000
Cost January 2012	(80,000)
Gain	170,000

Cash – non-chargeable asset

CGT liability

Gains	€
Goodwill	245,000
Building	170,000
Total	415,000
CGT €415,000 @ 10%	41,500

Note: retirement relief does not apply as the business was only owned for six years, but revised entrepreneur relief applies as the conditions have been satisfied.

(b) CAT liability

Janet

No CAT liability arises as Ronnie had owned the securities at 24 February 2003 and Janet is not Irish domiciled or ordinarily resident.

Jake

Taxable value of gift:

	€
Business	1,280,000
Less: business relief @ 90%	(1,152,000)
Taxable value	128,000
Cash	20,000
Total taxable value	148,000
Inheritance from mother	460,000
Total gifts/inheritances within Group A threshold	608,000
Group A threshold taxed @ Nil	(320,000)
Balance taxable @ 33%	288,000
CAT @ 33%	95,040
CAT attributed to previous inheritance (Note 1)	(46,200)
CAT in respect of current gift	48,840
Credit for CGT (Note 2)	(9,900)
CAT payable	38,940

Notes:

1. €460,000 – €320,000 = €140,000 @ 33% = €46,200
2. Credit for CGT:

CGT on disposal of business = goodwill of €245,000 @ 10% = €24,500
CAT attributable to goodwill – as the CGT relates only to the goodwill, the CGT can only be credited against CAT re goodwill, i.e. CAT re goodwill only is:

$$€48,840 \times \frac{€30,000 \text{ (i.e. } 300,000 \times 10\%)}{€148,000} = €9,900 \text{ (or } €30,000 \times 33\%)$$

Credit limited to lower of CGT or CAT, i.e. €9,900.
The credit for CGT will be clawed back if the goodwill of the van business is disposed of within two years.

Brendan

Taxable value of gift:	€
Vans	40,000
Building (Note 1)	250,000
Cash	50,000
Total taxable value	340,000
Inheritance from mother	460,000
Total gifts/inheritances	800,000
Group A threshold taxed @ Nil	(320,000)
Balance taxable @ 33%	480,000
CAT @ 33%	158,400
CAT attributed to previous inheritance (Note 2)	(46,200)
CAT in respect of current gift	112,200
Credit for CGT (Note 3)	(17,000)
CAT payable	95,200

Notes:

1. Business relief does not apply to the gift of vans and office buildings as the relief only applies to gifts of business interests not business assets.
2. €460,000 – €320,000 = €140,000 @ 33% = €46,200
3. Credit for CGT:
   CGT on disposal of building = €170,000 @ 10% = €17,000

   $$\text{CAT attributable to building} = €112,200 \times \frac{€250,000}{€340,000} = €82,500$$

   Credit limited to lower of CGT or CAT, i.e. €17,000.
   The credit for CGT will be clawed back if the building is disposed of within two years.

Question 17.4

XYZ Chartered Accountants
Main Street

4 June 2019

Mr Mark Murphy
Director
Murphy Electrical Wholesalers Ltd
Church Street

Re: Proposed transfer of shares to Jake Murphy

Dear Mark,

I refer to our recent telephone conversation in which you asked me to advise you on the tax consequences of the transfer of your entire shareholding in Murphy Electrical Wholesalers Ltd to your son, Jake.

Background

My understanding is that you inherited all the shares in Murphy Electrical Wholesalers Ltd on the death of your brother in June 1995. At that time the shares were valued at €2 million. The shares are now valued at €3.5 million and you are considering transferring your entire shareholding to your son, Jake.

Taxation consequences of transfer of shares

1. Capital Gains Tax
The gift of shares will be treated as a sale by you of your shares at market value for CGT purposes. I have estimated that the CGT arising will be €312,180 (see Appendix 1).

2. Stamp Duty
Stamp duty of 1% of the value of the shares will be payable by Jake, i.e. €35,000.

3. Capital Acquisitions Tax
Assuming your son has not previously received any taxable gifts from you or your wife, CAT will be payable at the rate of 33% on the excess of the taxable value of the shares received from you over €320,000. The taxable value of a gift is normally calculated as the market value of the property which is the subject of a gift less any consideration given and any liabilities payable out of the gift. However, if the property which is gifted consists of business assets or shares in certain unquoted companies, the taxable value is further reduced by 90%. This relief is known as business relief. The conditions which must be satisfied if business relief is to apply to the transfer of shares to your son are outlined in Appendix 2.

Assuming the only cost payable by Jake is stamp duty, if your son qualifies for business relief, the taxable value of the shares for CAT purposes will be €346,500, and his CAT liability will be nil, calculated as follows:

	€
Market value of shares	3,500,000
Less: stamp duty @ 1%	(35,000)
	3,465,000
Business relief @ 90%	(3,118,500)

Taxable value	346,500
Less: tax-free amount	(320,000)
Taxable	26,500
CAT @ 33%	8,745
Less: CGT credit (lower of €8,745 or €312,180)	(8,745)
CAT liability	Nil

If, however, business relief does not apply, Jake's CAT liability will be as follows:

	€
Market value of shares	3,500,000
Less: stamp duty @ 1%	(35,000)
	3,465,000
Tax-free amount	(320,000)
Taxable	3,145,000
CAT @ 33%	1,037,850
Less: CGT payable	(312,180)
CAT liability	725,670

As can be seen from these computations, Jake's CAT liability may be reduced by the CGT payable by you on the transfer of the shares to him. This credit for CGT will only apply if your son does not dispose of the shares within two years after the date of the gift.

Conclusion

As outlined, if Jake qualifies for business relief, a substantial CAT liability can be avoided. Accordingly, it is important that before any decision is taken to transfer the shares to Jake that we meet to go through these conditions to make sure that they are satisfied.

In making a decision to transfer the shares to Jake, you should also bear in mind that if he were to inherit the shares from you rather than by receiving them as a gift, **there would be no CGT liability**, and Jake's CAT position, before CGT credit, would be unchanged.

Accordingly, bearing in mind the significant CGT cost associated with the transfer, you might decide ultimately to wait a few years to gift him the shares or, alternatively, leave him the shares in your will. We can, however, discuss this aspect further when we meet as there are rules to be satisfied before full retirement relief applies.

Yours sincerely,

APPENDIX 1

Capital Gains Tax Liability on Transfer of Shares by Mr Mark Murphy to Mr Jake Murphy

	€	€
Market value of shares		3,500,000
Market value in June 1995	2,000,000	
Indexation factor 1.277		
Indexed value of €2 million		(2,554,000)
Capital gain		946,000
CGT @ 33%		312,180

Note: Mark Murphy does not qualify for retirement relief as he did not work full-time for at least five years; nor does he qualify for revised entrepreneur relief as he did not work for the company for not less than 50% of his time for three of the last five years.

Appendix 2

Business Relief – Conditions to be Satisfied

In order for a gift of shares in an unquoted company to qualify for business relief for CAT purposes the following conditions must be satisfied:

(1) The recipient of the gift must, after receiving the gift of shares, either:

   (a) control more than 25% of the voting shares in the company;
   (b) together with his relatives, control the company; or
   (c) hold at least 10% of the issued share capital and have worked full-time in the company for the five years prior to the gift or inheritance.

(2) The company's business must not consist wholly or mainly of:

   (a) dealing in currencies, securities, stocks or shares, land or buildings; or
   (b) making or holding investments.

   In determining whether a company's business consists wholly or mainly of one of (a) or (b) above, wholly or mainly can be taken as more than 50%. Each case is looked at separately, but broadly it can be taken that if more than 50% of a company's assets and more than 50% of its income is derived from business activities other than (a) or (b) above, the company will satisfy this test.

(3) The shares must have been owned by the person making the gift, or by him and his spouse, for at least five years prior to the gift.

(4) To the extent that the value of the shares is attributable to any non-trade assets owned by the company, that portion of the shares will not qualify for business relief. For example, a company valued at €5 million on an assets basis owns an investment property valued at €1 million. Only 80% of the value of any shares in this company transferred by way of gift or inheritance will qualify for business relief.

(5) To the extent that the value of the shares is attributable to any business assets which were not being used wholly or mainly for the business for a continuous period of two years prior to the date of the gift, or if acquired less than two years ago for the period since acquisition, must also be left out of account. An asset is not regarded as being used wholly or mainly for the purpose of the trade where it was used wholly or mainly for the personal benefit of the owner of the shares or any of his relatives. This provision is aimed at significant assets which have an impact on the value of the shares, e.g. a private yacht or a large house provided to a director/shareholder. Assets such as the typical company car while used for the personal benefit of a director/shareholder would not normally impact upon the value of the shares in a company.

(6) The company need not be incorporated in Ireland. It can be incorporated anywhere.

Chapter 18

Question 18.1

MEMORANDUM

To :	
From :	
Date :	
Re :	Capital Acquisitions Tax Queries

I refer to the matters recently raised by you.

(a) Accountable Persons

The person accountable for payment of the tax is the donee or successor, as the case may be.

(b) Delivery of Returns

A person who is accountable for CAT is obliged to deliver a return where the aggregate taxable value of all taxable benefits taken by a donee or successor which have the same group threshold exceeds 80% of the group threshold amount.

If the valuation date arises in the period from 1 January to 31 August, the pay and file deadline is 31 October in that year; if the valuation date arises in the period from 1 September to 31 December, the pay and file deadline is 31 October in the following year. If the return is filed using ROS, the filing date is extended: for 2019, it is 12 November 2019.

Even if the 80% threshold has not been exceeded, a person must deliver a return if required to do so by notice in writing from the Revenue Commissioners. They must comply within the time set out in the notice.

The disponer must deliver a return if requested by notice in writing from the Revenue Commissioners. They must comply within the time set out in the notice.

(c) Return Details

(i) The return must show:
  - (I) every applicable gift/inheritance;
  - (II) all property comprised in such gift/inheritance;
  - (III) an estimate of the market value of the property; and
  - (IV) such particulars as may be relevant to the assessment of tax in respect of such gift.

(ii) Also, the taxpayer must make on the return an assessment of such amount of tax, as to the best of his knowledge, information and belief, ought to be charged and paid.

(iii) Finally, he must pay any tax which he calculates is due.

(d) Defective Return

Where an accountable person, who has made a return becomes aware, at any time, that the return is defective in a material respect, by reason of anything contained or omitted from it, he shall, without being asked by the Revenue Commissioners:

(i) deliver to them an additional return;
(ii) make an amended assessment; and
(iii) pay the outstanding tax.

The above action is required within three months of becoming aware of the defect in the original return.

(e) Undervaluation of Property

A surcharge ranging from 10% to 30% will be levied where the market value of property is underestimated in returns for CAT purposes. The legislation contains a table setting out the percentage surcharge to be levied depending on the extent to which the property was undervalued.

The surcharge applies to the total amount of tax ultimately attributable to the property. In addition, interest penalties will apply to the tax underpaid as well as to the surcharge.

Signed:

Question 18.2

Before computing the CAT liabilities, it is necessary to calculate the split of the estate for each beneficiary.

		Total	Sheila($^2/_3$)	Ruth($^1/_6$)	Angela($^1/_6$)
		€	€	€	€
House		600,000	400,000	100,000	100,000
Mortgage thereon		(60,000)	(40,000)	(10,000)	(10,000)
		540,000	360,000	90,000	90,000
Newsagents		900,000	600,000	150,000	150,000
Government Stock		66,000	44,000	11,000	11,000
Holiday home		150,000	100,000	25,000	25,000
Residue:					
Cash	45,000				
Income tax liabilities	(15,000)				
Legal expenses	(6,000)				
Funeral expenses	(3,000)				
Net cash		21,000	14,000	3,500	3,500

Ruth and Angela also received the insurance proceeds of €140,000.

(a) CAT liabilities

Sheila

Sheila has no liability to CAT as she was the spouse of Robert. The fact that they had been separated for 10 years is irrelevant. They are still legally married.

Ruth

	€	€
Newsagents	150,000	
Business relief @ 90%	(135,000)	15,000
Life insurance €140,000 × 50%		70,000
House less mortgage (Note)		90,000
Government stock		11,000
Holiday home		25,000
Net cash		3,500

continued overleaf

Taxable value of inheritance	214,500
Group A threshold taxed @ Nil	(320,000)
CAT payable	Nil

Note:
House does not qualify for exemption from CAT as Ruth had an interest in another dwelling house at the date of the inheritance, i.e. the holiday home in Kerry.

Ruth has not previously received any taxable gifts or inheritances and the current benefit is below the threshold, so no CAT is payable in respect of the current inheritance.

Angela

	€	€
Newsagents	150,000	
Business relief @ 90%	(135,000)	15,000
Life insurance €140,000 × 50%		70,000
House less mortgage (Note)		90,000
Government stock		11,000
Holiday home		25,000
Net cash		3,500
Taxable value of inheritance		214,500
Group A threshold taxed @ Nil		(320,000)
CAT payable		Nil

Note:
House does not qualify for exemption from CAT as Angela had an interest in another dwelling house at the date of the inheritance, i.e. the holiday home in Kerry.

As Angela has not previously received any taxable gifts or inheritances and the current benefit is below the threshold, no CAT is payable in respect of the current inheritance.

(b) Payment of tax

If interest charges are to be avoided, CAT must be paid by 31 October 2020.

Chapter 19

Question 19.1

(a) Corporation tax liabilities

Lemmon Ltd

	12 months ended 31/12/2019		2 months ended 29/02/2020	
	€		€	
Case I (time-apportioned)	264,000	[12/14]	44,000	[2/14]
Case III (actual)	3,000		2,000	
Total income	267,000		46,000	
Chargeable gain	5,156			
Total profits	272,156		46,000	

continued overleaf

Corporation tax:

Case I: €264,000 @ 12.5%	33,000	Case I: €44,000 @ 12.5%	5,500
Chargeable gain: €5,156 @ 12.5%	644		
Case III: €3,000 @ 25%	750	Case III: €3,000 @ 25%	500
	34,394		6,000

Rentco Ltd

	Year ended 31/12/2019
Case V	€50,000
Corporation tax @ 25%	€12,500

Distributors Ltd

	8 months ended 29 February 2020
Case I	€20,000
Corporation tax @ 12.5%	€2,500

(b) and (c) Payment of CT liabilities and filing returns

Lemmon Limited

For the accounting period ending 31 December 2019 the preliminary tax is payable by 23 November 2019 and must be 90% of the corporation tax liability for the current accounting period. The balance is payable at the same time as the company is due to file corporation tax return (23 September 2020). If not paid, or underpaid, interest is charged at 0.0219% per day or part of day.

For the accounting period ending 29 February 2020 the accounting period is only two months, so 90% must be paid by 23 January 2020 and the balance is paid when return is filed (23 November 2020).

Rentco Limited

For the accounting period ending 31 December 2019, 90% of the current liability is due by 23 November 2019. Balance is to be paid when the return is due to be filed, i.e. 23 September 2020.

Distributors Limited

For the accounting period of 8 months ended 29 February 2020, 90% of the current liability is due by 23 January 2020. Remainder is to be paid when the return is due to be filed, i.e. 23 November 2020.

Chapter 20

Question 20.1

The corporation tax computation for 12-month accounting period ended 31 December 2019 would be as follows:

		€	€
Profit before tax per accounts			116,000
Add:	Depreciation	15,149	
	Motor leasing (Note 1)	240	
	Entertainment (Note 2)	1,050	

continued overleaf

	Finance lease charges (Note 3)	1,300	
	Legal fees (Note 4)	2,400	20,139
			136,139
Less:			
	Grant for extension of premises (Note 5)	10,000	
	Employment grant (Note 6)	1,000	
	Patent royalty (Note 7)	1,600	
	Dividends from Irish quoted shares (Note 8)	1,300	
	Profit on sale of van (Note 9)	1,000	
	Profit on sale of shares (Note 10)	2,000	
	Bank deposit interest (Note 11)	600	
	Finance lease payments (Note 3)	9,400	
	Capital allowances	7,272	(34,172)
Case I Schedule D			101,967
Case III Schedule D – bank interest (gross)			600
Case IV Schedule D – royalty (gross $= \frac{1,600}{80} \times 100$)			2,000
Total income			104,567
Chargeable gain (Note 12)			3,759
Total profits			108,326
Corporation tax:			
Case I:	€101,967 @ 12.5%	12,746	
Chargeable gain:	€3,759 @ 12.5%	470	
Cases III and IV:	€2,600 @ 25%	650	13,866
Less: income tax suffered on royalty €2,000 @ 20%			(400)
Corporation tax payable			13,466

As this is a small company, i.e. corporation tax payable in 2018 did not exceed €200,000, if interest charges are to be avoided, preliminary tax of €80,000 (100% of preceding period) or 90% of this period (i.e. 90% × €13,466 = €12,120) must be paid on/before 23 November 2019 and the balance of €1,346 must be paid on/before 23 September 2020.

Notes:

1. There is no motor expenses restriction. The lease payments are in respect of a Category B vehicle leased when its retail price was €25,000. Therefore, the amount disallowed is:

$$€6,000 \times \frac{€25,000 - €24,000}{€25,000} = €240$$

continued overleaf

2. Entertainment costs disallowed:

	€
Christmas gifts for suppliers	150
Entertainment costs incurred by MD	350
General customer entertainment	550
	1,050

Costs incurred for benefit of staff, i.e. Christmas party and prizes, are deductible.
3. Finance lease charges (i.e. interest) disallowed and gross payments made deducted.
4. Legal fees are of a capital nature and fall to be disallowed.
5. Grant for extension of premises is a capital receipt and not liable to corporation tax.
6. Employment grant is not taxable.
7. Patent royalty – this is not taxable under Case I. The gross amount is taxable under Case IV of Schedule D. However, the income tax suffered can be set off against the corporation tax chargeable. As only the net amount (i.e. the amount after deduction of standard rate income tax) has been credited in the income statement, then this is the correct amount to deduct.
8. Dividends from Irish quoted shares. Dividends received from other Irish companies are not liable to corporation tax.
9. Profit on sale of van is a capital profit and not a trading receipt and so is not taxable under Case I (see Note 12).
10. Profit on sale of shares is a capital profit and not a trading receipt and so is not taxable under Case I (see Note 12).
11. Bank deposit interest – this is taxable under Case III as it was not subject to DIRT.
12. Chargeable gain:
    (a) Sale of van – although a loss arose on the sale of the van, this is not an allowable loss. Relief for this loss will be given through capital allowances.
    (b) Sale of shares.

	€	€
Proceeds		6,000
Cost	4,000	
Indexation factor 2000/01: 1.144		
Indexed cost		(4,576)
Gain		1,424
Chargeable gain: €1,424 @ 33/12.5		3,759

Question 20.2

Zaco Ltd Corporation Tax Computation Year Ended 30 September 2019

		€	€
Profit per accounts			379,300
Add:	Repairs	5,200	
	Professional fees	300	
	Political donations	750	
	Entertainment	600	
	Depreciation	13,000	19,850
			399,150

continued overleaf

Less:	Dividends	3,000	
	Profit on sale of investments	5,200	
	Interest on tax overpaid	1,200	
	Profit on sale of fixtures and fittings	4,300	(13,700)
			385,450
Less:	Capital allowances		(9,846)
Case I Schedule D			375,604
Add:	Chargeable gains (Note)		Nil
			375,604
Corporation tax:			
Case I:	€375,604 @ 12.5%		46,950

Note:

Chargeable Gains

		€	€
Sale of investments:			
(a) Sale of Irish Treasury bonds			Exempt
(b) Quoted investment company shares			
	Proceeds	5,548	
	Cost		1,000
	Indexation factor: 1.232		
	Indexed cost	1,232	4,316
(c) Sale of plant			
	Proceeds	11,100	
	Cost	8,000	3,100
Total gains			7,416
Less: capital loss forward			(10,000)
Capital loss forward to 2020			(2,584)

Question 20.3

Overseas Limited

1. Corporation tax

	€
Case I: Branch trading profits	600,000
Case III: Branch interest income	20,000
	620,000
Chargeable gains	
Gain on branch assets: €32,000 @ 33/12.5	84,480
	704,480

continued overleaf

	Corporation tax:	
	€684,480 @ 12.5% = €85,560	
	€20,000 @ 25% = €5,000	90,560
2.	Capital gains tax	
	Sale of land – €50,000 @ 33%	16,500

Chapter 21

Question 21.1

Nifty Investments Limited
Accounts Year Ended 31 March 2019

	€	€
Profit per accounts		90,000
Add:		
Depreciation	10,000	
Interest	9,000*	
Patent royalties	8,000*	27,000
		117,000
Less:		
Loan interest	6,000*	
Bank interest	1,000*	
		(7,000)
		110,000
Less: Case I charge (Note 2)		(10,000)
Case I		100,000
Case III		1,000
Case IV (Note 1)		6,000
Income		107,000
Chargeable gain (Note 3)		26,400
Profits		133,400
Less: non-trade charge (Note 4)		(9,000)
Profits liable to tax		124,400
Corporation tax due on profits (Note 5)		15,550
Add: Income tax withheld by Nifty		2,000
Less: Income tax deducted from receipts		(1,200)
Total tax liability		16,350

*Add back or deduct the amount in the income statement.

continued overleaf

Notes:

1.	**Net received**	**Tax deducted**	**Taxable Case IV**
Loan interest	4,800	1,200	6,000

2.	**Net paid**	**Tax withheld**	**Deductible as a charge**
Patent royalties	8,000	2,000	10,000

3. As the tax rate for year ended 31 March 2019 is 12.5% and the CGT rate at the time of disposal is 33%, these are the rates at which you gross up the gain. €10,000 × 33/12.5 = €26,400.
4. As the interest is paid to an Irish bank, there is no requirement to withhold income tax. As the interest qualifies as a non-trade charge, it is deductible against total profits.
   When calculating corporation tax, it will be offset against any profits taxable at 25% first, as that would save most tax.
5. Corporation tax liability on €124,400:

	€
€98,000 @ 12.5%	12,250
€26,400 @ 12.5%	3,300
Corporation tax	15,550

The non-trade charge of €9,000 is offset first against the €7,000 liable at 25%. The balance of €2,000 is offset against income taxable at 12.5%, i.e.: €100,000 – €2,000 = €98,000.

Question 21.2

Alpha Ltd Corporation Tax Computation Year Ended 31 December 2019

			€	€
Case I	Profit per accounts			424,605
	Add:	Rent and rates	1,000	
		Repairs	15,000	
		Insurance	350	
		Loss on sale of investments	600	
		Legal expenses	2,000	
		Depreciation	13,260	
		Subscriptions (Note 1)	1,835	
		Other interest – not trade (Note 4)	7,000	
		Motor expenses (Note 2)	845	
		Sundry (Note 3)	2,201	
		Entertainment	1,191	
		Finance lease charges	1,700	46,982
				471,587

continued overleaf

Less:	Irish dividends		4,500	
	Interest on Irish Treasury bonds		2,500	
	Gain on sale of Irish shares		1,000	
	Enterprise Ireland employment grant – exempt		240	
	Interest on tax overpaid		475	
	Rents received		6,000	
	Deposit interest		1,500	
	Finance lease payments		12,200	(28,415)
				443,172
Capital allowances				(26,006)
Case I for period				417,166
Case III	Interest on Irish Treasury bonds			2,500
	Deposit interest			1,500
Case V	Gross rents		6,000	
	Less: rent and rates paid	1,000		
	Insurance	350	(1,350)	4,650
Chargeable gains (Note 5) 400 @ 33%/12.5%				1,056
Total profits				426,872
Less: charge (protected interest)				(7,000)
Profits liable to corporation tax				419,872

Corporation tax (Note 6)	€
€417,166 @ 12.5%	52,146
€1,056 @ 12.5%	132
€1,650 @ 25%	412
	52,690

Notes:

1. Subscriptions:

	€
Football club	20
Political	1,815
	1,835

2. Motor expenses:

Leasing charges

$$€21,126 \times \frac{€150,000 - €144,000^*}{€150,000} = €845$$

*€24,000 × 6 = €144,000

3. Sundry:

	€
Interest on late payment of VAT	1,630
Parking fines	30
Gifts to customers	541
	2,201

continued overleaf

4. Protected interest: non-trade charges are deductible against total profits. The conditions to be satisfied for a payment to be deductible as a non-trade charge are satisfied, i.e. use loan to acquire shares in a trading company, have a material interest (>5%), common director and no recovery of capital. €7,000 was paid, so that is the amount deductible.

5. Chargeable gains:

	€
Gain on Irish quoted shares	1,000
Less: Loss on UK shares	(600)
Gain	400

6. Corporation tax: non-trade charges are offset against total profits. The taxpayer can choose which source of income/gain against which to offset the non-trade charge. It is most tax efficient to offset the €7,000 against income taxable at 25% (€2,500 + €1,500 + €4,650 − €7,000) = €1,650.

Chapter 22

Question 22.1

Enya Limited

31/03/2016		€	€
Case I			60,000
Case III			10,000
Case V	2016	5,000	
	re. 2017	(4,000)	1,000
	Taxable income		71,000
Corporation tax: €60,000 @ 12.5%			7,500
€11,000 @ 25%			2,750
Corporation tax payable			10,250
31/03/2017			
Case I			70,000
Less: trading loss from 2018			(70,000)
Case I			–
Case III			5,000
Case V			–
Income			5,000
Corporation tax: €5,000 @ 25%			1,250
Less: relief on a value basis (loss memo)			(1,250)
Corporation tax payable			Nil

continued overleaf

31/03/2018		
Case I		–
Case III		10,000
Case V		6,000
Taxable income		16,000
Corporation tax: €16,000 @ 25%		4,000
Less: relief on a value basis (loss memo)		(4,000)
Corporation tax payable		Nil
31/03/2019		
Case I	10,000	
Less: loss	(10,000)	–
Case III		3,500
Case V		8,000
Taxable income		11,500
Corporation tax: €11,500 @ 25%		2,875

Loss Memo

Relevant trading loss for y/e 31/03/2018	130,000
Utilised by way of section 396A(3) against y/e 31/03/2017	(70,000)
Utilised by way of section 396B(3) against y/e 31/03/2018 €32,000 @ 12.5% = €4,000	(32,000)
Utilised by way of section 396B(3) against y/e 31/03/2017 €10,000 @ 12.5% = €1,250	(10,000)
Utilised by way of section 396(1) forward	(10,000)
Loss forward to 2020	8,000

Question 22.2

Hells Bells Ltd

Year ended 31 March 2019

	€	€
Case I		167,000
Section 396A(3) loss back (Note 1)		(125,250)
		41,750
Case III		10,000
Case V	4,000	
Less: loss	(3,000) (Note 2)	1,000
Total income		52,750
Chargeable gain		–
Total profit		52,750

continued overleaf

Corporation tax:	
€11,000 @ 25%	2,750
€41,750 @ 12.5%	5,218
Tax payable	7,968
Less: relief on a value basis (Note 4)	(3,094)
Corporation tax payable	4,874
Nine months ended 31 December 2019	
Case I	–
Case III	20,000
Case V	–
Total income	20,000
Chargeable gains (Note 3)	–
Taxable profits	20,000
Tax:	
€20,000 @ 25%	5,000
Less: relief on a value basis (Loss Memo)	(5,000)
Tax payable	Nil

Notes:

1. Loss available for carry back	€190,000
Trading profit of corresponding period	
€167,000 × 9/12ths	€125,250
Offset total	€125,250

2. A Case V loss can be carried back to a previous accounting period of the same length. A loss for nine months can be carried back against income for nine months, i.e.:

   €4,000 × 9/12ths = €3,000.

3.

	€
Gain	10,000
Less: capital loss forward	(19,000)
Capital loss forward	(9,000)

4. The maximum tax that can be saved is 9/12ths of the corporation tax, i.e. €7,968 × 9/12ths = €5,976. However, the losses still available are only €24,750. Therefore, the value of the losses is €24,750 × 12.5% = €3,094. This is the maximum reduction in corporation tax.

Loss Memo	€
Relevant trading loss for p/e 31/12/2019	190,000
Utilised by way of section 396A(3) against y/e 31/03/2019 (i)	(125,250)
Utilised by way of section 396B(3) against p/e 31/12/2019 (ii)	
€40,000 @ 12.5% = €5,000	(40,000)

continued overleaf

Utilised by way of section 396B(3) against y/e 31/03/2019 (iii)	
€24,750 @ 12.5% = €3,094	(24,750)
Loss forward to 2020	Nil

(i) to (iii) shows sequence of claims.

Question 22.3

Monk Ltd

Year ended 31 December 2019

	€
Case I	–
Case III	30,000
Case V	20,000
Total income	50,000
Chargeable gain	26,000
Taxable profits	76,000
Tax:	
€50,000 @ 25%	12,500
€26,000 @ 12.5%	3,250
	15,750
Less: relief on a value basis (loss memo)	(10,000)
Tax payable	5,750

The gain on development land cannot be sheltered as it is liable to CGT payable, i.e. €100,000 × 33% = €33,000.

Year ended 31 December 2018

Case I	340,000
Less: Case I loss forward section 396(1)	(20,000)
Case I	320,000
Less: section 396A(3)	(320,000)
Case I	–
Case III	5,000
Case V	15,000
Total income	20,000
Chargeable gain	12,000
Taxable profits	32,000
Tax:	
€20,000 @ 25%	5,000
€12,000 @ 12.5%	1,500
Tax payable	6,500

continued overleaf

Loss Memo	€
Relevant trading loss for y/e 31/12/2019	400,000
Utilised by way of section 396A(3) against y/e 31/12/2018	(320,000)
Utilised by way of section 396B(3) against y/e 31/12/2019	
€80,000 @ 12.5% = €10,000	(80,000)
Loss forward to 2020	Nil

Must claim under section 396A(3) first, as required by law, and then on a value basis in the current period.

Question 22.4

Monaghan Limited – Year ended 30 June

	2017	**2018**	**2019**
	€	€	€
Assessable Case I profit	180,000	Nil	140,000
Section 396(1) loss relief	(20,000)		(140,000)
Section 396A loss relief	(160,000)		
Case I	Nil	Nil	Nil
Case III – interest on Government stocks	5,000	30,000	10,000
Case V – rental income	10,500	20,000	20,000
Capital gains – as adjusted	10,200	40,000	50,000
Total profits	25,700	90,000	80,000
Less: non-trade charges	–	–	(50,000)
Taxable profits	25,700	90,000	30,000
Corporation tax @ 12.5% (Note 1)	1,275	5,000	3,750
Corporation tax @ 25%	3,875	12,500	
Corporation tax	5,150	17,500	3,750
Section 243B relief (Note 2)	(1,250)	(1,250)	(750)
Section 396B(3) relief (Note 3)	(3,900)	(16,250)	
Corporation tax liability	Nil	Nil	3,000

Notes:

1. Non-trade charges paid in y/e 30/06/2019 are offset against income liable at 25% first.
2. Excess trade charges in y/e 30/06/2017 and 30/06/2018 = €10,000
   Relief on a value basis in y/e 30/06/2017: €10,000 @ 12.5% = €1,250
   Relief on a value basis in y/e 30/06/2018: €10,000 @ 12.5% = €1,250
   Excess trade charges y/e 30/06/2019: €6,000 @ 12.5% = €750. Relief for €4,000 charges paid in July 2019 will be given in y/e 30/06/2020.
3. Losses for y/e 30/06/2018 available to carry forward and offset against profits arising in the year ended 30/06/2019 and subsequent years.

continued overleaf

	€
Case I adjusted loss	530,000
Utilised by way of section 396A relief y/e 30/06/2017	(160,000)
Utilised by way of section 396B relief:	
y/e 30/06/2018 €130,000 @ 12.5% = €16,250	(130,000)
y/e 30/06/2017 €31,200 @ 12.5% = €3,900	(31,200)
Losses available to carry forward to y/e 30/06/2019	208,800
Utilised against y/e 30/06/2019	(140,000)
Losses available to carry forward to y/e 30/06/2020	68,800

Chapter 23

Question 23.1

Corporation Tax Computation Period Ended 31/12/2019 – Z Ltd

	€
Case I	Nil
Case III income	20,000
Total profits	20,000
Corporation tax @ 25%	5,000
Less: loss relief on a value basis	(5,000)
Corporation tax	Nil

Corporation Tax Computation Period Ended 31/12/2019 – B Ltd

		€
Case 1	Adjusted trading profit	180,000
	Deduct: Case I losses forward	(16,000)
	Deduct: group relief surrendered by Z Ltd	(56,000)
		108,000
Case III	Interest	4,000
Case V	Rents	20,000
Profit liable to corporation tax		132,000
Corporation tax:		
€108,000 @ 12.5% = €13,500		
€24,000 @ 25% = €6,000		19,500

Loss Memo

	€
Loss	96,000
Used on a value basis in Z Ltd: €40,000 @ 12.5% = €5,000	(40,000)

continued overleaf

Claim section 420A balance of loss	(56,000)
Loss available	Nil

It should be noted that Z Ltd could have opted not to claim section 396B relief and instead surrender losses of €96,000 to B Ltd.

Question 23.2

A Ltd – Corporation Tax Computation Period to 31/03/2019

	€
Case I profits	Nil
Case III income	1,000
Case V income	20,000
Liable to corporation tax	21,000
Corporation tax @ 25%	5,250
Less: loss relief on a value basis	(5,250)
Corporation tax payable	Nil

B Ltd – Corporation Tax Computation Period to 31/03/2019

	€
Case I	56,000
Less: group loss surrendered by A Ltd	(48,000)
	8,000
Case III	2,000
Case V	25,000
Liable to corporation tax	35,000
Corporation tax:	
€8,000 @ 12.5%	1,000
€27,000 @ 25%	6,750
Corporation tax payable	7,750

C Ltd – Corporation Tax Computation Period to 31/03/2019

	€
Case I	48,000
Less: Case I loss forward	(26,000)
	22,000
Case III	3,000
Case V	2,000
Liable to corporation tax	27,000
Corporation tax:	
€22,000 @ 12.5%	2,750
€5,000 @ 25%	1,250
Corporation tax payable	4,000

continued overleaf

Loss Memo	
Loss	90,000
Used on a value basis in A Ltd	
€42,000 @ 12.5% = €5,250	(42,000)
Claim section 420A balance of loss to B Ltd	(48,000)
Loss available	Nil

Alternatively, part of the loss could have been surrendered to C Ltd to reduce its Case I income to nil.

The loss forward of €4,000 in A Ltd is carried forward to be used against trading income of the same trade in A Ltd.

Question 23.3

(a) Corporation Tax Computation

	Queen Group		
	Queen Ltd	*Pawn Ltd*	*Rook Ltd*
	€	€	€
Profit/(loss) per accounts	202,313	(2,030)	(80,586)
Disallow:			
Depreciation	12,000	10,000	16,000
Entertainment	1,350	1,200	1,650
Interest (Note 1)	400	10,720	–
	216,063	19,890	(62,936)
Less: grant release	(3,000)	–	–
	213,063	19,890	(62,936)
Capital allowances	(7,375)	(3,000)	(5,627)
Case I loss forward	–	(80,000)	–
	205,688	(63,110)	(68,563)
Group relief re trading losses (Note 2)	(68,563)	–	68,563
Case I	137,125	–	–
Case III deposit interest	23,846	–	–
	160,971	–	–

Corporation tax payable:	
Pawn Ltd	Nil
Rook Ltd	Nil
Queen Ltd:	
Profit for period	160,971
€137,125 @ 12.5% = €17,141	
€23,846 @ 25% = €5,961	
Corporation tax	23,102

continued overleaf

Notes:

1. The interest paid by Pawn Ltd is not allowed as 'a charge on income', as there is no common director. The amount charged in arriving at the profit is disallowed, as it is not a trading expense.
2. The trading loss of Rook Ltd can be offset against the trading income of Queen Ltd. Pawn Ltd has no income for this period, as it is covered by losses forward and these cannot be grouped.

(b) Losses Forward to 2020

	Losses Forward
Pawn Ltd	€63,110
Rook Ltd	Nil
Queen Ltd	Nil

(c) Payment of tax

As Queen Ltd is a small company (its prior period corporation tax did not exceed €200,000), preliminary tax is the lower of €55,000 × 100% or €23,102 × 90%, i.e. €20,792. The preliminary tax of €20,792 is due on or before 23 November 2019. The balance of €2,310 is due on/before 23 September 2020, at the same time as the tax return.

Chapter 24

Question 24.1

Dear Client,

I refer to your recent query in respect of the tax implications of Irish Cable Installations Ltd being sold in the coming weeks.

I assume the following to apply:

- Fibre Optic Developments Ltd purchased the property in 2014 at a cost of €3 million.
- The property was transferred to Irish Cable in November 2017, at a time when the property was valued at €4 million.
- Stamp duty and CGT group relief were claimed in November 2017, and as such no tax arose on the transfer of the property between both companies.
- Irish Cable is due to leave the VC Holdings Group before 31 December.
- The property is currently valued at €4.5 million.

It is now circa 25 months since the property was transferred to Irish Cable.

CGT and stamp duty must be considered in advance of the share sale closing.

Group Relief – Chargeable Gains

CGT group relief was claimed on the transfer of the property to Irish Cable and as such no CGT arose for Fibre Optic on the disposal in November 2017.

There is, however, provision that where Irish Cable leaves the VC Holdings CGT group within 10 years of the transfer, there will be a clawback of CGT relief provided for in November 2017. Irish Cable is due to leave the group before 31 December 2019.

The factory, on the event of the group relationship being broken, will be deemed to be sold and immediately re-acquired by the company leaving the group (i.e. Irish Cable) at its market value at the time of original acquisition by that company (i.e. €4 million in November 2017).

This, in effect, means that the gain on the original transfer from Fibre Optic to Irish Cable is triggered.

Indexation relief, if available, will be applied by reference to that date and not by reference to the date that Irish Cable actually leaves the group. In this case, however, as the property was acquired in 2014, no indexation relief will be available.

It is important to note that the liability in respect of this clawback rests with Irish Cable and is due to be paid with its corporation tax liability for the year ended 31 December 2019. The company may be required to make a top-up payment of preliminary tax on or before 31 January 2020 to meet its preliminary tax obligations. The clawback can be computed as follows:

Deemed market value consideration	€4,000,000
Less: cost (no indexation relief)	(€3,000,000)
Chargeable gain	€1,000,000
Tax payable:	
Taxed at effective rate of 33%	
€1,000,000 @ 33%*	€330,000

The base cost of the property will be €4 million on the event of a future disposal.
*The rate that applied when the asset was transferred, i.e. 33% in November 2017.

Disposal of Shares in Irish Cable by VC Holdings

VC Holdings is due to receive consideration of €20 million on the disposal of its 100% shareholding in Irish Cable.

VC Holdings acquired the share capital in Irish Cable for €500,000 in 2017.

A chargeable gain will arise as follows on disposal:

Proceeds	€20,000,000
Less: base cost	(€500,000)
Chargeable gain	€19,500,000

VC Holdings would ordinarily be liable to an effective rate of 33% on the chargeable gain arising on the disposal of its shares in Irish Cable.

There is, however, an exemption from tax on the disposal of certain shareholdings. This relief is known as the "participation exemption". The relief exempts a chargeable gain from tax in certain circumstances. The conditions for the relief are:

1. VC Holdings must be the parent company of Irish Cable at the time of disposal. This means that VC Holdings must have held a minimum shareholding in Irish Cable at the time of disposal or within two years prior to the disposal. This minimum holding must be at least 5% of the following:
   - the ordinary share capital of Irish Cable;
   - entitlement to distributable profits; and
   - assets available for distribution on winding up of the company.

   As VC Holdings owns 100% of the share capital, the minimum shareholding condition is met.
2. VC Holdings is required to have held the minimum holding for a continuous period of 12 months over the last 24 months. This condition is also satisfied.
3. Irish Cable must have carried on a trade, which it has.
4. Irish Cable must be resident in a Member State of the EU or a country with which Ireland has signed a tax treaty. Irish Cable is an Irish resident company, so this condition is met.
5. Irish Cable must not derive the greater part of its value from land and minerals in the State. We will need to ensure that this condition is satisfied.

If all of the above required conditions have been met, the chargeable gain of €19,500,000 will be exempt from Irish tax.

This results in a tax saving to VC Holdings of €6,435,000 (i.e. €19,500,000 @ 33%).

Stamp Duty

Stamp duty relief was claimed in November 2017 as both companies were 100% associated at the time of transfer. This effectively reduced the level of stamp duty arising to nil.

Companies are associated with one another if there is a minimum 90% direct or indirect relationship between them in terms of ordinary share capital, profits available for distribution and assets available for distribution on a winding up.

If both companies cease to be associated within two years of the date of the conveyance or transfer of the property, full stamp duty will become payable.

The property was transferred to Irish Cable in November 2017. It is now 25 months since the transfer and on this basis, a clawback of stamp duty will not arise in the event of Irish Cable being sold (and the association being broken).

Should you have any further queries, please do not hesitate to contact me.

Kind regards,

Chapter 25

Question 25.1

(a) DWT payable

Lance Investments Ltd

	Gross Dividend	**DWT**	**Notes**
	€	€	
Mr C (resident in the State)	60,000	12,000	1
Skeleton Investments Ltd	360,000	Nil	2
Irish registered charity	20,000		
Arrow Investments Ltd (resident in the State)	60,000	Nil	2
	500,000	12,000	

The total DWT payable by Lance Investments Ltd is €12,000.

Notes:

1. Irish resident individual not exempt from DWT.
2. Irish resident company, so exempt from DWT.

(b) The DWT must be paid before 14 December 2019.

(c) Arrow Investments Ltd must make a declaration to Lance Investments Ltd to the effect that the company, being the company beneficially entitled to the dividend, is a company resident in the State.

Skeleton Investments Ltd is not required to make any declaration to Lance Investments Ltd in order to be exempt from DWT as it qualifies as a "parent" company, i.e. it owns more than 50%.

Chapter 26

Question 26.1

(a) Tax effect on close company from loan

TCA 1997 provides that the company must account for tax as if the loan were a net annual payment after deduction of tax. For example, if the loan amounted to €8,000 in the accounts to 31 December 2019, then the calculation would be:

	€
Grossed-up loan	10,000
Income tax @ 20%	(2,000)
Loan	8,000

A return of these figures must be included in the company's annual corporation tax return (form CT1) for the year ended 31 December 2019. The tax due of €2,000 is collected as part of the corporation tax for that year and, therefore, assuming the company is a "small" company, unless preliminary tax is based on 100% of the previous year, €1,800 (90%) is payable on or before 23 November 2019 and the balance of €200 is payable on or before 23 September 2020 in order to avoid interest.

If and when the loan is repaid, the company may claim a refund of the sum of €2,000.

Exemption from this tax charge is, however, available where:

- the business of the company is, or includes, the lending of money, and the loan is made in the ordinary course of that business;
- a debt is incurred for the supply of goods or services in the ordinary course of the business of the close company, unless the credit given exceeds six months or is longer than the period normally given to the company's customers; or
- the borrower satisfies the following conditions:
  - total loans to borrower or spouse or civil partner do not exceed €19,050; and
  - the borrower works full-time for the close company or any of its associated companies; and
  - the borrower and/or his associates is not the beneficial owner of, or able to control more than 5% of, the ordinary shares of the company or an associated company.

(b) Corporation tax liability year ended 31/12/2019

	€
€500,000 @ 12.5%	62,500
€33,000 @ 25%	8,250
Corporation tax liability	70,750
Surcharge:	€
Case III and Case V	33,000
Less: corporation tax @ 25%	(8,250)
	24,750
Less: 7.5%	(1,856)
	22,894
Less: dividends paid within 18 months	(9,300)
	13,594

€13,594 @ 20% = €2,719 surcharge due

Question 26.2

(a) Corporation tax computation year ended 31/12/2019

	€	€
Net profit per accounts		32,900
Add: depreciation	15,000	
Sundry (Note 1)	800	15,800
		48,700
Less: interest on:		
Government securities	8,500	
Capital grants	1,500	(10,000)
		38,700
Less: capital allowances		(4,000)
Case I income		34,700
Case III income:		
Interest on Government securities		8,500
Total income		43,200
Corporation tax:		
€34,700 @ 12.5%	€4,337	
€8,500 @ 25%	€2,125	
Corporation tax payable		6,462

(b) Surcharge

	€
Case III	8,500
Less: tax @ 25%	(2,125)
	6,375
Less: 7.5% relief	(478)
	5,897
Less: distribution	(800)
	5,097
Surcharge @ 20%	1,019

(c) Specific Items

Note 1: the expense payment is treated as a "distribution" and added back in the Case I computation. Close Ltd will be required to deduct DWT at 20% from the payment of €800 to Y, who will be assessed to income tax, USC and PRSI as follows (assume Y's marginal income tax rate of tax is 40%, USC is 8% and PRSI is 4%):

Additional income tax payable:	€
Schedule F: €800 @ 40%	320
Less: DWT €800 @ 20%	(160)
	160
Add: USC €800 @ 8%	64
Add: PRSI €800 @ 4%	32
	256

Close Ltd is entitled to recover the DWT of €160 from Y. However, if Y is not going to repay the DWT to Close Ltd, the deemed distribution of €800 must be grossed up and the DWT payable will be €200, i.e. €800/0.8 – €800. Y will then be subject to income tax under Schedule F and USC and PRSI on €1,000 instead of €800 and will be entitled to a credit for DWT of €200 instead of €160.

Question 26.3

(a) Corporation tax computation year ended 31/12/2019

		€	€
	Net profit per accounts		1,870,000
	Add: Entertainment (Note 1)	11,900	
	Finance lease interest	2,000	
	Depreciation	100,000	
	Loss on sale of plant	20,000	
	Architects' fees	15,000	148,900
	Less: Finance lease payments	15,000	
	Profit on sale of building	1,480,000	
	Rents	200,000	(1,695,000)
			323,900
	Capital allowances		(50,000)
	Case I		273,900
	Case I losses forward		(210,000)
			63,900
	Case V (Note 2)		181,000
	Income		244,900
	Chargeable gain (Note 3)		Nil
	Total profits		244,900
	Corporation tax:		
	€63,900 @ 12.5% = €7,987		
	€181,000 @ 25% = €45,250		53,237
	Income tax on loan €550,000 × 20/80		137,500
			190,737
(b)	**CGT liability** (see Note 3)		364,848
(c)	**Surcharge computation**		
	Case V income		181,000
	Less: corporation tax @ 25%		(45,250)
			135,750
	Less: 7.5% relief		(10,181)
			125,569
	Surcharge due @ 20%		25,114

continued overleaf

Notes:

1. Entertainment disallowed:

	€
Entertaining customers	6,000
Entertaining suppliers	5,000
Christmas gifts for suppliers	900
	11,900

2. Case V income:

	€
Portion of premium subject to	
Corporation tax: $€50,000 \times \frac{(51-20)}{50}$	31,000
Rental income (€200,000 − €50,000)	150,000
Case V income	181,000

3. Chargeable gain:

Sale of plant

No allowable loss arises on the sale of the plant as full relief is given for the loss via capital allowances.

Sale of building

	€
Proceeds from building	1,500,000
Legal fees	(18,000)
	1,482,000
Cost May 1974: €50,000	
Indexation: 7.528	(376,400)
Gain	1,105,600
CGT @ 33%	364,848

As the building constitutes "development land", CGT is payable rather than corporation tax.

CGT liability: €1,105,600 @ 33% = €364,848.

Question 26.4

Servisco Ltd
Year Ended 31 December 2019
Corporation Tax Computation

	€
Case II professional income	430,000
Less: loss forward	(9,000)
Less: loss carried back (Note 1)	(10,000)
	411,000
Case III interest on Government stocks	50,000
Case V rents	100,000
	561,000
Chargeable gains: €54,000 × 33/12.5	142,560
	703,560

continued overleaf

Corporation tax:

€553,560 @ 12.5% = €69,195	
€150,000 @ 25% = €37,500	106,695

Note 1: loss carried back of €10,000 is offset against trading income taxed @ 12.5%.

Surcharge Computation

1. "Income for the accounting period" is:

		€
Case II	Professional income (Note 1A)	430,000
Case III	Interest on Government stocks	50,000
Case V	Rents	100,000
Total income for the accounting period (Note 1B)		580,000

Notes:

1A. income of the current period, i.e. ignore loss forward and loss back.

1B. as there are no current-year losses or current-year trade charges, income for the accounting period is the same as total income.

2. Distributable estate and investment income of the company is:

	€
Passive income	150,000
FII	7,500
	157,500
Less: corporation tax @ 25% of passive income	(37,500)
	120,000
Less: trading deduction (7.5%)	(9,000)
Distributable estate and investment income	111,000

3. Distributable trading income of the company is:

	€
Trading income	430,000
Corporation tax @ 12.5%	53,750
Distributable trading income	376,250

4. Surcharge is therefore calculated as:

	€
(a) 50% distributable trading income: €376,250 @ 50%	188,125
(b) Distributable estate and investment income (DEII)	111,000
	299,125
Dividend paid	(70,000)
Liable to surcharge	229,125
DEII	111,000
Dividends	(70,000)
Liable @ 20%	41,000

continued overleaf

Balance of €229,125 – €41,000 = €188,125, will be liable @ 15%. Therefore, surcharge is:

	€
€41,000 @ 20%	8,200
€188,125 @ 15%	28,219
	36,419

Question 26.5

Machinery Ltd
Corporation tax computation for year ended 31 December 2019

	€	€
Net profit from trading		627,000
Add: depreciation	59,790	
Loan interest treated as a distribution	2,171 (Note)	61,961
		688,961
Less: capital allowances		(10,700)
Case I		678,261
Case III bank interest		10,000
Case V rents		50,000
		738,261
Corporation tax:		
€678,261 @ 12.5% = €84,783		
€60,000 @ 25% = €15,000		99,783
Add income tax (Note)		648
Total due		100,431

Note:
Interest limit is lower of:
(a) 13% @ €20,000 = €2,600
(b) 13% @ €34,000 = €4,420

Therefore, interest limit = €2,600.

Loans from directors (and/or associates) with material interest:

	€
V. Duffy	4,000
Mrs V. Duffy	5,000
G. Duffy	5,000
S. Duffy	5,000
D. O'Connell	5,000
L.T. Smith	10,000
	34,000

continued overleaf

Interest on above loans = €4,771.
Distribution: €4,771 − €2,600 = €2,171. DWT at 20% (€434) must be deducted from this.

Income tax deducted from:	€
Interest of €2,600 @ 20%	520
Interest on other loan	
(€5,410 – €4,771) @ 20%	128
	648

Surcharge Computation	€
Estate and investment income: €10,000 + €50,000	60,000
Less: corporation tax @ 25%	15,000
	45,000
Less: 7.5% × €45,000	(3,375)
	41,625
Less: distributions made	(2,171)
Excess	39,454
Surcharge @ 20%	7,891

Question 26.6

1. Identify income for the accounting period

	€
Income (Cases II & III)	200,000
Less: trade charges (section 243A)	(60,000)
Income for accounting period	140,000

2. Calculate 'passive income'

$$€140{,}000 \times \frac{€100{,}000}{€200{,}000} = €70{,}000$$

3. Calculate distributable estate and investment income

	€
Passive income	70,000
Less: non-trade charges	(50,000)
Net passive income	20,000
FII	NIL
Estate and investment income	20,000
Less: corporation tax @ 25%	(5,000)
	15,000
Less: 7.5% trading deduction	(1,125)
DEII	13,875

4. Calculate distributable trading income (DTI)

	€
Income for accounting period	140,000
Less: passive income	(70,000)
Trading income	70,000
Less: CT on trading income @ 12.5%	(8,750)
Distributable trading income	61,250

5. Calculate amount liable to surcharge

	€
DEII	13,875
DTI × 50%	30,625
	44,500
Less: distributions paid/payable within 18 months of the accounting period	(30,000)
Liable to surcharge	14,500

6. Calculate surcharge

   All taxable at 15% as distributable estate and investment is less than dividend paid.

   Surcharge @ 15% = €2,175

Chapter 27

Question 27.1

Equities Ltd

		€	€
	Case III		15,100
Less:	Management expenses:		
	Accounting fees	1,000	
	Secretarial fees	2,000	
	Auditor's remuneration	6,000	
	Directors' remuneration: €155,100 @ 10%	15,510	
	Stockbroker's charges	3,000	(27,510)
Excess			(12,410)

The company can carry forward the excess of €12,410 to offset against profits of future accounting periods or to offset against total profits of another group member, if it is a member of a loss group.

Chapter 28

Question 28.1

Foreign Income Limited
Accounts Year ended 31 December 2019
Corporation Tax Computation

	€
Case I	800,000
Case III (€88,000 + €80,000)	168,000
Income	968,000
Corporation tax:	
€800,000 @ 12.5% = €100,000	
€88,000 @ 12.5% = €11,000 (Note)	
€80,000 @ 25% = €20,000	
Corporation tax	131,000

Note: As the dividend of €88,000 is received from a company resident in a country with which Ireland has a tax treaty and it is paid out of trading profits, it is taxed at 12.5%.

The dividend from Irish Maniacs Limited is exempt.

Payment of dividend

Foreign Income Ltd will be required to deduct DWT @ 20% (€10,800) from the dividend of €54,000 paid on 1 February 2019. The DWT must be paid to Revenue before 14 March 2019.

Index

CHARTERED
ACCOUNTANTS
IRELAND